The **AIR** & **SPACE** CATALOG

ANOTHER TILDEN PRESS BOOK FROM VINTAGE BOOKS/RANDOM HOUSE

The Map Catalog:
Every Kind of Map and Chart on Earth and Even Some Above It

The AIR & SPACE CATALOG

Joel Makower, Editor

Marilyn P. Fenichel, Senior Editor

A

TILDEN PRESS

BOOK

VINTAGE BOOKS

A Division of Random House, Inc.   New York

A Vintage Original, December 1989
First Edition

Copyright © 1989 by Tilden Press

All rights reserved under International and Pan-American
Copyright Conventions. Published in the United States by
Vintage Books, a division of Random House, Inc., New York
and simultaneously in Canada by Random House of
Canada Limited, Toronto.

LIBRARY OF CONGRESS CATALOGING-IN-PUBLICATION DATA

The Air & space catalog: the complete sourcebook to everything in the
   universe / Joel Makower, editor in chief; Marilyn Fenichel, senior
   editor.
      p.   cm.
   "A Tilden Press book."
   ISBN 0-679-72038-3: $16.95
   1. Aeronautics—Miscellanea.   2. Space flight—Miscellanea.
3. Astronomy—Miscellanea.   4. Weather—Miscellanea.   I. Makower,
Joel, 1952–   . II. Fenichel, Marilyn.   III. Title: Air and space catalog.
TL553.A35   1989b
500.5—dc20   89-40133
                                                                     CIP

Book design by Rogers Graphic Design, Washington, D.C.

Manufactured in the United States of America

10 9 8 7 6 5 4 3 2 1

INTRODUCTION

We are always looking up, it seems—to the clouds, the constellations, and beyond—to learn about where we've been and where we're going. We study the weather to a near obsession, carefully charting each day's readings and comparing them with those of last year, or whenever, looking for clues to (or consolation about) what life will be like tomorrow. We marvel at the miracle of flight, flocking to primitive or sophisticated technologies—from boomerangs and box kites to Beechcraft and Boeings—that allow us to participate in the experience. We cheer the world's astronauts and cosmonauts, taking them into our hearts and minds, often elevating them to hero status. And above all, we are constantly in awe of the wonders of the night's sky.

It is a truly wonderful world up there, and much like the limitless heavens themselves, the more you learn, the more you want to know. This book is dedicated to those who want to learn, and who want to know more.

We have divided *The Air & Space Catalog* into four major sections, covering astronomy, weather, aviation, and spaceflight. In each section we have attempted to provide useful information about the organizations, products, and other resources available on the subject, whether you are just starting out or are approaching expertise. Mixed in are some short articles and essays on a variety of related topics we think you'll find interesting and useful.

Although we believe that this is the most comprehensive reference book on air and space topics, it is by no means complete. But a book containing a list of every product available or every organization, product, or service on all these topics, should such a book be feasible, would be of limited use to most people. Instead, we have attempted to pare down the information to a manageable level, offering a variety of resources for those who want to delve further into a given subject.

Many of the agencies, associations, and companies we've described offer a wide range of products and services. Given space limitations, we were not always able to do justice to all these organizations; we confined ourselves to mentioning only a few noteworthy products or services. Also be aware that prices, addresses, phone numbers, and other vital information, while accurate at time of publication, are subject to change. You are encouraged to contact any organization that interests you for their latest catalog, price list, membership information, brochure, or whatever else they may have to offer.

We hope you will find enjoyment and enlightenment in the pages that follow. We welcome your comments and contributions, which we will incorporate in future, updated editions of *The Air & Space Catalog*. You may send them to The Air & Space Catalog, c/o Tilden Press, 1526 Connecticut Ave. NW, Washington, DC 20036.

CONTENTS

ACKNOWLEDGMENTS

In addition to our Board of Advisers (see opposite page), the editors would like to offer their sincere thanks and appreciation to a number of individuals who contributed ideas, resources, or support to this effort:

Laura A. Bergheim; Jodi S. Brover, The Cockpit; Susan M. S. Brown; Jim Cassell; Bob Dreesen, Air and Space Museum Library; Sol Hirsch, National Weather Association; Aleta Jackson, National Space Society; Hal Kane; Terri Lawrence; Kevin Mahoney; Shawn P. McCarthy; Bob McCracken, National Capital Astronomers; John Mosley, Griffith Observatory; Suzanne Niemeyer; Cathryn Poff; Nancy Roman, formerly with NASA; Brent Rytting, Jeppesen Sanderson; Rebecca Saletan, Random House; Margaret Sullivan, Astronomy Magazine; Ed Taylor, Smithsonian Resident Associate Program; Felicia Tiller; Seth Tuttle, National Science Foundation; and Linda Zaleskie.

BOARD OF ADVISERS

ASTRONOMY

ASTRONOMY

From the beginning of time, the sky has captured our imagination. The Egyptians observed the brightest star of the night, Sirius, and told time by its appearance. The Greeks worshiped the sky and all its bodies. Even today, we are still drawn to the sky's magic.

Modern-day astronomers do more than just admire the sky. They strive to see and understand. Often they become experts on one type of celestial object or one band of radiation that the universe sends us. Some astronomers focus on the moon or planets, others on the sun or other stars. Still others might learn about variable stars or double stars. Some may be tempted by the wonders of galaxies and quasars or the speed and grace of comets. Whatever the interest, the sky is a place of awe and mystery.

All the paraphernalia of astronomy enthusiasts—binoculars, telescopes, cameras, star charts, and on and on—are designed to make these celestial objects more accessible. And, according to practiced astronomers, they are worth trying to see. "The moon is one celestial object that lives up to expectations the first time it's seen in a telescope," says astronomy writer Alan MacRobert. "And it never fails to impress even casual viewers. One evening I showed the first-quarter moon in my 6-inch reflector to a visiting real-estate agent. She was flabbergasted by the sight. 'How long have they known about

this?' she asked. 'About 350 years,' I replied. 'Well,' she demanded, 'why don't they tell anyone?'"

"When you view the planets with a telescope, you'll be amazed at what you see," write the editors of *Astronomy Magazine*. "Mercury is a ruddy jewel of light never rising very high in the sky. Venus passes through slowly changing phases, reminiscent of an ivory-white, featureless moon. The bright orange disk of Mars shows white polar ice caps and gray-green surface features. Jupiter offers a colorful, banded disk and a retinue of satellites. Saturn presents a beautiful orange globe with its dazzling rings. Because of their enormous distances, Uranus and Neptune are tiny blue-green disks. Pluto is a mere point of light that resembles a faint star."

Many, many others wax poetic, romantic, and fanciful at the sights in the night's sky. And nearly all who take the time to look begin to understand the wonder that is possible with a little knowledge, time, and patience. In the pages that follow, we'll tell you about the work of national observatories and planetariums; how to buy telescopes and binoculars, books, periodicals, and software; and how to read star charts—all are meant to lead you within range of the spectacular.

You are about to discover the greatest show on earth.

OBSERVATORIES:
THROUGH THE LOOKING GLASS

Telescopes are the keys to unlocking the sky's secrets. They offer a way to penetrate the heavens and uncover the mysteries that lie beyond. Today's sky watchers use several basic kinds of telescopes: optical, radio, and infrared on earth, and ultraviolet, X-ray, and gamma ray from space.

OPTICAL ASTRONOMY

Since the seventeenth century, when Galileo first turned the telescope to the heavens, scientists have been exploring ways to perfect the instruments. Optics technology is now better than ever. As a result, today's telescopes can see objects billions of light years away.

Professional astronomers use gigantic, costly, and sophisticated state-of-the-art telescopes housed in large observatories. Each year thousands of professional scientists make their way to remote mountain peaks in Arizona, Hawaii, Chile, and other sites that boast the world's most favorable conditions for peering into the sky.

Until this century all astronomy relied on collecting visible light, the band of radiation our eyes can see. But more recently astronomers realized that the universe sends us information across the whole electromagnetic spectrum, a wide range of radiation that includes X rays, radio waves, and ultraviolet light—as well as visible light. The beauty of today's telescopes and their accompanying electronic gadgetry is that astronomers can capture these waves and obtain information that can tell them the distance, chemistry, evolutionary state, and age of most celestial objects. From this information we have come to understand dwarfs and giant stars, pulsating and variable stars, the structure of galaxies and the expanding universe, and a great deal about life on our own planet.

In the 1950s, as telescope astronomy advanced, it became even clearer that the cost of developing, building, and operating these state-of-the-art instruments was prohibitive for all but the very wealthy. So the federal government decided to provide public support in the form of research grants to establish a network of national centers for astronomy, funded by the National Science Foundation in cooperation with seven leading universities. The organization eventually became the Association of Universities for Research in Astronomy, also known as AURA. The mission of AURA was to establish, improve, and consolidate the principal government-sponsored observatories, all in an attempt to build and maintain the world's most sophisticated observatories.

AURA's first facility was Kitt Peak National Observatory, located on a mountain southwest of Tucson, Arizona, at an elevation of 6,888 feet. Opened in 1958, Kitt Peak has since become the largest optical astronomy facility in the world, with some of the scientific community's most impressive instruments. The Mayall telescope, with its 13-foot-wide mirror—the third largest optical reflector in the United States—and smaller telescopes that have been upgraded as new technology has been refined, have made possible a host of advancements and discoveries: measuring galaxies as far away as 12 billion light-years and detecting luminous arcs—the largest optical "illusions" ever seen—found near clusters of faraway galaxies.

Kitt Peak National Observatory. Courtesy AURA, Inc.

In 1963 the Cerro Tololo Inter-American Observatory in Chile opened its doors to allow astronomers the same quality view of the southern skies. On this mountaintop, with a telescope that is the twin of Kitt Peak's largest, visiting scientists and astronomers have learned about the births, lives, and deaths of stars and galaxies, and the age and fate of the universe. In 1976 Cerro Tololo unveiled its giant 13-foot reflector, the largest optical telescope in the Southern Hemisphere and the fifth largest in the world.

Control of another major telescope, at the solar observatory at Sacramento Peak, in Sunspot, New Mexico, was transferred in 1976 from the U.S. Air Force to the National Science Foundation. A few years later Sacramento Peak was joined to the facilities at Kitt Peak to form the National Solar Observatory.

In 1984, in an attempt to consolidate further the nation's astronomy centers, Kitt Peak National Observatory, Cerro Tololo Inter-American Observatory, and the National Solar Observatory were placed under the auspices of a new organization, the National Optical Astronomy Observatories (NOAO). They were joined by the Advanced Development Program, whose role was to act as a research-and-development arm for the new organization. NOAO is operated by AURA (which has since expanded to include 20 universities) in cooperation with the National Science Foundation. Its mission is to provide state-of-the-art observing facilities to our nation's astronomers and to develop innovative technologies that will pave the way for new discoveries.

In that spirit, under the auspices of AURA and the National Aeronautics and Space Administration (NASA), the Space Telescope Science Institute, in Baltimore, Maryland, has been charged with operating the Hubble Space Telescope. Although not the first telescope placed in orbit, this technological splendor, scheduled to be launched by the space shuttle, is to be the largest and most complex astronomical observatory in the sky. Scientists project

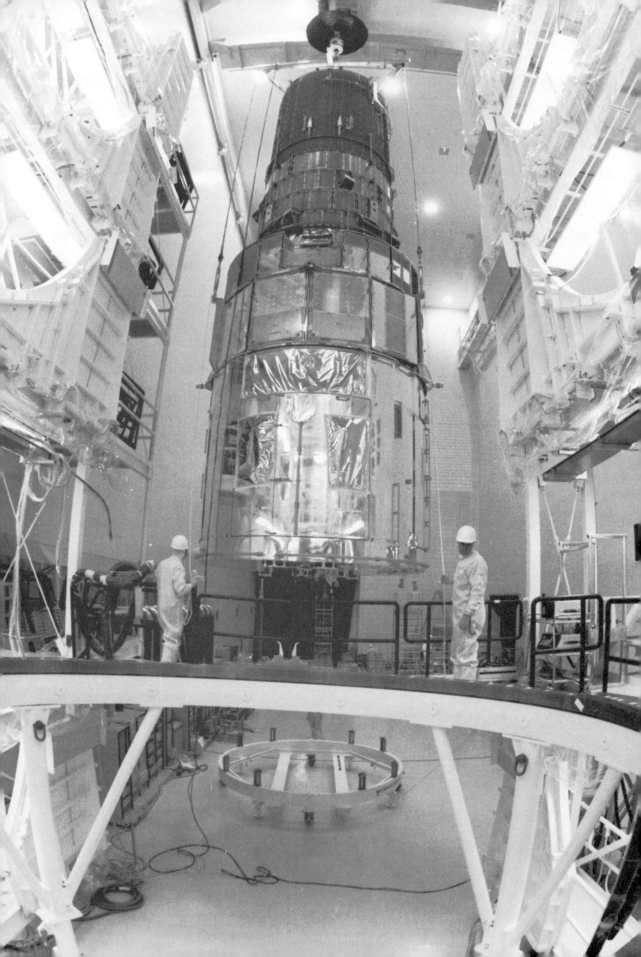

that the Hubble Space Telescope will be able to detect objects too faint for even the most sophisticated ground-based telescopes and to study at length detailed features of planets that passing space probes could glimpse only fleetingly. Deeper in space the telescope will be able to see crucial details of star clusters, galaxies, and quasars.

The Space Telescope Science Institute, opened in 1981, is staffed by astronomers, computer scientists, and technicians from the European Space Agency (which is a partner with NASA on the Hubble telescope), and the Computer Sciences Corp. The institute is on the campus of Johns Hopkins University.

All these facilities, with the exception of the Space Telescope Science Institute, have visitors' centers or offer tours. Here are addresses, phone numbers, and visitor information for the major national optical-astronomy centers:

Kitt Peak National Observatory (P.O. Box 26732, Tucson, AZ 85726; 602-325-9204) offers a walking tour that gives visitors a chance to view up close the giant Mayall telescope, the McMath solar telescope, and the 24/36 Burrell Schmidt telescope. Visitors cannot touch these scopes or look through them, however. The visitors' center has models of telescopes and a smaller solar scope that you can look through. Hours: weekdays, 8 a.m. to 4 p.m.; weekends and holidays, 10 a.m. to 4 p.m. Closed Christmas Day. Regularly scheduled tours are conducted on weekends and holidays.

Cerro Tololo Inter-American Observatory (Cerro Tololo, Cassilla 603, La Serena, Chile; 51-21-33-52) is located above a treacherous, winding road. For this reason visitors are discouraged from coming, and the facility offers no formal tours. For more information, contact the observatory directly.

National Solar Observatory (Sacramento Peak, Sunspot, NM; 505-434-1390. Or: NOAO Public Information Office, Box 26732, Tucson, AZ 85726; 602-325-9204) is open during the day and allows visitors to view the Big Dome, which houses instruments used to study the sun's surface, lower atmosphere, and outer atmosphere, or corona. The building's dome rotates automatically to keep the sun in view. A bell rings to warn visitors that the dome is about to turn. A guided tour is given each Saturday at 2 p.m. There is no charge for admission to the observatory or the tour.

Space Telescope Science Institute (3700 San Martin Dr., Baltimore, MD 21218; 301-338-4707) is a research facility with no buildings open to the public.

Association of Universities for Research in Astronomy (AURA, 1625 Massachusetts Ave. NW, Ste. 701, Washington, DC 20036; 202-483-2101) is the organization's corporate headquarters and has no facilities open to the public.

RADIO ASTRONOMY

Just as stars, planets, and other celestial objects emit or reflect visible light, different kinds of light waves, they also radiate or reflect waves that are invisible. These extremely weak signals from space are called *radio waves*. Since World War I scientists have developed sophisticated telescopes to pick up radio waves emitted by celestial objects. Using radio telescopes, radio astronomers try to describe the physical nature of these objects, how they grow or change or die. Their observations must agree with—or at least not

Left: The Hubble Space Telescope under construction at Lockheed Missiles and Space Company. Courtesy National Aeronautics and Space Administration.

The 140-foot radio telescope at Green Bank, West Virginia, the largest equatorially-mounted telescope in the world. Courtesy National Radio Astronomy Observatory.

conflict with—descriptions given by astronomers making observations in other parts of the spectrum.

How do radio telescopes work? The basic principle is that they pick up waves entering a curved antenna. From there the waves travel to a collector, where they are turned into electric currents. Then they are fed into a receiver—much like the one on your stereo that receives AM and FM waves—and are amplified and recorded.

A single radio telescope cannot "see" features of an object in much detail. To improve resolution, signals from two or more similar telescopes are combined to make what is called an *interferometer*. Radio waves from a given object are received by each telescope, and before they are recorded the signals are made stronger and multidimensional. Simply put, the more pairs of antennas used, the better the "picture" received. Highly sophisticated radio telescopes include many antennas arranged in a variety of

pairs, each designed to pick up a specific range of wavelengths. (Wavelengths are generally expressed in centimeters; the shorter the wavelength, the higher the frequency being detected.) These many "ears," combined with the earth's natural rotation, enable radio astronomers to gain accurate pictures of objects in the sky.

By the mid-1950s radio astronomy had become such an important part of science as a whole that a group of radio astronomers asked for the establishment of a national observatory, where large instruments could be built for use by all scientists. The result was the National Radio Astronomy Observatory (NRAO).

It was at Deer Creek Valley, near Green Bank, West Virginia, that the first NRAO radio telescopes were built. The Green Bank site has become the NRAO center for single-dish observations in the wavelength range of 2 to 90 centimeters (about 1 to 35 inches). In the early 1960s scientists discovered that receivers could be built to work at wavelengths as short as 1 millimeter (about 0.039 inch). Kitt Peak was the site selected for the telescope functioning in this range. At about the same time an interferometer was constructed at Green Bank. It was soon followed by the Very Large Array (VLA) telescope near Socorro, New Mexico, which includes some 27 separate antennas spread over about 25 square miles. The array is by far the most powerful radio telescope in the world. It has been used to observe the planets as well as radio stars, gas clouds—in which new stars form—and the remains of supernovas—violent explosions marking the "deaths" of stars.

NRAO's latest project is an instrument called the Very Long Baseline Array, which uses existing antennas at cooperating observatories spanning the United States from Hawaii to the Virgin Islands. This project is scheduled to begin full operation in the 1990s and will be managed out of the Socorro, New Mexico, facility.

Another facility, not connected with NRAO, is the National Astronomy and Ionosphere Center (NAIC), site of the world's largest telescope, near Arecibo,

Puerto Rico. Originally built by the Defense Department, NAIC is now sponsored by the National Science Foundation in conjunction with Cornell University.

Arecibo is an awesome sight. Located in a natural valley almost the right shape for a reflector, it is 1,000 feet in diameter and spans 25 acres. Its large dish allows it to broadcast radio signals along a beamed path. A feature added in 1974 gives it the capability of mapping the surfaces of the planets Mercury, Venus, and Mars. The observatory also specializes in pulsars—those strange objects that are actually spinning neutron stars, the remains of stars that have died.

Here are addresses, phone numbers, and hours of radio astronomy facilities:

National Radio Astronomy Observatory
Edgemont Rd.
Charlottesville, VA V22903
804-296-0211
Hours: 8:30 a.m. to 5 p.m.

National Radio Astronomy Observatory
P.O. Box 2
Green Bank, WV 24944
304-456-2011
Hours: 8 a.m. to 4:30 p.m.

The Very Large Array Radio Telescope near Socorro, New Mexico—the world's most powerful radio telescope. Courtesy National Radio Astronomy Observatory.

The millimeter-wave telescope on Kitt Peak, near Tucson, Arizona, which has played a key role in studying the cold gas of the Milky Way. Courtesy National Radio Astronomy Observatory.

National Radio Astronomy Observatory
949 N. Cherry Avenue
Campus Bldg. 65
Tucson, AZ 85721
602-882-8250
Hours: 7:30 a.m. to 4:30 p.m.

National Radio Astronomy Observatory
P.O. Box O
Socorro, NM 87801
505-988-1710
Hours: 8:30 a.m. to 4:30 p.m.

Arecibo Observatory
P.O. Box 995
Arecibo, PR 00613
809-878-2612
Hours: tours at 2 p.m. Tues. through Fri.; open house Sun. 1 to 4 p.m.

National Astronomy and Ionosphere Center
Administrative Offices, Space Science Bldg.
Cornell University
Ithaca, NY 14853
607-255-3734
Hours: 8 a.m. to 4:30 p.m.

INFRARED ASTRONOMY

Lying between optical and radio waves in the electromagnetic spectrum is another kind of wavelength—infrared radiation—which we commonly associate with heat. Celestial objects ranging from planets in the solar system to distant quasars are known to emit enormous quantities of infrared radiation. As a result, over the last 15 years infrared astronomy has been still another source of astronomical discoveries. By using infrared telescopes we have been able to see previously inaccessible aspects of celestial objects.

To help along progress, the Infrared Telescope Facility (University of Hawaii, Institute for Astronomy, 1175 Manono St., Hilo, HI 96720; 808-935-3373), a 10-foot telescope designed for maximum efficiency in the infrared range, was opened in 1979. Located on the summit of Mauna Kea on the island of Hawaii, the facility is operated and maintained for NASA under contract by the University of Hawaii.

Among other things, the telescope is used to make observations of the solar system to further the space program.

PRIVATE OBSERVATORIES

Along with the elaborate complex of government-funded observatories, there are privately endowed observatories. Many of these are affiliated with universities and are an integral part of an academic astronomy program. Others are used solely by professional astronomers.

Among the private observatories, a few warrant special mention.

Arizona, a Mecca for astronomers, boasts the following exceptional facilities:

Fred L. Whipple Observatory (P.O. Box 97, Amado, AZ 85645; 602-629-6741) is operated jointly by the University of Arizona and the Smithsonian Astrophysical Observatory, which is based in Cambridge, Massachusetts. The observatory is located on Mt. Hopkins, 35 miles south of Tucson, the second-highest peak in the Santa Rita Range of the Coronado National Forest. Research activities include spectroscopic observations of extragalactic, stellar, and planetary bodies, and solar energy research. The observatory conducts guided tours for the general public on Monday, Wednesday, and Friday from March through November. Tour rates are $5 for adults, $4.50 for Smithsonian associates, and $2.50 for children ages 6 through 12. Reservations are required and may be made up to four weeks in advance by either calling or writing.

The Multiple Mirror Telescope (P.O. Box 97, Amado, AZ 85645; 602-629-6741), one of the telescopes at the Whipple Observatory, represents a marvel in innovative design. Using six individual mirrors, the telescope is equivalent to a single 176-inch reflector, making it the world's third-largest optical telescope. It is especially effective in making observations in the infrared portion of the spectrum. This facility is run jointly by the Smithsonian Institution and the University of Arizona. Tours of the building that houses the telescope are given Monday, Wednesday, and Friday from 9 a.m. until 3 p.m. by appointment only. Fees are $5 for adults, $2.50 for children.

Steward Observatory (University of Arizona, Tucson, AZ 85721; 602-621-2288) is the research arm for the Department of Astronomy at the University of

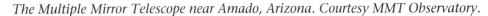

The Multiple Mirror Telescope near Amado, Arizona. Courtesy MMT Observatory.

Arizona. Public viewing through the 21-inch telescope is possible from 7:30 p.m. to 10:30 p.m. during the academic year. The observatory also offers guest lectures and courses during the academic year.

The University of Arizona also has observatories on Kitt Peak, near Mt. Bigelow, and on Mt. Lemmon. These are research facilities and are not open to the public.

California, another key location for astronomers, has the following noteworthy facilities:

Big Bear Solar Observatory (40386 North Shore Ln., Big Bear City, CA 92314; 714-866-5791) is owned and operated by the California Institute of Technology with support from the federal government. The observatory, specializing in studying the sun, is located in the middle of a lake to reduce the image distortion that occurs when the sun heats the ground. These conditions, along with the cloudless skies of southern California and the 6,700-foot elevation, make this one of the best sites in the world for studying the sun. Big Bear is particularly well known for its observations of solar activity and solar flares. This facility is not open to the public.

Lick Observatory (P.O. Box 85, Mt. Hamilton, CA 95140; 408-429-2201) has an extensive public program at its site on Mt. Hamilton. The visitors' gallery of the 120-inch Shane telescope is open daily from 10 a.m. to 5 p.m. The visitors' center is open from 1 to 5 p.m. From mid-June to mid-September, the observatory runs ten Friday-evening observing programs, which provide the only opportunity for the general public to look through any of its telescopes. A lecture usually accompanies the viewing session. Because of the

limited number of spaces for this program, the observatory requests that only individuals with a serious interest in astronomy attend. To obtain program tickets, write Summer Visitors' Program, Lick Observatory, P.O. Box 85, Mt. Hamilton, CA 95140.

Palomar Mountain Observatory (California Institute of Technology, 1201 E. California Blvd., Pasadena, CA 91106; 818-356-6811) is known for its 200-inch Hale Telescope, one of the world's largest. This instrument has observed asteroids and comets, stars of the Milky Way, other distant galaxies, and quasars, flickers in the universe so distant that their light takes billions of years to reach the earth. Because it is such an effective tool, it has become central to serious astronomical study. The observatory is open daily, except December 24 and 25, from 9 a.m. to 4:30 p.m. Visitors may tour the museum and view the Hale Telescope from a special gallery in the dome. Unfortunately, visitors may not look *through* the telescope.

Texas is famous for many things, and one of its attractions is the MacDonald Observatory (Box 1337, Ft. Davis, TX 79734; 915-426-3263), which offers a variety of programs to the public. Among them are the following:

❑ "Star Date," a daily radio series, includes two-minute capsules of information about astronomy, space, and astrophysics. The series airs on more than 200 radio stations in the United States and Canada. It is also available to schools for nonbroadcast purposes. For more information, call 512-471-5285.

❑ *Star Date Magazine*, published bi-

Right: Big Bear Solar Observatory, near Big Bear City, California. Courtesy Big Bear Solar Observatory, California Institute of Technology.

THE NATION'S OBSERVATORY

The U.S. Naval Observatory is one of the oldest scientific agencies in the country. It made its debut in 1830, and its original mission included caring for the navy's charts and navigational instruments. In 1844 it moved to the hill north of where the Lincoln Memorial now stands, and for 50 years it was the site of important scientific experiments. Using its 26-inch telescope, scientist Asaph Hall discovered Mars's two satellites; other scientists observed the solar eclipses and the transit of Venus here.

Over the years, as its facilities grew and spread outside Washington, D.C., the observatory's role has become firmly established. It is the official timekeeper for the United States and is also charged with the task of determining the precise positions and motions of the earth, sun, moon, planets, and stars. The observatory's Washington facility—the grounds of which double as the official home of the vice president of the United States—houses the historic 26-inch refractor that is used primarily for observing planetary satellites and for tracing double stars. In Flagstaff, Arizona, the observatory's 61-inch reflector is used to measure distances of faint objects and brightness and colors of stars. It was with this telescope that James Christy in 1978 discovered Pluto's lone satellite, Charon.

The six-inch transit telescope at the Naval Observatory.

The Naval Observatory's library is one of the leading astronomical libraries in the world. With more than 75,000 volumes, it also serves as an archive for many rare books and periodicals, dating back to the fifteenth century. The works of such astronomical greats as Newton, Galileo, Kepler, and Copernicus have become part of the observatory's collection.

Night tours are given on Monday night (except federal holidays) on a first-come, first-served basis. Tours begin at 7:30 p.m. during Eastern Standard Time and 8:30 p.m. during Eastern Daylight Time. Passes are handed out on arrival. Group reservations for up to 35 people are taken, but these are usually booked two to three months in advance.

For more information, contact the U.S. Naval Observatory, 34th St. & Massachusetts Ave. NW, Washington, DC 20392; 202-653-1507 or U.S. Naval Observatory, Flagstaff Station, P.O. Box 1149, Flagstaff, AZ 86002; 602-779-5132.

monthly by the University of Texas at Austin, includes information about the stars and planets and a star chart. A year's subscription is $12. For more information, write to Star Date, University of Texas at Austin, RLM 15.308, Austin, TX 78712.

❑ The W. L. Moody, Jr., Visitors' Information Center houses astronomy exhibits, films, and a gift shop. The center is open daily, 9 a.m. to 5 p.m., except Thanksgiving, Christmas, and New Year's Day.

❑ The visitors' center staff conducts solar viewing sessions daily at 11 a.m. Reservations are required and should be made at least six months in advance. Cost is $5 for adults, $4 for students and senior citizens, and $2.50 for children under 12.

In addition to these gems many other observatories conduct research activities and sponsor public programs. Here is a list of observatories, with addresses and phone numbers, organized by state. Some are not open to the public, so call before heading out to view the stars. Also, this list includes only observatories affiliated with universities and research institutions. Many planetariums have observatories for public viewing. (See "Planetariums" for more information.)

Arizona
Lowell Observatory
1400 W. Mars Hill Rd.
Flagstaff, AZ 86001
602-635-9272

McGraw Hill Observatory
P.O. Box 220
Sells Star Rte.
Tucson, AZ 85735
602-620-5360

California
Frank P. Brackett Observatory
Dept. of Physics and Astronomy
Claremont, CA 91711
714-621-8000

Chabot Observatory
4917 Mountain Blvd.
Oakland, CA 94619
415-531-4560

Leuschner Observatory
University of California
Berkeley, CA 94720
415-642-5275

Mt. Wilson Observatory
740 Holladay Rd.
Pasadena, CA 91106
818-793-3100

San Fernando Observatory
14031 San Fernando Rd.
Sylmar, CA 91342
818-367-9333

Sonoma State University Observatory
Dept. of Physics and Astronomy
Robert Park, CA 94928
707-664-2119

Table Mountain Observatory
P.O. Box 367
Wrightwood, CA 92397
619-249-3551

UCB—Hat Creek Observatory
Radio Astronomy Laboratory
Cassel, CA 96016
916-335-2364

Colorado
Black Forest Observatory
P.O. Box 35233
Colorado Springs, CO 90836
719-495-3828

Chamberlin Observatory
University of Denver
Denver, CO 80208
303-871-3557

Sommers-Bausch Observatory
Campus Box 391
University of Colorado
Boulder, CO 80309
303-492-6732

Connecticut
Van Vleck Observatory
Wesleyan University
Middletown, CT 06457
203-347-9411

Western Connecticut State University
Observatory
181 White St.
Danbury, CT 06810
203-797-2774

Delaware
Mt. Cuba Astronomical Observatory
P.O. Box 3915
Greenville, DE 19807
302-654-6407

Florida
Gibson Observatory
4801 Dreher Trail N.
West Palm Beach, FL 33405
407-832-1988

Georgia
Agnes Scott College Observatory
Dept. of Physics and Astronomy
Decatur, GA 30030

Fernbank Observatory
156 Heaton Park Dr. NE
Atlanta, GA 30307
404-378-4311

Hawaii
Canada-France-Hawaii Telescope Corp.
P.O. Box 1597
Kamuela, HI 96743
808-885-7944

Mauna Kea Observatory
Institute for Astronomy
2680 Woodlawn Dr.
Honolulu, HI 96822
808-948-8312

Illinois
Dearborn Observatory
2131 Sheridan
Northwestern University
Evanston, IL 60201
312-491-5633

Illinois Wesleyan University Observatory
Bloomington, IL 61702
309-556-3176

Northern Illinois University Observatory
Physics Dept.
De Kalb, IL 60115
815-753-1772

Indiana
Goethe Link Observatory
Indiana University
Swain Hall W. 319
Bloomington, IN 47405
812-335-6915

Holcomb Observatory
Butler University
4600 Sunset
Indianapolis, IN 46208
317-283-9282

The 88-inch telescope at Mauna Kea Observatory in Hawaii. Courtesy National Aeronautics and Space Administration.

John C. Hook Memorial Observatory
Indiana State University
Terre Haute, IN 47809
812-237-3294

McKim Observatory
DePauw University
Greencastle, IN 46135
317-658-4505

Iowa
Drake University Municipal Observatory
Des Moines, IA 50311
515-271-3033

Erwin W. Fick Observatory
Physics Dept.
Iowa State University
Ames, IA 50011
515-294-3668

Kansas
Lake Afton Public Observatory
1845 Fairmount
Wichita, KS 67208
316-689-3191

Clyde W. Tombaugh Observatory
Dept. of Physics and Astronomy
University of Kansas
Lawrence, KS 66045
913-864-4626

Kentucky
Roberts Observatory
Berea College
Berea, KY 40404
606-986-9341

Maryland
University of Maryland Observatory
Astronomy Program
College Park, MD 20742
301-454-3001

Massachusetts
Boston University Observatory
Astronomy Dept.
725 Commonwealth Ave.
Boston, MA 02215
617-353-4884

Harvard College Observatory
60 Garden St.
Cambridge, MA 02138
617-495-9059

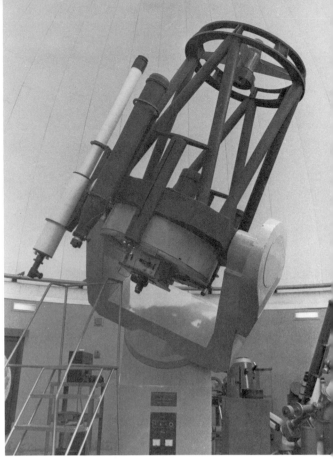

The 36-inch telescope at Fernbank Science Center in Atlanta.

Haystack Observatory
Rte. 40
Westford, MA 01886
508-692-4764

Hopkins Observatory
Williams College
Williamstown, MA 02167
413-597-2188

Maria Mitchell Observatory
3 Vestal St.
Nantucket, MA 02554
508-228-9273

Wallace Astrophysical Observatory
Dept. of Earth Sciences
MIT Rm. 54-426
Cambridge, MA 02139
617-253-6315

Woodside Observatory
13 Friend Ct.
Wenham, MA 01984
508-468-4815

Michigan
Brooks Observatory
Central Michigan University
Mt. Pleasant, MI 48859
517-774-3321

Michigan State University Observatory
Physics and Astronomy Dept.
East Lansing, MI 48824
517-353-4540

Minnesota
Macalester College Observatory
1600 Grand Ave.
St. Paul, MN 55105
612-696-6383

Mississippi
University of Mississippi Observatory
Physics Dept.
University, MS 38677
601-232-7046

Missouri
Laws Observatory
Dept. of Physics and Astronomy
University of Missouri
Columbia, MO 65211
314-882-3036

Nebraska
Behlen Observatory
Dept. of Physics and Astronomy
University of Nebraska
Lincoln, NE 67858
402-472-2788

New Hampshire
Shattuck Observatory
Dept. of Astronomy, Wilder Hall
Dartmouth College
Hanover, NH 03755
603-646-2034

University of New Hampshire Observatory
Physics Dept., DeMeritt Hall
Durham, NH 03824
603-862-1950

New Jersey
Princeton University Observatory
Peyton Hall
Princeton, NJ 08544
609-452-3800

New Mexico
University of New Mexico
Dept. of Physics
Albuquerque, NM 87131
505-277-2616

New York
Alfred University Observatory
Alfred, NY 14802
607-871-2208

Dudley Observatory
69 Union Ave.
Schenectady, NY 12308
518-382-7583

Fuentes Observatory
Cornell University
Ithaca, NY 14853
607-255-3557

North Carolina
Three College Observatory
University of North Carolina at Greensboro
Greensboro, NC 27412
919-334-5669

North Dakota
MSU Observatory
Minot State University
Minot, ND 58701
701-857-3071

Ohio
Cincinnati Observatory
3489 Observatory Pl.
Cincinnati, OH 45208
513-321-5186

Perkins Observatory
Box 449
Delaware, OH 43015
614-292-7876

SBP Observatory
Box 601
Cedarville, OH 45314
513-766-2211

Warner & Swasey Observatory
Case Western Reserve University
Cleveland, OH 44106
216-368-3729

Left: The telescope at Keeble Observatory of Randolph-Macon College in Ashland, Virginia.

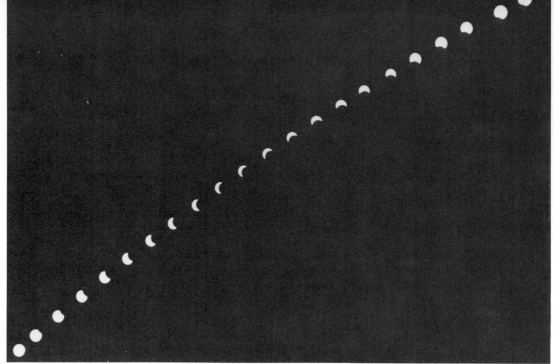

Portrait of a 1972 solar eclipse, photographed at the Goddard Space Flight Center in Greenbelt, Maryland, courtesy National Aeronautics and Space Administration.

Weitkamp Observatory
Otterbein College
Westerville, OH 43081
614-898-1516

Oregon
Pine Mountain Observatory
PMO Bend-Burns Star Rte.
Bend, OR 97701
503-382-8331

Pennsylvania
Allegheny Observatory
Observatory Station
University of Pittsburgh
Pittsburgh, PA 15214
412-321-2400

Bucknell University Observatory
Dept. of Physics
Lewisburg, PA 17837
717-524-1139

Edinboro University of Pennsylvania
   Observatory
Edinboro, PA 16444
814-732-2469

Keystone Junior College Observatory
Rte. 107
Fleetville, PA 18420
717-945-5141

Kutztown University Observatory
Kutztown, PA 19530
215-683-4438

Swarthmore College Observatory
Swarthmore, PA 19081
215-328-8272

Villanova University Observatory
Dept. of Astronomy and Astrophysics
Mendel Hall
Villanova, PA 19085
215-645-4820

Rhode Island
Community College of Rhode Island
500 East Ave.
Warwick, RI 03886
401-825-2178

South Carolina
Francis Marion College Observatory
Francis Marion College
Hwy. 301 N
Florence, SC 29501
803-661-1250

Melton Memorial Observatory
Dept. of Physics and Astronomy
University of South Carolina
Columbia, SC 29208
803-777-6446

Tennessee
A. J. Dyer Observatory of Vanderbilt University
1000 Oman Dr.
Brentwood, TN 37027
615-373-4897

Jones Observatory
Dept. of Physics and Astronomy
University of Tennessee at Chattanooga
Chattanooga, TN 37402
615-755-4546

Texas
Stephen F. Austin State University Observatory
Dept. of Physics and Astronomy
Box 13044
Nacogdoches, TX 75962
409-568-3001

Utah
Physics Dept. Observatory
201 James Fletcher Bldg.
University of Utah
Salt Lake City, UT 84112
801-581-7140

Vermont
Green Mountain Observatory
P.O. Box 782
Williston, VT 05495
802-878-3459

Virginia
Keeble Observatory
Randolph-Macon College
Ashland, VA 23005
804-752-7344

Leander McCormick Observatory
University of Virginia
P.O. Box 3818
Charlottesville, VA 22903
804-924-7494

Washington
Goldendale Observatory
1602 Observatory Dr.
Goldendale, WA 98620
509-773-3141

Wisconsin
Hobbs Observatory
Beaver Creek Reserve
Rte. 2, Box 94
Fall Creek, WI 54742
715-877-2212

Pine Bluff Observatory
4065 Observatory Rd.
Cross Plains, WI 53528
608-262-3071

The Lagoon Nebula, photographed in 1978 by the U.S. Naval Observatory. Courtesy National Aeronautics and Space Administration.

Washburn Observatory
University of Wisconsin at Madison
475 N. Charter St.
Madison, WI 54706
608-262-3071

Yerkes Observatory
373 W. Geneva St.
P.O. Box 258
Williams Bay, WI 53191
414-245-7476

Wyoming
Wyoming Infrared Observatory
Dept. of Physics and Astronomy
University of Wyoming
Laramie, WY 82071
307-766-6150

CANADA
Burke-Gaffney Observatory
St. Mary's University
Halifax, NS B3H 3C3
902-420-5633

Chimenhaga Observatory
Dept. of Physics and Astronomy
University of Victoria
P.O. Box 1700
Victoria, BC V8W 2Y2
604-721-7747

Devon Observatory
Dept. of Physics
University of Alberta
Edmonton, AB T6G 2J1
403-432-5286

Dominion Astrophysical Observatory
5071 W. Saanich Rd.
Victoria, BC V8X 4M6
604-388-0001

David Dunlap Observatory
Box 360
Richmond Hill, ON L4C 4Y6
416-884-2112

Rothney Astrophysical Observatory
Physics Dept.
University of Calgary
Calgary, AB T2N 1N4
403-931-2366

Gordon M. Southam Observatory
1100 Chestnut St.
Vancouver, BC V6J 3J9
604-738-2855

University of Western Ontario Observatory
Astronomy Dept.
London, ON N6A 3K7
519-679-2111

PLANETARIUMS

In 1923 Max Adler, a Chicago business-man, heard about an exciting new invention. Dr. Walther Bauersfeld, the scientific director of the firm of Carl Zeiss in Jena, had designed an optical projection device that could create the illusion of the night sky. Curious, Adler traveled to Germany to see the technique for himself. He was so impressed that he decided to purchase the device, paving the way for the first planetarium in the Western Hemisphere.

"The popular conception of the universe is too meager," declared Adler at the 1930 opening of Chicago's Adler Planetarium. "The planets and the stars are too far removed from general knowledge." Although we have since walked on the moon and scanned the heavens with sophisticated probes, for most people planetariums are still the only way to get close to the stars.

Today there are more than 500 planetariums in North America. Some are in schools, colleges, or community centers and may be used for educational purposes only. Others are located in elaborate science museums, which also offer astronomy exhibits, hands-on displays, and seminars and classes for a variety of audiences. But often the planetarium itself is the centerpiece.

In the planetarium's theater, viewers gaze up at a domed "sky" to witness constellations, planets, the moon, the center of the Milky Way, or countless other images. Using music, artwork, and as many as 20 slide projectors, planetarium shows aim to dazzle the senses.

Although all planetariums offer an important service to their communities, there are a few that boast exemplary facilities and programs. The descriptions below offer a glimpse into some of the larger and better-known facilities.

Adler Planetarium (1300 S. Lake Shore Dr., Chicago IL 60605; 312-322-0304). Located at the end of a half-mile-long peninsula that juts into Lake Michigan, the Adler Planetarium is an ideal spot from which to view the Windy City's impressive skyline. The twelve-sided building is a unique rainbow-granite structure crowned with a lead-covered copper dome. The main level of the planetarium, which is underground, was added in 1973 and houses the 456-seat Kroc Theater. The planetarium's ceiling contains the world's largest map of the universe.

The western half of the main level houses the Robert S. Adler Hall of Space Exploration. Exhibits include a collection of spacecraft models, a space suit worn on the *Apollo 10* mission, and a 4-billion-year-old moon rock. The mid level of the planetarium complex contains the Hall of Telescopes, which displays early telescopes—including the one used by Sir William Herschel to discover Uranus in 1781—and state-of-the-art astronomers' tools.

On the upper level is the Sky Theater, an auditorium constructed beneath a hemispheric projection surface. On this dome the planetarium's sophisticated Zeiss projector reproduces a highly realistic sky as it would appear from any place on the earth's surface at any point in time. Special effects, supplied by the Zeiss Mark VI projector, up to 150 other projectors, and a laser beam can be superimposed on this star-studded sky. The planetarium's early scientific instrument collection, gathered by Max Adler himself, is also on this level. The "New Universe" exhibit explores the structure of the universe, life cycles of stars, and our sun. Hours: Daily, 9:30 a.m. to 4:30 p.m.

Adler Planetarium in Chicago. Photo courtesy The Adler Planetarium.

(Friday until 9 p.m. from September 1 to June 15). Admission to the building and exhibits is free; the sky show is $3 for adults, $1.50 for children 6 through 17.

Directly east of the planetarium in the same complex, the Doane Observatory offers a 20-inch computer-controlled telescope that brings galaxies, nebulas, and planets into real-life focus for planetarium viewers. This is done by projecting images from the telescope on an area of the Sky Theater dome. This special program can be seen on Friday evenings at 8 p.m. Admission is $2.50 for adults, $1.50 for children 6 to 17.

Fels Planetarium of the Franklin Institute of Science Museum (20th St. and Ben Franklin Pkwy., Philadelphia, PA 19103; 215-448-1293). The Fels Planetarium was established in 1933, making it the second-oldest such facility in the country. Designed to seat 350 people under its dome, the planetarium produces at least two major public shows a year, as well as seasonal constellation shows and the popular Christmas presentation. The major shows cover topics ranging from the history of astronomy to UFOs and black holes. The accompanying astronomy exhibit includes a 30-foot layout of the planets; an interactive videodisk of solar flares, sunspots, and other solar phenomena; and displays explaining retrograde motion, celestial mechanics, and the composition of the atmosphere. In addition to the planetarium dome, Fels boasts the largest public observatory in the United States. The telescopes offer viewers a chance to see the sun, the moon, or a distant planet. A solar telescope reveals solar eruptions, explosions, and the effects of magnetic fields. Hours are September through June: weekdays, 9:30 a.m. to 4:30 p.m.; weekends, 10 a.m. to 5 p.m. July through August: daily, 10 a.m. to 5 p.m. Weekday shows are at 12:30 and 2 p.m. (no 2 p.m. show on Monday); weekends, noon, 1, 2, 3, and 4 p.m. Admission is $5 for adults, $4 for children 4 through 11, and $3.50 for senior citizens.

Reuben H. Fleet Space Theater and Science Center (Balboa Park, P.O. Box 33303, San Diego, CA 92103; 619-238-1233). Opened in 1973, the Fleet Space Theater was the first Omnimax theater in the world, featuring a 70-millimeter system projected on a gigantic screen. The theater rests beneath a massive 76-foot dome tilted 25 degrees to the horizon. Planetarium shows also take place in this theater. A star ball in the center of the theater can project as many as 10,000 stars onto the screen. Synchronized by a sophisticated computer program, the star ball provides a highly realistic view of the sky. Hours are daily, 9:40 a.m. to 7:30 p.m. Shows are presented hourly starting at 11:40 a.m. weekdays and 10:30 a.m. on weekends. Admission is $5 for adults, $3 for children.

Saturn, as seen at the Reuben H. Fleet Science Center in San Diego, California.

The Zeiss projector at the McLaughlin Planetarium, Toronto, Ontario.

McDonnell Star Theater (5100 Clayton Rd., Forest Park, St. Louis, MO 63110; 314-289-4439). The McDonnell Star Theater is one of six planetariums in the world that has a Digistar computer. This permits showing the view from anywhere in space at any time. McDonnell also offers shows especially designed for children under age 5. The star theater also has an outdoor science park with apparatus for hands-on learning. Hours are Monday through Thursday, 9:30 a.m. to 5 p.m.; Friday and Saturday, 9:30 a.m. to 9 p.m.; and Sunday, 11 a.m. to 5 p.m. There is no admission fee.

Fernbank Science Center (156 Heaton Park Dr. NE, Atlanta, GA 30307; 404-378-4311). Set on a 65-acre hardwood forest, the Fernbank Science Center includes an electron microscope laboratory, botanical gardens, and a computer laboratory, as well as a 500-seat planetarium and a 36-inch research telescope. Run by the DeKalb County school system, the center offers planetarium shows, general viewing of celestial objects through its telescope, and an astronomy film and lecture series. Exhibit hall hours are Monday, 8:30 a.m. to 5 p.m.; Tuesday through Friday, 8:30 a.m. to 10 p.m.; Saturday, 10 a.m. to 5 p.m.; and Sunday 1 to 5 p.m. Planetarium

shows are Tuesday through Friday, 8 p.m.; Saturday, 11 a.m. and 3 p.m.; Sunday, 3 p.m.; and Wednesday and Friday, 3 p.m. Admission to the planetarium is $2 for adults, $1 for students. Other parts of the center are free.

McLaughlin Planetarium of the Royal Ontario Museum (100 Queen's Park, Toronto, ON M5S 2C6; 416-586-5826). This planetarium seats 340 people and offers four new 40- to 45-minute star shows each year. The Astrocentre, the museum's permanent astronomical gallery, has a solar telescope; a stellarium, a dramatic display of different kinds of stars, from white dwarfs to black holes; and a photographic display illustrating the differences between the rocky terrestrial planets and the giant gaseous bodies. In addition, the planetarium boasts three Soviet-made spacecraft models, the first such models to be shown in North America. Planetarium hours are daily, 10 a.m. to 5 p.m. Admission is $3.50 for adults, $2 for students and children. Shows are presented Tuesday through Friday, 3 and 7:30 p.m.; weekends, 12:30, 3, and 7:30 p.m. Astrocentre admission is $2 for adults, $2 for students and children, and $6 for families.

Space Center (P.O. Box 533, Alamogordo, NM 88311; 505-437-2840). This facility includes the International Space Hall of Fame, the Clyde W. Tombaugh Space Theater, and the John P. Stapp Air and Space Park. The Space Hall of Fame tells the story of spaceflight by highlighting individuals who made it possible. Objects on display include samples of moon rock, a Skylab model, space shuttle food, and a look at a space station in the year 2001. An added feature of this unique museum is that each year, selected astronauts and scientists are inducted into the Hall of Fame. Outside, in the Air and Space Park, historic rockets and missiles such as the

Sonic Wind One, the actual rocket sled used by Stapp (referred to as "the fastest man alive"), is on display, as well as *Little Joe II*, used to test launch escape systems for manned flights at nearby White Sands Missile Range, and the Lance Missile, a U.S. Army combat weapon. Also outside is the Astronaut Memorial Garden, dedicated to the seven members of the space shuttle *Challenger*. The Space Theater, operated jointly by the Space Center and New Mexico University, has the capacity to project more than 2,300 stars, the sun, the moon, and the planets Mercury, Venus, Mars, Jupiter, and Saturn, as well as the Milky Way and many constellations. It can also demonstrate a variety of celestial phenomena, such as the daily apparent motion of the stars as the earth rotates, the annual motion of the earth around the sun, and the path of the sun through the sky on a daily and annual basis. Large-screen Omnimax films also are shown. Hours are 9 a.m. to 6 p.m. daily. Admission is $2.25 for adults, $1.50 for children 5 and under, and free for children under 5. Shows at the planetarium are presented Monday through Friday, at 10 a.m., noon, 2 p.m., and 4 p.m. On Friday, a 7 p.m. show is given. On weekends, show times are 10 and 11 a.m., noon, 2, 3, 4, and 7 p.m. Planetarium admission is $3.50 for adults, $2.50 for children 5 and over, and free for children under 5.

These planetariums also offer exemplary programs:

Abrams Planetarium (Michigan State University, East Lansing, MI 48824; 517-355-4672) presents programs on Friday and Saturday at 8 p.m.; Sunday at 4 p.m. Admission is $2.50 for adults, $2 for students and senior citizens, and $1.50 for children 12 and under. The planetarium also offers several programs for school-age children and publishes a monthly sky calendar illustrating planet and star movements.

Alberta Science Centre/Centennial Planetarium (P.O. Box 2100, Postal Station M, Calgary, AB T2P 2M5; 403-221-3700) is open daily, 1 to 5 p.m. during the winter, and until 9 p.m. during the summer. Shows are offered at 1:30 and 3 p.m. in the winter; a night show is offered at 8 p.m. in the summer, Monday through Thursday. Admission is $4 for adults, $2 for children, and $1 for senior citizens.

American Museum-Hayden Planetarium (81st St. at Central Park W, New York, NY 10024; 212-769-5920), was established in 1935 and offers sky shows, educational programs for children, and a range of astronomy courses for interested amateurs. The admission fee of $3.75 for adults (13 and older), $2.75 for students with ID and senior citizens and museum members, and $2 for children ages 2 through 12 (members' children $1.50) includes the 45-minute sky show and two floors of astronomical exhibits. The planetarium is open 9 a.m. to 5 p.m., with sky shows at 1:30 and 3:30 p.m., Monday through Friday; Saturday at 11 a.m. and 1, 2, 3, 4, and 5 p.m.; and Sunday at 1, 2, 3, 4, and 5 p.m. October through June. Performance times July through September are 1:30 and 3:30 p.m., Monday through Friday; Saturday 1, 2, 3, and 4 p.m.; and Sunday 1, 2, and 4 p.m.

Edmonton Space Sciences Centre (11211 142nd St., Edmonton, AB T5M 4A1; 403-452-9100) is open Sunday through Thursday 10 a.m. to 10 p.m.; Friday and Saturday, 10 a.m. to 10:30 p.m. Admission to the Devonian Theatre, which offers giant-screen, 70-millimeter Imax films, and the planetarium is $4 for adults, $2 for children and senior citizens. Laser shows are $5 for adults, $3 for children and senior citizens.

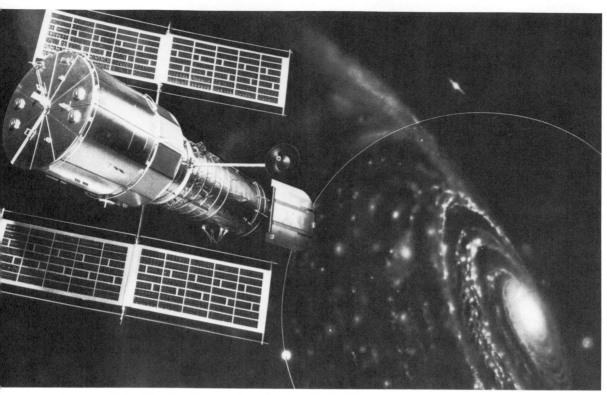

A scene at the Hayden Planetarium in New York City.

Albert Einstein Planetarium of the National Air and Space Museum (6th St. & Independence Ave. SW, Washington, DC 20560; 202-357-2700) offers shows that project simulated images of the sun, the moon, and the five planets visible to the naked eye, plus stars, quasars, galaxies, and black holes. Hours are 10 a.m. to 7:30 p.m. during summer months, and 10 a.m. to 5:30 p.m. the rest of the year (the exact dates change each year). Shows are continuous, seven days a week; check at the information desk for times. Admission is $2.25 for adults; $1.25 for children, students, and senior citizens.

Ferguson Planetarium of Buffalo State College (1300 Elmwood Ave., Buffalo, NY 14222; 716-878-4911) is intended for school use only. Hours are 9 a.m. to 3 p.m. weekdays. Admission is 50 cents for students, with a $10 group minimum.

Flandrau Planetarium (University of Arizona, Tucson, AZ 85721; 602-621-4515) offers exhibits of NASA memorabilia, one of the mirrors from the Multiple Mirror Telescope, and space art and photos. The planetarium presents shows at the following times: Tuesday through Friday, 10 a.m., 1:30, 2:30, 7:30, and 8:30 p.m. Saturday: 1:30, 2:30, 3:30, 7:30, and 8:30 p.m. Sunday: 1:30, 2:30, and 3:30 p.m. Admission is $3.75 for adults and $3 for students, senior citizens, and children. The museum is open 1 p.m. to 4 p.m. Monday; 10 a.m. to 4 p.m. Tuesday through Friday; and 1 to 5 p.m. Saturday and Sunday.

Griffith Observatory (2800 E. Observatory Rd., Los Angeles, CA 90027; 213-664-1191) offers general shows and school programs, as well as numerous science exhibits, including a 12-inch telescope open for public viewing. The museum is open in the summer 12:30 to 10 p.m. Sunday through Friday and 11:30 a.m. to 10 p.m. Saturday; in the winter, 2 to 10 p.m. Sunday through Friday and 11:30 a.m. to 10 p.m. Saturday. The observatory is closed on Monday. Admission is $2.75 for adults and $1.50 for children and senior citizens.

Hansen Planetarium (15 S. State St., Salt Lake City, UT 84111; 801-538-2104) has both the staff and the technology to offer highly sophisticated shows. Like McDonnell Star Theater (listed in the preceding section), Hansen has a Digistar computer, which allows for greater diversity in shows. Hansen also has space-related exhibits. Hours are Monday through Wednesday, 9 a.m. to 9 p.m.; Thursday through Saturday, 9 p.m. until after midnight; and Sunday, 1 to 4 p.m.. Admission is $4 for adults, $3 for children.

H. R. MacMillan Planetarium & Gordon Southam Observatory (1100 Chestnut St., Vancouver BC V6J 3J9; 604-738-4431 planetarium; 604-738-2855 general) offers shows, classes, and observing times at this elaborate science center. The planetarium is open Tuesday through Sunday, with shows offered at 1, 9:30, and 10:45 p.m. Admission is $3.50. The observatory is free, and viewing hours are subject to weather conditions.

Morehead Planetarium (CB 3480, Morehead Planetarium Bldg., University of North Carolina at Chapel Hill, Chapel Hill, NC 27599; 919-962-1236) offers shows, exhibits, and classes. The planetarium is open Sunday through Friday, 12:30 to 5 p.m. and 6:30 to 9:30 p.m. Saturday hours are 10 a.m. to 5 p.m. and 6:30 to 9:30 p.m. Admission is $3 for adults, $2.50 for students and senior citizens, and $2 for children ages 2 through 11.

Morrison Planetarium (California Academy of Science, Golden Gate Park, San Francisco, CA 94118; 415-750-7127) is considered northern California's largest "indoor universe." Shows provide realistic simulations of the night sky as observed from any place on earth, as well as depictions of numerous celestial events and cosmic phenomena. Shows are offered Monday through Friday, 2 p.m.; Thursday, 8 p.m.; Friday evening, 7:30, 9, and 10:30 p.m.; Saturday and Sunday, 1, 2, 3, 4, 5, 7:30, and 9 p.m., with an additional show Saturday at 10:30 p.m.. Admission is $2.50 for adults, $1.75 for children ages 6 through 17, and $1.25 for senior citizens.

Here is a listing of planetariums in North America. Call first to find out whether facilities in your area are open to the public.

Alabama
Robert R. Meyer Planetarium
Birmingham-Southern College
Arkadelphia Rd., Box A-36
Birmingham, AL 35254
205-226-4700

UNA Planetarium
University of North Alabama
Box 5050
Florence, AL 35632
205-760-4334

W. A. Gayle Planetarium
1010 Forest Ave.
Montgomery, AL 36106
205-832-2625

Alaska
Marie Drake Planetarium
1250 Glacier Ave.
Juneau, AK 99801
907-586-3780

Arkansas
University of Arkansas at Little Rock
  Planetarium
2801 S. University
Little Rock, AR 72204
501-569-3259

California
Chabot College Planetarium
Hayward, CA 94545
415-786-6881

J. Frederick Ching Planetarium
Hartnell Community College
Salinas, CA 93901
408-755-6800

George Clever Planetarium
San Joaquin Delta College
5151 Pacific Ave.
Stockton, CA 95207
209-474-5051

Diablo Valley College Planetarium
Astronomy Dept.
321 Golf Club Rd.
Pleasant Hill, CA 94553
415-685-1230

El Camino College Planetarium
16007 Crenshaw Blvd.
Torrance, CA 90506
213-715-3373

Los Angeles Harbor College Planetarium
1111 S. Figueroa Pl.
Wilmington, CA 90744
213-518-1000

Los Medanos College Planetarium
2700 E. Leland Rd.
Pittsburg, CA 94565
415-439-2181

Daniel B. Millikan Planetarium
Chaffey College
5885 Haven Ave.
Alta Loma, CA 91750
714-987-1737

Minolta Planetarium
21259 Stevens Creek Blvd.
Cupertino, CA 95014
408-996-4815

Mt. San Antonio College Planetarium
1100 N. Grand Ave.
Walnut, CA 91789
714-594-5611

Orange Coast College Planetarium
2701 Fairview Rd.
Costa Mesa, CA 92628
714-432-5611

Palomar College Planetarium
1140 W. Mission Rd.
San Marcos, CA 92069
714-744-1150

Planetarium Institute
Dept. of Physics and Astronomy
San Francisco State University
San Francisco, CA 94132
415-338-1852

Riverside Community College Planetarium
4800 Magnolia
Riverside, CA 92506
714-684-3240

San Diego State University Planetarium
Astronomy Dept.
San Diego, CA 92182
619-237-1233

Santa Monica College Planetarium
1900 Pico Blvd.
Santa Monica, CA 90405
213-452-9223

Santa Rosa Junior College Planetarium
1501 Mendocino Ave.
Santa Rosa, CA 95401
707-527-4365

Schreder Planetarium
1644 Magnolia Ave.
Redding, CA 96001
916-244-4600

University of Southern California Planetarium
Dept. of Astronomy
Los Angeles, CA 90089
213-743-2696

West Valley College Planetarium
14000 Fruitvale Ave.
Saratoga, CA 95070
408-867-2200

Colorado
Fiske Planetarium and Science Center
University of Colorado
Boulder, CO 80309
303-492-5002

Gates Planetarium
2001 Colorado Blvd.
Denver, CO 80205
303-370-6374

Harry Zacheis Planetarium
Adams State College
Alamosa, CO 81102
303-589-7921

U.S. Air Force Academy Planetarium
50 ATS/DOP
Colorado Springs, CO 80840
719-472-2779

Connecticut
Copernican Observatory and Planetarium
Central Connecticut State University
Danbury, CT 06050
203-827-7852

Gengras Planetarium
950 Trout Brook Dr.
West Hartford, CT 06119
203-236-2961

Southern Conn. State University Planetarium
501 Crescent St.
New Haven, CT 06515
203-397-4347

Wickware Planetarium
Eastern Connecticut State University
Willimantic, CT 06226
203-456-2231

Delaware
Mt. Cuba Planetarium
P.O. Box 3915
Greenville, DE 19807
302-654-6407

District of Columbia
Rock Creek Nature Center Planetarium
5200 Glover Rd., NW
Washington, DC 20015
202-426-6829

Florida
Astronaut Memorial Hall
1519 Clearlake Rd.
Cocoa, FL 32922
305-632-1111

Bishop Planetarium
291 10th St. W
Bradenton, FL 34205
813-746-4132

Buehler Planetarium
3501 SW Davie Rd.
Ft. Lauderdale, FL 33314
305-475-6680

Florida State University Planetarium
Dept. of Physics
Tallahassee, FL 32306
904-644-3734

Museum of Arts and Sciences Planetarium
1040 Museum Blvd.
Daytona Beach, FL 32014
904-255-0285

Nature Center and Planetarium
P.O. Box 06023
Ft. Myers, FL 33906
813-275-3183

South Florida Science Museum and Aldrin
    Planetarium
4801 Dreher Trail N
Palm Beach, FL 33405
305-832-1988

Space Transit Planetarium
3280 S. Miami Ave.
Miami, FL 33129
305-854-4242

St. Petersburg Junior College Planetarium
P.O. Box 13489
St. Petersburg, FL 33733
813-341-4320

University of South Florida Planetarium
Physics 154
Tampa, FL 33620
813-974-3010

John Young Planetarium
Orlando Science Center
810 E. Rollins St.
Orlando, FL 32803
305-896-7151

Georgia
Fulton Planetarium
2025 Jonesboro Rd. SE
Atlanta, GA 30315
404-691-8767

Georgia Southern College Planetarium
Physics Dept.
Statesboro, GA 30460
912-681-5292

Harper Planetarium
3399 Collier Dr. NW
Atlanta, GA 30331
404-699-4566

Patterson Planetarium
2900 Woodruff Farm Rd.
Columbus, GA 31907
404-568-1730

Rollins Planetarium
Young Harris College
Young Harris, GA 30582
404-379-3990

Savannah Science Museum
4405 Paulsen St.
Savannah, GA 31405
912-355-6705

Valdosta State College Planetarium
Dept. of Physics, Astronomy, and Geology
Valdosta, GA 31698
912-333-5756

Wetherbee Planetarium
100 Roosevelt Ave.
Albany, GA 31701
912-435-1575

Idaho
Ricks College Planetarium
Math and Physics Dept.
Rexburg, ID 83440
208-356-1910

Illinois
Cernan Earth and Space Center
Triton College
2000 5th Ave.
River Grove, IL 60171
312-456-5815

John Deere Planetarium
Augustana College
Rock Island, IL 61201
309-794-7327

Lakeview Science Planetarium
1125 W. Lake Ave.
Peoria, IL 60614

Physics Dept. Planetarium
Illinois State University
Normal, IL 61761
309-438-8758

Strickler Planetarium
Olivet Nazaren University
P.O. Box 592
Kankakee, IL 60901
815-939-5267

Apollo 6 spacecraft at the Fernbank Science Center in Atlanta, Georgia.

Herbert Trackman Planetarium
Joliet Junior College
1216 Houbolt Ave.
Joliet, IL 60436
815-729-9020

Indiana
Ball State University Planetarium
Dept. of Physics and Astronomy
Muncie, IN 47306
317-285-8871

E. C. Schouweiler Planetarium
2701 Sprint St.
Fort Wayne, IN 46808
219-432-3551

Koch Science Center and Planetarium
411 S.E. Riverside Dr.
Evansville, IN 47713
812-425-2406

Turkey Run State Park Planetarium
R.R. 1, Box 164
Marshall, IN 47859
317-597-2654

Iowa
Grout Museum Planetarium
503 South St.
Waterloo, IA 50701
319-234-6357

Luther College Planetarium
700 College Dr.
Decorah, IA 52101
319-387-1124

Science Center of Iowa
4500 Grand Ave.
Des Moines, IA 50312
515-274-4138

Kansas
Barton County Community College
  Planetarium
Great Bend, KS 67530
316-792-2701

Kansas Cosmosphere and Space Center
1100 N. Plaum
Hutchinson, KS 67501
316-662-2305

L. Russel Kelce Planetarium
Pittsburg State University
Pittsburg, KS 66762
316-231-7000

Peterson Planetarium
Division of Mathematics and Physical Sciences
Emporia State University
Emporia, KS 66801
316-343-1200

Washburn University Planetarium
Dept. of Physics and Astronomy
Topeka, KS 66621
913-295-6330

Wichita Omnisphere and Science Center
220 S. Main St.
Wichita, KS 67202
316-264-3174

Kentucky
Georgetown College Planetarium
Georgetown College
Georgetown, KY 40324
502-863-8146

Hardin Planetarium
Western Kentucky University
Bowling Green, KY 42101
502-745-4044

Arnim D. Hummel Planetarium
Eastern Kentucky University
Richmond, KY 40475
606-622-1547

Rauch Memorial Planetarium
University of Louisville
Louisville, KY 40292
502-588-6665

Louisiana
Lafayette Planetarium
637 Girard Park Dr.
Lafayette, LA 70503
318-268-5544

Louisiana Arts and Science Center Planetarium
502 North Blvd.
Baton Rouge, LA 70821
504-344-9465

Louisiana Tech University Planetarium
Ruston, LA 71272
318-257-4303

St. Charles Parish Library and Planetarium
91 Lakewood Dr.
Luling, LA 77070
504-785-8471

Maine
Southworth Planetarium
University of Southern Maine
96 Falmouth St.
Portland, ME 04103
207-780-4249

University of Maine Planetarium
Physics Dept. Wingate Hall
Orono, ME 04469
207-581-1341

Maryland
K. Price Bryan Planetarium
College of Notre Dame of Maryland
4701 N. Charles St.
Baltimore, MD 21210
301-435-0100

Maryland Science Center
601 Light St.
Baltimore, MD 21230
301-685-5225

Montgomery College Planetarium
Takoma Ave. & Fenton St
Takoma Park, MD 20012
301-587-4090

U.S. Naval Academy Planetarium
Annapolis, MD 21402
301-267-3586

Washington County Planetarium
823 Commonwealth Ave.
Hagerstown, MD 21740
301-791-4172

Watson-King Planetarium
Towson State University
Baltimore, MD 21204
301-321-3014

Massachusetts
Peter Andrews Planetarium
Deerfield Academy
Deerfield, MA 01342
413-772-0241

Bassett Planetarium
Dept. of Astronomy
Amherst College
Amherst, MA 01002
413-253-5351

Framingham State College Planetarium
State St.
Framingham, MA 01701
508-626-4764

Charles Hayden Planetarium
Science Park
Boston, MA 02114
617-723-2500

New England Science Center
222 Harrington Way
Worcester, MA 01604
508-791-9211

Springfield Science Museum
236 State St.
Springfield, MA 01103
413-733-1194

Michigan
Abrams Planetarium
Michigan State University
East Lansing, MI 48824
517-355-4672

Jesse Besser Museum and Sky Theatre
491 Johnson St.
Alpena, MI 49707
517-356-2202

Roger B. Chaffee Planetarium
233 Washington SE
Grand Rapids, MI 49503
616-456-3985

Robert T. Longway Planetarium
1310 E. Kearsley St.
Flint, MI 48503
313-762-1182

McMath Planetarium
Cranbrook Institute of Science
500 Lone Pine Rd.
Bloomfield Hills, MI 48013
313-645-3235

Ruthven Planetarium Theatre
University of Michigan
1109 Geddes
Ann Arbor, MI 48109
313-764-0478

Minnesota
Marshall Alworth Planetarium
University of Minnesota at Duluth
Duluth, MN 55812
218-726-7129

Minneapolis Planetarium
300 Nicollet Mall
Minneapolis, MN 55401
612-372-6644

Moorhead State University Planetarium
Moorhead, MN 56560
218-236-3982

Paulucci Space Theatre
Hwy. 169 & E. 23rd St.
Hibbing, MN 55746
218-262-6718

St. Cloud State University Planetarium
St. Cloud, MN 56301
612-255-2013

Southwest State University Planetarium
Marshall, MN 56258
507-537-6196

Mississippi
Russell C. Davis Planetarium
201 E. Pascagoula St.
Jackson, MS 39201
601-960-1550

Missouri
Kansas City Museum Planetarium
3218 Gladstone Blvd.
Kansas City, MO 64123
816-483-8300

St. Louis Science Center
5100 Clayton Ave.
St. Louis, MO 63110
314-289-4444

STAR MAGNITUDES

Astronomers refer to the brightness of stars as their magnitude. It's a rather complex system, but in general, the smaller the number, the brighter the star. The very brightest objects in the sky have zero or negative magnitudes. Sirius, the brightest star in the sky, for example, has a magnitude of -1.4. The earth's full moon has a magnitude of -13.0, and the sun -27.0.

With the naked eye, you can see stars as faint as the 6th magnitude. With a pair of binoculars, you can see stars of the 9th magnitude. And with an 8-inch telescope, you can see stars of the 13th magnitude.

To get you started, here is a list of the 1st-magnitude stars, brighter than 1.5. If you know where to look, you should be able to see them on a good night with your naked eye.

Sirius	-1.46	Betelgeuse	0.80, variable
Canopus	-0.72	Aldebaran	0.85
Centauri (A +B)	-0.29	Crucis (A +B)	0.87
Arcturus	-0.06	Spica	0.96
Vega	0.04	Antares	1.00, variable
Capella	0.08	Pollux	1.15
Rigel	0.14	Formalhaut	1.16
Procyon	0.37	Deneb	1.25
Archernar	0.48	Crucis	1.26
Centauri	0.60	Regulus	1.35
Altair	0.76		

When comparing star magnitudes, keep in mind that a star of one magnitude is actually 2.51 times brighter than a star of the next magnitude. That means, for example, that a star of the 1st magnitude is 2.51 x 2.51 x 2.51 x 2.51 brighter than a star of the 5th magnitude. After doing all that multiplying, you will see that 1st magnitude stars are 40 times brighter than 5th-magnitude stars.

Montana
Museum of the Rockies
Montana State University
Bozeman, MT 59717
406-994-2251

Nebraska
Jenson Planetarium
Nebraska Wesleyan University
Lincoln, NE 68504
402-466-2371

J. M. McDonald Planetarium
1330 N. Burlington
Hastings, NE 68901
402-461-2399

Lueninghoener Planetarium
Midland Lutheran College
900 N. Clarkson
Fremont, NE 68025
402-721-5480

Ralph Mueller Planetarium
University of Nebraska at Lincoln
Lincoln, NE 68588
402-472-2641

Nevada
Clark Community College Planetarium
3200 E. Chevenne Ave.
North Las Vegas, NV 90030
702-644-5059

Fleischmann Planetarium
University of Nevada at Reno
Reno, NV 89557
702-784-4812

New Jersey
County College of Morris Planetarium
Rte. 10 & Centergrove Rd.
Randolph, NJ 07869
201-361-5000

Robert J. Novins Planetarium
Ocean County College, CN 2001
Toms River, NJ 08754
201-255-0343

New Mexico
Hefferan Planetarium
806 Mountain Rd. NE
Albuquerque, NM 87102
505-247-3658

New York
Andrus Planetarium
511 Warburton Ave.
Yonkers, NY 10701
914-963-4550

Gustafson Planetarium
R.D. 3, Box 276
Fishkill, NY 12524
914-897-4320

Herkimer County Boces Planetarium
Gros Blvd.
Herkimer, NY 13350
315-867-2088

Jones Planetarium Theater
I. U. Willets & Searingtown Rds.
Albertson, NY 11507
516-747-5400

Link Planetarium
30 Front St.
Binghamton, NY 13905
607-772-0660

Longwood School District Planetarium
Middle Island-Yaphank Rd.
Middle Island, NY 11953
516-345-2741

Newburgh Free Academy Planetarium
201 Fullerton Ave.
Newburgh, NY 12550
914-561-8500

Northeast Bronx Planetarium
750 Baychester Ave.
Bronx, NY 11230
718-258-9283

Potsdam College Planetarium
Pierrepont Ave.
Potsdam, NY 13676
315-267-2281

Schenectady Museum
Nott Terrace Hts.
Schenectady, NY 12308
518-382-7890

Strasenburgh Planetarium
657 East Ave.
Rochester, NY 14603
716-271-4320

SUNY at Fredonia Planetarium
Jewett Hall
Fredonia, NY 14063
716-673-3370

SUNY College at Brockport Planetarium
Brockport, NY 14420
716-395-5578

SUNY Northcountry Planetarium
Box 44, Hudson Hall
Plattsburgh, NY 12901
518-564-3166

Vanderbilt Planetarium
180 Little Neck Rd.
Centerport, NY 11721
516-262-7800

Whitworth Ferguson Planetarium
Buffalo State College
1300 Elmwood Ave.
Buffalo, NY 14222
716-878-4911

North Carolina
Discovery Place and Nature Museum
301 N. Tryon St.
Charlotte, NC 28202
704-372-6261

Haines Planetarium
Nature Science Center
Museum Dr.
Winston-Salem, NC 27105
919-767-6730

Kelly Planetarium
Sciences Museum of Charlotte
1658 Sterling Rd.
Charlotte, NC 28209
704-372-6261

North Dakota
Center for Aerospace Science
Box 8216, University Station
Grand Forks, ND 58202
701-777-2791

Ohio
Ward Beecher Planetarium
410 Wick Ave.
Youngstown, OH 44555
216-742-3616

Bowling Green State University Planetarium
Dept. of Physics and Astronomy
Bowling Green, OH 43403
419-372-8666

Copernicus Planetarium
6832 Convent Blvd.
Sylvania, OH 43560
419-885-3211

Dayton Museum of Natural History
2629 Ridge Ave.
Dayton, OH 45414
513-275-7432

Muller Planetarium
Wade Oval, University Cir.
Cleveland, OH 44106
216-231-4600

Ohio State University Planetarium
Columbus, OH 43210
614-292-1773

Ohio's Center of Science and Industry
280 E. Broad St.
Columbus, OH 43215
614-221-6051

Schuele Planetarium
28728 Wolf Rd.
Bay Village, OH 44140
216-835-9912

Oklahoma
Kirkpatrick Planetarium
2100 N.E. 52nd St.
Oklahoma City, OK 73111
405-424-5545

Oregon
Chemeketa Community College Planetarium
4000 Lancaster Dr. NE
Salem, OR 97309
503-399-5161

Harry C. Kendall Planetarium
Oregon Museum of Science and Technology
4015 SW Canyon Rd.
Portland, OR 97221
503-222-2828

Mt. Hood Community College Planetarium
26000 S.E. Stark St.
Gresham, OR 97030
503-667-7297

Pennsylvania
Allegheny College Planetarium
Meadville, PA 16335
814-724-2632

Detwiler Planetarium
Lycoming College
Williamsport, PA 17701
717-321-4284

Fred W. Diehl Planetarium
Rte. 11
Danville, PA 17821
717-275-7570

Edinboro University Planetarium
Edinboro, PA 16444
814-732-2493

Indiana University Planetarium
Geoscience Dept.
115 Walsh Hall
Indiana, PA 15705
412-357-2379

McDonald Planetarium
666 Reeves Ln.
Warminster, PA 18974
215-441-6157

North Museum
Franklin & Marshall College
P.O. Box 3003
Lancaster, PA 17604
717-291-3941

Reading School District Planetarium
1211 Parkside Dr. S
Reading, PA 19611
215-371-5850

University of Maine Planetarium in Orono, Maine. Photo by Michael York, University of Maine.

Strait Planetarium
Mansfield University
Mansfield, PA 16933
717-662-4275

Ulmer Planetarium
Lock Haven University
Lock Haven, PA 17745
717-893-2075

West Chester University Planetarium
Dept. of Geology and Astronomy
West Chester, PA 19383
215-436-2727

Rhode Island
Cormack Planetarium
Providence, RI 02905
401-785-9450

Middletown Planetarium
Aquidneck Ave.
Middletown, RI 02840
401-846-6395

South Carolina
Gibbes Planetarium
Columbia, SC 29201
803-799-2810

Howell Memorial Planetarium
Bob Jones University
Greenville, SC 29614
803-242-5100

Settlemyre Planetarium
4621 Mt. Gallant Rd.
Rock Hill, SC 29730

Stanback Museum and Planetarium
South Carolina State College
Orangeburg, SC 29117

Tennessee
M. D. Anderson Planetarium
Lambuth College
Jackson, TN 38301
901-425-3283

East Tennessee State University Planetarium
Box 22-870A
Johnson City, TN 37614
615-929-4315

University of Tennessee Planetarium
Chattanooga, TN 37403
901-425-3283

Texas
Angelo State University Planetarium
Dept. of Physics
San Angelo, TX 76909
915-942-2136

Mariam Blakemore Planetarium
1705 W. Missouri
Midland, TX 79701
915-682-8611

Cooke County College Planetarium
1525 W. California
Gainesville, TX 76240
817-668-7731

Morgan Jones Planetarium
P.O. Box 981
Abilene, TX 79604
915-673-2751

Planetarium of Brazosport
P.O. Box 1464
Lake Jackson, TX 77566
409-265-7731

Sam Houston State University Planetarium
Huntsville, TX 77340
409-294-1686

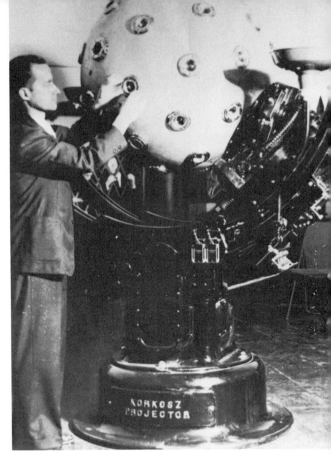

*Finishing the new "star projector" at the
Springfield (Mass.) Science Museum in 1937.*

San Antonio College Planetarium
1300 San Pedro Ave.
San Antonio, TX 78284
512-733-2910

St. Mark's School of Texas Planetarium
10600 Preston Rd.
Dallas, TX 75230
214-363-6491

Stephen F. Austin State University
  Planetarium
Dept. of Physics and Astronomy
P.O. Box 13044
SFA Station
Nacogdoches, TX 75962
409-568-3001

University of Texas at Arlington Planetarium
Physics Dept.
Box 19059
Arlington, TX 76019
817-273-2266

Utah
Sarah Summerhays Planetarium
Brigham Young University
492 ESC
Provo, UT 87602
801-378-2805

Vermont
Fairbanks Museum and Planetarium
Main St.
Essex Junction, VT 05819
802-748-2372

Virginia
Chesapeake Planetarium
300 Cedar Rd.
Chesapeake, VA 23320
804-547-0153

Eastern Mennonite College Planetarium
Harrisonburg, VA 22801
703-433-2771

Norfolk State University Planetarium
2401 Corprew Ave.
Norfolk, VA 23504
804-623-8240

Pittsylvania County School Planetarium
37 Pruden Ave. SE
Chatham, VA 24531
804-432-2761

Mary D. Pretlow Planetarium
Old Dominion University
Hampton Blvd.
Norfolk, VA 23508
804-440-4108

Science Museum of Virginia
2500 W. Broad St.
Richmond, VA 23220
804-257-1657

John C. Wells Planetarium
James Madison University
Harrisonburg, VA 22807
703-568-6109

J. Calder Wicker Planetarium
Fork Union Military Academy
Rte. 15, P.O. Box 278
Fork Union, VA 23055
804-842-3216

Washington
Eastern Washington University Planetarium
300 Patterson Hall
Cheney, WA 99164
509-335-3136

Geer Planetarium
3000 Landerholm Cir. SE
Bellevue, WA 98007
206-641-2321

Pacific Science Center
200 Second Ave. N
Seattle, WA 98109
206-433-2920

Washington State University Planetarium
Program in Astronomy
Pullman, WA 99164
509-335-3136

West Virginia
Dwight O. Conner Planetarium
2101 Dudley Ave.
Parkersburg, WV 26101
304-420-9595

Wisconsin
Buckstaff Planetarium
University of Wisconsin at Oshkosh
800 Algoma Blvd.
Oshkosh, WI 54901
414-424-4429

L. E. Phillips Planetarium
Dept. of Physics and Astronomy
University of Wisconsin at Eau Claire
Eau Claire, WI 54701
715-836-5731

University of Wisconsin at La Crosse
    Planetarium
Physics Dept., Cowley Hall
La Crosse, WI 54601
608-785-8669

University of Wisconsin at Stevens Point
    Planetarium
Dept. of Physics and Astronomy
Stevens Point, WI 54481
715-346-2208

Wyoming
Casper Planetarium
904 N. Poplar
Casper, WY 82601
307-577-0310

Distances in the Universe

When you look up at a star-filled sky, the universe appears to be packed with countless objects. But space, within galaxies and between them, is actually almost empty. There are, of course, billions of stars within each of the billions of galaxies spread across the universe. Yet the universe is so huge that these inconceivable numbers of galaxies and stars are lost in its depth.

Close to home, astronomical distances are relatively easy to comprehend. The average distance between earth and the moon, for example, is 240,000 miles. You could travel this distance by making ten trips around earth's equator. This journey would be long in human terms, but it could be made.

Now imagine a trip that can't be made—a journey to the edge of the universe. Moving outward from earth, we see the planets in our solar system spanning 8 billion miles. This distance is so vast that even light, traveling at 186,000 miles per second, takes 12 hours to cross it.

Farther out lie the closest stars. Twenty stars lie within 4 parsecs of the sun. (Astronomers use parsecs to measure distances in space. One parsec equals 20 trillion miles.) Although stars are so distant that their light takes several years to reach us, they are close compared with other objects in the galaxy.

The sun belongs to a system of billions of stars called a galaxy. Our galaxy is a flattened, spiral disk of stars called the Milky Way. The sun and its neighboring stars lie in a spiral arm of the Milky Way, 8,000 parsecs from the center of the galaxy. Light traveling from the center of the galaxy reaches us in just over 25,000 years.

Measuring some 35,000 parsecs across, the Milky Way holds between 200 billion and 400 billion stars as well as large amounts of interstellar gas and dust. So vast is this volume that all these stars and gas and dust are no more than a glittering band of light spanning the night sky.

And the Milky Way is only one of billions of galaxies. Just as stars are held together in galaxies, we find galaxies in clusters bonded by their mutual gravity. The Milky Way belongs to a small cluster of galaxies called the Local Group. Another galaxy in the Local Group, Andromeda, is the spiral galaxy closest to the Milky Way. Andromeda and the Milky Way are 670,000 parsecs apart, so light from the Andromeda spiral has traveled 2.2 million years before reaching us.

Clusters of galaxies are also bound together by gravity to form super-clusters. The universe contains enormous chains, strings, and sheets of super-clusters.

The astronomer can no more comprehend such vastness than the average person on the street can. Yet astronomers can and do think routinely about the universe, trying to fathom its vastness and to learn a little more about what happened unimaginable times and distances from us. We cannot help being awed by our universe, but we can be proud knowing we are doing our best to understand it.

University of Wyoming Planetarium
Dept. of Physics and Astronomy
Box 3905
Laramie, WY 82071
307-766-6150

CANADA
Doran Planetarium
Laurentian University
Sudbury, ON P3E 2C6
705-675-1151

Lockhart Planetarium
University of Manitoba
500 Dysart Rd.
Winnipeg, MB R3T 2M8
204-474-9785

Planetarium Dow
1000, rue St. Jacques Ouest
Montreal, PQ H3C 1G7
514-872-4530

Seneca College Planetarium
1750 Finch Ave. E
North York, ON M5S 5T7
416-491-5050

The Paulucci Space Theater in Hibbing, Minnesota.

HOW TO CHOOSE A TELESCOPE

by Alan MacRobert

Sooner or later, every beginning amateur astronomer faces a major decision: what to do about getting a telescope. When it comes to astronomy, this is probably the most critical move you will ever make. If chosen well, a telescope will open up a lifetime of pleasurable evenings exploring the sky. If chosen poorly, it is likely to bring frustration and disillusionment and eventually be sold at a loss in the classified ads: "mint condition, rarely used."

What makes for the right decision? This depends more on you than on the telescope itself. If you live in a fifth-floor city apartment with tiny closets and are fascinated by the moon and planets, you should get an entirely different instrument than if you live on a farm in Vermont with a nice empty shed and your true love is galaxies. The money you can spend, the weight you can lift, and the amount of observing you've already done with the naked eye and binoculars are also crucial.

A telescope's most important characteristic is its *aperture* (the size of the light-collecting mirror or lens), which determines its light grasp and resolving power. A 3-inch telescope can never show stars as detailed as a good 6-inch will. This suggests that choosing a telescope ought to be easy: get the biggest aperture you can afford. But in practice, it's not so simple. For example, a telescope's *f/ratio* or *focal length* is also an important consideration.

TELESCOPE TYPES

It is important first to understand the strengths and drawbacks of different optical designs. There used to be just two basic types of telescope to choose from, *refractor* and *reflector*. Now there is a third, the *catadioptric*. Each has reasons it should be sought or avoided.

Refractors. Refractors use a glass lens to focus light. The refractor was king until the early twentieth century, and it still has devotees. But in apertures (the diameter of the telescope's main lens or mirror) larger than 3 or 4 inches, its heyday has passed for several reasons.

The advantages of refractors are that they are rugged, require little or no maintenance, and have sealed tubes that keep out dust and image-degrading air currents. They have no obstruction in the light path to reduce contrast, but this advantage is offset by their chromatic aberration. At long focal lengths (f/12 or f/15) all aberrations are minimized,

A reflector telescope, made by Edmund Scientific.

making for extremely crisp images over a wide field of view. Large refractors are probably still unsurpassed for observing the moon, planets, and double stars.

The disadvantage of refractors is that they are *very* expensive for the aperture. They are quite big and heavy, require tall mountings (which are both expensive and prone to shakiness), and usually need a diagonal mirror at the eyepiece for comfortable viewing. The diagonal mirror inverts the image right-for-left and makes it that much harder to compare with charts.

Refractors still hold sway at very small apertures—up to about 3 inches—but beware of cheap ones. Even if their optics are good, their mounts are often so poor that the view will constantly shake, and they will be pure frustration to use. If you can't afford to spend more than $300 or so, get a pair of binoculars instead, or save the money toward a better telescope later.

Reflectors. By the middle of this century, the refractor's popularity had slipped to second place among amateurs, and the reflector (which uses a curved, circular mirror to focus light) was becoming the telescope of choice. The reflectors provide much more light grasp for the money and are simple enough for the do-it-yourselfer to build from scratch.

Among reflectors' advantages is that they still offer the most aperture per dollar. They have only two optical surfaces (not counting the eyepiece), meaning fewer places where optical flaws and other problems can degrade contrast and definition. (The fewer surfaces a light wave encounters, the less trouble it can get into.) The popular *Newtonian* design is low to the ground, allowing a stubbier, more stable mount. Because it has an even number of mirrors, the image is not mirror-reversed. In addition, dew is less likely to condense on the mirror on damp

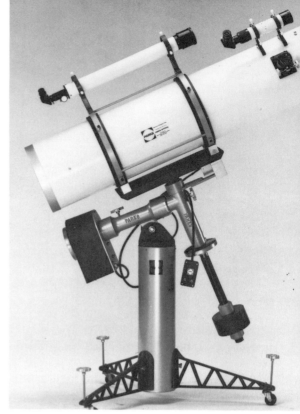

10-inch f/5 refractor, made by Parks Optical.

nights, since it is at the bottom of a long tube.

The disadvantage of reflectors is that they require the most care and maintenance. The open tube means dust on the optics, no matter how well the tube is sealed during storage (although small amounts of dust have surprisingly little effect on performance). The mirrors may often need realigning, an easy but sometimes tiresome procedure of turning screws on the mirror mounts. Every 5 to 20 years the mirrors will need to be sent off for realuminizing. Also, during observing, the open tube allows internal air currents that may harm image definition until the telescope comes to the same temperature as the surrounding air. And the field of good definition is somewhat limited; at low powers, stars suffer distortion near the field edge.

Older astronomy manuals state that reflectors are definitely inferior to refractors, and they sometimes equate a 6-inch mirror with a 3-inch lens. This may have been true in the past, but today a well-made Newtonian is nearly the equal of a refractor, at least in the long focal ratios of f/10 and up.

Catadioptrics. These are the newest wave in amateur telescopes. By combining an extremely short-focus mirror with a corrector plate, a big telescope can be compressed into a small package. In the standard designs, the mirror has a simple spherical surface figure, lending itself well to mass production. Several companies have taken advantage of this fact to turn the large astronomical telescope into a mass-marketed consumer item. One example is the commercially available Schmidt-Cassegrain.

The breakthrough that catadioptrics represent is in portability and convenience, not in visual performance. Although most people can manage to lug an 8-inch Newtonian in and out of doors, it is awkward, heavy, and subject to bangs and bumps on the way. An 8-inch Schmidt-Cassegrain comes in a padded footlocker that can be carried with one hand; the tripod is separate. The telescope can be stowed in a car or closet like a piece of luggage, whereas a Newtonian tends to displace everything around it. A catadioptric's sealed tube protects the mirrors, and the firm construction reduces alignment problems. The light, compact tube allows a clock drive to track the stars more reliably, making photography easier. The undistorted field of view is wider than that of a Newtonian, although some light is lost near the edges.

Among the disadvantages of catadioptrics is that their incoming light strikes seven optical surfaces (when the diagonal prism is used) rather than a Newtonian's two, and the secondary obstruction is bigger than that of any but short-focus Newtonians. Inevitably a slightly less crisp image results. The cost is higher than for a

8-inch Schmidt-Cassegrain telescope made by Meade Instruments Corp.

reflector of the same aperture, though still well below that of a refractor. With the diagonal in use, the image is mirror-reversed.

The other commonly sold catadioptric design is the *Maksutov*. This type gives a very wide, flat field with sharpness that can match that of a long-focus refractor. Hence some manufacturers have used this design for extremely high-quality (and expensive) small instruments. They are bought by those for whom convenience and perfection outweigh small aperture and higher price.

WHAT ARE YOU LOOKING AT?

The sun, moon, planets, and close double stars require high power and sharp resolution, and if these are your main interest, a long-focus reflector or refractor (f/12 and up) may be best. Faint comets, star clusters, galaxies, and nebulas generally need low powers, a wide field, and less critical resolution, and this is where short-focus (also known as "rich-field") instruments of f/6 and below come into their own.

If you have not specialized to the point of ruling out one type of observing, an all-purpose midrange telescope will serve best. But within any given telescope design, a higher f/ratio means a better image. You can always get low power by using a long-focus eyepiece, assuming the telescope was built to give a wide enough fully illuminated field. Also, a high f/ratio does not require expensive, highly corrected eyepiece designs. Then again, a high f/ratio means a longer, heavier, and more awkward telescope. Everything is a trade-off.

One factor may force your selection of interests: light pollution (caused by manmade lighting sources). The moon, major planets, and brighter star images have high surface brightness and are hardly affected by a bright sky. The fifth-floor city dweller could clamp a small refractor or catadioptric to the rail of a fire escape and enjoy as fine a view of the moon as could the Vermont farmer (discounting local air turbulence). But almost all deep-sky objects might be invisible to the city dweller.

WHERE DO YOU LIVE?

You don't just look through a telescope. You have to store it and carry it. You have to set it up *and* take it down at the end of a long day, when most people are ready for bed. If this is a lot of work, you won't observe very often no matter how burning your enthusiasm may be. Too many novices forget this and buy "white ele-phants" they hardly ever use.

Remember: *A 3-inch will show more than a 12-inch if you use it more.* And how good an astronomer you become depends on how much time you spend observing, not what you observe with.

Figure out where you'll use the telescope and where you'll store it. The farther these points are apart, the smaller and lighter the instrument you should get. Does the route involve stairs? Then think very carefully before getting any reflector bigger than a 6-inch. An enclosed, unheated porch or a clean, weatherproof shed are excellent for storage, since the telescope will be at nearly outdoor temperature before you use it.

Can you see the whole sky from one spot, or will you have to tote the telescope around to avoid trees and light? If you have a permanent observing site, consider installing a pier rather than lugging the tripod in and out. A concrete-filled pipe cemented deep into the ground will be steadier than a tripod. If the mount can withstand moisture, leave it atop the pier under a tarpaulin. The ideal solution is a shelter or observatory around the entire telescope. This is the only way really large instruments become practical.

Comfort is essential while observing, so plan to sit at the eyepiece. This means getting an adjustable tripod or, in a Newtonian, a rotating tube.

An equatorial mount is a great observing aid even without a clock drive; its motions define east-west and north-south in the field of view, making direction finding relatively easy. Setting circles should be included (but don't plan to rely on them; they take some learning and practice and are no substitute for knowing how to find things visually). Azimuth mounts are simpler and less bulky than equatorials, and these advantages are exploited to the utmost by the Dobsonian mount design.

Whatever mount you get, don't

Reflector telescope, made by Celestron International.

compromise on its size and strength. Nothing will kill your enthusiasm like a perpetually shaky view, whereas a solidly mounted telescope—one that wiggles only a little bit when you focus it—is a joy to use.

SHOPPING TIPS

Having narrowed your choices—perhaps to a 6-inch f/8 Newtonian, or a 4- to 8-inch catadioptric—get all the manufacturers' catalogs and compare details, paying careful attention to size and weight. Call different dealers for the best price, and insist on an *honest* appraisal of the delivery date.

If possible, star-test a telescope before buying. This is especially important when considering a used instrument not covered by warranty. Optical quality varies among manufacturers and even among identical-looking instruments from the same company. Here is an easy but very stringent test:

With the optics properly aligned and the telescope at the same temperature as the air, focus on a 2nd- or 3rd-magnitude star using a high power. Turn the knob by small, equal amounts—first to one side, then the other side of best focus. The shimmering out-of-focus diffraction rings should look just the same in both cases; they should be round and have the same distributions of light within them.

The best advice of all is to seek guidance from other amateurs. The Astronomical League and Western Amateur Astronomers are umbrella groups of amateur clubs that can direct you to the nearest astronomy club, whose members will be happy to offer frank opinions. You may even get the chance to try out a variety of telescopes, which will help you decide whether twice the aperture is really worth four times the cost and six times the weight. For local addresses of these organizations, contact the national offices; addresses may also be found under "Astronomical Societies."

Reprinted with permission of *Sky & Telescope.* Copyright 1983 Sky Publishing Corporation.

BINOCULARS: THE IDEAL STARTER

By Alan MacRobert

One December evening when I was 14 years old, I was playing with a large magnifying glass and happened to hold it up in line with a Christmas light on the other end of the house. Suddenly, the lens was filled with a blinding glare. How could such a dim light, I wondered, produce such a dazzle? Would it work on an even fainter light—a distant streetlight, say, or a star? I ran out into the cold night to try. The results were disappointing. But my father, who came out to see me holding the magnifying glass up to the stars, suggested I try the family binoculars instead. I did, and the sight that night of the Pleiades, Jupiter with its tiny moons, and the belt of Orion started me on an

11 x 80 center-focus binocular, from Swift Instruments.

astronomical path that continues to this day.

It seemed too easy. I'd never realized that ordinary binoculars could be an astronomical instrument. Like many American children at the start of the space age, I had learned the basics of astronomy. But *observing* celestial objects seemed to be something only scientists could do, or advanced sorts who built their own observatories. As I found out in the following months, however, a pair of binoculars opens up endless opportunities for serious sky exploring.

Binoculars are the ideal starter instrument because they're so simple to use. You see the image right side up and in front of you. The large field of view makes it easy to find what you point at. Yet binoculars reveal many sights that most people think require a telescope—including craters, mountains, and plains on the moon, planets and their satellites, comets, asteroids, double and variable stars, star clusters, nebulas, and galaxies.

The observing skills you'll gain while finding these things are the same as those needed to use a telescope. But binoculars are far cheaper as a first investment—not to mention being easier to carry outdoors or store in a closet.

CHOOSING YOUR BINOCULARS

Any optical aid will bring deeper views of the sky than the naked eye, and any binoculars that happen to be available, no matter how small, are enough to launch a rewarding observing program. But some kinds are much better for astronomy than others.

The variety of brands and models on the market can be bewildering. Prismatic binoculars have been made commercially for over 80 years, and manufacturers have long since incorporated whatever easy improvements are possible. So today, when a particular model offers special advantages, you can expect these to be offset by corresponding disadvantages in performance, convenience, or price. Choosing the right instrument is partly a matter of choosing where to compromise. Here are some things to consider:

Power. Every pair of binoculars has a two-number designation, such as 6 x 30 or 8 x 50. The first number is the magnifying power. The second is the diameter of the objective (front) lenses in millimeters.

Beginners usually assume that the higher the power the better. Higher powers do penetrate light pollution more effectively, and are best for double stars, star clusters, and certain other objects, such as the moons of Jupiter. But high powers also narrow the field of view (making it harder to find your way among the stars), magnify imperfections of

manufacture, and, worst of all, magnify the constant dancing of the stars when the instrument is held in the hands. For this last reason, 8 power is the maximum recommended for hand-held binoculars.

Aperture. The bigger the objective lenses, the brighter the stars, and here you should compromise least. Astronomical objects are usually hard to see—not because they are small and need more magnification but because they are faint and need more aperture (or a bigger lens). A pair of 7 x 50 "night glasses" collect twice as much light as the all-purpose 7 x 35s, and hence make everything appear almost a magnitude brighter. The corresponding disadvantage (aside from the higher price) is that they are bigger and heavier, making them less appropriate for daytime use. For hikes or the ballpark, 7 x 35s would be the better choice—or even 7 x 30s or 6 x 24s, sacrificing both power and aperture for light weight and convenience.

Giant 20 x 100 binoculars,
from Celestron International.

Quality versus price. Suppose you have decided on 7 x 50s. You may find three similar-looking instruments offered for $37, $150, and $800. Do these prices really reflect the range of value?

This is a matter of opinion: A pair that costs 20 times more than another will not show 20 times as much—but if it is subjected to bangs and bumps, it may keep its alignment 20 times longer. Especially away from the extremes, say in the $60 to $250 range, you usually get what you pay for.

In this range, many manufacturers offer A, B, and C lines of binoculars to provide a selection of values and prices. A cheaper instrument may be a good buy for a casual user. But quality is *very* important in the stringent applications of astronomy, so you should consider the better grades. If the manufacturer's catalog does not note the grades explicitly (such as by "good," "better," and "best"), price is often a reliable way to tell them apart. However, having decided on a make and model, you may get a bargain on it by checking with discount stores and dealers.

Used binoculars can be bought at great savings in secondhand stores and pawnshops, but you risk getting stuck with a lemon. The following tests, which can be done in less time than it takes to read them, will enable you to judge the value of any binoculars, new or used.

TESTING BINOCULARS

1. Pick up the instrument and compare its overall workmanship with that of other brands; some will seem more carefully made than others. Hold the two barrels and try to twist them slightly. If there is any play in the joints or anything rattles, reject the pair. Move the barrels together and apart; the hinges should work smoothly, with steady resistance. So should the focusing motions for both eyepieces. On center-focus binoculars, the eyepiece frame should not tilt when you turn the focus in and out.

2. Next, look into the large objective lenses with a light shining over your shoulder so the inside of the barrel is illuminated. Reject the pair if a film of dirt or mildew is visible on any glass surface. (A little dust on the outside is not a problem.) Look at the two reflections from the front and back of the lens. If the lens is antireflection coated—and it should be—both reflections will be purple or amber, not white. Move the binoculars around until you see a third reflection deeper inside, from the first surface of the prisms. This too should be colored, not white. Then, still looking in the front, aim the eyepiece at a nearby light bulb and move the glasses around to view a row of internal reflections. The ratio of colored to white images indicates the percentage of coated to uncoated surfaces. The coatings increase light transmission and contrast, both of which are important in astronomy. In very good models, all glass-to-air surfaces are coated.

3. Turn the binoculars around and repeat your examination of lenses and coatings from the eye end. Then, holding the glasses a foot or so in front of you, aim them at the sky or a bright wall. Look at the little disks of light floating in front of the eyepieces. These are the *exit pupils*. If they have four shadowy edges, rendering them squarish instead of round, the prisms are not the best and are cutting off some light. In good binoculars, the exit pupils are uniformly bright to their edges. They should be surrounded by darkness, not by reflections from inside the barrels.

4. Finally, look through the instrument, and focus each side separately; a noticeably filmy or gray image indicates an unacceptable contrast problem. If you wear glasses, leave them on only if you

need them to correct for astigmatism; if you keep them on, make sure you can get your eyes close enough to view the full field.

Each barrel should point in the same direction! If you see a double image—even for just a moment before your eyes compensate for the displacement—you have a reject. The eyestrain would be a constant headache (literally). For a somewhat better test, look at something through the binoculars, then slowly move them a few inches from your eyes while still viewing the object. It should show no tendency to become double, even when you close and reopen your eyes. Misalignment caused by flimsy prism supports is the *worst* problem of cheap binoculars; even a small knock can render a working pair worthless. More expensive instruments should stand up better to rough handling.

Note the size of the field of view: the wider the better. But the edges of a wide field usually have poor optical quality. Sweep the field at right angles across a straight line, such as a doorframe or telephone wire. Watch whether the line bows in or out near the edges. This distortion should be slight.

Look at sharp lines dividing light and dark, such as tree limbs or the edge of a building against a bright sky. Do they have red or blue fringes? No instrument is perfectly free from such chromatic aberration, but some are better than others.

ONE LAST WORD

Don't be discouraged if you can't find (or can't afford) perfection. Success in amateur astronomy depends on good attitudes more than good instruments. This was driven home to me some years ago after I moved into downtown New Haven, Connecticut. The skies were awful, my pair of 7 x 50s was mediocre, and there was no place to use them except through a plastic bubble skylight in the roof of my apartment. The plastic turned star images into shapes I felt no true amateur would deign to look at. But they were there all right, and I was so intrigued at being able to observe *anything* under such conditions that I kept at it. It turned out that stars could be detected to 8th magnitude, and I wound up spending a year following variables, hunting clusters and doubles, comparing stellar colors, and becoming more familiar with the sky than ever before. So take what you've got and enjoy it.

Reprinted with permission of *Sky & Telescope*. Copyright 1983 Sky Publishing Corporation.

WHERE TO BUY TELESCOPES AND BINOCULARS

Although it would be possible to provide a complete list of all manufacturers of binoculars and telescopes, such a list wouldn't be very helpful; it would be too long and confusing for most people. Here are some of the best-known companies. When possible, we've included prices and model numbers for their notable products. This price list is by no means all-inclusive. If you don't see something you like here, contact the company for a catalog or additional information and prices. Note that all prices listed here are suggested retail prices and are subject to change.

Asko/RVR Optical (P.O. Box 62, Eastchester, NY 10709; 914-337-4085) is a manufacturer of big telescopes. It offers Cassegrain models from 17.7 inches to 27.6 inches. Its catalog includes focusing mechanisms, ventilation systems, and many other accessories for advanced applications.

aus Jena, imported by Europtik, Ltd. (P.O. Box 319, Dunmore, PA 18512; 717-347-6049) offers German-made precision high-end binoculars. Of particular interest is the 12 x 50 B Dodecarem Series ($610), which offers excellent light-gathering properties, and the 8 x 50 B Octarem ($580). Both are wide-angle glasses.

Bausch & Lomb/Bushnell (300 N. Lone Hill Ave., San Dimas, CA 91773; 800-423-3537; 714-592-8000), although known mostly for its binoculars, also offers a variety of refractor telescopes and its Banner series of spotting scopes, which look a bit like a pair of half-binoculars. The company offers some excellent waterproof binoculars, and a nice 7 x 50 wide-angle pair (model 13-7505). For in-depth stargazing, check out the Sportview 16 x 50 (13-1665), the Astronomical 11 x 80 (11-1180), or the Astronomical 20 x 80 (11-2080).

Brandon/VERNONscope & Co. (Candor, NY 13743; 607-659-7000) is the maker of the Brandon 94-millimeter f/7 Apochromatic Refractor telescope, the "ultimate" portable scope. It is very versatile and can be used to view the moon, the planets, and deep sky objects. The tube assembly is compact at 99-millimeter and weighs only 8 pounds. The focal ratio of f/7 was chosen for overall viewing versatility, and the 640-millimeter focal length allows for a wide range of specifications to suit all observing requirements. The tube assembly and eyepiece can be purchased together for $1,595. Parts are also sold separately. Send for a price list for more complete information.

California Telescope Co. (P.O. Box 1338, Burbank, CA 91507; 818-505-8424), a well-known retailer, sells a wide range of telescopes, including Meade Instruments, Celestron International, Bausch & Lomb, Tele Vue Optics, and Edmund Scientific. Prices range from $995 to $4,000. The company has many accessories in stock and a catalog is available.

Celestron International (2835 Columbia St., Torrance, CA 90503; 800-421-1526; 213-328-9560) makes several types of telescopes and binoculars, but it is best known for the C5, C8, and C14 Schmidt-Cassegrain telescopes. A good starter telescope is Celestron's appropriately named Firstscope 80 (model 21023), a sturdy refractor with slow-motion controls on flex cables. Also check out the Comet Catcher reflector (21004) and the extremely portable C90 Astro Maksutov-Cassegrain. Binocular astronomers will want to take a peek at the Celestron Giant Series, which offers a range of big binoculars, from 11 x 80 up to 20 x 100.

Company Seven (14300-117 Cherry Lane Ct., Laurel, MD 20707; 301-953-2000), a retailer, offers a wide selection of telescopes, including Meade Instruments, Celestron, and Bausch & Lomb. All price ranges are available. The catalog costs $3.

Edmund Scientific (101 E. Gloucester Pike, Barrington, NJ 08007; 609-573-6259) manufactures and distributes scientific equipment and other products, including a couple of telescopes under its own label: a 60-millimeter f/8 refractor (P31,611; $299.95) and a 3-inch, f/6 reflector (P31,308; $199.95). Edmund also carries the uniquely designed Astroscan hybrid reflecting telescope (P2001; $359), with a bottom that looks like a bowling ball. It

can be set in its base at any angle for easy viewing, or slung over a shoulder by its strap for easy transport into the countryside. It is a favorite first telescope for amateurs because it is durable and easy to use.

Martin's Star Tracker (3163 Walnut St., Boulder, CO 80301; 303-449-3350) has a new line of high-resolution telescopes, the MST-6 and the MST-10, copied from a design by *Astronomy Magazine* editor Richard Berry. The MST-6 is a long-focus (f/8 or f/10) 6-inch Newtonian reflector designed for viewing planets and double stars. The MST-10 has a 10-inch diameter aperture, f/4.5, as well as a fully rotational tube system. The MST-6 sells for $1,695; the MST-10 for $1,895.

Meade Instruments Corp. (1675 Toronto Way, Costa Mesa, CA 92626; 714-556-2291) offers one of the widest ranges of equipment of any company. Meade

Left: beginner's telescope, from Edmund Scientific. Right: 8-inch Schmidt-Newtonian telescope, from Meade Instruments Corp.

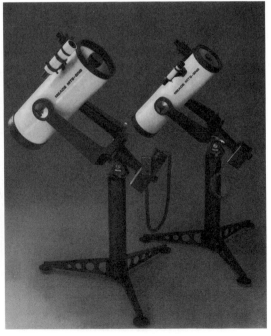

makes both telescopes and binoculars, including a well-supported series of Schmidt-Cassegrain design catadioptric telescopes. Several of these are sold in packages that include motor drives, assorted eyepieces, tripods, and carrying cases. List prices range from $1,300 to $5,200. Meade's Giant Series binoculars all come with carrying cases and photo tripod adapters. The biggest is the 30 x 80 (06230; $570).

Parks Optical (270 Easy St., Simi Valley, CA 93065; 805-522-6722) offers a full line of refractors, reflectors, catadioptrics, and binoculars. Its Comet Finder ($350) is a compact and practical scope with zoom capability, whereas the Jovian-4 ($599) is a sturdy catadioptric. Parks offers a pair of 6-inch reflectors ($799) and an 8-inch reflector ($1,099). The company's Giant Binocular series includes two 11 x 80 models, a 14 x 80, and a 20 x 80, with prices ranging up to $500.

Questar Corporation (P.O. Box 59, New Hope, PA 18938; 215-862-5277) offers catadioptric telescopes in all shapes and sizes. But the company's greatest gift to astronomy may be its Standard model, a 3 1/2-inch catadioptric scope with a map of the heavens printed on its tube. This scope ($2,677, or $1,795 for the field model) is often used in astronomy class-rooms.

Star Instruments (P.O. Box 597, Flagstaff, AZ 86002; 602-774-9177) offers Newton-ian telescopes ranging from $400 (10-inch-diameter aperture; f/4 or f/5) to $6,100 (24-inch diameter, f/4 or f/5); classical Cassegrains from $600 (10-inch diameter, f/5) to $7,300 (24-inch diameter, f/16); and Ritchey-Chretien telescopes from $700 (10-inch, f/8.4) to $10,000 (24-inch, f/8).

Star Liner Co. (1106 S. Columbus Blvd.,

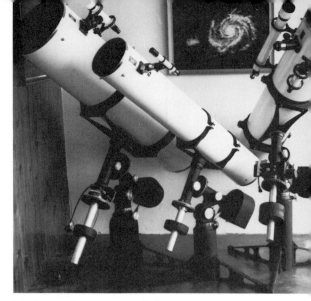

Various telescopes made by Star Liner Co.

Tucson, AZ 85711; 602-795-3361) makes big telescopes that carry big price tags. For example, several universities use Star Liner scopes for viewing the night sky beyond the typical "amateur" range. Prices are, well, astronomical, ranging up to $80,000.

Swift Instruments (952 Dorchester Ave., Boston, MA 02125; 800-446-4544; 617-436-2960) manufactures both binoculars and telescopes. Of the latter, its good starter refractors include the Aerolite Student Model (860; $310) and the Swift Astronomical Refractor (859; $675). If you are looking for compact power, there's the relatively inexpensive Swift Short Tube Catadioptric (865; $350).

Tectron Telescopes (2111 Whitfield Park Ave., Sarasota, FL 34243; 813-758-9890) builds 20-inch and 25-inch lightweight Dobsonian telescopes, with a focal ratio of f/5. Prices are $3,200 for the 20-inch and $5,500 for the 25-inch. Crating charge is $150.

Tele Vue (20 Dexter Pl., Pearl River, NY 10965; 914-735-4044) makes a nice personal telescope called the Oracle 3, a 3-inch-diameter refractor. It boasts good resolution and contrast through a multi-coated triplet objective lens. It may be attached to a standard camera tripod. Also noteworthy is Tele Vue's Genesis refractor. It has a 4-inch-diameter aperture, f/9, with magnification from 9x to 260x and offers a selection of eyepieces.

DISCOUNT HOUSES

Buying optical equipment from discount houses, like buying anything else at discount, can be risky, particularly if you are a novice. You can get a good price, to be sure, but don't look for much in the way of service. These sources are best when you already know what you want and how to use it, and don't need or expect much in the way of assistance. Among the principal discounters are:

Ad-libs Astronomics
2401 Tee Cir.
Norman, OK 73069
800-422-7876; 404-364-0858

Chicago Optical & Supply Co.
9114 N. Waukegan Rd.
P.O. Box 1361
Morton Grove, IL 60053
312-827-4846

Northern Sky Telescopes
5667 Duluth St.
Golden Valley, MN 55422
800-345-4202; 612-545-6786

Orion Telescope Center
421 Soquel Ave.
P.O. Box 1158
Santa Cruz, CA 95061
800-447-1001; 800-443-1001 in CA

Pauli's Discount Optics
29 Kingswood Rd.
Danbury, CT 06811
203-746-3579

Scope City
679 Easy St.
Simi Valley, CA 93065
805-522-6646

Sunwest Space Systems
P.O. Box 20500
St. Petersburg, FL 33742
813-577-0629

Roger W. Tuthill, Inc.
Box 1086Q
Mountainside, NJ 07092
800-223-1063; 201-232-1786

For more information about selecting telescopes, write to the Astronomical Society of the Pacific (390 Ashton Ave., San Francisco, CA 94112; 415-337-1100) for its detailed booklet *Selecting Your First Telescope*. A $4 donation is requested.

A 16-inch long catadioptric telescope, from Swift Instruments.

BUILDING FUN TELESCOPES FOR LESS THAN $10

by Robert Monaghan

Telescopes started out as a playground accident: the spectacle maker's children played with some discarded lenses and by chance hit upon a combination that made distant objects look close. Within a few years word of the discovery spread to Italy, where an ambitious scientist, one Galileo Galilei, turned an "optic tube" skyward and started a major revolution in astronomy.

Too few of us play with lenses anymore. We prefer to buy ready-made telescopes and computerized cameras and then casually follow the directions for their use instead of experimenting with bits and pieces of optical equipment and learning from our experiments.

Here are some simple ideas for things you can make and do with lenses, things you can really enjoy trying. There's something here for any curious person: a beginner, an old pro, or someone in between. The optics may be surplus, obsolete, or gathering dust in your closet or camera bag. Obsolete junk has one big advantage: it's really cheap. Break out the junk and start experimenting! And don't be surprised if some of these crazy ideas become a part of your stock of astronomical equipment.

Start off by dredging up that old 8-millimeter movie camera, the kind with a screw-in lens. Remember that relic from the days before home video? If you find an old camera with a three-lens turret, you're in luck, but the really obsolete, non-Super-8-know-nothing camera is perfect. These usually go for a couple of dollars at yard sales.

Why search for these ancient 8-millimeter cameras? The answer is simple:

The lens, used backward, makes a very acceptable eyepiece. A normal lens for such cameras is roughly 13-millimeter focal length at f/2. The aperture is around 7-millimeter in diameter when fully open. The lenses are high-quality, highly color-corrected formulas designed to put images on 8-millimeter film that will be blown up to wall size. It's relatively easy to make good-quality glass lenses in such small sizes. Even so, the original lens often costs a substantial sum, especially converted into today's dollars. Because they're obsolete, they're a real bargain.

Do you have an old 2.4-inch refractor? You know, the kind you saw being sold as "Comet Clobberer" during the Halley craze but one that is 20 years old? Try this: Compare the 8-millimeter movie camera lens with your economy 0.965-inch eyepiece. The first time I did this I was amazed. The movie camera lens gave greater sharpness and clarity than the eyepiece did, and it hadn't cost me a cent. Most of the old color fringing was gone too. So for a couple of bucks at most, you'll have an amazingly good quality eyepiece. Your old Comet Clobberer, equipped with its obsolete 8-millimeter camera lens, now turns out to be a nice scope. You might even feel the urge to start using it again. Sure, I know a standard eyepiece might be even better, but try finding one for the cost of a burger.

To make your junk-box eyepiece more permanent, use some metal or plastic tubing, epoxy, black paint, a black cardboard stop (optional), and voilà!— you've just built your own experimental eyepiece. It may even become your favorite.

An inexpensive, simple-design telescope. Courtesy Astronomy *magazine, Kalmbach Publishing Company.*

STARTING TO BUILD

Now let's try building a telescope. What can you use for an objective lens? You need a good magnification ratio, and a fair amount of "glass" area would add to its appeal. Low cost is essential too. Where can you find such a beast? Enter the photographer's screw-in diopter lens set. These were used for close-up photog-

raphy before macrozoom lenses were invented. Millions of diopter lens sets are lying around gathering dust—inconvenient and "obsolete." (There's that magic word again!) Practically any such lens will do for experiments—you needn't be particular. Any filter size is fine too. So what if the lens was made for an Exacta camera? The larger the glass area the better. One or two dollars per lens seems to be the going price in stores and ads, which really isn't bad for a 50-millimeter diameter lens with a focal length of 1000-millimeter. The camera store will call it a +1 diopter lens.

At the hardware store pick up a 1-meter length of 2-inch-diameter PVC pipe for the tube, a pipe coupler to serve as a lens retaining ring and dew cap, and a 2-inch-to-1-inch coupler to hold your 8-millimeter-movie-camera-lens eyepiece. The magnification will be 1000-millimeter/13-millimeter, or about 80x. Assemble it, and you have built yourself a fun telescope. It's about twice as powerful as the one Galileo used and probably better optically. For $10 you can afford to let this scope take a beating (translation: it's a perfect scope for kids). Or would you rather have them play with yours?

Want low magnification? You can get it by using a longer focus eyepiece or a shorter focus objective. Will the 50-millimeter lens from that decrepit SLR your brother-in-law dropped in the lake (and you fished out) fill the bill? The camera doesn't work anymore, so try the lens. What can you lose? If it works, you'll get 1000-millimeter/50-millimeter or 20x.

If you buy a three-lens close-up kit, you can build quite a variety of scopes. Get the clerk in your favorite camera store to dig around in that box of stuff the store couldn't sell last time it held an 80 percent off sale. Aha, here they are—three close-up lenses for $8.95. Offer $5. Note that the focal length of diopter-rated close-up lenses is 1000 millimeters divided by the strength of the lens in diopters, so a lens rated +2 diopters has a focal length of 1000 millimeters divided by 2, or 500 millimeters. With one eyepiece coupler unit and three lens-and-tube sections you can make three scopes for about $15, or $5 each.

These scopes will have magnifications from 15x to 80x, a nice complement to the magnification you can get with your primary scope but beyond that of ordinary binoculars. You should be able to see craters on the moon, the phases of Venus, the ovalness of Saturn (if not its ring system), Jupiter's disk and satellites, hundreds of double stars, and dozens of deep-sky objects.

Optically, though, diopter lenses leave quite a bit to be desired, especially in terms of color correction. More obsolete junk to the rescue. Unearth that 135-millimeter f/2.8 telephoto lens you don't use anymore. It's a high-quality, well color-corrected optical assembly. Set it to infinity and attach it to your 8-millimeter movie camera eyepiece lens. How? Mount the eyepiece on the rear lens cap, preferably the older, metal style.

Drill out a central hole and epoxy in an appropriate bit of PVC pipe or metal tubing. Blacken the inside with flat black spray paint. Plug in your "eyepiece" and set the focus: You've got a nice 10- by 40-millimeter finder with excellent optics.

For really low magnification, dig out that 50-millimeter normal lens, attach your eyepiece to it, and you've got a dandy 4x finder. This is an especially satisfying way to recycle obsolete screw-thread camera lenses in today's bayonet-mount world. Radio antenna clamps and muffler clamps are a big help in mounting such finders on a telescope, although you may well think of something better. Be creative.

A 200-millimeter f/4 camera lens gives you a nice 16x scope with a respectable 50-millimeter aperture. Since virtually any lens from any camera will work, feel free to experiment. Haunt flea markets. Visit a few pawnshops. Poke around a surplus store. Scrounge from your photographer friends. Take your junk to a swap meet and see if you can trade it for somebody else's junk. Discovery is a thrill.

Once you've built a couple of telescopes and spotting scopes, you may want to investigate making a few more eyepieces. Lenses for 16-millimeter movie cameras were frequently traded in for zoom lenses. Many are gathering dust in camera stores with prices around $10. Typically these are f/2 or faster 25-millimeter lenses. They are high quality, highly color corrected, and quite a bargain. Any design we've mentioned for an 8-millimeter movie lens ought to work with a 16-millimeter camera lens—and the price is just a few dollars more. Again, have fun experimenting with all of them.

If you don't have a nice loupe for examining those tiny, millimeter-size astro images on your slides, you can make one. Cut the sides of a 2-inch-to-1-inch PVC pipe adapter to form a little tripod and slide your movie lens eyepiece in. A lens mounted on a coupler can be used directly on a light table.

Experiment with whatever optics you can find around the house, in the attic and closets, and in neighborhood garage sales. Sure, you'll find stuff you'll never use. But you might also turn up a real winner for just a few bucks!

If you're an old pro, here's your reward for browsing through this article. These 8-millimeter and 16-millimeter lenses are superb copy lenses for making one-step duplicates of astronomical slides. Construction is simple: Remove your present lens from its bellows or extension tubes. Mount the 8-millimeter movie camera lens on a camera body cap over the bellows with the inner surface of the lens facing out.

Using this rig is easy. Place a slide on a light table and use standard bellows-focusing techniques. You can blow up an astrophoto 500 to 2,000 percent with crisp definition, good contrast, and excellent color fidelity. Try it. You probably already have the lens. Even if you don't, all you have to lose is a couple of dollars. I predict you'll be pleased with your bargain bellows-enlarging lens, especially after you price an equivalent bellows lens. What you save in cold cash will please you even more.

If you're a serious astrophotographer, consider using an 8-millimeter or 16-millimeter movie lens for eyepiece-projection photography. These lenses were designed to project supersharp images in tiny film, and they work beautifully in reverse for enlarging tiny planetary images. You can use them in a commercial eyepiece-projection rig or put together something of your own.

The telescopes you build with obsolete optics may not be world-class creations. They may be a bit wiggly around the edges or show somewhat more chromatic aberration than you'd like. But you've gained something you couldn't get in a store-bought scope: the fun of doing. Try whatever lenses you can find and experiment with different combinations. So what if the images are a bit fuzzy? You'll learn how telescopes work and why.

Use these cheap but good-quality scopes as gifts for the kids or as ideas for the budding astronomer. One final thought: when you've done your thing with them, don't put them back in the junk box. Pass your creations on to some of the neighborhood kids. Give them a chance to learn and play too. It's only fair. After all, aren't kids the ones who invented telescopes in the first place?

Reprinted with permission from *Astronomy*. Copyright 1987 by Kalmbach Publishing Co.

PHOTOGRAPHING THE HEAVENS

Astrophotography is not easy, but it isn't impossible if you learn the fundamentals. To get started you need a camera that can make time exposures, a cable release that allows you to open the shutter for time exposures, a stable tripod, and a sky that doesn't suffer from too much light pollution.

STAR TRAILS

Perhaps the most intriguing celestial pictures to obtain are of star trails. Load your camera with a slow-to-moderate-speed color film, such ISO 100 slide or print film. Go out on a dark, moonless night and aim your camera at a bright group of stars. Set the lens to f/2.8, and then make one 5-minute exposure and one 10-minute exposure. Try this for stars in the north, south, east, and west, as well as for star groups that look particularly interesting to you. Include some foreground objects in your scene, such as a mountain, a stand of trees, or a hilly horizon.

When you have the film developed, you will notice that the stars in the north show up as concentric trails. Star trails near the east and west, however, appear straight, and those near the southern horizon, opposite the celestial pole, are curved downward slightly. You will also see that the star trails are noticeably colored. This is because starlight builds up on the film during the exposure, recording the subtle colors of the individual stars.

STAR FIELDS WITHOUT TRAILING

You can take photographs of constellations and groups of stars and planets if you keep the exposures short. The length of the exposure depends on the speed of your film, your camera lens, and the part of the sky you are shooting.

For example, with ISO 100 film at f/1.8, a 50-millimeter lens will not record any appreciable trailing of circumpolar stars for as long as 30 seconds. However, exposures can last 60 seconds when you use a wide-angle 18-millimeter lens for the same area of sky. At the celestial equator, maximum exposures of 10 and 40 seconds are possible with a 50- and an 18-millimeter lens respectively.

THE MOON AND THE PLANETS

The moon is a very accommodating subject if you have a telephoto lens of at least 100-millimeter focal length. (Lenses shorter than this record the moon as nothing more than a tiny dot on film.) If the moon is in the crescent phase, exposures should be about 1/60 of a second at f/8 with ISO 200 speed film. At quarter phase (and at the same lens opening), use exposures of 1/125 second. And at full moon use exposures of 1/500 second.

Also, be sure to make exposures at speeds on both sides of the suggested setting. Thus, if a 1/30-second exposure is called for, also make exposures at 1/15 and 1/60 second. This technique, called *bracketing*, increases your chances of getting a successful photograph. Remember too that your camera's light meter may be able to "read" the scene. Try it.

Lunar and planetary conjunctions make beautiful fixed-camera photos, especially when the photos are taken in the muted colors of twilight with a silhouetted horizon in the frame. Use a normal or long focal-length lens and a slow-to-moderate-speed film. As an example, a shot of the crescent moon and a nearby bright planet (say Venus) in a

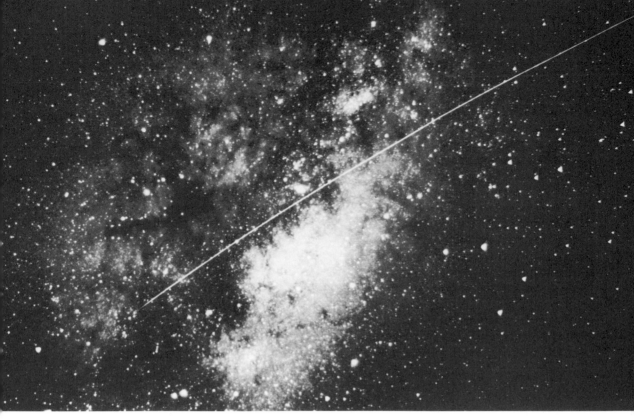

The trail of an Echo satellite in the Milky Way, photographed by the U.S. Naval Observatory. Courtesy National Aeronautics and Space Administration.

dusky sky can be made using ISO 64-speed film at f/2.8 and a 3-second exposure—but don't forget to bracket the exposure. For a fainter planet, use longer exposures; if you have a faster film, use shorter exposures.

As you explore the universe with your binoculars or telescope, you will observe many celestial sights you will want to record on film. They may be the rubble-strewn surface of the moon, a planetary conjunction set amid the deepening dusk, a glittering cluster of stars, or just a "snapshot" of a favorite constellation you may want to take out occasionally to show your friends. With a little practice and perseverance, you can capture these small corners of the universe and call them your own.

Reprinted with permission from *Astronomy*. Copyright 1987 by Kalmbach Publishing Co.

STAR CHARTS AND MAPS

For thousands of years observers have tried to unlock the secrets of the heavens. And with that effort has come a never-ending stream of celestial charts and maps. Today there are maps showing the landscapes of the planets and satellites that our spacecraft have visited and charts that show the bright stars with which we share the Milky Way galaxy. Still others catalog the positions of other galaxies. The charts are redrawn every 50 years (a period known as an *epoch*), with additional updating done in the intervening years.

There are several kinds of star charts. Some are decorative, made to be put on a wall to pique the interest of curious passersby. The most stunning chart of this variety is the *Map of the Universe*, published by **Celestial Arts** (P.O. Box 7327, Berkeley, CA 94707; 800-841-2665; 415-845-8414). Printed on black paper, this brightly colored map glows in the dark. Major constellations and zodiacal signs are vividly illustrated, as are comet paths, meteor showers, and other celestial wonders. A 16-page booklet accompanying the map explains how to decipher it for maximum use.

For beginners, a novel and effective way to get to know the sky is an audio star chart. Called *Tapes of the Night Sky* ($19.95 from **Astronomical Society of the Pacific**, 390 Ashton Ave., San Francisco, CA 94112; 415-337-1100), the two cassette tapes feature four "guided tours" of the bright stars and constellations of each season and come with a 60-page book of instructions, transcripts, maps, and readings.

Young astronomers may find it easier to work with a planisphere, a wheel that is dialed to the time and date of the visible stars and constellations in the sky. Planispheres may be the most basic and helpful astronomical tool for the novice.

Many amateur astronomers interested in using star charts for outdoor gazing turn to star atlas field guides. Often these are printed on vinyl or on another kind of durable paper that can withstand inclement weather and other hazards that may be encountered outdoors. As you peruse what's available, think about how much information you need. A weekend observer may need charts that only show stars visible with the naked eye. Such charts are less cluttered and a lot easier to use. If you plan to take your chart outside, to use while viewing, make sure that it is visible at night (stars printed in white on a black field) and that it is compact enough to accompany you, your telescope, and other necessities. If you plan to use the chart to make observations, make sure that you bring along a flashlight with a red filter so you can use the atlas without being blinded by white light. Using a red light while observing is the mark of an experienced amateur.

WHERE TO FIND THEM

With these tips in mind, you may want to check out the different star charts listed here. **Sky Publishing Corporation, Kalmbach Publishing Co.**, and **Willmann-Bell, Inc.** are the three major companies publishing reputable star charts used by amateur astronomers. Government agencies also publish star charts, as well as maps of planets and the solar system. The **National Geographic Society** offers individual maps, and two beautiful star charts in its comprehensive *Atlas of the World*. Finally, a few additional companies sell planispheres and other unique types of star charts. Following are descriptions of what's out there to make your journey through the stars easier and more enjoyable.

Sky Publishing Corporation offers a wide range of publications for both the amateur and the more advanced astronomer. Its monthly magazine, *Sky & Telescope*, includes timely articles on space research, telescope making, astrophotography, planetariums, and more. Each issue contains a map of the whole sky that is especially useful for locating the constellations. Sky Publishing has a Book Faire division that specializes in quality astronomical books and publications from numerous other publishers. It also has its own publishing arm, which distributes star charts and atlases among other things. To order materials from the catalog, write to Sky Publishing Corporation, 49 Bay State Rd., Cambridge, MA 02238; 617-864-7360. Here are some selections from their catalog:

❏ *Norton's Star Atlas and Reference Handbook*, edited by Gilbert Satterthwaite, Patrick Moore, and Robert Inglis (06780; $29.95), is a favorite among serious stargazers. Now in its 17th edition, the book serves as a handy reference book for explanations of unfamiliar terms, as well as maps that show more than 8,400 stars, 600 deep-sky objects, and constellations from pole to pole. In addition to the numerous charts, the book contains information about astronomy concepts, observation techniques, mysteries of the solar system, the composition of stars, and telescopes and accessories.

❏ *Sky Atlas 2000.0*, by Will Tirion (black-and-white version 4631x; $15.95; color version, 46336; $34.95), is considered a necessity for the practicing astronomer. A 27-page collection of 13-by-18-inch charts, the book includes more than 43,000 stars and 2,500 deep-sky objects. The atlas also is available in a field version, which reverses the normal black-on-white format for easier nighttime stargazing.

❏ *Atlas Borealis* and *Atlas Australis*, by Antonin Becvar ($49.95 each), plot the location, spectral class, and brightness of more than 320,000 stars in the northern and southern skies and in the equatorial region. Comets, asteroids, and other deep-sky phenomena are also included. Each volume contains twenty-four 13 1/2-by-19-inch charts.

❏ *Atlas Stellarum 1950.0*, by Hans Vehrenberg, comprises two volumes: *Stellarum North* (49051; $145) and *Stellarum South* (4906X; $80). Both include a collection of photo-offset black-and-white images and illustrate star positions in the northern and southern skies respectively. The charts are scaled to 2 arc-minutes per millimeter on a transparent grid and magnify the sky 14 times.

❏ *Atlas of Selected Areas* (49000; $33) is a compilation of 206 regions in the celestial sphere. Each region contains one star of 8th or 9th magnitude, and each page maps a general field as well as a magnified version of the same region. Selected areas are spaced at every half hour of right ascension.

❏ *Photographic Star Atlas—The Falkau Atlas*, by Hans Vehrenberg, is available in several versions: white-on-black volume (A version) of the northern and southern skies and black-on-white version (B version) of the northern skies. All volumes include both photographs and charts (northern sky A version, $48 each; southern sky B version, $40 each).

❏ *Handbook of Constellations*, by Hans Vehrenberg and Dieter Blank (49086; $39.45), presents 55 dark gray maps of the entire sky. Other information includes maximum and minimum brightnesses, spectral types, periods, and some epochs.

❏ *Sky Catalogue 2000.0*, edited by Alan

Hirschfeld and Roger Sinnott, is available in two volumes. Volume 1 lists stars to magnitude 8, and volume 2 presents data on double stars, variable stars, and non-stellar objects. Both volumes use data from the NASA-Goddard SKYMAP project, with volume 1 listing timely star positions, magnitudes, and spectral classes, and volume 2 offering a variety of data on more than 3,100 galaxies. Both volumes are available in paperback and cloth for $29.95 and $49.95, respectively.

❏ *Sky & Telescope Guide to the Heavens*, which comes out annually, weaves a chart of astronomical events into the astronomical year. Planetary movements, the waxing and waning of the moon, meteor shower activity, and star magnitude and location are charted on an easy-to-read color foldout. Also included is a day-by-day guide to celestial activity. The guide is available for $5.95.

Kalmbach Publishing Co. (P.O. Box 1612, Waukesha, WI 53187; 414-796-8776) produces a wide range of astronomy materials, including magazines, books, and posters. Keep in mind that purchasers in the United States must include an additional $1.50 for postage and handling and that foreign residents must add an additional 15 percent, or a minimum of $3. Wisconsin residents must also add a 5 percent sales tax. Here are a few samples from Kalmbach's list:

❏ *The Star Book*, by Robert Burnham ($8.95), is a good basic field guide to the constellations of the Northern Hemisphere. Half of the 18 pages illustrate the changes in the night sky for both the early and late halves of the four seasons. The other half describe the constellations and their history. Illustrations are white on blue for easier nighttime reference. The accompanying text explains clearly how to identify stars and constellations.

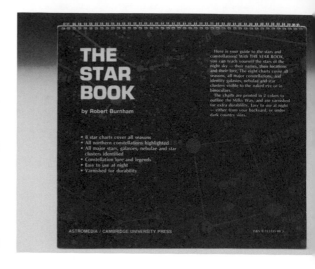

❏ *Leslie Peltier's Guide to the Stars: Exploring the Sky With Binoculars* ($11.95) is a detailed guide on how to use binoculars to see constellations, stars, variable stars, the sun, the planets, the moon, and comets and meteors. Easy-to-read seasonal star charts and diagrams are included.

❏ *Our Galaxy: The Milky Way Poster* ($16.95) shows the entire sky that is visible from planet earth. What sets this star chart apart is that everything in the sky is shown in relation to the Milky Way. The poster shows more than 9,000 stars, all 88 constellations, and more than 250 of the brightest and most significant deep-sky objects.

Willmann-Bell, Inc. (P.O. Box 35025, Richmond, VA 23235; 804-320-7016) is one of the largest retail book dealers in astronomy-related materials in the world. It carries 1,500 titles, many of which are also carried by Sky Publishing and Kalmbach Publishing. The catalog costs $1. The company's own star chart, *Uranometria 2000.0*, by Will Tirion, Barry Rappaport, and George Lovi ($34.95), charts the heavens in two volumes. Volume 1 shows the Northern Hemi-

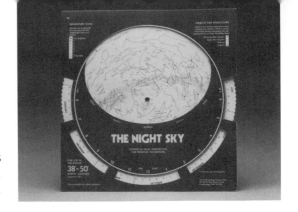

sphere to -6 degrees. Volume 2 shows the Southern Hemisphere to +6 degrees. Each volume contains 259 charts.

OTHER STAR CHARTS

This section includes simplified star charts or planispheres that are particularly useful for the beginning astronomer. You should write to each company to obtain their latest catalog and price list.

American Map Corporation (46-35 54th Rd., Maspeth, NY 11378; 718-784-0055) offers Hallwag's highly detailed full-color astronomy charts with their own heavy-duty cover. Available are charts of the moon, the stars, and the solar system. Each chart comes with a separate illustrated instruction booklet. The charts are $9.95 each.

Celestial Arts (P.O. Box 7327, Berkeley, CA 94707; 800-841-2665; 415-845-8414) offers four 36-by-36-inch posters showing a map of the universe, the solar system, the phases and faces of the moon, and the cosmos as perceived by the Aztecs. The two maps have the added benefit of glowing in the dark. Prices for the maps are $9.95.

David Chandler Co. (P.O. Box 309, La Verne, CA 91750; 714-946-4814) has created a night sky planisphere that allows you to dial in on the constellations of your choice according to the current date and time. Chandler's 10-inch chart is double-sided to accommodate both the northern and southern sky view, and four different versions are available for the following latitudes: northern United States/Canada/Europe; southern United States; Mexico/far southern United States; and South America/Australia/New Zealand. Chandler's book *Exploring the Night Sky with Binoculars* provides additional information about stargazing. Suggested retail price for the planisphere is $3.25;

for the book, $3.95. These are also available through *Sky Publishing Catalogue* and the Astronomical Society of the Pacific.

National Geographic Society (17th & M Sts. NW, Washington, DC 20036; 800-368-2728; 301-921-1330 in Maryland) offers the state-of-the-art *Atlas of the World*, which includes two magnificent star charts of both the northern sky and the southern sky. Magnitudes up to 6 are included, as well as quasars, pulsars, stars, nebulas, and even a possible black hole. Also included in the Atlas is a map of the solar system and maps of both the near side and far side of the moon. Other astronomical maps sold separately are:

❑ *The Earth's Moon*, 42 by 28 inches, reproduced on both paper and plastic, comes with descriptive notes and diagrams. The paper version is $3; plastic is $4.

❑ *Mars*, 38 by 23 inches, revealing its cratered topography. Price is $3.

❑ *The Solar System/Saturn*, $22^{1}/_{2}$ by 17 inches, is printed on both sides and includes illustrations and text. Price is $3.

❑ *The Universe/Sky Survey*, $22^{3}/_{4}$ by 34 inches, has illustrations and text on both sides. Price is $3.

The NightStar Company (1334 Brommer St., Santa Cruz, CA 95062; 800-STAR-122; 408-462-1049) manufactures three models of star globes that are made of soft plastic, deflated, and sealed into the shape of a bowl. The models have a movable surface that can be adjusted for any time and place on earth. They include the whereabouts of all 88 constellations. There are several models available: *NightStar Traveler* ($26) is compact enough to fit in your

pocket or backpack. The package includes a full-featured foldable two-color (white on dark blue) map with simplified instructions. *NightStar Classic* ($39) is the top-of-the-line model; it includes a comprehensive activities handbook, two planet finder overlays showing one full year of planetary movements, and two snap-on dials that offers the option of presetting the sky for any time, date, or latitude. *NightStar Traveler Deluxe* ($39) combines features of both models. It comes with the same handbook as the *Classic* and is as compact as the *Traveler*.

Two additional NightStar products are *Learning Astronomy with NightStar* ($7), an easy-to-follow activities booklet for beginning students of the stars, and *Astronomy and the Imagination* ($15), which is packed with fascinating astronomical facts that can be appreciated by viewing the sky with the naked eye.

NorthStar Imports Company (P.O. Box 60100, Reno, NV 89506; 702-972-5111) offers the following star charts:

❏ *Philips' Planisphere* (10-inch diameter, $8.25) and *Philips' Mini-Planisphere* (5-inch diameter, $4.95) have two revolving disks each that illustrate the night sky when matched up with the date and time noted around the edges. Built of heavy plastic, they are available for four latitudes (32.0 degrees north, 42.0 degrees north, 51.5 degrees north, and 35.0 degrees south). All are designed to help

amateur astronomers identify the stars and constellations; follow hourly, daily, and annual progressions; and plot the positions of the stars.

❏ *Signpost to the Stars*, by George Philip ($4.95), is a beginners' guide to the major stars and constellations.

❏ *Stars at a Glance*, by George Philip ($2.50), is a handy introduction to sky watching that includes detailed illustrations and discussions of the movements of the stars and planets visible in the Northern Hemisphere.

❏ *Philips' Chart of the Stars* ($4.95) is a 45-by-36-inch star chart featuring a large Mercator projection of the middle heavens. Stars are shown in white against a dark blue field, with constellations shown as black lines. Also included are 12-inch diameter projections of the North and South Polar stars that fold to 6 1/2 by 10 1/4 inches in a durable laminated cover.

Replogle Globes, Inc. (2801 S. 25th Ave., Broadview, IL 60153; 313-343-0900), the world's largest manufacturer of globes, offers a 12-inch moon globe and a 12-inch celestial globe. Developed under the auspices of NASA, the moon globe (38245; $28.95) has a three-dimensional look that

reveals craters, seas, and mountains. The celestial globe (38848; $32.95) locates 1,200 stars from 1st to 4th magnitude and shows constellations, star clusters, new stars, and double stars.

Star Finders, Inc. (2406 Lawrence St., Eugene, OR 97405; 503-686-6754) produces a glow-in-the-dark star chart (22 by 28 inches; $9) of the northern sky for learning the stars indoors. It shows all the constellations of the Northern Hemisphere. Star Finders also produces a brass-and-vinyl planisphere ($12) for learning the same stars and constellations outdoors. The planisphere comes with a red plastic filter for use with a flashlight.

Sunstone Publications (R.D. 3, Box 100A, Cooperstown, NY 13326; 607-547-8207) offers ASTRO-DOME R ($9.95), a three-dimensional map of the night sky developed by schoolteacher Klaus Hunig. With easy-to-follow directions, the precut pages transform into an attractive miniature planetarium depicting the stars and constellations of the Northern Hemisphere. ASTRO-DOME measures 20 inches in diameter when assembled and includes a 24-page *Constellation Handbook* explaining the history and details of the major constellations. The map glows in the dark and is intended for children 12 and up.

To Know the Stars, by Guy Ottewell ($7 from Astronomical Workshop, Furman University, Greenville, SC 29613; 803-294-2208), presents a simple introduction to constellations and their mythology, the dynamics of the solar system, and general suggestions for star gazing.

GOVERNMENT SOURCES
The **Government Printing Office** has the following astronomical charts and maps:

❏ *Astronomical Phenomena for the Year* comes in three volumes covering 1986 through 1988. Each volume contains information on the sun, the moon, planets, eclipses, Gregorian calendar and Julian day, time zones, and related phenomena. (1986: S/N 008-054-00112-2, $2.75; 1987: S/N 008-054-00118-1, $3; 1988: S/N 008-054-00123-8, $3.)

❏ *Atlas of Mercury* contains photographs of the planet Mercury taken by the *Mariner 10* spacecraft. (S/N 033-000-00695-1; $21.)

❏ *Stars in Your Eyes: A Guide to the Northern Skies* explains how to locate several summer constellations of the northern sky and includes famous mythological lore. S/N 008-022-00155-7; $1.50.

ASTRONOMY SOFTWARE

by John Mosley

We can watch the sky, but we can't control it. We see the stars and planets as they appear tonight, from one place on one planet, and (except for meteors or the rare eclipse) we see no motion. With the proper personal computer software, however, we can take control of the sky; we can travel through space and time and see things we never will from our back-yard. And we can find out how the universe is really put together. The best astronomy programs, which cost the same as the best telescope eyepieces, give you more useful power in a more convenient package than the Naval Observatory had when the first satellite was launched. And the future is bright; today's best programs will be obsolete in less than five years.

The earliest personal computer astronomy programs were limited to one or perhaps two functions. A program might calculate planet positions, work out the details of a solar eclipse, show the relative positions of Jupiter's moons, plot a chart of the stars for a particular place and time, or calculate the positions of a comet, but it did only that one thing. A program did its task slowly (it might take 90 seconds to calculate the positions of all the planets), and computer-produced star charts showed only a few hundred or perhaps a thousand stars. People then owned a dozen programs and switched among them.

Today the best programs are comprehensive; they wrap into one package a list of features that is staggering to those of us who grew up with slide rules. They far exceed the computational capabilities of the best Zeiss planetarium (although the display is a bit smaller), and some are accurate enough for serious astronomical and historical research. They will plot up to a quarter million stars and calculate planet positions to within a hundredth of a degree of arc for thousands of years. They give you a powerful window on the universe.

Astronomy software has found an important place in the classroom. Some programs are designed for the primary or secondary school market and come with teachers' lesson plans. Others would be useful only if the teacher were sufficiently familiar with both the subject and the software to develop his or her own plans. A word of caution, however: some educational programs are among the worst available and must be avoided. Select carefully, seek recommendations, and do not buy from a catalog description.

Few people will buy a specific personal computer to run astronomy software. Instead, they will find software that runs on a computer they already own. However, if you *were* to start from scratch and buy a computer and astronomy software together, I recommend *Visible Universe* for the IBM PC and compatibles and *Voyager* for the Macintosh. Keep in mind, however, that innovative new programs are published all the time.

It is not easy to know which program to buy. Most astronomy and computer magazines do not review astronomy software on a regular basis. Three that do are *Astronomy*, which prints reviews on an irregular basis; *Sky & Telescope*, which runs reviews bimonthly; and *Mercury*, which runs a lengthy review approximately biannually. For information and recommendations, (a) read reviews in back issues of these magazines and in the major computer magazines (use the annual index); (b) contact your local astronomy club; and (c) contact your local planetarium or science museum. If you have a modem, join the Astronomy

Forum of CompuServe. By doing so you can not only download many programs that are in the public domain but find other forum members who will share their experiences and offer advice. And there are over two dozen local astronomy bulletin boards in the United States and Canada (contact an astronomy club or planetarium for phone numbers of those nearest to you, or see "In Touch: Bulletin Boards and Hotlines").

Few if any of the programs listed here are available at computer or software retail stores or from mail-order outlets, even by special order. The market is too limited to interest retailers, who must deal in volume. And most astronomy programs, including the best, are written and sold by individuals whose profit margin is too low to offer attractive wholesale discounts. Buy direct from the vendor.

These are the major astronomy programs currently on the market. Many are available for more than one type of computer. Write to the vendors for brochures and current prices. For a current list of over 100 astronomy programs for all personal computers, send $2 and a legal-size return envelope with 65 cents in postage (outside of North America, send $5 in U.S. funds and no postage) to: John Mosley, 13623 Sylvan St., Van Nuys, CA 91401. The list is updated bimonthly.

Apple II

Astro Link (P.O. Box 1978, Spring Valley, CA 92077; 619-698-9174). *Indoor Astronomy*: variable magnification high-resolution color star atlas including 6,000 stars and 2,000 deep-sky objects; more can be added; prints telescope finder charts.

Earthware Computing Services (P.O. Box 30039, Eugene, OR 97403; 503-344-3383). *Star Search*: detailed educational simulation of the geological and biological exploration of a hypothetical planet around Epsilon Eridani.

Educational Activities, Inc. (P.O. Box 392, Freeport, NY 11520; 516-223-4666). *Stars for All Seasons*: tutorial demonstrating constellation identification and celestial motions with planetarium-type display; for grades 5 through 12.

Charles Kluepfel (11 George St., Bloomfield, NJ 07003). *Eclipse Map*: detailed calculations and display of solar eclipses in numerical and graphic form. *Moon and Sun*: complete lunar and solar positions and circumstances of partial and total lunar and solar eclipses and occultations. *World Map*: sunrise/sunset lines; ecliptic, subsolar, and sublunar points; lunar nodes and lunar perigee point on high-resolution world map.

Lightspeed Software (2124 Kittredge St., Ste. 185, Berkeley, CA 94704; 415-540-0671). *The Observatory*: variable-magnification planisphere showing sun, moon, planets, 310 stars, and Messier objects, corrected for precession.

MECC (3490 Lexington Ave., North St. Paul, MN 55126; 612-481-3500). *Sky Lab*: instructional astronomy laboratory for grades 7 through 9; with manual.

Microillusions (17408 Chatsworth St., Granada Hills, CA 91344; 818-360-3715). *Sky Travel*: variable-scale chart showing the sky (1,200 stars, constellations, all planets) from any location at any time, with coordinates; eclipses, occultations, transits, and so on included.

Mindscape, Inc. (3444 Dundee Rd., Northbrook, IL 60062; 312-480-7667). *The Observatory*: features a "software telescope" through which one can view the sky from anywhere on earth during any moment in history, from the moons of Jupiter to Halley's comet.

Prentice-Hall, Inc. (Englewood Cliffs, NJ

Planetary Programs and Tables from −4000 to +2800

Pierre Bretagnon
Jean-Louis Simon

Foreword by
Jean Meeus

07632). *Astronomy Disk*: set of 16 educational programs for high school and university; includes Expedition to Mars, Satellites, Comets, Rocket, Build a World, Spectral Types, Double Stars, Inside Stars, Evolution of Stars.

School Management Arts, Inc. (P.O. Box 1, Boston, MA 02195; 617-969-0966). *Daily Planet*: instructional curriculum of 16 astronomy lessons, with manual.

Willmann-Bell, Inc. (P.O. Box 35025, Richmond, VA 23235; 804-320-7016). *Planetary Programs*: high-precision planet positions.

Atari
Atari Corporation (1196 Borregas Ave.,

Sunnyvale, CA 94088; 408-745-2000). *Atari Planetarium*: color variable scale chart showing the sky (1,200 stars, constellations, all planets) from any location at any time, with coordinates; eclipses, occultations, transits, and so on included.

Robtek Limited (1983 San Luis Ave., Ste. 24, Mountain View, CA 94043; 415-968-1345). *Skyplot*: planisphere containing 15,000 stars; shows transits, eclipses, and so on; can view stars from up to 326,000 light-years from earth. Requires Atari ST.

Commodore
Astro Link (P.O. Box 1978, Spring Valley, CA 92077; 619-698-9174). *Indoor Astronomy*: variable-magnification high-resolution color star atlas including 6,000 stars and 2,000 deep-sky objects; more can be added.

Deltron, Ltd. (155 Deer Hill Rd., Lebanon, NJ 08520; 201-236-2098). *Sky Travel*: color variable scale chart showing the sky (1,200 stars, constellations, all planets) from any location at any time, with coordinates; eclipses, occultations, transits, and so on included. For Commodore 64 and 128.

Infinity Software, Inc. (1331 61st St., Ste. F, Emeryville, CA 94604; 415-420-1551). *Galileo*: color planetarium showing up to 9,100 stars and deep-sky objects plus all planets, sun, moon as seen from any location; also rising and setting times. Requires Amiga with 512K minimum.

Charles Kluepfel (11 George St., Bloomfield, NJ 07003). *Eclipse Map*: detailed calculations and display of solar eclipses in numerical and graphic form. *Moon and Sun*: complete lunar and solar positions and circumstances of partial and total lunar and solar eclipses and occultations. *World Map*: sunrise/sunset lines; ecliptic, subsolar, and sublunar points; lunar nodes and lunar perigee point on high-resolution world map. For Commodore 64.

OMNI (3826 Woodland Park Ave. N, Seattle WA 98103). *OMNI*: set of 16 chained public domain programs, including gravity simulations, meteor shower, binary star, Saturnian and Uranian satellite systems, solar rotation, and so on. For Amiga 512.

Science Software (7952 W. Quarto Dr., Littleton, CO 80123; 303-972-4020). *Astros*: simulated tracking and and operation of Amateur Space Telescope; plus suite of programs to calculate eclipses, solve Kepler's equations, convert times, calculate planet positions and diameters, calculate comet positions (including Halley's), locate Jupiter's moons, determine satellite positions, predict performance of model rockets and hot air balloons, and more. For Commodore 64 /128 and Amiga.

IBM PC AND COMPATIBLES

Astrosoft, Inc. (P.O. Box 4451, Hayward, CA 94540). *Astrosoft Computerized Ephemeris*: suite of programs to calculate sun, moon, planet positions, distances, and appearances; eclipses; time conversions; Jupiter's moons; with a catalog of 2,000 stars and deep-sky objects and solar system data. Shareware.

Darrel Bartelheimer (P.O. Box 591609, Houston, TX 77259; 513-222-1745). *Astrophysical Simulations:* High school-level simulations of motions and interactions of objects in gravitational fields .

David Chandler Co. (P.O. Box 309, La Verne, CA 91750; 714/946-4814). *Deep Space*: production of custom three-dimensional star charts (uses stereo viewer) to 7th magnitude in five projection systems, with coordinate lines; calculation of

coordinates and plotting of comet orbits from orbital elements.

Computer Assist Services (1122 13th St., Golden, CO 80410; 303-279-9073). *The Sky*: adjustable planisphere for any location, plus variable-scale orrery; many features. *Sky Calc*: calculation of sun, moon, and planet positions and other data; moon phases; Jupiter's moons; eclipses; time and calendar conversions; coordinate conversions; rising and setting times; printing of calendars; and so on.

Dynacomp, Inc. (1064 Gravel Rd., Webster, NY 14580; 716-671-6160). *Optics One*: ray-tracing program for over two dozen optical systems. *Solarsim*: dynamic three-dimensional simulation of solar system as viewed from any time and position; 250 asteroids and comets and 800 background stars and nebulas.

Lewis-Michaels Engineering (48 Delemere Blvd., Fairport, NY 14550; 716-425-3470). *Genesis Project*: integrated software package that generates star charts (choice of nine projections) to 11th magnitude with planets, Near Galactic Catalog objects and comets; planet tables; telescope design; and so on.

Parsec Software (1949 Blair Loop Rd., Danville, VA 24541; 804-822-1179). *Visible Universe*: powerful comprehensive program that plots accurate sun, moon, and planet positions; constellation outlines; rising and setting times, eclipse paths, and much more for 17,200 objects.

Picoscience (41512 Chadbourne Dr., Fremont, CA 94539; 415-498-1095). *Superstar*: displays of up to 259,000 stars to magnitude 9.5, 22,000 variable stars, 8,000 Near Galactic Catalog objects, sun, moon, all planets plus some comets and asteroids; calculation of precise coordinates.

Below: Genesis Project, from Lewis-Michaels Engineering.

School Management Arts, Inc. (P.O. Box 1, Boston, MA 02195; 617-969-0966). *Daily Planet*: instructional curriculum of 16 astronomy lessons, with manual.

Southwest Astronomy (4242 Roma NE, Albuquerque, NM 87108). *Nightsky*: plotting of 2,000 stars, planets, sun and moon; listing of planet positions, rising and setting times, Jupiter's satellites and Red Spot; clocks; exposure times; and so on.

U.S. Naval Observatory (Nautical Almanac Office, Code FA, Washington, DC 20390). *Floppy Almanac*: calculation of data found in the *American Ephemeris* (positions, rising and setting times, magnitudes, and son on for sun, moon, and planets, plus 1,536 stars) to *American Ephemeris* accuracy.

Willmann-Bell, Inc. (P.O. Box 35025, Richmond, VA 23235; 804-320-7016). *Planetary Programs*: high-precision planet positions for period -4000 to +2800. *Newcomb and Gnewcomb*: front-end programs for *Planetary Programs* to calculate and display rising and setting times, conjunctions, elongations, and so on.

Z2 Computer Solutions (5540 Sunny Oaks Dr., San Jose, CA 95123; 408-225-0552). *Z2 Astronomy*: high-precision stellar, solar, lunar, and planetary positions from 4001 B.C. to A.D. 8000; determination of conjunctions and so on.

MACINTOSH
Carina Software (830 Williams St., San Leandro, CA 94577; 415-352-7328). *Voyager*: powerful planetarium includes 9,100 stars, 2,000 deep-sky objects in three projections, all planets, with information on each; viewing possible from any point in or near the solar system (e.g., earth from Mars); planet positions, rising and setting times; plotting of comet orbits from elements; redrawing of star fields in two seconds. Requires 1MB.

Elton Software Macintosh (P.O. Box 649, Lafayette, CO 80026; 305-665-3444).

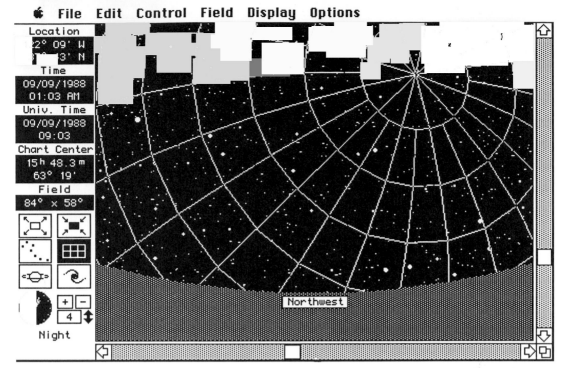

File Edit Control Field Display Options

Location
2° 09' W
    3' N
Time
09/09/1988
01:03 AM
Univ. Time
09/09/1988
09:03
Chart Center
15ʰ 48.3ᵐ
63° 19'
Field
84° x 58°

Night

Northwest

Sample screen from Voyager, the Interactive Desktop Planetarium, *from Carina Software.*

MacStronomy: variable-zoom planisphere showing all planets and 9,000 stars plus Messier objects; includes moon phases, planet rising and setting times, constellation outlines; coordinate conversions.

Microillusions (17408 Chatsworth St., Granada Hills, CA 91344; 818-360-3715). *Sky Travel*: variable-scale chart showing the sky (1,200 stars, constellations, all planets) from any location at any time, with coordinates; eclipses, occultations, transits, and so on included.

Jeff Rommereide (343 Elma Ave., Laurel Springs, NJ 08021; 609-784-0149). *Gravitation Ltd.:* two-dimensional simulation of gravitational interaction of multiple objects, with many fascinating examples. Shareware.

ASTRONOMY PUBLICATIONS

Every hobby spawns its fair share of popular literature, and astronomy is no exception. From highly specialized publications to those intended for beginners, astronomy magazines cover a wide range of subjects. The space program, observation techniques, the idiosyncrasies of celestial objects, and tips for budding star gazers all receive coverage on the pages of these publications. Here are brief descriptions of what's out there, and what they each publication offers:

Air & Space (Smithsonian Institution, 900 Jefferson Dr., Washington, DC 20560; 202-287-3733) stresses space travel but usually covers some aspect of astronomical interest as well. Regular features include a commentary about air and space, exhibits at the Smithsonian, moments and milestones in space travel, and book reviews. Geared to the general public, the magazine frequently descends from outer space to include airplanes, issues related to the aircraft industry, and collectibles that have become popular here on earth. Published bimonthly. Subscription is $18 in the United States, $24 elsewhere. Single copy, $3.50.

Astronomy (Kalmbach Publishing Co., 1027 N. 7th St., Milwaukee, WI 53233; 414-272-2060) is geared to the beginning amateur astronomer. Regular features include a detailed description of the night sky, tips on naked-eye viewing, the latest on equipment, a calendar of monthly events, and book reviews. Features highlight timely events. Published monthly. Subscription is $24 in the United States, $33 elsewhere; $39 for two years ($57 elsewhere), $55 for three years ($82 elsewhere). Single copy, $2.50.

Deep Sky (Kalmbach Publishing Co., P.O. Box 1612, Waukesha, WI 53187; 414-796-8776) is intended for those with a love of and expertise in deep-sky astronomy, a term that refers to nebulas, star clusters, galaxies, and anything else beyond the solar system that encompasses quantities of stars. Articles cover helpful hints on deep sky viewing, astrophotography, and news from the research literature. Published quarterly. Subscription is $12 for one year, $21 for two years in the United States; $14 for one year, $25 for two years elsewhere. Single copy, $3 in the United States, $3.50 elsewhere.

How to Build Your Own Observatory (Kalmbach Publishing Co., P.O. Box 1612, Waukesha, WI 53187; 414-796-8776) is composed of reprints from *Telescope Making*. Articles are written largely by hobbyists themselves and cover all aspects of observatory building. $7.95.

Mercury (Astronomical Society of the Pacific, 390 Ashton Ave., San Francisco, CA 94112; 415-337-1100) specializes in articles explaining the latest developments in astronomy, usually written by astronomers engaged in the work they are describing. *Mercury* is edited to be accessible for the beginner in astronomy who has just a little bit of a science background. Published six times a year. Subscription is $27 in the United States and $35 elsewhere; it includes 12 issues of the *Abrams Planetarium Sky Calendar and Chart*, as well as the *ASP Catalog*.

Odyssey (Kalmbach Publishing Co., 1027 N. 7th St., Milwaukee, WI 53233; 414-272-2060) is designed for children with a serious interest in space. Articles are

similar to those in adult periodicals, but the length and complexity have been modified to make them suitable for a young audience. *Odyssey* is lively and fun, with easy-to-read diagrams, games, and experiments, along with interesting and informative pieces. Published monthly. Subscription is $21 for one year in the United States, $25 elsewhere. Single copy, $2.

Sky & Telescope (Sky Publishing Corporation, 49 Bay State Rd., Cambridge, MA 02138; 617-864-7360) is a comprehensive astronomy publication geared to the advanced amateur astronomer. Articles cover the gamut from news events to astrophysics, spacecraft hardware to space imagery. In addition, every issue includes a monthly sky chart. A great magazine, almost a must, for the serious astronomer. Published monthly. Subscription is $21.95 in the United States, $24.95 in Canada and Mexico, and $36.95 elsewhere. Single copy, $2.50 in the United States, $3 elsewhere.

Telescope Making (Kalmbach Publishing Co., P.O. Box 1612, Waukesha, WI 53187; 414-796-8776) is the magazine "for, by, and about telescope makers." The publication is in black and white and is written by those with an avid interest in the hobby. Richard Berry, editor of *Astronomy* magazine, takes the time out of his busy schedule to compile the articles out of a deep love for telescope making. The magazine has a homey feel to it, and in addition to technical diagrams showing how to make appropriate hardware, it includes pictures of telescope makers, their families and friends. Published quarterly. Subscription is $12 for one year in the United States, $14 elsewhere. Single copy, $4 in the United States, $4.50 elsewhere.

In addition to those just listed, the major science magazines—among them *Discover, Omni, Science, Science News,* and *Scientific American*—also cover astronomical developments. Their coverage tends to be more extensive during periods of space exploration. Check local newsstands.

In Touch:
Bulletin Boards and Hotlines

If you want to keep up with the latest in astronomy news, a good way to hook up and tune in is through computer bulletin board systems and telephone hotlines. CompuServe, a major national data-base company, offers astronomy information, as do several independent organizations. Telephone hotlines are mostly sponsored by astronomy clubs, universities, and planetariums. They offer news about events, tours, and space exploration.

One of the largest national astronomical bulletin boards is operated by **CompuServe Information Service**. It contains information on space exploration, space education, and astronomy, among many other things. Under each subject area, the service provides message boards, text files, data libraries, and the opportunity to participate in "on-line" conferences. CompuServe can be accessed from most cities throughout the United States at baud rates of 300, 450, 1200, and 2400 (depending on your location and the kind of modem you have). Hourly rates for connection time are $6 at 300 and 450 baud and $12.50 at 1200 and 2400; there may be additional telephone hookup surcharges. For more information, call 800-848-8199 (617-457-0802 in Ohio) or write CompuServe Inquiry Brochure, Dept. MA1017, P.O. Box 20212, Columbus, OH 43220.

Bulletin Board Systems
Here is a selected list of astronomy-related bulletin board systems. Unless otherwise noted, you can access these services at no charge by calling the telephone number after setting your modem protocol to 8 bits and a baud rate of 300 or 1200.

Alpha Bulletin Board: 303-367-1935 (Aurora, CO). Access: 300, 1200, and 2400 baud; type *Alpha* at log-in prompt. Sponsor: Alpha SciNet. This bulletin board, for serious users only, allows read-only access to space and amateur radio sections of the Unix network, which has over 11,000 sites worldwide. Also allows space and ham radio discussions among users.

Amsat Bulletin Board: 515-961-3325 (Indianola, IA). Access: 300, 1200, or 2400 baud; use *AMSAT* for password. Sponsor: Radio Amateur Satellite Corp. (AMSAT). Includes AMSAT news, orbital patterns for selected satellites, and relevant NASA reports.

Apple Astronomy Bulletin Board: 713-526-5671 (Houston, TX). Sponsor: Houston Museum of Natural History. Includes a visual sky guide, news about space, cosmology, and on-line astronomical news.

Astro Bulletin Board: 202-547-4418 (Arlington, VA). Sponsor: Kurt Riegel. Includes astronomical data file and a message board.

Day's End Bulletin Board: 303-650-5636 (Westminster, CO). Access: 300, 1200, and 2400 baud. Sponsor: Chris Day. Includes comprehensive astronomy section and MS-DOS utilities.

Digital Newsletter Bulletin Board: 612-291-0567 (St. Paul, MN). Provides space exploration coverage and up-to-the-day schedules and information during space shuttle missions.

Howard's Notebook Bulletin Board:
816-331-5868 (Belton, MS). Sponsor: Jim
Howard. Astronomy section includes text
files. Frequently used by members of the
Astronomical Society of Kansas City.

Kalamazoo Astronomical Society RCP/
M Bulletin Board: 616-342-4062 (Kalamazoo, MI). Sponsor: Kalamazoo Astronomy Society. Files include a weekly sky
report, local museum information, and
planetary information. Several on-line
astronomy-related programs.

Killer Bulletin Board: 214-827-4670,
827-1994, or 821-0390 (Bedford, TX).
Sponsor: Unix Connection Public Bulletin
Board. Allows access to the UseNet community and the Unix shell, with the
ability to program on-line in many
different computer languages.

L-5 (Magie) Bulletin Board: 309-343-
3799 (Galesburg, IL). Sponsor: Prairieland
Computer Club and Midwest Information
Systems. Allows network access to
Telenet, Tymnet, CompuServe, Genie,
and others.

L-5 Gateway Bulletin Board: 412-667-
3984 (Pittsburgh, PA). Access: 300, 1200,
and 2400 baud. Sponsor: L-5 Society
(National Space Society). Supplies information from the Space Studies Institute
and the National Space Society.

L-5 SpaceNet Bulletin Board: 408-262-
7177 (Milpitas, CA). Sponsor: California
Space Development Council and the L-5
Society (National Space Society). Supports
desktop publishing for all space and
astronomy organizations with source text
in the public domain. Has many on-line
files showing the latest developments in
pro-space organizations.

M-Net Bulletin Board: 313-994-6333
(Ann Arbor, MI). Sponsor: Public Access

Unix. Allows public access to the UseNet
community.

NASA-Lewis Educational Computer
Bulletin Board: 216-433-8035 (Cleveland, OH). Sponsor: NASA—Lewis Educational Services Office. Allows users to ask
questions about astronomy and the space
program. Press releases, bibliographies,
and technical reports included. No
uploads.

NASA Spacelink: 205-895-0028
(Huntsville, AL). Sponsor: Marshall Space
Flight Center. Provides news releases,
information on shuttle status, space
exploration, NASA installations, and
educational services and materials.

Naval Observatory Bulletin Board: 202-
653-1079 (Washington, DC). Access:
Requires 7 bits, even parity, and 2 stop
bits. All commands must be preceded by
Alpha. Sponsor: U.S. Naval Observatory.
Includes a variety of astronomy-related
files organized in a unique way.

NOAA Bulletin Board: 303-497-5000
(Boulder, CO). Sponsor: National Oceanic
and Atmospheric Administration, Space
Environment Laboratory. Has daily
summaries and forecasts of solar and
geophysical activity. Information on
high-frequency radio propagation is
updated every six hours.

Pittsburgh L-5 Bulletin Board: 412-464-
1397 (Pittsburgh, PA). Access: 300, 1200,
and 2400 baud. Sponsor: Pittsburgh L-5
Society (National Space Society). Offers
monthly sky events; planet, comet,
asteroid, moon, and stellar data; recent
developments; extraterrestrial biology;
and more.

Quantum Link. Call 800-782-2278 for
subscription information. Includes sym-
posia twice a month with guest "speak-

Telephone Hotlines

These services—offered by organizations, astronomy clubs, and observatories—provide astronomy news, observation information, and news about space exploration. Most are updated weekly or monthly. When calling, keep in mind that long-distance rates apply.

Astronomical Society of the Pacific: 415-337-1244 (San Francisco, CA)
Chicago Astronomical Society: 312-259-2376 (Arlington Heights, IL)
Detroit Astronomical Society: 313-837-0130 (Detroit, MI)
Griffith Observatory: 213-663-8171 (Los Angeles, CA)
Houston Astronomical Society: 713-661-6180 (Houston, TX)
Kendall Planetarium: 503-228-7827 (Portland, OR)
NASA Johnson Space Center: 713-483-8600 (Houston, TX)
National Space Society: 202-543-1995 (Washington, DC)
Pacific Science Center: 206-443-2920 (Seattle, WA)
Sky & Telescope: 617-497-4168 (Cambridge, MA)
Smithsonian Astrophysical Observatory: 617-497-1497 (Cambridge, MA)

ers," a message board, an on-line listing of current sky events, and a library with more than 100 programs. Not a free service.

Scooter's Scientific Exchange: 215-657-5586 (Willow Grove, PA). Sponsor: Brian Moldover. Offers on-line conference for the general scientific community. Many research-oriented computer programs.

Silent Side Bulletin Board: 602-962-7698 (Mesa, AZ). Sponsor: Chris Mitchell. Provides information from the Saguaro Astronomical Club, monthly astronomy events, and club news.

Space Network: 303-494-8446 (Boulder, CO). Access: 300, 1200, and 2400 baud. Sponsor: Mars Institute of the Planetary Society. Provides information from the Mars Institute, Space Studies Institute, National Space Society, Mars Underground, World Space Foundation, Jet Propulsion Laboratory, and International Planetarium Society. Specializes in space exploration and development, missions,

research, and education about Mars.

Star-Net Bulletin Board: 612-681-9520 (Minneapolis, MN). Access: 133, 1200, and 2400 baud. Sponsor: Chuck Cole. A nonprofit scientific exchange group that includes astronomy, technology, management, and general-interest sections, as well as a library of public-domain astronomy programs, major astronomy data bases, observing alerts, on-line prediction programs, and astrophoto aids. Use fee is $30 a year, but potential users may try the system before subscribing.

StarPort Bulletin Board: 203-698-0588 (Old Greenwich, CT). Access: 300 to 9600 baud (USR HST modem). Sponsor: Jim Bolster. Offers information on astronomy, science fiction, UFOs, satellites, Search for Extraterrestrial Intelligence, and more.

Well Bulletin Board: 415-332-6106 (Sausalito, CA). Access: 300, 1200, and 2400 baud. Sponsor: Whole Earth Lectronic Link. Offers full access to the UseNet community. Fee is $8 a month.

Astronomical Societies

For many budding astronomers, the biggest problem is knowing where to begin their study of the heavens. Do you build a library? Buy binoculars or a telescope? "No," say experienced astronomers. The best place to start is joining a local astronomy club. There are more than 200 astronomy clubs in North America. Although they vary widely in size and activities, all strive to bring together people with common interests to learn about the hobby and to pursue it together.

Most astronomy clubs have informal monthly meetings that feature guest speakers; sponsor "star parties," in which members spend an evening together observing the heavens; and publish a newsletter about upcoming activities and other information. Some run a local observatory or hold special events for school groups and the public. Specialized clubs might build a telescope together.

Here is a list of selected astronomy clubs in North America. The organizations listed first are the biggest and serve the whole amateur astronomy community. The second listing includes representative local clubs. If no clubs near you are listed, you might want to call a local planetarium, telescope store, or college astronomy department for suggestions. Or contact one of the national organizations listed.

The following large clubs offer a wide range of services to the astronomy community:

Astronomical League (Merry E. Wooten, Executive Secretary, 6235 Omie Cir., Pensacola, FL 32504; 904-477-8732). The league is designed to coordinate activities of amateur astronomical societies. Its membership includes some 170 clubs, which represent about 8,000 individual members. Member organizations are grouped into geographic regions that can hold conventions of several societies. At present the regions are Northeast, Mideast, Southeast, North Central, Mid States, Southwest, Mountain Astronomical Research Society (MARS), and Northwest. Each year the league holds a national convention to discuss relevant astronomical information. This convention also has displays of homemade telescopes, instruments, astrophotographs, and other items, and offers field trips. The climax of the event usually is a "star party," at which both amateurs and professionals compare notes about the stars. The league also publishes a quarterly newsletter, *Reflector*, which includes local society activities and national events. Other membership benefits include a 10-percent discount on all astronomical and related science books published in the United States, access to a subscription service of astronomical handbooks and major publications, educational guides, and league pamphlets. Individual membership is $15, although most of the league's members are local clubs, which pay a per-person fee based on their size.

Astronomical Society of the Pacific (390 Ashton Ave., San Francisco, CA 94112; 415-337-1100). One of the oldest astronomical organizations in the world, the society has members in every state and in more than 70 foreign countries. Members include professional astronomers, educators at all levels, active amateurs, and thousands of other interested individuals. Membership benefits include subscription to the bimonthly magazine *Mercury*; a monthly sky calendar and star map; the ASP catalog, featuring a wide variety of astronomical materials; discounts for the society's annual meetings; 24-hour recorded telephone hotlines; and the

Courtesy Astronomy *magazine, Kalmbach Publishing Co.*

opportunity to support many public education activities, such as a newsletter and workshops for educators, resource services for the media, and bibliographies and information packets for students, libraries, and other interested individuals. Membership is $27 a year in the United States, $35 elsewhere for *Mercury* and the sky calendars; $54 in the United States, $64 elsewhere for technical publications as well.

Royal Astronomical Society of Canada (RASC, 136 Dupont St., Toronto, ON M5R 2V2; 416-924-7973). The society is a national organization of 3,000 amateur and professional astronomers. Founded in 1840, RASC received its royal charter in 1903 and began expanding with the addition of "centres of the society" across Canada, although its national office and library remain in Toronto. Today there are more than 20 centers in Canada. The society's most important event is its annual three-day general assembly, hosted by a different centre of the society

each year. The society also publishes the annual *RASC Handbook,* which is an essential reference for observing the sky in North America. Each center determines its own fees, ranging from $7.50 to $32. Membership covers star parties, access to observatories, and subscription to news-letters.

Western Amateur Astronomers (WWA, c/o Margaret Matlack, 13617 E. Bailey, Whittier, CA 90601; 213-696-9227). Founded in 1949, WAA is an umbrella organization of some 60 astronomy clubs, which include 3,000 members in the far western regions of the United States. WAA sponsors conferences, such as the annual Riverside Telescope Makers Workshop, geared to people who make their own telescopes and get together to discuss improvements and new concepts in telescope design. Members find communi-cation through the group with other organizations very useful. Membership is free. To join, organizations should send a letter of intent.

Here is a sample of representative clubs:

Alabama
Auburn Astronomical Society
1963 Canary Dr.
Auburn, AL 36830

Birmingham Astronomical Society
P.O. Box 36311
Birmingham, AL 35236
205-979-9343

Mobile Astronomical Society
P.O. Box 190042
Mobile, AL 36619
205-973-1325

Muscle Shoals Astronomical Society
302 N.E. Commons
Tuscumbia, AL 35674
205-383-6717

Von Braun Astronomical Society
Box 1142
Huntsville, AL 35807
205-881-0793

Alaska
Astronomical Units
Box 82210
Fairbanks, AK 99708
907-456-6586

Arizona
Leisure World Astronomers
1792 Leisure World
Mesa, AZ 85206
602-981-3136

Phoenix Astronomical Society
6945 E. Gary Rd.
Scottsdale, AZ 85254
692-996-3617

Saguaro Astronomy Club
11815 North St.
Scottsdale, AZ 85254

Tucson Amateur Astronomy Association
7222 E. Brooks Dr.
Tucson, AZ 85730
602-790-5053

Arkansas
Arkansas-Oklahoma Astronomical Society
P.O. Box 31
Ft. Smith, AR 72902
501-452-4614

Ark-La-Tex Skywatchers
Rte. 2, Box 9
Ashdown, AR 71822
501-898-3178

Sidewalk Astronomers's 24-inch telescope, with Venus setting over San Francisco.

Astronomical Society of Northwest Arkansas
P.O. Box 316
Lincoln, AR 72744

Mid-South Astronomical Research Society
P.O. Box 5142
Little Rock, AR 72225
501-376-3021

California
Andromeda Astronomical Society
P.O. Box 118
Morongo Valley, CA 92256

Antelope Valley Astronomy Club
P.O. Box 426
Lancaster, CA 93534
805-256-4261

Arcata Society of Amateur Astronomers
499 1/2 Bayview Rd.
Arcata, CA 95521
714-884-0657

Astronomers of Humboldt
College of the Redwoods
Eureka, CA 95501

Astronomical Association of Northern
  California
731 Camino Ricardo
Moraga, CA 94556
415-376-3007

Astronomical Association of San Diego
P.O. Box 7919
Ocean Beach, CA 92107

Astronomical Society of Southern California
P.O. Box 2046
San Marcos, CA 92069
619-741-6128

Astronomical Society of the Desert
College of the Desert
43-500 Monterey Ave.
Palm Desert, CA 92260
619-346-2524

Bear Valley Astronomical Society
P.O. Box 874
Big Bear Lake, CA 92314

Celestial Observers
9534 Gierson Ave.
Chatsworth, CA 91311
818-882-6172

*Courtesy Fairbanks Planetarium, St.
Johnsbury, VT.*

Central Coast Astronomical Society
P.O. Box 1415
San Luis Obispo, CA 93406
805-528-6682

Central Valley Astronomers
5790 E. Tarpey Dr.
Fresno, CA 93727
209-291-7879

Chabot Telescope Makers Workshop
25555 Hesperian Blvd.
Hayward, CA 94545

China Lake Astronomical Society
P.O. Box 1783
Ridgecrest, CA 93555
619-375-5681

Eastbay Astronomical Society
4917 Mountain Blvd.
Oakland, CA 94619
415-533-2394

Excelsior Telescope Club
265 Roswell
Long Beach, CA 90803

Fremont Peak Observatory Association
10281 Parlett Pl.
Cupertino, CA 95014
408-7146-6493

Idyll-Gazers Astronomy Club
P.O. Box 1245
Idylwild, CA 92349
714-659-3562

Kern Astronomical Society
2901 Renegade Ave.
Bakersfield, CA 93306
805-871-7116

Los Angeles Astronomical Society
2800 E. Observatory Rd.
Los Angeles, CA 90027
213-926-4071

Marin Stargazers
27 Morning Sun
Mill Valley, CA 94941

Modesto Society of Astronomical Observing
1521 Clevenger Dr.
Modesto, CA 95356

Mother Lode Astronomical Society
P.O. Box 176
Altaville, CA 95221

Mt. Diablo Astronomical Society
P.O. Box 4542
Mountain View, CA 94040
415-566-3116

Polaris Astronomical Society
22018 Ibarra Rd.
Roodland Hills, CA 91364
818-347-8922

Pomona Valley Amateur Astronomers
546 Prospectors Rd.
Diamond Bar, CA 91765
714-860-5373

Riverside Astronomical Society
P.O. Box 7213
Riverside, CA 92503
714-689-6893

Sacramento Valley Astronomical Society
P.O. Box 575
Rocklin, CA 95677
916-624-3333, ext. 2291

San Bernardino Valley Amateur Astronomers
1345 Garner Ave.
San Bernardino, CA 92411

San Diego Astronomy Association
P.O. Box 23215
San Diego, CA 92123

San Diego L5
P.O. Box 4636
San Diego, CA 92104

San Francisco Amateur Astronomers
114 Museum Way
San Francisco, CA 94114
415-752-9420

San Francisco Sidewalk Astronomers
1801 Golden Gate Ave.
San Francisco, CA 94115
415-567-2063

San Jose Astronomical Association
3509 Calico Ave.
San Jose, CA 95124
308-371-1307

San Mateo Astronomical Society
P.O. Box 974, Station A
San Mateo, CA 94403

Santa Barbara Astronomy Club
Carroll Observatory at Westmont College
P.O. Box 3702
Santa Barbara, CA 93130

Santa Cruz Astronomical Society
235 Auburn Ave.
Santa Cruz, CA 95060

Santa Monica Amateur Astronomy Club
1415 Michigan Ave.
Santa Monica, CA 90404
213-450-1944

Sonoma County Astronomical Society
P.O. Box 183
Santa Rosa, CA 95404
707-528-1034

Space Frontier Society
64 Monterey Blvd.
San Francisco, CA 94131

STARS
City College of San Francisco
50 Phelan Ave.
San Francisco, CA 94112
415-239-3242

When the Stars Shine: Astronomy Day

Each year astronomy buffs across the country pick a day in spring to haul their telescopes out to the streets and shopping malls to encourage the uninitiated to take a look at the heavens. The spring ritual has become known as Astronomy Day.

Conceived in northern California and now celebrated throughout the world, Astronomy Day activities and dates vary from city to city and country to country. Typically local clubs hold seminars on new developments in space and astronomy, and observatories open their doors to viewers eager to catch a glimpse of the sun by day or the moon by night. There are also telescopes set up in schools, parks, and other public places so everyone can have a chance to take a look at planets, star clusters, and nebulas. All this celestial activity is bound to lure even the most recalcitrant.

The Astronomical League, under the auspices of an Astronomy Day coordinator, determines the day most places recognize as Astronomy Day by determining the date of the first-quarter moon between mid-April and mid-May, then picking the closest Saturday.

For more information about Astronomy Day in your area, contact a local astronomy club, planetarium, observatory, science museum, or college astronomy department.

Stockton Astronomical Society
P.O. Box 243
Stockton, CA 95201
209-473-8234

Stony Ridge Observatory
3019 Welsh Way
Glendale, CA 91206
818-248-7067

Tamalpais Astronomical Society
31 Crane Dr.
San Anselmo, CA 94960

Torrance Astronomical Society
1905 Havenmeyer Lane
Redondo Beach, CA 90278

Tri-Valley Astronomers
5315 Deseree Ave.
Livermore, CA 94550

Tulare Astronomical Association
P.O. Box 515
Tulare, CA 93275
209-685-0585

University of California at Davis Astronomy
  Club
Physics Dept.
Davis, CA 95656
916-752-1788

Ventura County Astronomical Society
P.O. Box 982
Simi Valley, CA 93063

Western Observatorium
13215 E. Penn St., Ste. 411
Whittier, CA 90602
213-698-0468

Colorado
Denver Astronomical Society
P.O. Box 10814
Denver, CO 80210

Longmont Astronomical Society
P.O. Box 9029
Longmont, CO 90501
303-772-1470

Rocky Mountain Astrophysical Group
P.O. Box 25233
Colorado Springs, CO 90836
719-550-9804

Southern Colorado Astronomical Association
812 "O" St.
Pensore, CO 81240

Connecticut
Astronomical Society of Greater Hartford
Gengras Planetarium
950 Trout Brook Dr.
West Hartford, CT 06119

Astronomical Society of New Haven
P.O. Box 3005
New Haven, CT 06515

Fairfield County Astronomical Society
Stamford Museum Observatory
39 Scofieldtown Rd.
Stamford, CT 06903
203-322-1648

Mattatuck Astronomical Society
Mattatuck Community College
Math-Science Division
750 Chase Pkwy.
Waterbury, CT 06708

Thames Amateur Astronomical Society
P.O. Box 5118
Westport, CT 06880

Delaware
Delaware Astronomical Society
P.O. Box 652
Wilmington, DE 19899
215-444-2966

District of Columbia
STOSTH
U.S. Naval Observatory
Washington, DC 20392

Florida
Ancient City Astronomy Club
5124 Shore Dr.
St. Augustine, FL 32084
904-797-7110

Astronomical Society of the Palm Beaches
South Florida Science Museum
4801 Dreher Trail N
West Palm Beach, FL 33405

Bay County Astronomy Club
424 E. 19th St., No. 106
Panama City, FL 32405

Brevard Astronomical Society
P.O. Box 1084
Cocoa, FL 32923
407-242-8854

Callahan Astronomical Society
Rte. 3, Box 1062
Callahan, FL 32011

Central Florida Astronomical Society
810 E. Rollins St.
Orlando, FL 32803
305-323-8890

Escambia Amateur Astronomers Association
6235 Omie Cir.
Pensacola, FL 32504
904-484-1154

Indian River Astronomical Society
1201 Sunnypoint Dr.
Melbourne, FL 32935
407-254-2556

Local Group of Deep Sky Observers
2311 23rd Ave. W
Bradenton, FL 34205
813-747-8334

Mars Astronomy Club
7407 Del Bonita Ct., No. 69
Tampa, FL 33617
813-985-9289

Northeast Florida Astronomical Society
P.O. Box 16574
Jacksonville, FL 32245
904-249-8968

St. Petersburg Astronomy Club
594 59th St. S
St. Petersburg, FL 33707
813-343-1594

Southern Cross Astronomical Society
13841 SW 106th St.
Miami, FL 33186

South Florida Amateur Astronomers
  Association
16001 West St., Rd. 84
Ft. Lauderdale, FL 33326
305-431-6905

Planetarium of the Virginia Living Museum, Newport News, VA.

Treasure Coast Astronomical Society
1100 Theresa St.
Stuart, FL 34996
407-287-2224

Georgia
Astronomy Club of August
P.O. Box 96
Evans, GA 30809
404-793-3420

Athens Astronomical Association
160 Plantation Dr.
Athens, GA 30605
404-543-3753

Atlanta Astronomy Club
5198 Avanti Ct.
Stone Mountain, GA 30088
404-498-1240

Middle Georgia Astronomical Society
Rte. 3, Box 1705
Byron, GA 31008
912-956-2141

Oglethorpe Astronomical Association
Savannah Science Museum
4405 Paulsen St.
Savannah, GA 31405
912-355-6705

Hawaii
Hawaiian Astronomical Society
P.O. Box 17671
Honolulu, HI 96817

Maui Astronomy Club
325 Olokani St., Makawao
Maui, HI 96768
808-572-1939

Mauna Kea Astronomical Society
R.R. No. 1, Box 525
Captain Cook, HI 96704
808-328-9201

Idaho
Boise Astronomical Society
10879 Ashburton Dr.
Boise, ID 83709
208-377-5220

Idaho Falls Astronomical Society
1710 Clarendon Ln.
Idaho Falls, ID 83404
208-524-6317

Illinois
Argonne Astronomy Club
6 N. 106 White Oake Ln.
St. Charles, IL 60176
312-584-1162

Astronomical Society at University of Illinois
1011 W. Springfield
Urbana, IL 61801
217-351-7898

Central Illinois Astronomical Association
Illinois College
Jacksonville, IL 62650

Chicago Astronomical Society
P.O. Box 48504
Chicago, IL 60648
312-966-6214

Illinois Benedictine College Astronomical
   Society
5700 College Rd.
Lisle, IL 60532
312-969-6410

Joliet Astronomical Society
P.O. Box 3893
Joliet, IL 60435
815-729-0568

Lake County Astronomical Society
603 Dawes
Libertyville, IL 60048
312-362-0959

Mt. Olive Astronomical Society
412 W. 4th St.
Mt. Olive, IL 62069
217-999-2224

Naperville Astronomical Association
205 N. Mill St.
Naperville, IL 60540
312-355-5357

Northwest Suburban Astronomers
4960 Chambers Dr.
Barrington, IL 60010

Peoria Astronomical Society
1125 W. Lake Ave.
Peoria, IL 61604
309-347-7285

Popular Astronomy Club
John Deere Planetarium
Augustana College
Rock Island, IL 61201
309-786-6119

Quincy Astronomical Society
22 Summer Creek
Quincy, IL 62301
217-222-8832

The sun's outer corona, photographed through the reflecting telescope of the NASA Langley Research Center's Sky Watcher's Astronomy Club.

Rockford Amateur Astronomers
P.O. Box 1874
Rockford, IL 61110
815-962-6540

Skokie Valley Astronomers
910 Glenwood Ln.
Glenview, IL 60025
312-998-1627

Space Science Explorers
910 Glenwood Ln.
Glenview, IL 60025
312-998-1627

Twin City Amateur Astronomers
P.O. Box 755
Normal, IL 61761
309-454-4164

Indiana
Evansville Astronomical Society
P.O. Box 3474
Evansville, IN 47733

Ft. Wayne Astronomical Society
P.O. Box 6004
Ft. Wayne, IN 46896
219-747-0774

Indiana Astronomical Society
Mooresville, IN 46158
317-831-8387

Michiana Astronomical Society
P.O. Box 262
South Bend, IN 46624
219-233-4667

Northern Indiana Astronomical Group
St. Francis College
Achatz Science Hall
P.O. Box 6004
Ft. Wayne, IN 46896

Wabash Valley Astronomical Society
2367 Yeager Rd. No. 102
West Lafayette, IN 47906
317-463-3741

Iowa
Ames Area Amateur Astronomers
1208 Wilson Ave.
Ames, IA 50010
515-232-8705

Cedar Rapids Amateur Astronomers
1513 Parkwood Ln., NE
Cedar Rapids, IA 52402
319-857-4698

Des Moines Astronomical Society
2307 49th St.
Des Moines, IA 50310
515-274-1873

Quad Cities Astronomical Society
P.O. Box 3706
Davenport, IA 52808
319-324-4661

Sioux City Astronomical Society
1001 S. Cornelia St.
Sioux City, IA 51106
712-276-0671

Southeastern Iowa Astronomy Club—
  Burlington Chapter
610 Walnut
Burlington, IA 52601
319-753-2509

Kansas
Kansas Astronomical Observers
Wichita Omnisphere
220 S. Main
Wichita, KS 67202
316-264-3174

Northeast Kansas Amateur Astronomers
  League
P.O. Box 951
Topeka, KS 66601

Kentucky
Blue Grass Amateur Astronomy Society
1490 N. Forbes Rd.
Lexington, KY 40511
606-252-6143

Midwestern Astronomers
1643 Elder Ct.
Ft. Wright, KY 41011
606-331-0052

Louisiana
Baton Rouge Astronomical Society
12635 Parnell Ave.
Baton Rouge, LA 60815
504-291-1685

High Culture: Archaeoastronomy

It is common knowledge that ancient peoples, from the Egyptians to the Greeks, the Mayans to the Aztecs, were fascinated with the night sky. They studied it, built monuments to it, wrote poetry about it, and even worshiped it. Today we admire their achievements and have used their discoveries as a basis for scientific research. The scientists investigating ancient perceptions of the sky are pioneers in the interdisciplinary area known as archaeoastronomy.

Archaeoastronomy is the study of the astronomical practices, celestial lore, mythologies, religions, and cosmologies of ancient cultures and the surviving indigenous peoples of today. To explore these areas, astronomers may team up with anthropologists, or art historians may form partnerships with astrophysicists. These teams use the tools of their disparate disciplines and depend on all aspects of a culture's legacy—written records, archaeological remains, art, and architecture—to draw conclusions about the past.

What kinds of questions capture the imaginations of archaeoastronomers? They may try to determine whether the builders of Stonehenge in England incorporated an eclipse-prediction system into the design of their fascinating structure. Or they may investigate whether the symbols found on a disk from Phaistos, Crete, represent a zodiac from the second millennium B.C. As archaeoastronomers study the data, they are discovering how science and cosmological thought evolved among ancient peoples.

If you are interested in learning more about archaeoastronomy, you may want to contact the **Center for Archaeoastronomy** (P.O. Box X, College Park, MD 20740; 301-864-6637). Founded in 1978 at the University of Maryland, the center is designed to advance research, education, and public awareness of these studies. Since 1985 the center has become an independent unit. *Archaeoastronomy*, the journal of the center, was founded in 1977 and is the only publication in the United States devoted exclusively to archaeoastronomy. Designed as a medium of information exchange for professional and amateur alike, the journal contains articles, field reports, book reviews, conference notes, and a complete review and listing of what has appeared in the current literature. Subscriptions to the semiannual journal are $20 per volume ($30 for libraries and institutions); add $3 per volume for orders outside the United States.

Pontchartrain Astronomy Society
12635 Parnell Ave.
Baton Rouge, LA 70072
504-340-0256

Red River Astronomical Society
1426 Alma St.
Shreveport, La 71108
318-865-2433

Maryland
Baltimore Astronomical Society
601 Light St.
Baltimore, MD 21230
301-766-6605

Bowie Astronomical Society
12700 Bridle Pl.
Bowie, MD 20715

Cumberland Astronomy Club
350 Bedford St.
Cumberland, MD 21502

Goddard Astronomy Club
Code 511
NASA-Goddard Space Flight Center
Greenbelt, MD 20771
301-286-6713

Harford County Astronomical Society
P.O. Box 906
Bel Air, MD 21014
301-457-5597

Tri-State Astronomers
823 Commonwealth Ave.
Hagerstown, MD 21740
301-791-4172

Westminster Astronomical Society
3481 Salem Bottom Rd.
Westminster, MD 21157
301-848-6384

Massachusetts
Aldrich Astronomical Society
12 Kay
Grafton, MA 01519

Amateur Telescope Makers of Boston
8 Pond St.
Dover, MA 02030
508-785-0352

Amherst Area Amateur Astronomers
  Association
P.O. Box 335
North Amherst, MA 01059
413-253-5057

Astronomical Society of the Berkshires
Box 41
Mt. Washington, MA 01258

Cape Cod Astronomical Society
531 Monomoscoy Rd.
Mashpee, MA 02649
508-477-2448

South Shore Astronomical Society
P.O. Box 429
Jacobs Ln.
Norwell, MA 02061
617-588-0673

Springfield Stars Club
107 Lower Beverly Hills
West Springfield, MA 01089
413-734-9179

Michigan
Astronomical Society of Hillsdale County
3260 N. Dunes Rd.
Hillsdale, MI 49242
517-439-1295

Capital Area Astronomy Club
Abrams Planetarium
Michigan State University
East Lansing, MI 48824
517-355-4676

Detroit Astronomical Society
14298 Lauder
Detroit, MI 48227
313-981-4096

Friends United Through Astronomy
8191 Woodland Shore, Lot No. 12
Brighton, MI 48116
313-227-9347

Grand Rapids Astronomical Association
4 Alten NE
Grand Rapids, MI 49503
616-454-7645

Kalamazoo Astronomical Society
315 S. Rose
Kalamazoo, MI 49001

Marquette Astronomical Society
1203 W. Fair Ave.
Marquette, MI 49855
906-225-1066

Michigan Spacelog
1109 Geddes Ave.
Ann Arbor, MI 48109
313-426-5396

Muskegon Astronomical Society
P.O. Box 363
Muskegon, MI 49443
616-798-7680

Sunset Astronomical Society
3622 Towerline Rd.
Bridgeport, MI 48722
517-777-2824

A tour of the U.S. Naval Observatory's 26-inch telescope in Washington, D.C.

Toledo Astronomical Association
8534 Covert Rd.
Petersburg, MI 49270
313-857-6204

Warren Astronomical Society
P.O. Box 474
East Detroit, MI 48021
313-344-2854

Minnesota
Arrowhead Astronomical Society
University of Minnesota at Duluth
Duluth, MN 55812
218-726-7129

Minnesota Astronomical Society
30 E. 10th St.
St. Paul, MN 55101
612-451-7680

Minnesota Valley Amateur Astronomers
Rte. 4, Box 14A
New Ulm, MN 56073
507-359-2488

Moorhead-Fargo Astronomical Club
P.O. Box 238
Concordia College
Moorhead, MN 56560
218-299-3391

3M Astronomical Society
14601 55th St. S
Afton, MN 55001
612-733-2690

Mississippi
Jackson Astronomical Association
6207 Winthrop Cir.
Jackson, MS 39206
601-982-2317

Missouri
Astronomical Society of Kansas City
P.O. Box 400
Blue Springs, MO 64015
815-228-4238

Prairie View Astronomical Society
931 N.W. Valley Ln.
Riverside, MO 64150
816-587-0054

Rural Astronomers of Missouri
Rte. 1, Box 601
Winfield, MO 63889
314-668-8674

St. Louis Astronomical Society
4562 Clearbrook Dr.
St. Charles, MO 63303

Montana
Astronomical Institute of the Rockies
6351 Cayon Ferry Rd.
Helena, MT 59601
406-442-2208

Nebraska
Omaha Astronomical Society
5025 S. 163 St.
Omaha, NE 68135
402-896-4417

Prairie Astronomy Club
P.O. Box 80553
Lincoln, NE 68501
402-467-4222

Nevada
Astronomical Society of Nevada
825 Wilkinson Ave.
Reno, NV 89502
702-329-9946

Carson Star Searchers
P.O. Box 1436
Carson City, NV 89701

Elko Nevada Astronomical Society
550 S. 12th, No. 22
Elko, NV 89801
702-738-7916

Las Vegas Astronomical Society
Clark County Community College
    Planetarium
3200 E. Cheyenne Ave.
Las Vegas, NV 89030
702-459-8401

New Hampshire
Keene Amateur Astronomers
12 Gardner St.
Keene, NH 03431
603-352-5058

New Hampshire Astronomical Society
22 Center St.
Penacook, NH 03303
603-753-9225

New Jersey
Amateur Astronomers
W. M. Spezzy Observatory
1033 Springfield Ave.
Cranford, NJ 07016
201-549-0615

Amateur Astronomers Association of Princeton
P.O. Box 2017
Princeton, NJ 08540
609-396-3630

Astronomical Society of the Toms River Area
Ocean County College
Toms River, NJ 08754
201-255-0343

Montclair Telescope Club
46 Oakley Terr.
Nutley, NJ 07110
201-667-0038

New Jersey Astronomical Association
P.O. Box 214
High Bridge, NJ 08829
215-253-7294

North Jersey Astronomical Group
P.O. Box 4021
Clifton, NJ 07012
201-523-0024

Sheep Hill Astronomy Association
P.O. Box 111
Boonton, NJ 07005
201-335-5990

Small Scope Observers Association
4 Kingfisher Pl.
Audubon Park, NJ 08106
609-547-9487

STAR Astronomy Society
Monmouth County Park System
Newman Springs Rd.
Lincroft, NJ 07738
201-872-2670

Tychonian Observers
Glassboro State College
Glassboro, NJ 08028
609-863-7348

Willingboro Astronomical Society
P.O. Box 1457
Merchantville, NJ 08109
609-829-4345

New Mexico
Alamogordo Amateur Astronomers
1210 Filipino
Alamogordo, NM 88310
505-434-0115

Albuquerque Astronomical Society
P.O. Box 54072
Albuquerque, NM 87153
505-299-0891

Astronomical Society of Las Cruces
P.O. Box 921
Las Cruces, NM 88004
505-526-2968

New York
Albany Area Amateur Astronomers
1529 Valencia Rd.
Schenectady, NY 12309
518-374-8744

Amateur Astronomers Association of New York
1010 Park Ave.
New York, NY 10028
212-535-2922

Amateur Observers Society of New York
707 S. 9th
Lindenhurst, NY 11757
516-957-3713

Astronomical Society of Long Island
1011 Howells Rd.
Bay Shore, Long Island, NY 11706
516-586-1760

Astronomical Society of New York City
HOSS Planetarium
153 Arlo Rd.
Staten Island, NY 10301
718-727-1967

Broome County Astronomical Society
Roberson-Kopernik Observatory
Underwood Rd.
Vestal, NY 13850
607-748-3685

Buffalo Astronomical Association
Buffalo Museum of Science
Humbolt Pkwy.
Buffalo, NY 14211

Elmira-Corning Astronomical Society
17 W. Hazel St.
Corning, NY 14830
607-962-5435

Martz Memorial Astronomical Association
176 Robin Hill Rd.
Frewsburg, NY 14738
716-386-4566

Mohawk Valley Astronomical Society
867 Bleecker St.
Utica, NY 13501
315-793-0753

Niagara Frontier L5 Society
40 King's Trail
Buffalo, NY 14221
716-689-9140

Rockland Astronomy Club
110 Pascack Rd.
Pearl River, NY 10965

Syracuse Astronomical Society
1115 E. Colvin St.
Syracuse, NY 13210
315-458-1454

Tri-Lakes Astronomical Society
P.O. Box 806
Saranac Lake, NY 12983
518-891-0339

Wagner College Astronomy Club
361 Howard Ave.
Staten Island, NY 10301
317-390-3341

Westchester Astronomy Club
511 Warburton Ave.
Yonkers, NY 10701
914-963-4550

North Carolina
Astronomical Society of Rowan County
1636 Parkview Cir.
Salisbury, NC 28144

Astronomy Club of Cumberland County
2308 Colgate Dr.
Fayetteville, NC 28304
919-485-8515

Cape Fear Astronomy Club
120 Coventry Rd.
Wilmington, NC 28405
919-791-7058

Catawba Valley Astronomy Club
12 East St.
Granite Falls, NC 28630
704-396-7656

Charlotte Amateur Astronomers Club
P.O. Box 36673
Charlotte, NC 28236

Cleveland County Amateur Astronomical
  Society
1012 Hunter Valley Rd.
Shelby, NC 28150
704-487-7751

Forsyth Astronomical Society
504 Gayron Dr.
Winston-Salem, NC 27105
919-744-7141

Gaston Amateur Astronomers
Schiele Museum
P.O. Box 953
Gastonia, NC 28054

Greensboro Astronomy Club
4301 Lawndale Dr.
Greensboro, NC 27408
919-454-1820

Raleigh Astronomy Club
P.O. Box 10643
Raleigh, NC 27605
919-832-NOVA

Stanley County Astronomical Society
P.O. Box 1269
Albemarle, NC 28001
704-982-3728

Thomasville Area Astronomy Club
Rte. 3, Box 273
Trinity, NC 27370

North Dakota
Dakota Astronomical Society
P.O. Box 2539
Bismarck, ND 58502
701-256-3620

Ohio
Astronomy Club Akron
5070 Manchester Rd.
Akron, OH 44319
216-644-0230

Chagrin Valley Amateur Astronomical
  Society
P.O. Box 11
Chagrin Falls, OH 44022
216-942-7599

Cincinnati Astronomical Society
5274 Zion Rd.
Cleves, OH 45002
513-661-3252

Columbus Astronomical Society
P.O. Box 16209
Columbus, OH 43216
614-262-9713

Cuyahoga Astronomical Association
P.O. Box 29089
Parma, OH 44129

Lewis Astronomy Club
NASA M.S. 654-1
21000 Brookpark Rd.
Cleveland, OH 44135
216-433-2072

Lima Astronomy Club
127 E. North
Kenton, OH 43326

Mahoning Valley Astronomical Society
1076 S.R. 534
Newton Falls, OH 44444
216-742-3616

Miami Valley Astronomical Society
Dayton Museum of Natural History
2629 Ridge Ave.
Dayton, OH 45414

Ohio Turnpike Astronomers Association
1494 Lakeland Ave.
Lakewood, OH 44107

Richland Astronomical Society
R.D. 10, Touby Rd.
Mansfield, OH 44903
419-756-0158

Sandusky Valley Amateur Society
319 S. Vine St.
Fostoria, OH 44830
419-435-9261

Tuscarawas County Astronomical Society
R.F.D. 1, Box 1361
New Philadelphia, OH 44663
216-339-7335

Wilderness Center Astronomy Club
P.O. Box 202
Wilmot, OH 44689

Oklahoma
Arbuckle Astronomy Society
Star Rte., Box D-2
Lone Grove, OK 73443
405-657-8509

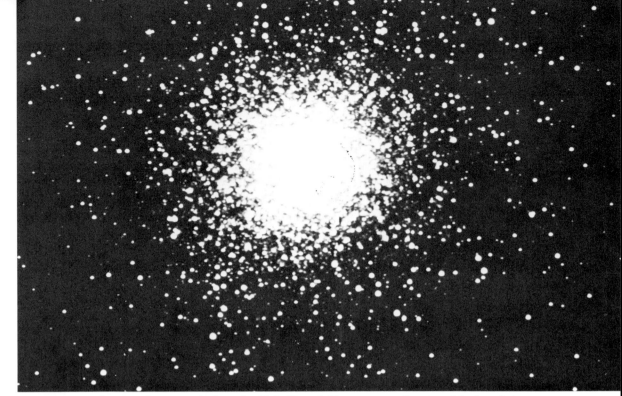

Hercules star cluster, photographed at the U.S. Naval Observatory. Courtesy National Aeronautics and Space Administration.

Astronomy Club of Tulsa
P.O. Box 470611
Tulsa, OK 74147
918-742-7577

Bartlesville Astronomical Society
225 S.E. Fenway Pl.
Bartlesville, OK 74006
918-333-1966

Central Oklahoma Astronomy Club
P.O. Box 628
Purcell, OK 73080
405-527-6584

Northwest Oklahoma Astronomy Club
1719 Pawnee
Enid, OK 73703
405-233-5707

Oklahoma City Astronomy Club
2100 N.E. 52nd St.
Oklahoma City, OK 73111
405-424-5545

Oregon
Central Beach
20352 Illahee Dr.
Bend, OR 97702
503-382-3094

Eugene Astronomical Society
Ln. Planetarium
P.O. Box 2680
Eugene, OR 97402
503-741-0501

Northwest Astronomy Group
55371 McDonald Rd.
Vernonia, OR 97064
503-429-2430

OMSI Astronomers
4015 S.W. Canyon Rd.
Portland, OR 94221
503-667-2350

Portland Astronomical Society
2626 S.W. Luradel St.
Portland, OR 94219

Pennsylvania
Astronomers Association of Pittsburgh
P.O. Box 314
Glenshaw, PA 15116
412-224-2510

Astronomical Society of Harrisburg
1915 Enfield St.
Camp Hill, PA 17011
717-975-9799

Beaver Valley Astronomy Club
818 6th Ave.
New Brighton, PA 15066
412-843-8931

Berks County Amateur Astronomical Society
Reading School District Planetarium
Parkside Dr.
South Reading, PA 19611
215-375-9062

Delaware Valley Amateur Astronomers
6233 Castor Ave.
Philadelphia, PA 19149
215-831-0485

Kiski Astronomers
2 Aluminum City Terr.
New Kensington, PA 15068
412-337-0509

Lackawanna Astronomical Society
620 E. Rock Rd.
Allentown, PA 18103
215-398-7295

Sir Isaac Newton Astronomical Society
P.O. Box 591
Kane, PA 16735

Rhode Island
Celestial Observers of Rhode Island
82 Sterling St.
Pawtucket, RI 02860
401-521-5680

Skyscrapers
47 Peeptoad Rd.
North Scituate, RI 02857
401-942-7893

South Carolina
Carolina Skygazers Astronomy Club
Museum of York County
4621 Mt. Gallant Rd.
Rock Hill, SC 29730
803-329-2121

Low Country Stargazers
58 Kiawah Loop
Charleston AFB, SC 20404
803-552-6848

Midlands Astronomy Club
321 Watermark Pl.
Columbia, SC 29210
803-799-8703

South Dakota
Black Hills Astronomy Society
3719 Locust
Rapid City, SD 57701

Tennessee
Barnard Astronomical Society
P.O. Box 90042
Chattanooga, TN 37412
615-629-6094

Bays Mountain Amateur Astronomers
Rte. 4
Kingsport, TN 27660
615-229-9447

Bledsoe Creek Astronomy and Telescope Club
Rte. 2, Newton Ln.
Gallatin, TN 37066

Bristol Astronomy Club
824 Hidden Valley Rd.
Kingsport, TN 27663
615-239-3638

Memphis Astronomical Society
1229 Pallwood Rd.
Memphis, TN 38122

Middle Tennessee Astronomical Society
1305 Sycamore St.
Manchester, TN 37355
615-728-7321

Orion
4412 Damas Rd.
Knoxville, TN 37921

Smoky Mountain Astronomical Society
P.O. Box 6204
Knoxville, TN 37914
615-637-1121

Texas
Abilene Astronomical Society
1109 Highland Ave.
Abilene, TX 79605
915-677-5713

Amarillo Astronomy Club
5303 S. Milam
Amarillo, TX 79110

Association of Amateur Astronomers
Texas A&M University
Dept. of Physics
College Station, TX 77843

Astronomical Society of East Texas
P.O. Box 4900, No. 151
Tyler, TX 75712
214-566-5317

Austin Astronomical Society
P.O. Box 12831
Austin, TX 78711

Brazosport Astronomical Society
400 College Dr.
Lake Jackson, TX 77566
713-483-9218

Corpus Christi Astronomical Society
3814 Marion St.
Corpus Christi, TX 78415
512-852-7643

Denton County Astronomical Society
225 Green Springs Cir.
Sanger, TX 76266
817-458-4058

Ft. Bend Astronomy Club
P.O. Box 942
Stafford, TX 77477

Ft. Worth Astronomical Society
P.O. Box 161715
Ft. Worth, TX 76161
817-860-6858

General Dynamics Astronomy Club
3400 Bryant-Irvin Rd.
Ft. Worth, TX 76109
817-451-4896

Houston Astronomical Society
8522 Bluegate Dr.
Houston, TX 77025

JSC Astronomical Society
3702 Townes Forest
Friendswood, TX 77546
713-482-3909

San Angelo Amateur Astronomy Association
P.O. Box 60391
San Angelo, TX 76906
915-944-3148

San Antonio Astronomical Association
6427 Threau's Way
San Antonio, TX 78239
512-654-9874

South Plains Astronomy Club
1920 46th St.
Lubbock, TX 79412
806-763-6800

Texas Astronomical Society
P.O. Box 25162
Dallas, TX 75225
214-368-6982

Texas Observers of Ft. Worth
1501 Montgomery St.
Ft. Worth, TX 76107
817-732-1631

Valley Astronomical Society
7005 N. 31st St.
McAllen, TX 78504

Utah
Ogden Astronomical Society
2336 W. 5650 S
Roy, UT 84067
801-773-8106

Salt Lake Astronomical Society
15 S. State St.
Salt Lake City, UT 84111
801-538-2104

Southern Utah Astronomy Group
147 South 300 E
Cedar City, UT 84720
801-586-7707

Vermont
Springfield Telescope Markers
4 Russell Ave.
St. Johnsbury, VT 05819
802-748-8369

Vermont Astronomical Society
P.O. Box 782
Silliston, VT 05495
802-878-3459

Virginia
Astronomical Society of Tidewater
4205 Faigle St.
Portsmouth, VA 23703
804-484-6152

Black Bay Amateur Astronomers
3808 Flag Rd.
Chesapeake, VA 23323
804-485-4242

Farquier Astronomy Society
Rte. 2, Box 680
Catlett, VA 22019

Halifax Skywatchers
P.O. Box 22
Nathalie, VA 24577
804-349-3700

Langley Skywatchers
221 Raleigh Ave.
Hampton, VA 23661

Lynchburg Astronomy Club
4648 Locksview Rd.
Lynchburg, VA 24502

Northern Virginia Astronomy Club
6028 Ticonderoga Ct.
Burke, VA 22015
703-866-4985

Piedmont Astronomy Club
P.O. Box 865
Bassett, VA 24055
703-647-8976

Richmond Astronomical Society
709 Timken Dr.
Richmond, VA 23239
804-741-3689

Roanoke Valley Astronomical Society
3721 Colony Ln. S.W.
Roanoke, VA 24018
703-989-3474

Shenandoah Valley Astronomy Club
305 S. Dogwood Dr.
Harrisonburg, VA 22801
603-568-3845

Skywatchers Astronomy Club
109 Mill Point Dr.
Hampton, VA 23669
804-865-2184

Tidewater Amateur Telescope Makers
677 Charlecote Dr.
Virginia Beach, VA 23462
804-424-9430

TCC Astronomical Society
3710 Bamboo Rd.
Portsmouth, VA 23703
804-484-6084

Triangulum Astronomical Society
P.O. Box 7463
Fredericksburg, VA 22404
703-373-8862

Washington
Olympic Astronomical Society
2312 5th St.
Bremerton, WA 98312

Seattle Astronomical Society
852 N.W. 6th St.
Seattle, WA 98115
206-523-2787

Southwest Washington Astronomical Society
2421 Leisure Ln.
Centralia, WA 98531
206-736-6144

Spokane Astronomical Society
S. 4140 Cook St.
Spokane, WA 99223
509-448-9694

Tacoma Astronomical Society
7101 Topaz Dr. S.W.
Tacoma, WA 98498
206-588-9504

Tri-City Astronomy Club
1905 Luther Pl.
Richland, WA 99352
509-943-5304

Wisconsin
LaCrosse Area Astronomical Society
P.O. Box 2041
LaCrosse, WI 54602
608-785-8669

Madison Astronomical Society
205 Cameo Ln.
Madison, WI 53714
608-241-1444

Milwaukee Astronomical Society
W248 S7040 Sugar Maple Dr.
Waukesha, WI 53186
414-662-2987

Neville Museum Astronomical Society
Neville Public Museum
210 Museum Pl.
Green Bay, WI 54303
414-336-5878

Northeast Wisconsin Stargazers
109 Skyline Dr.
Appleton, WI 54915
414-757-6710

Rock Valley Astronomical Society
Rte. 2, 335 Russell Rd.
Janesville, WI 54545
608-752-2155

Wehr Astronomical Society
9401 W. College Ave.
Franklin, WI 53132
414-425-8550

Wyoming
Cheyenne Astronomical Society
3409 Frontier St.
Cheyenne, WY 92001
307-634-2509

CANADA
Lethbridge Astronomy Society
2015 13th Ave. S
Lethbridge, AB T1K 0S4

Manitoba Astronomy Club
190 Rubpert Ave.
Winnipeg, MB R3B 0N2
204-956-2830

Prince George Astronomical Society
3330 22nd Ave.
Prince George, BC V2M 3Z1
604-562-2131

RASC-Calgary Centre
P.O. Box 2100
Calgary, AB T2P 2M5

RASC-Edmonton Centre
Edmonton Space-Science Centre
11211 142nd St.
Edmonton, AB T5M 4A1

RASC-Halifax Centre
1747 Summer St.
Halifax, NS B3H 3A6

RASC-Kingston Centre
P.O. Box 1793
Kingston, ON K7L 3J6

RASC-Kitchener-Waterloo Centre
49 Sorrel Pl.
Waterloo, ON N2L 4H2

RASC-London Centre
P.O. Box 842, Station B
London, ON N6A 4Z3

RASC-Montreal Centre
P.O. Box 1752, Station B
Montreal, PQ H3B 3K3

RASC-Niagara Centre
24 Hawthorne Ave.
St. Catharines, ON L2M 6A9

RASC-Ottawa Centre
Herzberg Institute of Astrophysics
100 Sussex Dr.
Ottawa, ON K1A 0R6

RASC-Quebec Centre
C.P. 9396
Sainte-Foy, PQ G1V 4B5

ASC-Saskatoon Centre
Sub. P.O. No. 6, Box 317
Saskatoon, SK S7N 0W0

RASC-Societé d'Astronomie de Montréal
P.O. Box 206, St. Michel
Montreal, PQ H2A 3L9

RASC-Toronto Centre
McLaughlin Planetarium
100 Queens Park
Toronto, ON M5S 2C6

RASC-Vancouver Centre
Gordon Southam Observatory
1100 Chestnut St.
Vancouver, BC V6J 3J9

RASC-Victoria Centre
6300 Springlea Rd.
Victoria, BC V8Z 5Z4

RASC-Windsor Centre
453 E. Belle River Rd., R.R. 2
Belle River, ON N0R 1A0

RASC-Winnipeg Centre
P.O. Box 215
St. James Post Office
Winnipeg, MB R3J 3R4

Steel City Star Gazers
448 E. 13th St.
Hamilton, ON L9A 4A5
416-388-0872

SCIENTIFIC AND EDUCATIONAL SOCIETIES

In addition to the many amateur clubs and umbrella organizations, there also are several national organizations with mandates to promote the study of astronomy. Some include both amateurs and professionals; others are intended for one group or the other. Most hold regular meetings, sponsor workshops, and publish a newsletter. Here is a list of a few key organizations, with a brief overview of what they do and how they serve the astronomy community.

American Association of Physics Teachers (AAPT, 5112 Berwyn Rd., College Park, MD 20742; 301-454-5327) is the world's largest association of physics teachers, with members from nearly every country and 40 branches in the United States and Canada alone. Its approximately 10,000 members come from colleges and high schools. AAPT publishes the *American Journal of Physics, The Physics Teacher,* and *AAPT Announcer.*

American Association of Variable Star Observers (AAVSO, c/o Dr. Janet A. Mattei, 25 Birch St., Cambridge, MA 02138; 617-354-0484) is an amateur astronomy organization with a worldwide membership. The association aims to encourage and support variable-star observing and to compile, computerize, publish, and distribute to the astronomy community variable-star observations. The stars in the association's observing program vary greatly in brightness, so members may use equipment ranging from binoculars to large-aperture telescopes. Membership is open to anyone over age 16 and costs $50; junior membership (ages 16 through 21) is $25. Membership includes a packet of materials for setting up individual observing

programs. Members are alerted to the discovery of exploding stars and are encouraged to participate in special observing programs requested by professional astronomers. Publications include *The Journal of the AAVSO* ($20 per year in the United States; $24 elsewhere), *The AAVSO Bulletin* ($20 per year in the United States; $24 elsewhere), *Solar Bulletin* ($20 per year in the United States; $24 elsewhere), *AAVSO Circular* ($10 per year in the United States; $14 elsewhere), and *AAVSO Reports and Monographs* ($30 per year in the United States; $34 elsewhere). Subscription rates to receive all publications are $100 per year in the United States; $120 elsewhere.

American Astronomical Society (AAS, 2000 Florida Ave. NW, Ste. 300, Washington, DC 20009; 202-328-2010) is the major organization of professional astronomers in North America. The organization boasts a membership of 4,300 and is designed to promote astronomy and closely related branches of science. Members include physicists, mathematicians, geologists, and engineers. AAS holds two meetings a year and offers grants, awards, and prizes for excellence in astronomy. It publishes *The Astronomical Journal, The Astrophysical Journal, The American Astronomical Society Photo Bulletin,* and a newsletter. The education office, in conjunction with the Astronomical Society of the Pacific, publishes a newsletter for teachers and provides visiting professional astronomers to non-science-oriented colleges.

American Meteor Society (c/o Dept. of Physics and Astronomy, SUNY, Geneseo, NY 14454; 716-245-5211) collects and analyzes meteor observations made by individual members from diverse locations and by others who submit their findings for analysis. The organization publishes an annual report and occasional research reports, and supports publication of the newsletter *Meteor News*. Subscriptions to the newsletter are $3.95 a year in the United States, $6 elsewhere, including Canada, by surface mail; $9 a year by air mail. (To subscribe, write *Meteor News*, Rte. 3, Box 1062, Callahan, FL 32011.)

Association of Lunar and Planetary Observers (ALPO, c/o Dr. John E. Westfall, P.O. Box 16131, San Francisco, CA 94116; 415-566-5768). Founded in 1947, the association is an informal, international group of students of the sun, the moon, planets, asteroids, meteors, and comets. ALPO aims to stimulate, coordinate, and promote the study of these bodies using methods and instruments available to amateur astronomers. Advanced amateurs specializing in particular areas are welcome, as are novices and professional scientists. ALPO publishes the annual *ALPO Solar System Ephemeris*, as well as a quarterly journal containing articles on observatories, projects, and scientific discoveries. Its membership dues include a subscription to the journal and are $12 for one volume (6 issues) and $21 for two volumes (12 issues) in North America. Rates are $14 and $25 elsewhere.

International Dark-Sky Association (3545 N. Stewart, Tucson, AZ 85716) is devoted to combating light pollution, a problem for both amateur and professional astronomers. The association is a clearinghouse of information and advice.

International Planetarium Society (c/o Mark Petersen, P.O. Box 3023, Boulder, CO 80307; 303-786-9366) is for people who work in planetariums and science museums concerned with sharing astronomy information with the public. It publishes *The Planetarium* magazine and various resource books and holds regional and national meetings.

National Deep Sky Observer's Society (c/o Alan Goldstein, 3123 Radiance Rd., Louisville, KY 40220; 502-458-5541). The society was founded in 1976 to serve as a clearinghouse for deep-sky observers. The group sponsors observing programs, research projects, and network opportunities. It publishes a bimonthly newsletter, *Betelgeuse*.

Sunsearch (c/o Steve Lucas, 14400 S. Kolin Ave., Midlothian, IL 60445; 312-396-1499). Geared to the advanced amateur astronomer, Sunsearch is a small group that aims to locate exploding stars, or supernovas, beyond the Milky Way. Using star charts and sophisticated equipment, the group's members spot these stars and then confirm their findings with major observatories.

ASTRONOMY STUFF

Like most serious enthusiasts, astronomy buffs love to show off their wares. On T-shirts and slide sets, art pieces and calendars, stargazers discuss and display the subject closest to their hearts. Some products are considered "educational," but just as many are intended simply for fun. Many are made and sold directly by professional or amateur astronomers.

Here is a list of selected astronomy products. Let your fantasies soar. Remember: the sky's the limit.

ASTRONOMY ART
Novagraphics (P.O. Box 37197, Tucson, AZ 85740; 800-821-1989, ext. 1014; 602-743-0500) features space art by Kim Poor and other artists. Subjects include the planets and their moons, star clusters, and renderings of the primeval earth. Prices range from $5 for posters to $115 for matted images.

Philatelic Collectors, Inc. (P.O. Box 128, Valley Stream, NY 11580; 516-725-2161) offers a collection of stamps from around the world in its "Halley's Comet Collection" catalog ($9.95). These colorful stamps show the comet, its discoverer, Sir Edmund Halley, and related space exploration. You'd be surprised how many countries have issued such stamps—more than 80 countries, at last count. Stamps are available in sets and sheets. Prices range from $2 to more than $100, but most are under $10. The variety and artistry of these stamps is a fascinating tribute to the comet's once-in-a-lifetime appearance.

EDUCATIONAL PRODUCTS
Astro Cards (P.O. Box 35, Natrona

Heights, PA 15065; 412-295-4128) features index-card finder charts ($7.50 for 75 cards); an observer's logbook ($18.75), an attractive three-ring binder with observation forms for the solar system, deep sky objects, and constellations; and a wide range of slide sets with cassettes and videotapes. The subject areas of both kinds of programs focus on the missions of the space program. The price for each slide set with cassette is $14.95; videotapes, $29.95. Also available are slide sets of 20 images with teacher's guide ($9.50) and deluxe albums of 100 images that range from $19.95 to $29.95.

Above: Artist's rendition of Halley's comet over Antarctica, from Novagraphics. Below: Space stamps from Philatelic Collectors, Inc.

Perhaps Astro Cards's most unique offering is a bimonthly magazine called *The Observer's Guide*. Designed for the avid telescope viewer, the magazine includes data chart pages with in-depth reviews of deep-sky objects within a featured constellation, complete data about sky objects, astrophotos, and constellation charts. Subscriptions are $12 a year, $21 for two years in the United States; $18 a year, $33 for two years in Canada. Add $1 for immediate first-class delivery of the current issue.

Astronomical Society of the Pacific (390 Ashton Ave., San Francisco, CA 94112; 415-337-1100) offers slide sets and cassettes about the solar system, computer software, videotapes, teaching kits, posters, and calendars. Prices vary widely: $25 to $87 for slide sets; $47 to $70 for software; $9 to $19 for planet kits; $5 to $8 for posters, and about $7.50 for calendars. One of the more innovative slide sets is a new package about Mars ($12.45), featuring color views of the red planet sent back by Viking probes. The set comes with captions, a set of eight activities, and audiovisual aids. Write for a complete illustrated catalog.

Bausch & Lomb/Bushnell (300 N. Lone Hill Ave., San Dimas, CA 91773; 800-423-3537; 714-592-8000) offers hands-on science products for children. Astronomy-related products include a portable planetarium with narrated tape (18-3330; $34.95), a star watcher's decoder set with 12 windows of constellations (18-0400; $39.95), and binoculars and telescopes for beginners (Telescope, 18-1560, $124.95; Binoculars, 18-7356, $49.95).

Hansen Planetarium Publishing Division (1098 South, 200 West, Salt Lake City, UT 84101; 801-538-2104) sells posters, astronomical calendars, and star charts. Prices range between $3 and $25.

Above: Astronomical Society of the Pacific's slide set. Below: Celestial star globe from Hubbard Scientific.

Hubbard Scientific (P.O. Box 104, Northbrook, IL 60065; 312-272-7810; 800-323-8368; 312-272-7810) offers several kinds of astronomy materials. Highlights from the catalog of this manufacturer of educational scientific products include a gear-driven planetarium that demonstrates the basic relationship between the sun, earth, and moon ($83.50); a celestial star globe that demonstrates the relationships of earth, stars, planets, and galaxies ($109); astronomy study prints with important information about day and night, phases of the moon, and tides (set of 12, $16.50); and a 44-by-44-inch star chart that shows the northern skies on one side and the southern skies on the other. Available to schools, colleges, and nonprofit institutions. Free catalog.

MMI Corporation (P.O. Box 19907, Baltimore, MD 21211; 301-366-1222). MMI furnishes astronomy and geology teaching materials to secondary schools, colleges, research institutions, observatories, planetariums, national parks, and other institutions. Products include slides ranging in subject from the topography of the earth to deep-sky objects (prices from $14 for a single slide set to $134.95 for a comprehensive series); six videos on astronomy subjects ($175); computer software (from $35 to $81.77); and celestial globes (from $24 to $995). The top-of-the-line 8700-P20 Einstein planetarium includes a planetarium projector, the model P-20 floor-based dome, operating manual, lesson plans, a battery-operated light provider, and the *Educator's Workshop Guide,* offering 196 pages of lesson plans, questioning strategies, teaching techniques, and indoor and outdoor planetarium activities ($1,695). Different-sized domes are available.

MMI Corp.'s Einstein Planetarium Projector.

National Geographic's educational filmstrip and video set.

National Geographic Society (17th & M Sts. NW, Washington, DC 20036; 800-638-4077; 301-921-1330 in Maryland) offers filmstrips and videos to educators only. Filmstrips include a two-volume set on the universe for grades K through 2 (30013; $62.95); a four-volume set on the planets for grades 3 through 6 (30020; $110.95); and an eight-part series covering everything from the planets to expanding galaxies for grades 7 through 12, available in two parts: the first set (04772; $130.95) and the second (04788; $85.95). There's a 10 percent discount if you buy both sets (04798, $195.20). One filmstrip in this series, *The Planets,* is available on CAV videodisk and comes with a user's guide (50365; $87.50). Videos and films include one on the moon for grades 2 through 6 (video: 51186, $59.95; film: 50085, $196.50) and one on the solar system for older children (video: 51204, $69.95; film: 50092, $248.50).

Science Graphics (P.O. Box 7516, Bend, OR 97708; 503-388-2225) distributes astronomy teaching slides, all selected from NASA imagery centers. Recent offerings include 66 slide sets comprising more than 2,000 slides featuring geological studies, artists' conceptions, computer and infrared images, and explanatory diagrams of the planets, the moon, earth, galaxies and quasars, and the dynamics of the sun. Other sets document scientists in history, comets, archaeoastronomy, and the work of observatories. Prices range from $25 to $65, with an average of 30 slides in each set. A *Science Graphics Astronomy Catalog* is available for $3.

NOVELTIES AND SOUVENIRS

Celestial Innovations (H.C.R. Box 3228, 67 Beverly Cir., Oracle, AZ 85623; 602-896-9109) offers a handy item you probably didn't know you needed: a binocular system that allows the binoculars to rest on your chest while remaining close to your eyes. The net gain is that the binoculars remain steady and your hands are freed up to take notes or to rest as your eyes do the work. The Model 80 system ($649.99) includes support, 11 x 80 binoculars, and a soft-sided binocular case. The Model 50 system ($279.99) includes 10 x 50 binoculars, with support and case. The support alone is $120.

Chest Works (1391 N. 72nd St., Wauwatosa, WI 53213; 414-476-6986), operated by astronomer Tom Gill, produces unique space-oriented designs for T-shirts, sweatshirts, polo shirts, and satin jackets. The designs are all whimsical and creative and feature witty sayings such as "Astronomy Is for Night Owls," "Deep Sky Observers Are Nebulous," and, of course, "Astronomers Do It with Heavenly Bodies." Prices are $7.95 for T-shirts, $12.95 for sweatshirts, $10.95 for polo shirts, and $29.95 for satin jackets. (Add $2 for postage and handling for one to two

items, $3 for three or more items; Wisconsin residents add 5 percent tax.) Gill also publishes a newsletter called *Sky Forum* for astronomers to discuss pertinent issues, such as telescope types, naked-eye astronomy, clubs, museums and planetariums, magazines, NASA, and more. Subscriptions are $6 a year, with at least 4 issues a year.

Cotton Expressions, Ltd. (1579 N. Milwaukee Ave., Chicago, IL 60622; 312-252-2545) specializes in zany designs for sweatshirts and T-shirts. Some of its best-sellers include star charts—the summer constellations and the winter constellations—that glow in the dark and are

printed upside-down so the wearer can read the shirt while wearing it. The company features the work of Sidney Harris, a well-known cartoonist on scientific topics. Prices start at $9.

Deen Publications (P.O. Box 831991, Richardson, TX 75083; 214-231-0338) offers a unique product: a 1,000-piece jigsaw puzzle of the summer Milky Way.

The puzzle offers a way to learn about constellations and deep-sky objects indoors and costs $12 (add $3 for UPS or priority mail; foreign purchasers $6 for surface, $15 for air). Deen also offers a 50-slide set of the constellation drawings done by Johannes Bayer in his *Uranometria*, published in the 1600s ($30).

Robert A. Haag Meteorites (P.O. Box 27527, Tucson, AZ 85726; 602-882-8804) offers meteorites of different shapes, sizes, and textures, found all over the world, for those who have a hankering for a piece of the rock. The specimens represent most known types of meteorites, and many were originally found by amateur enthusiasts. Prices vary widely, depending on type and size. Also included in the catalog are interesting tidbits about meteorites.

HC Designs, Inc. (P.O. Box 33245, Baltimore, MD 21218; 301-889-0460) is a design and mail-order house offering T-shirts, sweatshirts, nightshirts, and tote bags featuring astronomical designs. A brochure is available for $1.

Illuminations (P.O. Box 1000, Cambridge, MA 02139; 800-343-5502; 617-864-6180) produces "Glow in the Dark Stars," a set of 140 self-adhesive stars, moons, planets, comets, and quasars that you can place on your bedroom ceiling (or wherever). They absorb and store light, then release it when

the lights are turned off. They actually appear to twinkle. Price by mail is $4.50, including shipping costs, per package.

The Nature Company (headquarters: P.O. Box 2310, Berkeley, CA 94702; 800-227-1114; 25 stores nationwide) offers books, slides, videos, and lighthearted astronomical knickknacks that aim to please and amuse. For example, three hand-blown glass paperweights feature the moon and tides, Saturn, and the nighttime sky ($89 to $98). Another offering is a quartz man's or woman's watch that displays stars and the constellations of the northern skies against a background of midnight blue ($59). There are also telescopes, star charts, T-shirts, and other items. Write for a free catalog.

Orbic Systems (109 Eltingville Blvd., Staten Island, NY 10312; 718-356-2328) produces model solar systems in the form of mobiles as well as desk models of the sun and of individual planets and their satellites. Specialties of the house include the deluxe solar family mobile, which includes 44 satellites and a Halley's comet model (0010-352; $160, plus $5 shipping and handling). Another favorite is the space-saver mobile, smaller than the deluxe model and less detailed, but with the same high-quality workmanship (0010-410; $48, plus $2 shipping and handling).

Science & Art Products (P.O. Box 1166, Malibu, CA 90265; 800-356-1733; 213-456-2496) specializes in photographs of space imprinted on T-shirts, sweatshirts, jackets, and caps. Also available are deep-space and planetary photographs printed on Kodak paper and designed as photo-strip bookmarks ($4.98 for package of four). Each is laminated and has an astronomical description on the back. T-shirts and sweatshirts sell for $13.95 and $21.95 respectively. Space caps are $5.95,

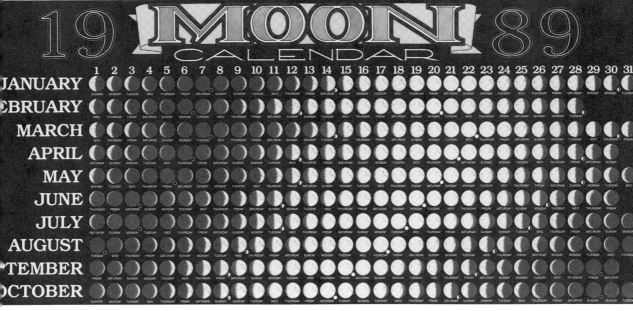

Johnson Publishing's moon calendar.

and fleece-lined jackets are $45. (Add $1.50 postage and handling for T-shirts, sweatshirts, and jackets; $1 for space caps; and 50 cents for packages of space markers.)

Whirlwind Designs (65 Inman St., Cambridge, MA 02139; 617-868-0946) produces sky imagery silk-screened on T-shirts and sweatshirts. Designs include the northern lights and UFOs. Prices are $9.95 per shirt (add $1.50 postage for one shirt, plus 50 cents for each additional shirt).

ASTRONOMICAL CALENDARS

Astronomical Society of the Pacific (390 Ashton Ave, San Francisco, CA 94112; 415-337-1100) has a calendar called "Quest for Space" ($7.50) that features 12 full-color astronomy or space photos by science photographer Roger Ressmeyer. The calendar keeps tracks of sky events and astronomy and space anniversaries. ASP also sells the calendar produced by Hansen Planetarium ($8.50), which features high-quality photographs taken with the world's largest telescopes and NASA probes. In addition, there is a poster of the phases of the moon in silver printed on blue ($7.25).

Astronomical Workshop (Furman University, Greenville, SC 29613; 803-294-2208) offers two handy reference guides from Guy Ottewell and company: an *Astronomical Calendar* ($12) and *Mankind's Comet: Halley's Comet in the Past, the Future, and Especially the Present* ($11). Both are witty and easy to read, and feature helpful diagrams. The annual calendar includes sky maps, a timetable of astronomical comings and goings, and constellation clues. The book includes a cultural and scientific history of the once-each-lifetime comet and offers thoughts about its path and appearance.

Astronomy Magazine (Kalmbach Publishing, Co., P.O. Box 1612, Waukesha, WI 53187; 414-796-8776) produces an astronomical calendar that features important sky occurrences and interesting tidbits about celestial objects. The annual calendar sells for $8.95.

Johnson Publishing (1880 S. 57th Ct., Boulder, CO 80301; 800-662-2665) produces a stunning moon calendar, showing the phase of the moon for every day of the year. The 21-by-32-inch black-and-white poster is $7.95, including postage. A companion 128-page text, *The Moon Book,* is $8.20 postpaid. Still another product is "Moon Wrap," attractive wrapping paper featuring the phases of the moon. A set of ten sheets, 22 by 34 inches each, is $9.95.

Books

There are hundreds of astronomy books published every year; some are wonderful, others are less than scientifically accurate. Regular reviews of astronomy books are published in such magazines as *Astronomy, Mercury, Science Books and Films,* and *Sky & Telescope.* You can special-order books that sound good at most local bookstores. Or you might look through the catalogs of such companies as Sky Publishing, Willmann-Bell, MMI, or the Astronomical Society of the Pacific, which often feature the best astronomy titles. Don't neglect your local *used* bookstore, which may have a special section on astronomy and space. One particular such store is **Warren Blake Old Science Books** (131 Sigwin Dr., Fairfield, CT 06430; 203-259-3278), which offers hardbound volumes on both popular and scholarly science subjects. Astronomy listings include a first edition of an 1855 astronomy textbook, astrophysics for the layperson of the 1880s, and a 1848 Middle East cartography of the fifth century Greeks. Prices range from $35 to $375.

A Brief Glossary of Commonly Used Astronomical Terms

Asteroid: Any of the thousands of small, rocky objects that orbit the sun, most of them between the orbits of Mars and Jupiter (although some pass closer to the sun than earth does and others have orbits that take them well beyond Jupiter). The largest asteroid is one called Ceres; it's about as wide as the state of Texas.

Astronomical Unit: A unit of distance equal to the average spacing between the earth and sun. Usually abbreviated "A.U.," it is equal to about 93 million miles (about 150 million kilometers), and is a distance that light takes about eight minutes to cover. It is a handy size to use for expressing distances in the solar system. (For example, the diameter of the orbit of the most distant planet, Pluto, is about 80 A.U.)

Astrophysics: The part of astronomy that deals with the physical processes that regulate activity in the universe. For example, study of the thermonuclear fusion reactions that power stars is part of astrophysics, as is analysis of the interactions of light and matter in stars and nebulas.

Big Bang: The primeval explosion that most astronomers think gave rise to the universe as we see it today, in which clusters of galaxies are moving apart from one another. By "running the film backward"—projecting the galaxies' motions back in time—astronomers calculate that the Big Bang happened about 10 to 20 billion years ago.

Binary Star: A system of two stars orbiting each other. Binary (and triple, and even higher numbers of) stars are very common; astronomers estimate that about half of all stars are members of multiple-star systems. The nearest "star" to our solar system, Alpha Centauri, is actually our nearest example of a multiple star system; it consists of three stars—two very similar to our sun and one dim, small red star—orbiting around one another.

Black Hole: An object whose gravitational pull is so strong that—within a certain distance of it—nothing can escape, not even light. Black holes are thought to result from the collapse of certain very massive stars at the ends of their lives, but other kinds have been postulated as well: **mini black holes,** for example, which might have been formed in that turbulence shortly after the Big Bang. **Supermassive black holes**—with masses millions of times the sun's—may exist in the cores of large galaxies.

Comet: A small chunk of ice, dust, and rocky material (only a few miles across) which, when it comes close enough to the sun, can develop a tenuous "tail." The tail of a comet is made of gas and dust that have been driven off the comet's surface by the sun's energy and the tail always points away from the sun (no matter what direction the comet is moving). Comets spend most of their time very far away from the sun, and are active only for a short period (a few months at most), as they move quickly around the sun on their elongated orbits.

Constellation: A pattern of stars on the sky, named for a person, animal, or object

Photograph of the comet Kohoutek taken by the Lunar and Planetary Laboratory photography team in January 1974. Courtesy National Aeronautics and Space Administration.

(usually from mythology). Astronomers use constellations to designate directions in space; for example, the Great Galaxy "in Andromeda" lies in the direction from us marked by the pattern of stars we call Andromeda (the princess of Ethiopia in Greek mythology). Just as patterns we see in the clouds are not permanent, neither are the star patterns of constellations, because the stars move (albeit very slowly on the scale of a human lifetime). The constellations of 100,000 years ago were quite different from today's. Astronomers now divide the sky into 88 sectors, each of which is named after the traditional constellation in it.

Cosmology: The branch of astronomy that deals with the origin, large-scale properties, and evolution of the observable universe.

Crescent Moon: See "Phases of the Moon."

Eclipse: The blocking of all or part of the light from one object by another. For example, a **lunar eclipse** occurs when the earth's shadow falls on the moon, preventing sunlight from illuminating all of the moon's surface. A **solar eclipse** occurs when the moon passes directly between us and the sun, keeping part or all of the sun's light from reaching us. Lunar eclipses can occur only when the moon is on the opposite side of the earth from the sun (at full moon), whereas solar eclipses can happen only at new moon. See "Phases of the Moon."

Equinox: Either of the two instants during the year when the sun is directly over the earth's equator. In the spring the

U.S. Naval Observatory photo of the center of Andromeda galaxy, 1978.

vernal equinox occurs around March 21, and in the fall the **autumnal equinox** occurs around September 21 (the specific dates vary slightly from year to year). On the equinoxes, the lengths of day and night are very nearly equal all over the world. Spring and fall officially begin at the instants of the vernal and autumnal equinoxes.

Galaxy: A large assemblage of stars (and sometimes interstellar gas and dust), typically containing millions to hundreds of billions of member stars. A galaxy is held together by the gravitational attraction of all its member stars (and other material) to one another. Most galaxies are either of a flattened, spiral form or a fatter, ellipsoid shape without a spiral pattern. The **Milky Way Galaxy,** of which our sun is a part, is a spiral galaxy with a disk about 100,000 light-years across, containing roughly 400 billion stars. Our sun is in the disk, about two-thirds of the way from the center, and it takes about 200 million years to orbit the center of the Milky Way once.

Globular Cluster: A large congregation of stars (containing hundreds of thousands to about a million stars) that is spherical in form. About 150 globular clusters are members of our Milky Way Galaxy, distributed in a round halo around the galaxy's disk. Globular clusters, which can also be detected in other galaxies, are made up of very old stars (twice the age of the sun or more).

Light-Year: The distance light travels in one year in a vacuum, about 186,000 miles per second (about 300,000 kilometers per second). A light-year is about 6 trillion miles (about 9.5 trillion kilometers) long.

Local Group: The relatively small cluster of galaxies of which our Milky Way is a part. It is known to contain about two dozen member galaxies, but most of these are "dwarf" galaxies, considerably smaller than our own. There are only two large galaxies in the Local Group: the Milky Way and the Andromeda Galaxy (about 2 million light-years away from us in the direction of the sky marked by the constellation Andromeda). The Local Group is about 3 million light-years across and is itself a part of a supercluster of galaxies centered on a huge aggregate called the Virgo Cluster.

Magellanic Clouds: The two closest galaxies to us that are satellites of the Milky Way. They are irregular in form and relatively small (only about one-fifth as broad as the Milky Way's disk). They are roughly 100,00 light-years away from our galaxy in a direction that can be seen easily only from earth's Southern Hemisphere. The first Europeans to record their existence were Ferdinand Magellan's crew in the early 1500s; to them, the two galaxies looked like small clouds separated from the Milky Way.

Magnitude: A way of expressing the brightnesses of astronomical objects, inherited from the Greeks. In the magnitude system, a lower number indicates a brighter object (for example, a 1st-magnitude star is brighter than a 3rd-magnitude star). Each step in magnitude corresponds to a brightness difference of about 2.5. Stars of the 6th magnitude are the faintest the unaided human eye can see.

Meteor: A bit of solid debris from space, burning up in earth's atmosphere because of friction with the air. (The luminous streaks meteors trace across the sky are commonly called **shooting stars**, although they have nothing to do with the stars.) Before entering earth's atmosphere (with a typical speed of about 25,000 miles per hour) the body is called a

meteoroid. If any of the object survives its fiery passage through the air, the parts that hit the ground are called **meteorites.**

Milky Way: A faint band of hazy light that can be seen from clear, dark locations and that stretches all the way around the sky. When looked at through binoculars or a small telescope, it is seen to be composed of vast numbers of individual, faint stars. It is actually the disk of our own galaxy—seen from our perspective (within the disk), the flat lens shape of the galaxy appears to surround us. Astronomers often use the term **Milky Way** to refer to our entire galaxy, rather than to just its appearance in our sky. (See "Galaxy.")

Moon: The earth's large natural satellite. (Although **moon** is sometimes used to denote any object orbiting a planet, many astronomers prefer that the term **satellite** be used in such generic cases.)

Nebula: A cloud of gas and/or dust in interstellar space. (The word *nebula* in Latin means "cloud".) Nebulae can make themselves apparent by glowing (as **emission nebulas**), by scattering light from stars within them (as **reflection nebulas**), or by blocking light from things behind them (as **obscuration** or **dark nebulas**).

U.S. Naval Observatory photo of the Orion nebula, 1978.

Neutron Star: A crushed remnant left over when a very massive star explodes. Made almost entirely of neutrons (sub-atomic particles with no electric charge), these stellar corpses pack about twice as much mass as there is in the sun into a sphere. A spoonful of their material would weigh more than all the automobiles in the United States put together. Some neutron stars are known to spin very rapidly, at least at the beginning, and can be detected as **pulsars**: rapidly flashing sources of radio radiation or visible light. The pulses are produced by the spinning of the neutron star, much as a lighthouse beacon appears to flash on and off.

Nova: A star that abruptly and temporarily increases its brightness by a factor of hundreds of thousands. Unlike super-novas (much more violent explosions, which destroy the stars that produce them), stars that "go nova" can do so more than once. Novas are thought to occur in binary stars in which one member is a compressed dwarf star (such as a white dwarf or a neutron star) orbiting close to a much larger star. According to this theory, material from the larger star's outer layers accumulates on the dwarf's surface, becoming even hotter and more compressed by the dwarf's strong gravity until the "stolen" material explodes. See "Binary Star," "Neutron Star," "Super-nova," and "White Dwarf."

Observatory: A place where telescopes are housed. Major astronomical observatories are now located primarily on remote mountaintops to escape the bright light of cities and to take advantage of the steady and clear viewing that high altitudes generally afford. Most "radio observatories" need not be located at high altitudes, though, since most of the radio waves that can be studied from earth make it all the way through our atmosphere easily. See "Radio Astronomy" and "Telescope."

Orbit: The path of one body around another (such as the moon around the earth) or around the center of gravity of a number of objects (such as the sun's 200-million-year path around the center of the galaxy).

Parsec: A unit of distance equal to about 3.26 light-years (or, more precisely, 206,256 astronomical units). Technically, a parsec is defined as the distance from which the earth and sun would appear to be separated from each other by 1 second of arc—about the size a dime would appear to be if it were viewed from a distance of 2 miles.

Phases of the Moon: The changing appearance of the moon as it orbits the earth. At **new moon**, the moon is on the same side of the earth as the sun is, and we see only the part of the moon that is in shadow (another term for new moon is **dark of the moon**). A quarter of an orbit later (about a week after new moon), we see the moon illuminated by sunlight from the side. Thus one-half of the disk of the moon that faces us is in sunlight—the right side as seen from earth's Northern Hemisphere. This phase is called **first quarter**. About two weeks after new moon, our satellite has traveled around to the other side of its orbit, and the side facing us also faces the sun and is fully illuminated as we see it; that phase is called **full moon**. Three-quarters of a lunar orbit after new moon, at **last quarter**, the moon is again illuminated from the side (the left side as seen from the Northern Hemisphere). About a week after that, the moon is new again, and the cycle starts over. Between first quarter and last quarter, when more than half of the side of the moon facing us is in sunlight, the moon is said to be **gibbous**. From last quarter to first quarter, when more than half of the side of the moon facing us is in shadow, it is said to be a **crescent**.

The full moon, taken from the Apollo 11 spacecraft from 10,000 miles away, returning from its historic 1969 moon landing. Courtesy National Aeronautics and Space Administration.

Planet: A major object that orbits around a star. In our solar system, there are nine such objects: Mercury, Venus, Earth, Mars, Jupiter, Saturn, Uranus, Neptune, and Pluto. (There are no official specifications for how big an object must be to be called a planet rather than, for example, an asteroid.) Although no individual planet has ever been seen orbiting another star, we wouldn't expect to see one, given the limits of current technology. It is suspected, though, that planets are common companions of stars.

Planetarium: A theater in which a special device in the center of the room projects a simulation of the nighttime sky onto a dome above the audience. Planetariums generally can show how the nighttime sky looks from anywhere on the earth's surface at any time (for thousands of years into the past and future).

Pulsar: See "Neutron Star."

Quasar: One of a class of very distant (typically billions of light-years away), extremely bright, and very small objects. The term **quasar** means "quasi-star"—that is, something that looks like a star but can't actually be a star. A typical quasar produces more light each second than an entire galaxy of stars does, and it does so from a region of space that is perhaps as small as our solar system. Precisely how quasars produce their prodigious amounts of energy is not known, but astronomers suspect that their brilliance may be connected with the violent effects of very massive black holes at the centers of distant, dim galaxies on material right around them. See "Black Hole."

Radio Astronomy: The study of radio waves from objects in the universe. Radio and visible-light waves are the only kinds of lightlike radiation that can reach the ground easily from space. Partly because of this, radio astronomy became the first nonvisible branch of astronomy, with large radio telescopes (instruments that can gather and focus radio waves from space) being developed in the 1950s.

Red Giant: A very large, distended, and relatively cool star that is in the final stages of its life. A typical red giant, if placed where the sun is in our solar system, might extend past the orbit of Mars. The relatively cool temperature of its outer layers (perhaps only 2,000 degrees Centigrade, as compared with the sun's 6,000 degrees) would make it look orange or red instead of yellowish white. (The sun is predicted to become a red giant about 5 billion years from now.)

Red Shift: The lengthening (or stretching) of light waves coming from a source moving away from us. (If a source of light is moving toward us, the opposite effect—called a **blue shift**—takes place.) Light from all galaxies outside the Local Group is red shifted, indicating that they are moving away from us (and from each other). This phenomenon is called expansion of the universe.

Satellite: An object orbiting around another, larger one. For example, smaller bodies orbiting around planets are called those planets' satellites (or occasionally, moons—but some astronomers frown on this use of the word moon because they feel it should denote earth's natural satellite exclusively). Probes we launch into orbit around the earth are called **artificial satellites.**

An artist's rendering of possible solar system exploration missions. Courtesy National Aeronautics and Space Administration.

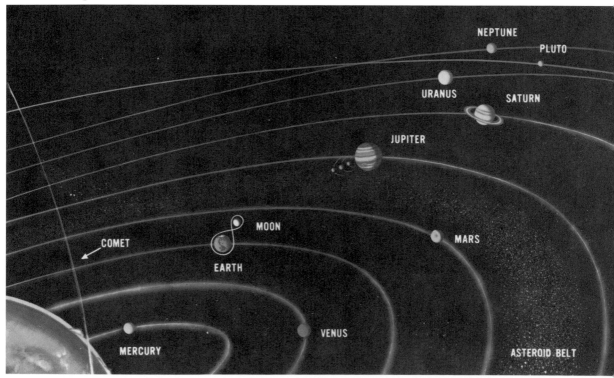

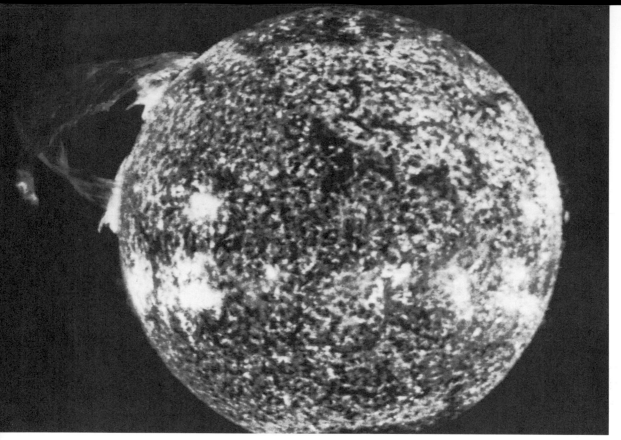

Photograph of the sun, taken from Skylab 4, showing a spectacular solar flare. Courtesy National Aeronautics and Space Administration.

Second of Arc: A very small angle which is equal to one-sixtieth of a minute of arc (which, in turn, is one-sixtieth of a degree). A line in the sky from horizon to horizon extends 180 degrees. A dime seen from a distance of 2 miles has an apparent diameter of about a second of arc.

SETI: An abbreviation for the "Search for Extraterrestrial Intelligence." (In the Soviet Union and some other places, this area of research has been called **CETI,** for "Communication with Extraterrestrial Intelligence.") At present, astronomers are undertaking this search by trying to find radio waves from space that may be artificial (that is, intelligently coded).

Solar System: The sun and all things orbiting it, including the nine major planets, their satellites, and all the asteroids and comets.

Solstice: Either of the two instants during the year when the sun as seen from earth is farthest north or south of the equator. The **summer solstice** (when the sun is over the Tropic of Cancer) occurs around June 21; the **winter solstice** (when the sun is over the Tropic of Capricorn) happens around December 21. In the Northern Hemisphere summer and winter officially begin at the instants of the summer and winter solstices.

Spectroscopy: See "Spectrum."

Spectrum: The band of colors, from violet through red, obtained by passing white light through a prism (or another device that spreads light out into its component colors). Astronomical **spectroscopy,** the study of the spectra of astronomical objects, is a very powerful tool in determining characteristics of stars, nebulas,

Diffuse nebula in the constellation Cassiopeia. White streak on the left is a meteor trail in the earth's upper atmosphere. Courtesy National Aeronautics and Space Administration.

and so on, because details of their spectra can reveal many of the physical conditions (temperature, pressure, and so on) existing within them.

Star: A large, hot ball of gas that generates energy in its core by nuclear reactions. (The sun is an example of a star.)

Star Cluster: A group of stars held together by their mutual gravitational attraction. In the Milky Way there are two kinds of star clusters: those called **open** (or **galactic**) star clusters, which are generally sparsely populated and exist only in the disk of the galaxy, and the larger, older **globular** clusters. (See "Globular Cluster.")

Sun: The star at the center of our solar system.

Supernova: An explosion that marks the end of a very massive star's life. When it occurs, the star can outshine all the other stars in a galaxy in total for several days and may leave behind only a crushed core (perhaps a neutron star or a black hole). Astronomers estimate that a supernova explosion takes place about once a century in a galaxy like our Milky Way. Although most supernovas in our galaxy are probably hidden from our view by interstellar gas and dust, astronomers can detect supernova explosions in other galaxies relatively frequently.

Telescope: An instrument designed to gather light (or other kinds of radiation) from a large area and bring it to a focus, where the radiation can be analyzed. The primary purpose of most astronomical telescopes is to provide the brightest possible images, since most things that astronomers study are very faint. Thus, the "size" associated with a telescope (such as the 200-inch on Palomar Mountain) refers to the diameter of its light-gathering area.

Universe: In astronomy, the sum total of all things that can be directly observed or whose physical effects on other things can be detected.

Variable Star: A star that changes its brightness. There are several classes of variable stars, including **periodic variables** (which change their brightnesses on a regular schedule, ranging from hours to many years) and **irregular variables** (which abide by no fixed schedule). Careful, long-term monitoring of variable stars is one major way in which amateur astronomers have made important contributions to research astronomy.

White Dwarf: The collapsed remnant of a relatively low-mass star (roughly one and a half times the sun's mass and less), which has exhausted the fuel for its nuclear reactions and shines only by radiating its stored-up heat. A typical white dwarf may have as much mass as the sun but have a size equivalent to the earth's. Its density is roughly equivalent to that of a soda can into which a 747 airliner has been squeezed. (The sun is expected to become a white dwarf at the end of its life.)

This "Map of the Universe" shows astronomical and astrological phenomena. The Milky Way and other highlights glow in the dark in this poster-sized map, which comes with a 16-page booklet. See "Star Charts and Maps," page 68. Copyright 1981 by Thomas Filsinger. Published by Celestial Arts, P.O. Box 7327, Berkeley, CA 94707.

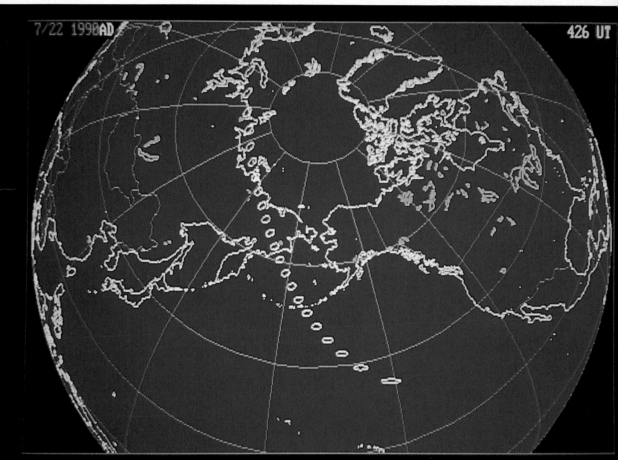

Total Eclipse of the Sun July 22, 1990/ Russia, North Atlantic

"The Visible Universe," as seen through the computer program published by Parsec Software. The program enables users to plot the positions of more than 17,000 celestial objects. See "Astronomy Software," page 74.

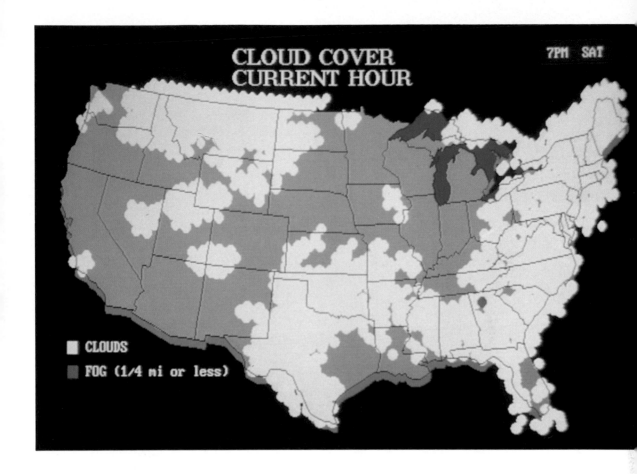

Weather Service data as viewed through WeatherBank, a dial-up information service providing up-to-the-minute data. See "Software and On-line Services," page 169.

Three cloud types, as photographed by the National Oceanic and Atmospheric Administration: Large towering (top), stratus (middle), and cirrus (bottom). For more on cloud charts, see "Weather Stuff," page 172.

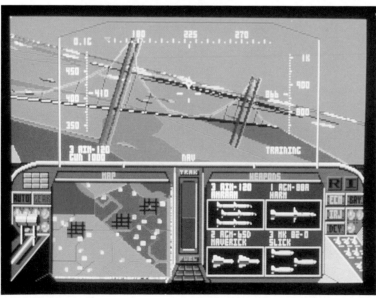

Two popular flight simulator programs for personal computers. Top: Microsoft® Flight Simulator. *Screen shots ©1983-1988 Bruce A. Artwick and Microsoft Corporation. Reprinted with permission of Microsoft Corporation. Below:* Micro Prose's F-19 Stealth Fighter. *See "Flight Simulators," page 262.*

The husband-and-wife stunt-flying team of Bob and Pat Wagner, a popular spectacle at air shows. See "Air Shows," page 223. Experimental Aircraft Association photograph by Jim Koepnick.

Two views of the Smithsonian Institution's National Air and Space Museum in Washington, D.C.: Minuteman III and Scout D missiles (top), and a vintage-World War II fighter. See "Aviation Museums," page 222.

Two vintage aircraft: Lockheed Constellation (top), first flown in 1943, courtesy Lockheed Aeronautical Systems Company; and the Curtiss P-40N Cu Warhawk (photo by Dave Gustafson), courtesy Kalamazoo Aviation History Museum. See "Aviation Museums," page 222.

WEATHER

WEATHER

How's the weather? It's a question that's far more than a conversation starter. Forecasting the weather is a multibillion-dollar worldwide industry, and the quality of those forecasts in turn affects trillions of dollars—everything from crops to construction to commerce of all types.

Long ago we depended on our own observations to make weather predictions. We came to understand that the loud chirp of crickets meant that a warm day lay ahead. Or if we looked up at the sky and saw a ring around the sun, we knew rain or snow was imminent. Needless to say, such predictions, although grounded in scientific fact, are not sufficiently accurate or reliable for those whose livelihoods depend on predictable weather patterns.

The quest for accurate weather prediction is an endless one, a quest that has been frustrating at best for scientists around the world. With the help of computer technology, meteorologists have made giant strides in forecasting, but even the best forecasts are still wrong about 35 percent of the time. And it's not just tomorrow's—or even next weeks'—weather that's important to know. Nearly all of the world's great industrial nations are engaged in a competition to create the most accurate medium- and long-term forecasts possible. The United States, long the leader in meteorology, has watched its European and Japanese counterparts pass it by. Part of the problem is technological: the European Center for Medium Range Weather Forecasts, a 17-nation cooperative project based in Reading, England, currently uses a state-of-the-art computer three times more powerful than that used by the U.S. National Meteorological Center outside Washington, D.C., although the agency has plans to upgrade the computer.

Still, there's plenty of weather information available to just about anyone who cares to ask. Each day's newspaper brings a wealth of basic but vital information: temperature, precipitation, air pressure, humidity, and wind speed and direction. Dozens of weather organizations and commercial weather services can provide more in-depth information. And thousands of amateur weather watchers—not to mention campers, boaters, pilots, sports enthusiasts and a host of other interested individuals—have learned to make reasonably accurate estimates of what's to come weatherwise, using everything from mythology to microcomputers.

In the pages that follow are a wealth of other resources on the weather: the federal government's organization of weather information collection and prediction, as well as that of private meteorologists and amateurs; professional organizations; weather products; weather lore, and more. Just about everything under the sun.

UNCLE SAM THE WEATHERMAN

Tomorrow's weather forecast—the one you hear on radio, see on TV, read in the papers, or obtain by "calling the phone company"—almost always originates with the federal government, one of the world's biggest weather watchers. There are tens of thousands of individuals at a variety of government agencies involved in collecting, analyzing, interpreting, and disseminating weather information.

Somewhere out there, as you are reading this, the government is gathering weather information. It is collected around the clock, every day of the year, at airports, military bases, and other strategic points around the country. Additional information comes from instruments carried by weather balloons, ships, airplanes, ocean buoys, and weather satellites. Some of the information—like that from airports and some ground stations—is updated every hour. Other ground stations and oceangoing ships usually update their information four times a day.

The Weather Bureau forecast office in Washington, D.C. in 1926. Courtesy National Oceanic and Atmospheric Administration.

An automated forecaster's console at National Weather Service headquarters in Maryland. Courtesy National Oceanic and Atmospheric Administration.

Weather balloons are sent aloft from selected stations—70 locations in the United States, more than 700 worldwide—twice daily. All told, there are more than 200 fully staffed weather stations in the United States and 12,000 additional substations that gather information.

All this information is fed to the National Weather Service's central weather computer, located in Suitland, Maryland. There it is combined with still more information sent from international weather sources. International reports are coordinated by the World Meteorological Organization, in Geneva, Switzerland. This organization acts as a clearinghouse for weather data coming more than 10,000 land stations, some 7,000 ships, and 850 stations designed to monitor upper-air observations. Global observations from space are made by about five geostationary and five polar-orbiting satellites.

All of these numbers are "crunched" in the computers of the National Weather Service, which then analyzes the data and selects detailed weather information for distribution through its various communication networks—over telephone lines,

via computers, and in print. This is the most current weather information available.

Although a number of government and private agencies have a hand in collecting weather data, processing it all for civilian use is the task of the National Oceanic and Atmospheric Administration (NOAA). The National Weather Service is part of NOAA, and NOAA, in turn, is one of the largest divisions in the U.S. Department of Commerce. The central office of the National Weather Service is located in Washington, D.C. and it has regional offices in several cities.

With all these different organizations and facilities, the government's weather-collecting business is extremely complex. To try to make sense of it all, here's a breakdown of how these various agencies work:

U.S. DEPARTMENT OF COMMERCE
The U.S. Department of Commerce is a vast government agency whose head, the Secretary of Commerce, reports directly to the president. The National Oceanic and Atmospheric Administration is one of several subagencies in the Commerce

Department. Others include the Bureau of the Census, the Travel and Tourism Administration, the International Trade Administration, and the Patent and Trademark Office.

The **National Oceanic and Atmospheric Administration** (NOAA) has several main departments:

❑ **National Ocean Service** (NOS, *Atlantic Marine Center*: 439 W. York St., Norfolk, VA 23510; 804-441-6616. *Pacific Marine Center*: 1801 Fairview Ave. E, Seattle, WA 98102; 206-442-7657) distributes U.S. nautical and aeronautical charts created by NOAA. These materials are crucial for sailors and pilots, who must navigate under all kinds of weather conditions. Four catalogs of nautical charts are available free: *Atlantic and Gulf Coasts, Alaska, Great Lakes and Adjacent Waterways,* and *Bathymetric Maps and Special Purpose Charts.* A *Catalog of Aeronautical Charts and Related Publications* also is free. These publications can also be purchased at authorized dealers around the country and direct from NOS.

❑ **National Weather Service** (NWS, 8060 13th St., Gramax Bldg., Silver Spring, MD 20910; 301-427-7622), the backbone of the weather-forecasting system, is the place to go when you want to know what to expect from the weather. Here's how they forecast the weather: information garnered from NOAA's hundreds of weather stations, radar sites, ocean data buoys, cooperative weather-reporting ships, environmental satellites, volunteer observers, and international forecasts all goes to the National Meteorological Center (NMC, 5200 Auth Rd., Camp Springs, MD 20233; 301-763-8016), where these more than 10,000 weather observations are incorporated into atmospheric models to produce forecasts from 48 hours to ten days in advance. This process happens every day. All the data are put on comprehensive weather maps, which are then sent to meteorologists all over the country. The NMC also produces monthly and seasonal temperature and precipitation predictions. Because weather forecasting is still such an inexact science, NWS is constantly working to upgrade its systems and to replace old weather satellites and computer systems with state-of-the-art systems. By improving technology the Weather Service hopes to improve its predictions of serious storms and of our daily weather.

As a public service NWS offers a number of free brochures about different kinds of storms: thunderstorms, hurricanes, and tornadoes. These brochures provide safety tips on what to do if you are caught in the "eye" of the storm. The NWS also makes vast quantities of observational data available to the public through various data lines, all of which have annual fees and connection charges in the thousands of dollars.

❑ **National Climatic Data Center** (NCDC, Federal Building., Asheville, NC 28801; 704-259-0682) offers much information to researchers, private institutions, and industry. The center is the custodian of all U.S. weather records as well as foreign records. It also has a stockpile of cloud photos and environmental satellite data. Summaries of these data are provided by state, region, and nation. Climatic information available includes hourly surface observations from land stations, pinpointing such phenomena as sky cover, visibility, and precipitation; daily climatological observations from cooperative observing stations; upper-air observations from radiosondes, and pilot balloon winds and aircraft reports; and hourly and daily solar radiation data. Data bases available include surface-land summary of the month; extreme wind speeds; and temperature and precipitation charts. Statistical and special studies include *Daily Means and Extremes of Temperature, Summary of Winds Aloft*, and *Summary of Meteorological Observations*. Other publications also are available. NCDC puts out a comprehensive manual, *Selective Guide to Climatic Data Sources*, that lists all its many products. Call NCDC for prices.

❑ **National Severe Storms Laboratory** (1313 Halley Cir., Norman, OK 73069; 405-360-3620), located in the heart of tornado country, is a research facility that has become a leader in severe thunderstorm research. It boasts the world's highest meteorologically instrumented tower, which stands at 4,725 feet tall, and the world's only 10-centimeter-wavelength Doppler radar system, which can be used to detect strong winds and tornadoes, allowing for more timely and accurate warnings. The facility studies thunderstorm life cycles, tornado formation, storm electricity, aircraft safety, and techniques to improve early storm-warning systems.

❑ **National Marine Fisheries Service** (*Northeast region*: 14 Elm St., Gloucester, MA 01930; *Southeast region*: 9450 Koger Blvd., St. Petersburg, FL 33702; *Northwest region*: 7600 Sand Point Way, Seattle, WA 98115; *Southwest region*: 300 S. Ferry St., Terminal Island, CA 90731; *Alaska region*: P.O. Box 1668, Juneau, AK 99802) is responsible for fisheries resource management, fishing industry regulation, international fisheries monitoring, protected species and habitat conservation, enforcement, resource investigations, data and information management, and maintaining four fisheries.

❑ **National Environmental Satellite, Data, and Information Service** (National Climatic Data Center, Satellite Data Services Division (SDSD), Washington, DC 20233; 301-763-8111) is responsible

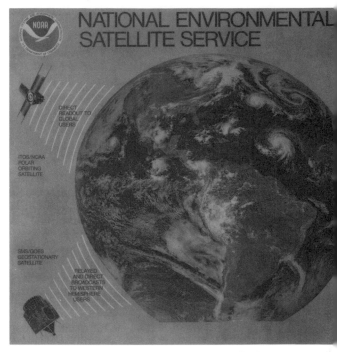

Courtesy National Oceanic and Atmospheric Administration.

for satellite operations, satellite data processing and distribution, research and applications, systems development, operation of the National Climatic Data Center, the National Oceanographic Data Center, and the National Geophysical Data Center. The information managed by this division begins with what was collected in 1960 by TIROS, the first series of earth-watching spacecraft. Since then hundreds of images of our earth have been taken every day and are now available as negatives, film loops, or digital data on magnetic tape. Today there are more than 8 million separate images, 25,000 computer-compatible tapes, and 400 mass-storage tapes from 30 satellites. These images are of special interest to people studying climatology, coastal zone management, oceanography, and agriculture; lawyers involved in weather-related litigation; and editors interested in illustrating publications and advertising materials. There is a publication, *Catalog*

WEATHER FORECASTS FOR U.S. CITIES

Albany, NY	518-476-1122	New York, NY	212-315-2705
Albuquerque, NM	505-243-1371	Oklahoma City, OK	405-360-8106
Atlanta, GA	404-936-1111	Omaha, NE	402-571-8111
Birmingham, AL	205-942-8430	Philadelphia, PA	215-627-5578
Bismarck, ND	701-223-3700	Phoenix, AZ	602-957-8700
Boise, ID	208-342-8303	Pittsburgh, PA	412-644-2881
Boston, MA	617-567-4670	Portland, ME	207-775-7781
Buffalo, NY	716-634-1615	Portland, OR	503-236-7575
Caribou, ME	207-496-8931	Raleigh, NC	919-860-1234
Charleston, WV	304-344-9811	Redding, CA	916-221-5613
Cheyenne, WY	307-635-9901	Reno, NV	702-793-1300
Chicago, IL	312-298-1413	St. Louis, MO	314-928-1198
Cincinnati, OH	513-241-1010	Salt Lake City, UT	801-575-7669
Cleveland, OH	216-931-1212	San Antonio, TX	512-828-3384
Columbia, SC	803-976-8710	San Francisco, CA	415-936-1212
Denver, CO	303-639-1212	Savannah, GA	912-964-1700
Des Moines, IA	515-288-1047	Seattle, WA	206-526-6087
Detroit, MI	313-941-7192	Sheridan, WY	307-672-2345
Elko, NV	702-738-3018	Shreveport, LA	318-635-7575
El Paso, TX	915-778-9343	Sioux Falls, SD	605-336-2837
Eugene, OR	503-484-1200	Topeka, KS	913-234-2692
Ft. Worth, TX	817-336-4416	Washington, DC	202-936-1212
Great Falls, MT	406-453-5469	Wichita, KS	316-942-3102
Indianapolis, IN	317-222-2362		
International Falls, MN	218-283-4615	**RESORT FORECASTS**	
Jackson, MS	601-936-2121		
Jacksonville, FL	904-757-3311	Cape Cod, MA	617-771-0500
Little Rock, AR	501-834-0316	Key West, FL	305-296-2011
Los Angeles, CA	213-554-1212	Myrtle Beach, SC	803-744-3207
Louisville, KY	502-363-9655	Nags Head, NC	919-995-5610
Lubbock, TX	806-762-0141	Ocean City, MD	301-289-3223
Memphis, TN	901-757-6400	Orlando, FL	305-851-7510
Miami, FL	305-661-5065	Rehoboth, DE	302-856-7633
Milwaukee, WI	414-744-8000	St. Augustine, FL	904-252-5575
Minneapolis, MN	612-452-2323	St. Petersburg, FL	813-645-2506
New Orleans, LA	504-465-9212	Virginia Beach, VA	804-853-3013

of Operational Satellite Products (NESS 109), available for no charge from SDSD to inform the interested customer of what's out there. Generally, prices for data tapes showing a specific geographic area and taken by the TIROS series, polar-orbiting satellites, or geostationary satellites run from $55 for a 9-track 1600/6250 BPI computer-compatible tape to thousands of dollars for special orders. Still photographs showing hurricanes, airflow patterns, fog, air pollution, and severe

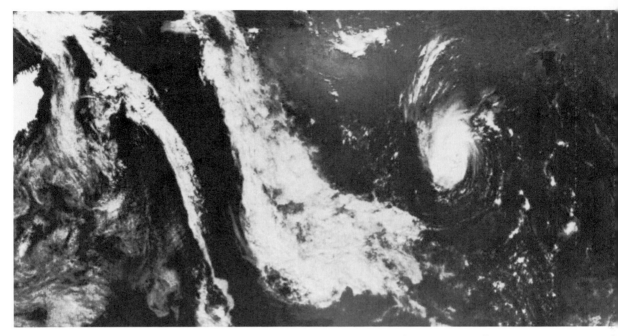

Information received from an orbiting weather satellite, NOAA-4, of Hurricane Belle, August 8, 1976, and received on an Automatic Picture Transmission system ground receiver. Courtesy National Oceanic and Atmospheric Administration.

storms range from $22 for a 10-inch-by-10-inch negative to $51 for a 16-millimeter movie loop. You can order through the National Climatic Data Center.

SDSD also publishes a variety of charts about sea and land weather conditions. You can order these annually, semiannually, or quarterly. Highlights from the list include *Multi-Channel Sea Surface Temperature Charts* (annual $25; semiannual $15; quarterly $10); *Northern Hemisphere Snow & Ice Charts* (annual $25; semiannual $15; quarterly $10); *Great Lakes Weather & Ice Charts* (annual $25; semiannual $15; quarterly $10); and *Polar Regional Ice Charts* (annual $25; semiannual $15; quarterly $10).

For those interested in learning more about the weather, SDSD offers rentals of 16-millimeter films for $35. Examples include *Advances in the Understanding of Weather Systems, The Global Weather Experiment—North Atlantic Hurricanes*, and *Fog Identification and Interpretation.*

Visitors are welcome at SDSD to look for a particular satellite image. You should call in advance, though, especially if you will need help.

❏ **Office of Oceanic and Atmospheric Research** is responsible for climatic and atmospheric research, sea grant and extramural programs, and environmental research labs. This branch of NOAA is particularly interested in developing new techniques to forecast tornadoes, flash floods, winter storms, and hurricanes. It operates the following facilities:

• **Atlantic Oceanographic and Meteorological Laboratories** (4301 Rickenbacker Cswy., Virginia Key, Miami, FL 33149; 305-361-4400) focuses on the study of hurricanes.
• **Environmental Research Laboratories** (3100 Marine St., Boulder, CO 80302; 303-497-6286) works to determine the sources and movement of

HURRICANE WARNINGS

Here is some sound advice if you are at risk of running into a hurricane. These guidelines were developed by the American Red Cross:

• Find out if your area is at risk of flooding from a hurricane. Remember that hurricane season lasts from June through November. August and September are peak hurricane months.
• Keep a portable radio, flashlight, extra batteries, emergency supplies, first aid, kit, canned food, and bottled water on hand.
• Prepare a family evacuation plan.
• Prepare instructions on how to turn off your utilities.
• Keep insurance policies and important documents in a secure place.

If a hurricane *watch* is issued:

• Board or tape up your windows.
• Bring inside objects that could fly away, such as garbage cans, bicycles, toys, and lawn furniture.

• Purchase a supply of fresh water and batteries.
• Fill your car with gasoline.
• Evacuate immediately if told to do so.

If a hurricane *warning* is issued:

• Evacuate immediately if told to do so.
• Stay away from windows, and stay inside if told not to evacuate.
• Beware of the calm eye of the hurricane. Stay inside. The calm lasts for only a short time. The most severe part of the hurricane comes immediately before and after the eye passes.

When the hurricane is over:

• Watch for downed power lines.
• Wear sturdy shoes and protective clothing.
• Use your flashlight to spot damage.
• Ask a professional to check your water, gas, electric, and sewage lines.

pollutants in the atmosphere, with special emphasis on acid rain, urban smog, and the greenhouse effect.
• **Geophysical Fluid Dynamics Laboratory** (P.O. Box 308, Princeton, NJ 08542; 609-452-6500) studies the general circulation of the ocean and atmosphere, thermal convection, and numerical weather prediction.
• **Great Lakes Environment Research Laboratory** (2300 Washlenaw Ave., Ann Arbor, MI 48104; 313-668-2235) is concerned with ecology modeling and climatology.
• **Pacific Marine Environmental Research Laboratory** (Bin C 15700, 7600 Sand Pt. NE, Seattle, WA 98115; 206-526-6239) studies the conditions of our oceans.
• **Space Environment Lab** (Radio Bldg., Boulder, CO 80302; 303-497-3311) is interested in forecasting the space environment and polar-cap events. The lab also maintains a data base of recent solar-geophysical data.

❏ **National Hurricane Center** (NHC, 1320 S. Dixie Hwy., Rm. 631, Coral Gables, FL 33146; 305-666-0413) is responsible for providing hurricane forecast and warning services. Researchers at the center collect meteorological and oceanographic analyses and satellite data of tropical storms and hurricanes. The NHC's forecaster's unit provides a 24-hour hurricane watch, predicts development and movement of storms, issues aviation, military, and marine advisories, plans daily aircraft reconnaissance into hurricanes, provides courses in tropical cyclone forecasting and storm surges, and carries out dozens of other hurricane-related duties, including satellite data analysis of the storms. The center holds computerized data tracking cyclones from 1886, which are available for public use at no charge.

OTHER GOVERNMENT AGENCIES

National Center for Atmospheric Research (NCAR, P.O. Box 3000, Boulder, CO 80307; 303-497-1000), operated by the University Corporation for Atmospheric Research under sponsorship by the National Science Foundation, aims to enhance research in the atmospheric sciences by identifying, developing, and providing to the scientific community advanced facilities and services. The center also does research to find solutions to environmental problems. Among other things, the center is conducting research into the deteriorating ozone layer and is working to develop new weather instruments.

NCAR runs two additional facilities: the **High Altitude Observatory** (HAO) and the **National Scientific Balloon Facility** (NSBF). HAO mostly measures solar activity, such as the 11-year cycle of sunspots and solar prominences. NSBF, whose launch facility is in Palestine, Texas, sends more than 80 scientific balloons aloft each year. Large enough to engulf a football field, scientific balloons carry sophisticated instruments that measure activity in different of the spectrum high above our atmosphere.

NCAR offers hour-long tours at noon from June 6 through October 1, Monday

Launching a balloon containing a radiosonde. Courtesy National Oceanic and Atmospheric Administration.

through Saturday. Visitors can see examples of weather and solar instruments, NCAR's computing facilities, displays on severe storms, and exhibits about the warming of the earth. Guided tours for groups are available by reservation only. For those who like to explore alone, the facility is open from 8 a.m. to 5 p.m. on weekdays and 9 a.m. to 3 p.m. on weekends and holidays. The library is open to the public during those hours as well. There is no admission fee.

Air Force Geophysics Laboratory (Hanscom AFB, Bedford, MA 01731; 617-377-3606) is an extensive complex that explores "the science of the earth in its solar-terrestrial environment." In simpler terms, this is where the air force takes a long, hard look at any form of weather or other natural phenomenon that could affect its mission. It looks at variations in the rotation of the earth, gravity, iono-spheric physics, solar flares, earthquakes, severe storms, and more. The lab maintains an extensive library of research material and books. It also has a vast supply of weather data in storage.

People who have an interest in weather may not know about the **National Technical Information Service** (NTIS, 5285 Port Royal Rd., Springfield, VA 22161; 703-487-4600), another branch of the Department of Commerce. NTIS has a huge stockpile of information that is available to anyone who asks for it, usually for a fee. Among other things, the service is the federal government's central source for machine-readable data files and government software, with more than 1.5 million available files. In addition, NTIS stockpiles U.S. and foreign reports on research, development, and engineering.

To wend your way through NTIS's vast holdings, it is best to know exactly what you want. If you call the main phone number, a helpful and informative person will answer your questions and take your order. Prices vary from a few dollars for a brief report to several thousand for a magnetic tape full of data. It usually takes about two weeks to receive an item. For a general overview of what NTIS has, the best place to start is the publication *NTIS Products and Services* (NTIS PR-827). It is free and lists many other free publications available through the service. There is also an NTIS bookstore in Springfield, Virginia.

If you are looking for government reports on weather, turn to *Government Reports Announcements and Index* (PR-195). This comprehensive compendium is updated annually and is available at most federal depositories. You can also buy it for a mere $600.

PUBLICATIONS, FILMS, AND VIDEOS
The **Government Printing Office** sells a

WHEN LIGHTNING STRIKES

The crash of thunder and the flash of lightning usually are ominous enough to concern even the most adventuresome. And that is just as well: lightning is among weather's worst killers. But a few simple precautions can help keep trouble away until it all blows over. Here are some handy tips from the experts:

• Stay inside. Go outside only if it is absolutely necessary.
• Keep away from open doors and windows, radiators, fireplaces, stoves, metal pipes, sinks, and electric appliances.
• Keep away from metal objects such as golf clubs and fishing rods. Golfers, pay close attention: Your cleated shoes are effective lightning rods.
• If you are riding a tractor, dismount immediately. Don't try to pull metal equipment during a thunderstorm.
• Don't work on fences, telephone or power lines, pipelines, or structural steel fabrication.
• Stay away from water. If you are in a boat, find your way to shore immediately.
• If you are traveling, stay in your automobile. Automobiles are good protection against lightning.
• Stay away from hilltops, open spaces, wire fences, metal clotheslines, and exposed sheds.
• If you are stranded outside, avoid the highest object around you. Stay away from trees; it is safer to stay in the open than to seek protection under trees.

variety of weather-related publications. To order any of these, write to Superintendent of Documents, U.S. Government Printing Office, Washington, DC 20402, or call 202-783-3238. Here is a sampling from the list:

❏ *Aviation Weather for Pilots and Flight Operations Personnel* (S/N 050 007-00283-1; $8.50), created in 1975, explains basic weather facts for pilots. A supplement, *Aviation Weather Services* (S/N 050-007-00705-1; $6), created in 1985, includes more recent information.

❏ *Cloud Code Chart* (S/N 003-018-00050-4; $2.25), created in 1972 and reprinted in 1980, includes a picture of each cloud type, the name, a brief description, and the cloud code figure according to the International System of Cloud Classification.

❏ *Daily Weather Maps Weekly Series* (S/N 703-021-00000-0; subscription prices: $60 per year in the United States, $75 per year elsewhere; single-copy prices; $1.50 in the United States, $1.88 elsewhere) offers daily weather maps created by the National Weather Service. Explanations of the maps and symbols are included .

❏ *Explanation of the Daily Weather Map* (S/N 003-017-00505-4; $2), created in 1982, explains symbols and other details of daily weather maps.

❏ *Operations of the National Weather Service* (S/N 003-018-0011-0, $7.50), created in 1985, describes the meteorological and hydrological programs of the National Weather Service.

❏ *World Weather Extremes* (S/N 008-022-00230-8; $4.50), created in 1985, provides maps of weather extremes on a worldwide basis and for the United States and Canada.

How Close Is It?

You can figure out how many miles away a flash of lightning occurred by counting the numbers of seconds between the flash and the following thunder and then dividing by 5. For example, if the time between the lightning and the thunder is 15 seconds, the lightning is about 3 miles away. When you see lightning and don't hear any thunder, the thunderstorm is more than 15 miles away.

NASA Teacher Resource Centers have 16-millimeter films for free loan on subjects such as hurricanes, tornadoes, floods, and meteorology from space; filmstrips are available for sale. Below are addresses for each of the regional centers:

Alabama, Arkansas, Iowa, Louisiana, Missouri, Tennessee
Alabama Space and Rocket Center, Attn.: NASA Teacher Resource Room, Huntsville, AL 35807; 205-837-3400. Bossier Parish Community College, Attn.: NASA Teacher Resource Center, 2719 Airline Dr., Bossier City, LA 71111.

Alaska, Arizona, California, Hawaii, Idaho, Montana, Nevada, Oregon, Utah, Washington, Wyoming
NASA Ames Research Center, Attn.: Teacher Resource Center, Mail Stop 204-7, Moffett Field, CA 94035, 415-694-6077. NASA Jet Propulsion Laboratory, Attn.: Teacher Resource Center, JPL Educational Outreach, Mail Stop CS-530, Pasadena, CA 91109; 818-354-6916.

Colorado, Kansas, Nebraska, New Mexico, North Dakota, Oklahoma,

Hail storm over Colorado. Courtesy National Oceanic and Atmospheric Administration.

South Dakota, Texas
NASA Lyndon B. Johnson Space Center, Attn.: Teacher Resource Center, Mail Stop AP-4, Houston, TX 77058; 713-483-3455 or 483-4433. U.S. Space Foundation, Attn.: NASA Teacher Resource Center, P.O. Box 1838, Colorado Springs, CO 80901.

Connecticut, Delaware, District of Columbia, Maine, Maryland, Massachusetts, New Hampshire, New Jersey, New York, Pennsylvania, Rhode Island, Vermont
Champlain College, Attn.: NASA Teacher Technology Resource Center, 174 S. Willard Street, Burlington, VT 05402. City College, Attn.: NASA Teacher Resource Room, NAC 5/208, New York, NY 10031. NASA Goddard Space Flight Center, Attn.: Teacher Resource Laboratory, Mail Stop 130-3, Greenbelt, MD 20771, 301-344-8981. NASA Industrial Applications Center, Attn.: Christa McAuliffe Teacher Resource Institute, 823 William Pitt

Union, University of Pittsburgh, Pittsburgh, PA 15260. National Air and Space Museum, Attn.: Education Resource Center, P-700, Office of Education, Washington, DC 20560.

Florida, Georgia, Puerto Rico, Virgin Islands
NASA John F. Kennedy Space Center, Attn.: Educator Resource Library, Mail Stop ERL, Cape Canaveral, FL 32899, 305-867-4090 or 9383.

Illinois, Indiana, Michigan, Minnesota, Ohio, Wisconsin
Center for Information Media, Attn.: NASA Teacher Resource Center, St. Cloud State University, St. Cloud, MN 56301. Central Michigan University, Attn.: NASA Teacher Resource Center, Mt. Pleasant, MI 48859. Children's Museum, Attn.: NASA Teacher Resource Center, P.O. Box 3000, Indianapolis, IN 46206. Mankato State University, Attn.: NASA Teacher Resource Center, Curriculum and Instruction, Box

52, Mankato, MN 56001. Museum of Science and Industry, Attn.: NASA Teacher Resource Center, 57th St. & Lakeshore Dr., Chicago, IL 60637. NASA Lewis Research Center, Attn.: Teacher Resource Center, Mail Stop 8-1, Cleveland, OH 44135; 216-267-1187. Northern Michigan University, Attn.: NASA Teacher Resource Center, Olson Library Media Center, Marquette, MI 49855. Oakland University, Attn.: NASA Teacher Resource Center, 115 O'Dowd Hall, Rochester, MI 48063. Parks College of Aeronautical Technology, Attn.: NASA Teacher Resource Center, Rte. 157 at Falling Springs Rd., East St. Louis, IL 62201. Science, Economics and Technology Center, Attn.: NASA Teacher Resource Center, 818 W. Wisconsin Ctr., Milwaukee, WI 53233. University of Evansville, Attn.: NASA Teacher Resource Center, School of Education, 1800 Lincoln Ave., Evansville, IL 47714. University of Wisconsin at La Crosse, Attn.: NASA Teacher Resource Center, College of Education, La Crosse, WI 54601.

Kentucky, North Carolina, South Carolina, Virginia, West Virginia
NASA Langley Research Center, Attn.: Langley Teacher Resource Center, Mail Stop 146, Hampton, VA 23665; 804-865-4468. University of North Carolina at Charlotte, Attn.: Lorraine Penninger, NASA Teacher Resource Center, J. Murrey Atkins Library, Charlotte, NC 28223.

Mississippi
NASA National Space Technology Laboratories, Attn.: Teacher Resource Center, Building. 1200, NSTL, MS 39529; 601-688-3338.

United States Army Audio-visual Centers (Ft. George G. Mead, MD 20755; Ft. Gordon, GA 30905; Ft. Sam Houston, TX 78324; Presido of San Francisco, CA 94129; Ft. Richardson, AK 98749; Schoefield Barracks, HI 96557) all have 16-millimeter films for free loan on subjects such as clouds, weather disasters, and storm survival.

NOAA ship Oceanographer. *Courtesy National Oceanic and Atmospheric Administration.*

STATE WEATHER OFFICES

The National Climate Program Act, passed by Congress in 1978, authorized the 50 states to get involved in the business of climate analysis. The act was based on the realization that the federal National Climatic Data Center could not supply each state with all the information it might need. Both state and local governments needed a closer connection to the vagaries of daily weather.

Today all states but Pennsylvania have state climatic offices. These offices are charged with providing pertinent information to such "clients" as local governments, construction companies, airports, and public utilities. Their principal fields of interest include improving flood management, increasing pilot information, and determining the best time to transport gas or oil. Sometimes state offices perform these services directly. Other times, they utilize the services of private meteorology consulting firms. When the work has been done and the necessary weather data has been collected, the state offices send their findings to one of the regional offices throughout the country. From there they go to the National Climatic Data Center, where the information is kept on file for use by other states.

The state program is managed by the National Climate Program Office, part of the National Oceanic and Atmospheric Administration, based in Rockville, Maryland. This office is in direct contact with the five regional centers, located at the following research facilities:

❏ **High Plains Regional Climate Center,** CAMAC, 237 Chase Hall (0728), University of Nebraska, Lincoln, NE 68583.

❏ **Midwestern Regional Climate Center,** 2204 Griffith Dr., Champaign, IL 61820.

❏ **Western Regional Climate Center,** Desert Research Institute, P.O. Box 60220, Reno, NV 89506.

❏ **Northeast Regional Climate Center,** Atmospheric Science Unit, Box 21, Bradfield Hall, Cornell University, Ithaca, NY 14853.

❏ **Southeastern Regional Climate Center,** South Carolina State Climatology Office, 1201 Main St., Ste. 1100, Capital Ctr., Columbia, SC 29201.

An additional center, to serve the south-central part of the country, is being planned and will be located in New Orleans, Louisiana.

State climatologists have their own professional society, the American Association of State Climatologists. The "headquarters" of this organization rotates from year to year, depending on where its president resides. The association gives state climatologists a chance to compare notes about issues facing the state system, as well as issues confronting their individual states. The organization has about 200 members. Membership ($25) includes a newsletter, published twice a year.

PRIVATE METEOROLOGY COMPANIES

Before World War II meteorology was the sole province of Uncle Sam, spurred by the air force, navy, and other military branches, which each trained its own cadre of meteorologists to assist in the war effort. Weather, after all, is a key factor in a war, whether it is being fought on air, land, or sea. After the war many of these meteorologists left government service and set up shop in the private sector. Thus began the commercial weather-forecasting industry.

Among the first two firms to open their doors in the late 1940s were Weather Services Inc. and Weather Corporation of America. As Peter Leavitt, a senior meteorologist with Weather Services Inc., puts it, "We started out in the snow and ice business." Their early clients were state and local governments, which needed to know when to alert their snow-removal teams. Gas and electric utilities followed, relying on private weather companies to tell them about sudden dips in the temperature, which might lead their customers to use more fuel, or about violent thunderstorms, which could disrupt power lines. Weather Corporation of America was the pioneer in this effort.

Over the years weather-forecasting companies have come and gone, some being swallowed up by bigger firms. In 1962 the older, more established companies met a formidable competitor in Joel Myers, who founded Accu-Weather while still a graduate student at Pennsylvania State University. Starting as a small operation, with Myers making his first forecast from a telephone booth, Accu-Weather has expanded to become one of the largest private forecasting companies in the world.

These days, there are many other firms in the weather business, some filling a special niche. OceanRoutes, for example, specializes in plotting routes for ocean liners, taking into account such variables as tides and wind currents. Freese-Notis Weather, Inc., has developed a specialty in agricultural commodities, supplying farmers with information that can help them plan their growing seasons and shipping schedules. A few companies have found their way into the courtroom, where they practice forensic meteorology, a relatively new specialty, providing expert testimony in matters in which weather may have played a role—a plane crash thought to have been caused by wind shear, for example, or a car accident during a snowstorm.

Most weather firms also serve newspapers and radio and television stations, construction companies, environment-related companies, and the nuclear power industry. A growing number of companies, including Weather Services Inc., offer on-line services to such clients and to the aviation industry. And most companies boast their fair share of fun clients—sports teams, sponsors of key athletic events, and movie studios.

Many weather forecasters belong to the **American Meteorological Society** (AMS, 45 Beacon St., Boston, MA 02108; 617-227-2425), a professional organization that certifies meteorologists. (Your local TV weatherperson may use the organization's initials after his or her name when it is flashed on the screen.)

Here are the main offices of AMS's certified meteorology companies. Each offers a variety of products and services. You should contact individual companies to obtain relevant sales information.

Accu-Weather, Inc.
619 W. College Ave.
State College, PA 16801
814-237-0309

Aerocomp, Inc.
3303 Harbor Blvd.
Costa Mesa, CA 92626
714-957-6596

Aeromatrix Inc.
3640 E. Huron River Dr.
Ann Arbor, MI 48104
313-971-2244

Aeromet, Inc.
P.O. Box 701767
Tulsa, OK 74170
918-299-2621

Aerovironment Inc.
825 Myrtle Ave.
Monrovia, CA 91016
818-357-9983

Air Science Consultants, Inc.
347 Prestley Rd.
Bridgeville, PA 15017
412-221-6002

Applied Meteorology, Inc.
9000 Southwest Fwy., Ste. 326
Houston, TX 77074
713-777-0106

Atek Corporation
900 28th St., Ste. 202
Boulder, CO 80303
303-449-5588

Atmospheric Research & Technology
6040 Verner Ave.
Sacramento, CA 95841
916-338-0550

Atmospherics Inc.
5652 E. Dayton Ave.
Fresno, CA 93727
209-291-5575

W. Boynton Beckwith
14728 Caminito Orense Oeste
San Diego, CA 92129
619-672-1565

Lyle E. Brosche
1347 Silver Lake Dr.
Melbourne, FL 32940
305-259-1615

Richard E. Cale
P.O. Box 3070
Cerritos, CA 90703
213-926-6149

Climatological Consulting Corporation
9900 Mosby Rd.
Fairfax, VA 22032
703-273-1977

Colorado International Corp.
P.O. Box 3007
Boulder, CO 80307
303-443-0384

Courtney Consultants, Inc.
520 Carriage Dr.
Atlanta, GA 30328
404-256-2487

Loren W. Crow Consultants, Inc.
3064 S. Monroe St.
Denver, CO 80210
303-753-6500

Spencer Duckworth
2506 Seville Ct.
Davis, CA 95616
916-756-9558

Environmental Research & Technology, Inc.
696 Virginia Rd.
Concord, MA 01742
800-722-2440, 617-489-3750

Sidney R. Frank Group
444 David Love Pl.
Santa Barbara Municipal Airport
Goleta, CA 93117
805-964-4477

Freese-Notis Weather, Inc.
1453 NE 66th Ave.
Des Moines, IA 50313

Galson Technical Services, Inc.
6601 Kirkville Rd.
East Syracuse, NY 13057
315-432-0506

THE OLD FARMER'S ALMANAC

Who hasn't heard of the *The Old Farmer's Almanac,* that American institution now 197 years old that attempts to do what no decent meteorologist would ever dare try: forecast the weather for an entire year. Dividing the country into regions, the almanac gives a complete summary of what each season will be like and also includes predictions for each month. Most of the time, these predictions are the butt of jokes by the professionals, but every so often the almanac hits it just right. After all these years the almanac does know something about the weather.

The Old Farmer's Almanac is a fount of information about more than just weather prognostications, as 9 million devoted readers will attest. It fulfills the same function as many astronomical calendars, with complete information about the positions of the planets, eclipses, bright stars, and principal meteor showers. For each month there are times for the setting sun and the waxing and waning of the moon, plus a list of holidays and essays offering helpful hints to farmers. Other fun facts: killing frosts and growing seasons, tide corrections, agricultural trends, and prize-winning recipes. *The Old Farmer's Almanac* has something for just about everyone.

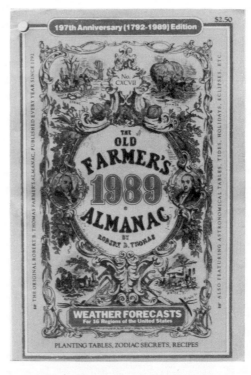

The almanac is written by Robert B. Thomas, who welcomes questions about the weather and other subjects all year long. Write The Old Farmer's Almanac, Dublin, NH 03444. What kinds of letters does Thomas get? One faithful correspondent wrote in that our calendar is off by .03 of a day. The way to remedy this, the reader suggested, was to eliminate leap year every 80,000 years. Thomas is looking into it.

A. H. Glenn Associates
New Orleans Lakefront Airport
New Orleans, LA 70126
504-241-2222

Global Weather Dynamics, Inc.
2400 Garden Rd.
Monterey, CA 93940
408-649-4500

Gerald W. Grams, Ph.D.
2696 Cosmos Dr.
Atlanta, GA 30345
404-894-3897

Hales and Co.
609 Lorient Dr.
West Chester, PA 19382
215-696-4833

Einar L. Hovind
4152 Primavera Rd.
Santa Barbara, CA 93110
805-964-8218

L. Ray Hoxit, Ph.D.
P.O. Box 836
Arden, NC 28704

International Center for the Solutions of
  Environmental Problems
3818 Graustark
Houston, TX 77006
713-527-8711

The C. T. Main Corporation
Prudential Center
Boston, MA 02199
617-262-3200

McVehil-Monnett Associates, Inc.
5655 S. Yosemite St., Ste. 104
Englewood, CO 80111
303-220-7213

Meteorological Applications
12926 Allerton Ln.
Silver Spring, MD 20904
301-384-1875

Meteorological Evaluation Services, Co.
165 Broadway
Amityville, NY 11701
516-691-3395

Meteorological Standards Institute
841 Seventh Ln.
Fox Island, WA 98333
206-549-2179

Metro Monitoring Services
143 E. Rowland Ave., Ste. 6
Covina, CA 91723
818-332-8411

Murray and Trettel, Inc.
414 W. Frontage Rd.
Northfield, IL 60093
312-446-7800

North American Weather Consultants
3761 S. 700 East, Ste. B
Salt Lake City, UT 84106
801-263-3500

Nowcasting
3760 Morrow Ln., Ste. F
Chico, CA 95928
916-893-0308

NUS Corporation
Park West 2, Cliff Mine Rd.
Pittsburgh, PA 15275
412-788-1080

OceanRoutes, Inc.
680 W. Maude Ave.
Sunnyvale, CA 94086
408-245-3600

Jerry Pardue
4065 Gilman Ave.
Louisville, KY 40207
502-893-5551

Robert L. Peace, Jr.
2050 New York Dr.
Altadena, CA 91001
818-798-3435

R*Scan Corporation
1200 Washington Ave. S
Minneapolis, MN 55415
612-333-1424

Sigma Research Corporation
394 Lowell St., Ste. 12
Lexington, MA 02173
617-862-0920

Simpson Weather Associates, Inc.
809 E. Jefferson St.
Charlottesville, VA 22902
804-979-3571

J. M. Sorge, Inc.
3301 U.S. Hwy. 22
Somerville, NJ 08876
201-218-0066

Stone & Webster Engineering Corp.
P.O. Box 2325
Boston, MA 02107
617-589-2701

TRC Environmental Consultants, Inc.
800 Connecticut Blvd.
East Hartford, CT 06108
203-289-8631

WEATHERWISE

Everyone talks about the weather—but who actually would write a magazine about it?

David M. Ludlum would, and did. A lifelong weather buff, Ludlum in 1948 published the first issue of *Weatherwise*, the first and still the only weather magazine for general readers. (The title comes from Benjamin Franklin's remark in Poor Richard's Almanac: "Some are weather-wise, some are otherwise.") For more than 40 years, Ludlum and his successors have been helping people to better understand the world of meteorology.

Today's *Weatherwise,* published in association with the American Meteorological Association, is a far cry from its 20-page maiden issue. Now a full-fledged bimonthly, it continues to fulfill Ludlum's promise of bringing the weather down to earth, so to speak. Filled with weather maps, photographs, profiles, and articles aimed at those without technical backgrounds, it offers a side of the business of weather few people get to see.

In recent years, *Weatherwise* has focused on research applications and technological advances, from Doppler and nexrad radar to acid rain and El Nino. Historical pieces feature the Blizzard of 1888 and the Great Snow of 1717, among other infamous moments in weather history. But it's not just the articles for which one turns to the magazine. Its advertisements can be an equally enlightening experience, with offers of equipment, maps, and historical treatises, some produced and sold by amateur weather buffs.

All told, it's enough to make a rainy day more enjoyable—and more understandable.

A one-year subscription to *Weatherwise* (Heldref Publications, 4000 Albemarle St. NW, Washington, DC 20016; 202-362-6445) is $23 for individuals, $38 for institutions; add $7 outside the United States.

Weather Applications
8520 41st W
Tacoma, WA 98466
206-564-3724

Weather Consultants Incorporated
P.O. Box 3414
Santa Rosa, CA 95402
707-538-1080

Weather Corporation of America
5 American Industrial Dr.
St. Louis, MO 63043
314-878-5150

WeatherData, Inc.
833 North Main St.
Wichita, KS 67203
316-265-9127

Weather Research Center
3710 Mt. Vernon
Houston, TX 77006
713-529-3076

Weather Services Corporation
131A Great Rd.
Bedford, MA 01730

Roy F. Weston, Inc.
Weston Way
West Chester, PA 19380
215-692-3030

Wilkens Weather Technologies Div.
Air Routing International Corp.
2925 Briarpark
Ste. 610, Houston, TX 77042
800-231-5787, 713-977-0800

PROFESSIONAL WEATHER ORGANIZATIONS

The **American Meteorological Society** is the weather industry's major professional organization. Wearing a variety of hats, the AMS aims to provide information to professionals about the latest techniques and developments in the atmospheric sciences and related fields through professional journals; offer leadership for students, the scientific community, and the general public; and disseminate employment information. But perhaps the AMS's most significant contribution is serving as a network for the meteorological community.

Through its 75 local chapters the AMS coordinates national and international meetings, specialized conferences and workshops, and exhibit programs. The society also prepares vocational guidance material, film clips, and popular monographs. To promote professional excellence, the AMS provides for the certification of consulting meteorologists (see "Private Meteorology Companies") and grants its seal of approval in radio and television weathercasting. The organization also publishes professional employment listings.

AMS publications include the following: *AMS Newsletter, Bulletin of the American Meteorological Society, Employment Announcements, Historical Monographs, Journal of Atmospheric and Oceanic Technology, Journal of Climate and Applied Meteorology, Journal of Physical Oceanography, Journal of the Atmospheric Sciences, Meteorological & Geoastrophysical Abstracts, Meteorological Monographs, Monthly Weather Review,* and *Weather and Forecasting.*

Basic dues, which include the *AMS Bulletin,* are $30 for members or associate members and $15 for students. There are additional fees for publications. For more information, contact AMS, 45 Beacon St., Boston, MA 02108; 617-227-2425.

The **National Weather Association** (NWA) is open to anyone interested in the weather, although most members actually work in the weather business, usually in forecasting, research, or applied meteorology. Founded in 1975, the association represents the viewpoints and philosophy of operational weatherpeople and encourages the exchange of information and ideas among practical meteorologists.

NWA publishes four *National Weather Digest* magazines each year and eight newsletters. The magazine includes papers on technical issues, whereas the newsletter provides information about the organization's daily activities. Membership dues are $20 a year. For information, contact NWA, 4400 Stamp Rd., Rm. 404, Temple Hills, MD 20748; 301-899-3784.

The **National Council for Industrial Meteorologists** (NCIM), with its 45 members, represents the official voice of private meteorologists. The organization's mandates include protecting the interests of consulting and industrial meteorologists, investigating new legislation affecting the meteorology industry, and emphasizing professional standards. Membership is limited to private meteorologists. Applicants must either be certified consulting meteorologists or pass written tests and an oral examination. For further information, contact NCIM, 6000 E. Evans Ave., Bldg. 1, Ste. 261, Denver, CO 80222; there is no phone. Armand R. Iaccheo (Weather Corporation of America, 5 American Industrial Dr., St. Louis, MO 63043; 314-878-5150) also can provide information about NCIM.

THE HUMAN DIMENSION
IN HURRICANE FORECASTING

by Mike Clary

A joke going around the National Hurricane Center (NHC) predicts that the weather forecaster of the future will need a bachelor's degree in computer science, a two-year degree in electronics, and three credits in meteorology. "The meteorology," deadpans hurricane forecaster Bob Case, "is just in case the computer breaks down."

Indeed, as Case and his colleagues at the NHC in Coral Gables, Florida, brace for the heart of this year's tropical season, they command and unprecedented array of high-tech hardware. From a new $58 million weather satellite to a push-button telephone system that automatically dials 88 preprogrammed numbers, forecasters have never had so many silicon chips to play with.

But meteorologists are not fearful for their jobs. Not yet, anyway. For while a whirring Cyber 205 may be able to compute a killer storm's likely track, it is still a human being who has to make the life-or-death decisions.

"Let's say you've got a category 3 or 4 storm [winds 111 to 155 miles per hour and/or a storm surge of 9 to 18 feet] rapidly approaching the coast between North Carolina and New Jersey on Labor Day weekend," says veteran hurricane specialist Gilbert Clark. "You've got maybe a million people on the beaches, narrow roads and people unfamiliar with the area. Now the machine says the storm will probably recurve, and pass to the east. But there's no guarantee. "This situation has the potential to turn into the worst disaster I can think of. A decision to evacuate these people must be made, and made in time. And that's a decision we have to make ourselves."

According to Robert Sheets, acting director of the NHC, it is not enough that forecasters and analysts be able to use and understand computers; they must also know when the computers are likely to be wrong. "We have to keep the human dimension in there, and mix man's analytical ability with the physics of the atmosphere," says Sheets.

This emphasis on what Sheets terms "the interactive relationship between people and technology" comes from the top in the National Weather Service (NWS). Earlier this year, in a talk to the American Meteorological Society, NWS Director Richard E. Hallgreen said technology had helped bring weather forecasting "from what was essentially an art 40 years ago to what is clearly a science today."

The advancing science of meteorology has presented forecasters with some astonishing new capabilities. And it has handed them some sobering new responsibilities as well. Says Halgreen: "The complex problems that are being generated by humans on this planet require information from meteorologists that we are not yet able to provide. . . . [We] still have a long way to go."

More than 2,000 years ago Archimedes wrote, in reference to the lever: "Give me where to stand, and I will move the earth." In a modern-day echo of that dictum, today's forecaster says, Give me enough data, and I will perfectly forecast the weather. Therein lies the problem; over the tropical oceans there just isn't enough data.

Over the continental United States

Hurricane Katrina, photographed by NOAA satellite off the coast of Baja California, 1975. Courtesy National Oceanic and Atmospheric Administration.

enough detailed balloon soundings of upper-air conditions are made each day to sample every 40,000 square miles; the data are fresh and plentiful, and weather forecasts are largely reliable. But over the tropics detailed balloon soundings are available only for every 4 million square miles. That paucity of hard data from the turbulent waters of the Atlantic Ocean—where the most dangerous hurricanes are usually spawned—produces what tropical meteorologists routinely call "the forecast problem."

According to Bob Sheets, the volatility of the tropics results from unstable air produced by differences in air temperature. That instability, coupled with the ready supply of moisture, results in a restless mix. Add the heat of summer, and then take away the upper-level wind shear that in winter knocks the tops off thunderstorms, and conditions are explosive.

"In the tropics," says Sheets, "the difference between an ordinary day and one that will kick off a disturbance is very slight."

Predicting which disturbances will spawn a tropical storm, and then forecasting where that storm will go, is part of the hurricane specialists' mission. And that's the part, they say, that is done with less success than they or the public would like.

What hurricane forecasters do very well now is measure and monitor storms once they have formed. And thanks to technology, they expect increasingly to handle that part of the job better than ever. New tools in use include:

GOES-East weather satellite. Since 1984, when a small lamp burned out and disabled the previous GOES-East, forecasters have been working around a blind spot in watching the tropics. The new satellite, launched into geostationary orbit in February, provides continuous surveillance of the Atlantic while also sounding the atmosphere. This 1,100-pound, all-seeing satellite is the forecaster's most invaluable tool in spotting disturbances that produce storms.

McIDAS. This is a computerized system to combine data from the GOES-East satellite and other sources, allowing NHC forecasters to develop a cross-sectional picture of the atmosphere that gauges wind speed and direction and air temperature and pressure from 22,300 miles down to the surface. Moved this year from the University of Wisconsin to the National Meteorological Center in Washington, D.C., the system is now available around the clock for hurricane forecasting. McIDAS is an acronym for Man-Computer Interactive Data Acquisition System.

Satellite Weather Interactive System. Called SWIS, this system combines satellite imagery and graphics into high-speed film loops that show the development and motion of thunderstorms. By watching high-resolution color monitors, forecasters can "read" these images to determine the height of cloud tops and air temperature and judge the potential for storm development.

Improved aircraft reconnaissance. This season two U.S. Air Force C-130 turboprop planes based at Keesler Air Force Base in Biloxi, Mississippi, have been fitted with on-board computers and sensing equipment that provide one-minute observations for forecasters for instantaneous analysis of tropical storms. When these long-range aircraft are inside a storm, information gathered by computer is bounced off a satellite, fed into computers at the NHC, and plotted to provide information on air temperature, and wind speed and direction.

Future efforts to improve NHC forecasters' performance in predicting the path of dangerous storms center on a new in-house computer system with direct links to both the GOES-East and GOES-West satellites. That system will be in operation in two to five years, according to Sheets. To get ready for the new age, the NHC is filling staff positions with me-

---

How Windy Is It?

Meteorologists use the Beaufort Scale of Wind Force to describe windy conditions:

Category	Miles Per Hour	Result
Calm	under 1	Smoke rises vertically
Light breeze	4 to 7	Wind is felt on face; leaves rustle, vanes move
Gentle breeze	8 to 12	A light flag extended
Moderate breeze	13 to 18	A small branch moves
Fresh breeze	19 to 24	A small tree sways
Strong breeze	25 to 31	Large branches move; umbrellas out of control
Near gale	32 to 38	Whole trees move
Gale	39 to 46	Twigs break off trees
Strong gale	47 to 54	Slight structural damage occurs
Whole gale	55 to 63	Considerable structural damage occurs

The Tiron N weather satellite. Courtesy National Oceanic and Atmospheric Administration.

teorologists with computer-programming backgrounds.

"So much data [on atmosphere] comes in now that there's no way we can digest it all without computers," says Sheets. "But computers can't do everything. At some point a person has to step in and say, *The front is over here, not there,* and force the computer to recognize that. And then the computer adjusts."

The evolving partnership between humans and technology has moved meteorology a world apart from the days of the "single station forecaster," who took temperature, wind, and barometric pressure readings, then looked at the sky for signs of changing weather patterns.

For the modern weather forecaster—inundated with data in a computer-cooled workstation—forecasting everything from hurricanes to local showers involves a more sophisticated process, at least three parts technology to one part intuition. Still, cautions Sheets, forecasters cannot afford to forget the basics, or neglect the obvious. "We still have windows here in the office," he says, "because looking out the window is still the best way to see if it's raining."

From *Weatherwise* magazine, vol. 40, issue 4, August 1987, pp. 197-199. Reprinted with permission of the Helen Dwight Reid Educational Foundation. Published by Heldref Publications, 4000 Albemarle St. NW, Washington, DC 20016. Copyright 1987.

AMATEUR WEATHER CLUBS

For an ever-growing number of people, watching the weather is an avocation with deep, personal meaning.

Steven D. Steinke, one of the founders of the American Association of Weather Observers (AAWO), the largest amateur weather-watching organization in the country, understands this kind of people — he's one of them. "Weather watching is an introspective hobby," he says, "with people working alone, taking readings and keeping accurate records. What's been particularly nice about the organization is that these loner types have found kindred spirits with whom to share their feelings about the weather."

Like many weather watchers, Steinke became interested in the weather as a young boy. But his motivation was spurred on by a unique twist of fate. "My family was trapped in a tornado," says Steinke, "and I experienced firsthand the effect the weather can have. I've been hooked ever since."

Founded five years ago, the **American Association of Weather Observers** (401 Whitney Blvd., Belvidere, IL 61008; 815-544-9811) acts as a clearinghouse for people interested in pooling weather data. Information submitted by members is published monthly in the organization's newsletter, *American Weather Observer.* It also becomes part of the organization's permanent data base, available to members. The newsletter includes other information close to weather watchers' hearts: new tools of the trade, reports from other organizations, and a weather map based on members' data, among other things. The group has about 1,500 members, who pay $12 a year ($18 for those not members of AAWO-affiliated groups), which includes membership and a dozen issues of the *Observer.*

As the association grows it is serving as an umbrella organization for the small sky-watching clubs that exist around the country. Here is a list of AAWO-affiliated organizations:

American Meteorological Society
45 Beacon St.
Boston, MA 02108

Atlantic Coast Observer Network
92 Village Hill Dr.
Dix Hills, NY 11746

Blue Hill Observatory Weather Club
Box 101
East Milton, MA 02186

Chesterfield Co. Weather Network
P.O. Box 808
Chesterfield, SC 29709

Interior of Eastern NY AMS
SUNY at Albany
Dept. of Atmospheric Sciences
1400 Washington Ave.
Albany, NY 12222

KBIM Sun Country Weather Watchers
P.O. Box 910
Roswell, NM 88201

KCNC-TV Weatherwatchers
1044 Lincoln St.
Denver, CO 80203

KKTV-Weather Spotters
P.O. Box 2110
Colorado Springs, CO 80901

KTVI-Weather Network
5915 Berthold Ave.
St. Louis, MO 63110

KTVY Television Weather Watchers
500 E. Britton Rd.
Oklahoma City, OK 73113

Long Island Weather Observers
2 Stanley Ct.
Lake Ronkonkoma, NY 11779

THE WEATHER CHANNEL

For weather watchers who can't get enough about the ever-changing drama unfolding outside, now there's a way to obtain up-to-the-minute information on a 24-hour basis. The Weather Channel, offered by many cable television companies, provides detailed weather information all day and all night.

The format of the show is much like that of the eleven o'clock news, but it includes a great deal more information. You can hear the skiing forecasts, boating forecasts, tide levels, business and travel information for key cities, aviation weather, and much more. Since its inception in 1982, it has been picked up by 3,200 affiliates and reaches 36 million homes.

To learn more about the Weather Channel, write or call 2840 Mt. Wilkinson Pkwy., Atlanta, GA 30318; 404-434-6800. Or contact your local cable company.

Mt. Washington Observatory
1 Washington St.
Gorham, NH 03581

National Weather Association
440 Stamp Rd., Rm. 404
Temple Hills, MD 20748

North Jersey Weather Observers
P.O. Box 619
Westwood, NJ 07675

Northeast OH AMS Chapter
1667 Cedarwood Dr., Apt. 109
Westlake, OH 44145

Skywatchers Club of California
390 N. Second St., No. 201
San Jose, CA 95112

Virginia Weather Observation Network
Central Virginia AMS
University of Virginia
Charlottesville, VA 22903

WDIV-TV4 Weatherwatchers
622 Lafayette Blvd.
Detroit, MI 48231

WDBJ Weatherwatchers
2001 Colonial Ave.
Roanoke, VA 24105

Western Montana News Weather Watchers
KECI-TV
P.O. Box 5268
Missoula, MT 59806

WITI-TV6 Weatherwatchers
9001 Green Bay Rd.
P.O. Box 17600
Milwaukee, WI 53217

WTJM Weather Center Observers
P.O. Box 693
Milwaukee, WI 53210

Clubs usually meet once a month. The main activity at meetings is comparing notes about weather phenomena. Many clubs also supply local weather information to TV and radio stations. To find out more about clubs in your area, write to Steven D. Steinke, 401 Whitney Blvd., Belvedere, IL 61008.

BUILD YOUR OWN WEATHER STATION

by Louis D. Rubin, Sr., and Jim Duncan

Few hobbies are as interesting, educational, and consistently attractive as weatherwatching. Also, setting up a small weather station is inexpensive, and the upkeep is practically nothing.

Why not learn, firsthand, as much as possible about the weather—today, tomorrow, next year—the subject that concerns everyone more than anything else? Once understood, the weather can be a real pleasure.

Professional forecasters employ several fundamental instruments in preparing their daily or extended forecasts. Without these instruments, records of the weather could not be properly assembled. Such records are very valuable, for they provide comparisons of conditions from year to year—such as temperatures, rainfall, snow accumulations, wind velocity, and humidity—and these factors can be of great worth to agriculture, industry, or any phase of endeavor that can benefit from knowing past happenings that may relate to the present and to the future.

BAROMETERS

The barometer is the most important of the weather instruments. It indicates atmospheric pressure. Its reading can change within minutes, as during a passing storm.

One type of barometer is the **mercury barometer**, activated by the expansion and contraction of a mercury column. This movement is produced by the rise or fall of air pressure, indicating the approach or passage of storms.

Another type is the **aneroid barometer**. This device is activated by air pressure on a vacuum contained within thin metal membranes. Any variation in the air pressure causes the "elastic"

Digital barometer from Sensor Instruments Co.

membranes to respond. This movement is transmitted by a spring attached to an indicating needle.

THERMOMETERS

Thermometers and barometers were invented many years before these instruments were fashioned to register temperature accurately. Not until 1714, when the German physicist Gabriel Daniel Fahrenheit devised a glass-tube thermometer, using a column of mercury for the indicator, was accuracy accomplished. Fahrenheit designed his reading scale to show 32 degrees Fahrenheit as freezing and 212 degrees Fahrenheit as the boiling point of water. The acceptance of this thermometer and its scaling has endured.

The centigrade thermometer, first described by the Swedish astronomer Anders Celsius in 1742, differs from the Fahrenheit thermometer in that the divisions are in one hundred parts, with zero corresponding to 32 degrees Fahrenheit and 100 degrees corresponding to 212 degrees Fahrenheit.

In a measure, we can determine if

the temperature has risen or fallen without consulting the thermometer by simply glancing through the window at the skies. If the sky was clear at night but by morning has become cloudy, than we might guess that the temperature has risen overnight. This is because the forming clouds prevented the heat radiation from leaving the earth. By contrast, if we observed cloudiness at night but by morning the sky has cleared, we can surmise that it is cooler outside than when we went to bed.

The most interesting thermometer to obtain for our weather station is the **maximum and minimum thermometer**. This instrument is moderate in cost. The most compact ones are the U-type with a double reading—one side showing how high the temperature went during any period, and the other side showing how low the reading went. With such a thermometer we can, with accuracy, tell exactly how cold, or how hot, the air was during the night and day. The lowest reading usually comes just before sunrise—not the best time to crawl from the covers to check the temperature.

For ordinary use, the small **mercury thermometer** is probably the best, because it is both accurate and inexpensive.

Another interesting thermometer is the **indoor-outdoor type**. It enables us to read the temperature on the outside and the inside of a building simultaneously.

Wind vane from Mason & Sullivan.

WIND VANES

The simplest way to determine the wind's direction is to wet a finger, hold it aloft, then feel which side becomes cool. That is the side from which the wind is coming.

An inexpensive wind vane can be made from scrap wood or metal and mounted so that it will move freely with the wind or from the top of a pole, pipe, or pivot set on any roof or chimney. Low-cost attractive vanes also can be readily purchased.

Most of the mechanical vanes that you can buy work from the outside, but have a "remote" readout, either digital or dial, that can be wired to the inside of your house.

A companion instrument for the wind vane is the **anemometer**. This device indicates the speed of the wind, helpful in foretelling the weather, especially when used in conjunction with cloud formations.

Rain Gauges

There are many types and styles of rain gauges; the simplest and cheapest is a plastic cup with graduated markings on the side; this is adequate for normal use. More elaborate, and of course expensive, gauges have remote readout capability and precisely calibrated measuring sensors.

No matter which style rain gauge is used, measurements are usually made in hundredths of an inch. On the plastic cylinder rain gauge, the markings on the side can be easily read to determine just how much rain has come down.

No fancy equipment is required to measure snowfall. Simply take out a ruler, and stick it in the snow to determine how deep it is.

Relative humidity is measured with a **hygrometer** or **psychrometer**. It determines how much water vapor is in the air, compared to the maximum amount that the air can hold at the same temperature, and expresses it as a percentage. A simple digital or dial-type hygrometer is easy to buy, and makes a useful addition to the home weather station.

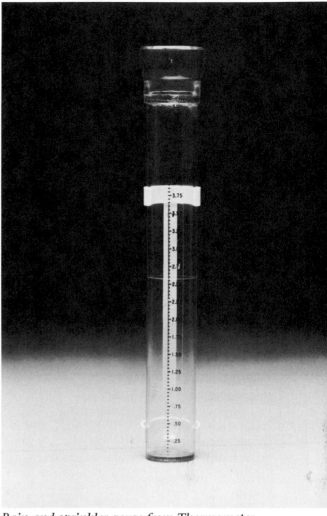

Rain and sprinkler gauge from Thermometer Corporation of America.

DO-IT-YOURSELF WEATHER EQUIPMENT

Weather has held a certain fascination for the human race ever since Noah built his ark. Back then people didn't understand much about the weather, but today we can monitor quite a few variables. Temperature, wind speed, humidity, cloud cover, dew point, and a whole host of other weather phenomena can now be measured and analyzed. As with so many other modern technologies, the price of weather instruments has dropped as their sophistication and accuracy have increased. As a result, there has been a steady rise in "backyard" weather forecasting.

There are charts to help track hurricanes, posters to identify clouds, kits explaining weather terms, and instruments galore to help you get this data. For the more ambitious weather watcher, there are computer software programs that include data lines from the National Weather Service and the tools to decipher this complex information. Whatever your interest in the weather, a wide range of products will help sharpen your observing techniques to penetrate nature's oldest secret.

We've divided the following product descriptions into sections, beginning with relatively simple, low-tech items, and increasing in sophistication—and cost.

BACKYARD WEATHER INSTRUMENTS

The people in the weather-instrument business are mostly mail-order houses offering a variety of products. Some companies specialize in instruments for the amateur, others in instruments that require technical know-how.

American Weather Enterprises (P.O. Box 1383, Media, PA 19063; 215-565-1232)

carries a line of basic weather instruments—barometers, thermometers, hygrometers, anemometers, and rain gauges. For all these instruments, prices vary considerably. A top-of-the-line barometer sells for $350, whereas a simple marine spinnaker barometer goes for $37.50. Thermometers range from $25 to $289; hygrometers, $16.50 to $359; anemometers begin at $300. Simple rain gauges are a bargain—they can be had for $12.98—but a remote reading digital rain gauge will set you back $449. American

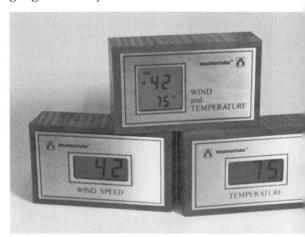

Basic weather instruments from American Weather Enterprises.

Weather Enterprises also sells weather stations that measure one or more variables electronically. These units range from $415 to $2,100. Other offerings include weather recording equipment ($299 to $695), sundials ($29.95 to $225), wind chimes ($27.50 to $42.50), and weather vanes ($65 to $75).

Carolina Biological Supply Company (2700 York Rd., Burlington, NC 27215; 800-547-1733; 919-584-0381) offers a full range of weather instruments, from barometers to hygrometers, rain gauges to anemometers. This company also has a complete weather station. Prices for instruments range from $31.95 to $295. The complete weather station costs $781.35.

Edmund Scientific (101 E. Gloucester Pike, Barrington, NJ 08007; 609-573-6260) offers thermometers ranging in price from $19.95 to $249.95 (for one that records temperatures); barometers ($29.95 to $39.95); and complete weather stations ($98 to $495).

Mason & Sullivan/Classics in the Making (586 Higgins Crowell Rd., West Yarmouth, MA 02673; 617-778-1056) is the place to go for whirligigs, kits, hot-air engines, and old-fashioned weather instruments. How about a storm bottle and thermometer kit? This $59 item is designed after the earliest known forecasting instrument. Then there's the "weatherglass," a $34 hand-blown pressure instrument often called the poor man's barometer.

Maximum Wind and Weather Instruments (30 W. Samuel Barnett Blvd., New Bedford, MA 02745; 617-999-2226) offers digital and hand-held weather instruments measuring wind, overall weather conditions, and tides. Suitable for home or office. Prices range from $165 to $570 for anemometers; $180 to $280 for barometers; $280 to $335 for thermometers; and $1,200 for all instruments in a complete weather station.

Rainwise (Bar Harbor, ME 04609; 207-288-5169) sells individual instruments and complete weather stations. Highlights from the list include a hygrometer driven by a synthetic hair movement, making it accurate to within 5 percent ($104); a thermometer with gradations in both

Examples of equipment from Rainwise.

Celsius and Fahrenheit ($79); and a rain gauge that you never have to empty ($54.90). Simply push the reset button to zero, and a new counting period begins. Rainwise's weather station monitors seven different weather phenomena and provides digital readouts, all designed for wall mounting ($1,200). The weather station without computer hookup costs $990.

Saunders and Cooke, Inc. (P.O. Box 1459, Portsmouth, NH 03801; 603-436-0011) makes handcrafted barometers in eighteenth-century style. Prices range from $425 to $680.

digital barometer costs $298; digital thermometers, $298 to $325; and the digital humidity system, $398 with a 50-foot cable and $425 with a 100-foot cable. The computer interface costs $75.

The Sharper Image (650 Davis St., San Francisco, CA 94111; 800-344-4444; 415-344-4444; and more than 50 stores nationwide) has a weather station monitored by a quartz clock. Price is $59.

Simerl Instruments (238 West St., Annapolis, MD 21401; 301-849-8667) specializes in different types of anemometers. This company pioneered hand-held electric/electronic anemometers more than 30 years ago. Its top-of-the-line

Model BTC hand-held anemometer, from Simerl Instruments.

Reproduction of eighteenth-century barometer from Saunders and Cooke, Inc.

Sensor Instruments Co. (41 Terrill Pk., Concord, NH 03301; 800-633-1033; 603-224-0167) offers high-quality weather instruments for the serious amateur. The

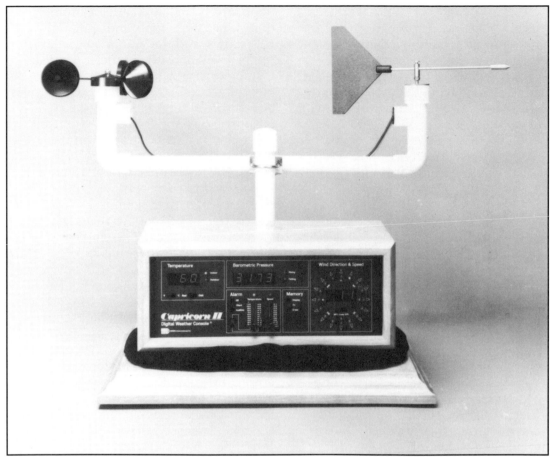

Capricorn II digital weather console, from Hinds International, Inc.

model is used by the air force, and other military services specify it for their weather squadrons. Less expensive models range from $10 to $125.

StormWatch (89 Mansfield St., Framingham, MA 01701; 617-872-3317) sells state-of-the-art weather instruments, ranging in price from $7.25 for a simple rain gauge to $2,126 for a computerized weather station.

Thermometer Corporation of America (280 Cane Creek Rd., Fletcher, NC 28732; 704-684-5178) makes Taylor weather instruments, a line of mostly inexpensive barometers, thermometers, hygrometers, wind speed and direction indicators, and

rain and sprinkler gauges. Prices range from $12.50 and up.

WeatherMeasure Weathertronics/Qualimetrics, Inc. (P.O. Box 230, Princeton, NJ 08542; 609-924-4470) offers a fat 310-page catalog that is chock-full of geo-physical instruments and systems. Looking for weather balloons and gas to fill them? Prices range from $3 to $253 for various size balloons, while a chemical reaction hydrogen gas generator lists for $4,995. How about humidity sensors? The catalog has 13 pages of them, from $50 to $1,150. There's something for everyone.

Wind & Weather Catalogue (Albion St. Watertower, P.O. Box 2320, Mendocino,

CA 95460; 707-937-0323) has weather instruments with early American appeal. Where else can you find a hammered copper weather vane shaped like a pig ($650) or a circa-1870 American wooden forecast barometer ($2,800)? This company also has digital weather instruments ranging in price from $13 to $65. Although there is a great variety of weather instruments listed here, Wind & Weather specializes in weather vanes and sundials.

ELECTRONIC INSTRUMENTS

Most of these companies manufacture weather instruments for use by industries, government agencies, or the military:

Alden Electronics (40 Washington St., Westboro, MA 01581; 508-366-8851) makes big weather instruments aimed at professionals. It has a complete line of weather satellite ground-receiving stations, shipboard APT systems, and color graphics packages for use with satellite data. Of particular interest is Alden's portable weather satellite system for a variety of ground station needs. Alden also makes a wide range of facsimile recorders. Prices range from $995 to $3,695.

Bay Technical Associates, Inc. (Hwy. 603, P.O. Box 387, Bay St. Louis, MS 39520; 601-467-2937) has helped pioneer electronic environmental-sensing devices. The line includes devices for pressure, temperature, and current and directional wind-speed data ($2,000 each). Bay Technical also makes a weather station that provides measurements of air temperature, barometric pressure, wind speed, and wind direction. The complete weather station ($5,900) can be mounted on land, buoys, or moving vessels.

Hinds International, Inc. (P.O. Box 929, Hillsboro, OR 97123; 503-648-1355) makes a weather instrument package,

Capricorn II Digital Weather Console, that is used by schools, industries, municipalities, and the military. But it also can be used by backyard meteorologists. Outdoor instruments relay their measurements back to a wood-grain box that gives constant readings of temperature, air pressure, wind speed and direction, and wind-chill factor. The Capricorn II can be hooked up to a computer to record readings. The weather station's $995 price includes the display console, outdoor sensors, and mast attachment. (You supply the mast.) Options include a computer interface ($295), software ($85), and various cable attachments.

VIZ Manufacturing Co. (335 E. Price St., Philadelphia, PA 19144; 215-844-2626) makes sensors for use with radiosonde transmitters that are often attached to weather balloons. Much of the company's equipment is designed for low-cost automatic upper-atmosphere soundings. The Mark II microsonde measures temperature, pressure, wind, and humidity. Separate, larger sensors are also available for more detailed measurements. Radiosondes can be tracked with VIZ's own W-9000 meteorological processing system, complete with antennas and software. Prices range from $80 to $100.

WEATHER BY FAX

It's not generally known, but you can use a shortwave radio to pick up much more than just voice transmissions or Morse code. For example, some weather stations transmit in a facsimile, or fax, mode, which means that they send photos and maps over shortwave radio bands. These are picked up by news and weather services around the country, but anyone with a little know-how can tap into the system. For some shortwave radios, you won't need a special antenna. Here are two sources:

How Cold Is It?

Here is a simplified equation to help you determine the wind-chill factor:

$$Tw = TA - (1.5 \times VA)$$

Tw = wind chill
TA = air temperature
VA = wind speed

Example: If the temperature is 20 degrees Fahrenheit and the wind is 30 miles per hour,

Tw = 20 minus (1.5 x 30)
= 20 minus 45
Tw = –15

Stephens Engineering Associates Inc. (7030 220th St. SW, Mountlake Terrace, WA 98043; 206-771-2182) offers the SEAFAX weather facsimile digital signal processor, with high-resolution printouts. The system must be attached to a single-side band radio receiver and a printer. Price is $995, or $1,145 with IBM-compatible serial output.

Universal Amateur Radio Inc. (1280 Aida Dr., Reynoldsburg, OH 43068; 614-866-4267) offers the Information-Tech M-800 ($349), which can be hooked up to a shortwave radio and an Epson printer for a crisp, clear weather map. A variety of other electronic gear is also included in the Universal catalog.

SOFTWARE AND ON-LINE SERVICES

The National Weather Service offers various data lines that you can subscribe to for up-to-the-minute weather information. The problem is that most of this data is in coded form; you can't really read it without special computer software and hardware to help you decipher the information being sent. Fortunately, a number of companies offer hardware and software packages to help translate the data. Others offer menu-driven systems that are not dependent on NWS data. Each of these systems has its own strengths and limitations.

Accu-Data (Accu-Weather Inc., 619 W. College Ave., State College, PA 16801; 814-237-0309) is a complete, real-time weather data base that interfaces with most terminals, personal computers, and business computers. Available data from Accu-Data include hourly surface observations; digitized radar signals; upper-air data; worldwide observations; DIFAX, LFM/NGM, MOS, and other modal output; plain-language and coded forecasts; severe weather bulletins; watches and warnings; climatological summaries; and marine data. Data are transmitted as both charts and maps. The data base is compatible with both IBM and Apple computers. There are three different prices for Accu-Data. Commercial users pay $69 an hour and secondary schools $42 an hour, both with access to a toll-free 800 number. Hobbyists pay $16.95 an hour, but they must also pay long-distance charges. (All three prices are for 1200 baud.) In addition, Accu-Weather sells a software package for Macintosh computers called *Accu-Weather Forecaster,* which lets you quickly download national weather data from Accu-Weather, then display it in easy-to-read maps, graphs, charts, and forecasts. The software package retails for $89.95 from Accu-Weather, and is also available from discount computer mail-order outlets for considerably less.

Hal Communications Corp. (P.O. Box 365, Urbana, IL 61801; 217-367-7373) makes the WX-1000 Weather Box and several types of interface cards. The

Weather Box ($1,995) receives selected information from a data line and stores it. Information can be retrieved using an on-site computer via radio or modem. The instrument can be programmed for the specific data requirements of the user, including sounding an alarm for a priority weather reading. The interface and Hal's own specially designed modem help users connect the Weather Box to computers and communications systems.

National Geographic Society (NGS, 17th & M Sts., Washington, DC 20036; 800-368-2728, 202-857-7000) distributes a product called the Weather Machine. Aimed at high school science classes, the Weather Machine allows students to get a select packet of weather data culled from the National Weather Service's Domestic Data Service and held in a special National Geographic computer. This system means that users don't have to subscribe to government data lines. The NGS data

are designed for use on the Apple IIc, IIe, or IIgs computer. They can be translated into color computer maps superimposed over a map of North America. Readings include temperature, air pressure, wind speed and direction, dew point, cloud cover, and more. A modem is needed if users plan to tap into the daily updates offered. A detailed curriculum is part of the package.

OceanRoutes (Weather Network Division, 680 W. Maude Ave., Sunnyvale, CA 94086; 408-245-3600), accessed via TYMNET, a communications network provided by McDonnell-Douglas, incorporates information from the National Weather Service, the National Oceanic and Atmospheric Administration, and the Federal Aviation Administration. It is used primarily by transportation companies and radio and TV meteorologists. There is a $15 setup fee and minimum monthly usage is rated at $1.50 per minute at 2400

Screen from WeatherPro *software, from TMI Inc.*

baud, $1 per minute at 1200 baud, and 58 cents a minute at 300 baud.

Petrocci Freelance Associates (651 N. Houghton Rd., Tucson AZ 85710; 602-296-1041) makes *Weather Pro Weather Track,* and *Weather Stat* software packages ($34.95 each). You may use the software to collect, compile, and manipulate National Weather Service data and to calculate and chart daily highs, lows, precipitation, and daily heating and cooling on a variety of graphs.

Satellite Data Systems (110 Wayne Ave., Ste. 1209, Silver Spring, MD 29010; 301-588-9000) markets two software packages and data services, *WXBrief* and *WXBase,* which run on IBM PC AT or PS/2 (and compatible) computers. *WXBrief* is a complete aviation weather-briefing system and provides information such as route weather, weather charts, weather trends, flight trends, weather in selected cities, and location information. Cost of the system begins at $95 a month; the software itself is $695. *WXBase* is a complete weather-data management system. It receives data from a Siscorp micro earth station moments after they are made available by the National Weather Service, FAA, or Accu-Weather. Functions of the system include display or print inventory, selection maintenance, weather applications, and communications control. The software is $1,900, with a monthly charge of $95. Satellite Data Systems boasts about having provided the *Voyager* with up-to-the-minute weather information so accurate that *Voyager* pilots believe it may have saved their lives.

TMI Inc. (4000 Kruse Way Pl., Bldg. 2, Ste. 120, Lake Oswego, OR 97035; 503-635-3966) publishes *PC Weather, PC WeatherPro,* and *PC Weather Toolkit. PC Weather* ($475) offers a graphic display of wind speed and direction, inside and outside temperature, and wind chill and gusts. It allows you to track weather conditions and can alert you to changes in temperature and wind speed. *PC Weather* is sold as a packaged system that includes a circuit card with on-board barometer, anemometer, and wind vane assembly, two temperature probes, display software, and installation hardware and documentation. The rain gauge is optional. *PC WeatherPro* ($575) is a more in-depth package. It includes the rain gauge and an enhanced software program that offers data-logging and analysis capabilities. More than 300 days of information can be stored on a single floppy disk. *PC Weather Toolkit* ($150) allows you to combine and average the data gathered by the *PC WeatherPro* system. A fourth component, *File Link,* allows you to create your own weather-gathering and display programs by accessing the data kept internally in the *PC Weather* software. For all IBM-compatible machines.

WeatherBank, Inc. (2185 South 3600 W., Salt Lake City, UT 84119; 801-973-3132) offers a dial-up information service called WeatherBrief. The service contains all National Weather Service products and can be connected at 300, 1200, or 2400 baud. The software package is free, but there is a $10 delivery and handling charge. On-line time is billed at 20 cents a minute.

Weathervane Software (P.O. Box 277, Grafton, MA 01519; 508-839-6777) is the publisher of *Atlantic Hurricane Watcher* ($30), a menu-driven program that allows you to plot and compare the tracks of hurricanes on a color or black-and-white map of the United States, western Atlantic Ocean, Caribbean, and Gulf of Mexico. IBM-PC compatible.

WEATHER STUFF

These products are designed to inform and entertain, sometimes in unique and winning ways. You are advised to contact each of these companies for their latest catalogs and price lists. Another good source of products is the ads in the back of *Weatherwise* magazine.

Here's a sampling of what's out there:

American Weather Enterprises (P.O. Box 1383, Media, PA 19063; 215-565-1232) sells books, software, and educational materials, in addition to weather instruments. Some choice items from the catalog include a sturdy wall chart (55 by 33 inches) that details global atmospheric influences, meteorological motion, severe weather, clouds and precipitation, examples of pollution, aviation meteorology, and more in an easy-to-understand flowchart design ($16.50) and Geochron, an attractive chalkboard-sized electronic map that continually shows the exact time of day and amount of sunlight anywhere in the world (basic unit is $1,200; deluxe models up to $2,000).

Blue Hill Meteorological Observatory (P.O. Box 101, East Milton, MA 02186; 617-698-5397) stocks a hurricane tracking chart that includes a 16-by-20-inch map of North America along with instructions on how to plot a hurricane's course using longitude and latitude. There is also a hurricane survival checklist and a list of

Cloud chart, from Cloud Chart Inc.

current hurricane names. The 1988 version of the chart included information about the 1938 New England hurricane. The nonprofit observatory offers weather-related publications, including a quarterly bulletin, available to all members; membership is $10 a year. Write for a free brochure.

Cloud Chart Inc. (P.O. Box 29294, Richmond, VA 23233; 804-282-5902) produces clouds galore. Pictures of clouds, that is. Cloud photos are Cloud Chart's business, and the company's specialties are wall charts and laminated 11-by-15-inch cards. The charts show various cloud formations around the world, coded and indexed with official World Meteorological Organization names and numbers. Each photo on the chart includes a caption describing the pictured cloud and offering a brief forecast. Chart groups are written for different grade levels, from elementary through high school. Charts are $2 to $3 each; classroom kits, including lesson plan guides, are $22.

Hammond, Inc. (515 Valley St., Maplewood, NJ 07040; 800-526-4953, 201-763-6000) makes maps and books of all shapes and sizes. Of special interest to weather watchers is the Hammond Weather Kit, complete with chart and wheel. The 25-by-28-inch weather chart offers graphic explanations of popular weather terms, including cloud types, weather fronts, tornado formation, and more. The weather wheel helps amateurs create their own forecasts.

Rencroc, Inc. (P.O. Box 588632, Seattle, WA 98188; 206-242-2319) produces Weatherslam ($9.95), "a card game where the sky's the limit." The game, for ages 8 through adult, pits players against the four seasons of the year. Players try to survive hurricanes, typhoons, and other storms so as to gain a "seasonal trump."

The weather-based card game "Weatherslam," from Rencroc, Inc.

Sky Guide (P.O. Box 30027, Greenwood Station, Seattle, WA 98103; 206-782-8485) identifies all cloud types and illustrates them on a poster with pictures taken around the world. The poster's size, 25 by 38 inches, makes this the largest cloud chart we've found. The price is $7.95, including shipping by first-class mail.

The Weather School (5075 Lake Rd., Brockport, NY 14420; 716-637-5207) offers the WeatherCycler, developed by the Department of Earth Sciences at the State University of New York at Brockport. The main part of this kit is an 8 1/2-by-11-inch heavy-duty card with a sliding insert to help users visualize why weather patterns develop. In addition, there is a key for deciphering common weather map symbols and several windows to help show weather changes as a front moves over, bringing a high- or low-pressure system with it. Two versions are available, one for aviation students and one for classroom use. Several sailing, pilot, and weather magazines have commended the

Clouds: A Guide to the Sky

CLOUD NOTES

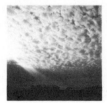

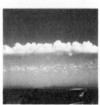

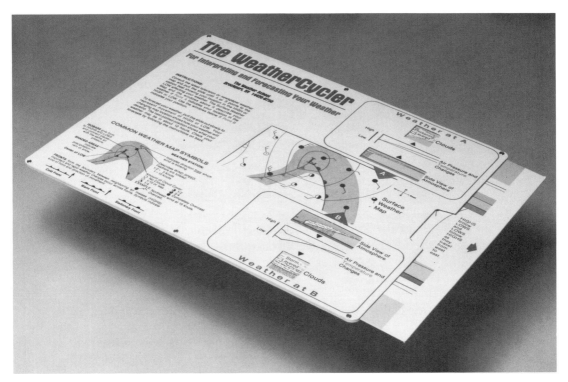

The WeatherCycler forecasting tool, from The Weather School.

WeatherCycler as a basic reference tool for weather forecasting. Prices are $6.95 for the slide chart and instruction booklet, $8.95 for a kit that includes a 12-page set of study activities, and $9.45 for the pilot's study kit. Other products, such as overhead projections and teacher's guides, are also available.

Whirlwind Designs (65 Inman St., Cambridge, MA 02139; 617-868-0946) offers a weather piece of whimsy: sky phenomena T-shirts. Designs include lightning bolts, northern lights, and tornadoes, silk-screened on cotton shirts in white, royal, navy, blue, or gray. Shirts are $9.95; $18 for two.

Left: Cloud chart from Sky Guide.

EDUCATIONAL AND AUDIOVISUAL PRODUCTS

The following organizations produce materials intended for classroom use. Some are available to educators only. You are advised to write to each company to obtain their latest catalog and prices.

Carolina Biological Supply Company (2700 York Rd., Burlington, NC 27215; 800-547-1733, 919-584-0381) makes videos and filmstrips about the weather. One comprehensive video ($199) includes information about the changing seasons and intense storms. The filmstrip series "Weather" includes three filmstrips on elements of weather and weather instruments ($75). Another series, "Understanding the Weather" ($168), has four filmstrips that cover forecasting, instruments, and storms.

Coronet Film & Video (108 Wilmot Rd., Deerfield, IL 60015; 800-621-2131; 312-940-1260) offers films and videos for sale or rent. Primary grade films and videos include whimsical titles such as "Where Does the Rain Go After It Falls?" "Why Doesn't Grass Grow on the Moon?" and "Can I Sit on a Cloud?" Prices are $320 for 16-millimeter films and $250 for videos. Programs for junior high and high school students cover violent storms, clouds and precipitation, and global forecasting. Prices are $400 for 16-millimeter films, $250 for videos.

Educational Images Ltd. (P.O. Box 3456, West Side, Elmira, NY 14905; 800-527-4264; 607-732-1090) has slide sets on the water cycle ($39.95), air pollutants ($99.95), clouds and weather ($79.95), and the greenhouse effect ($32.50). Filmstrips include those on acid rain ($69.95), cold weather survival, and weather in the wilderness (packaged

together for $79.95); the last two titles come in video as well, also for $79.95.

Encyclopaedia Britannica Educational Corporation (425 N. Michigan Ave., Chicago, IL 60611; 800-621-3900; 312-321-6640) offers a video on weather forecasting ($300) and a five-part filmstrip package aptly called "Weather" that covers the water cycle, changes in the atmosphere, and weather, climate, and people. The filmstrip series is $194; in video, $207.

Environmental Films (R.F.D. 2, St. Johnsbury, VT 05819; 802-748-2505) sells a filmstrip on tornadoes of the United States. Price is $30 plus shipping.

The Everyday Weather Project (State University of New York at Brockport, Brockport, NY 14420; 716-395-2352). Designed by the same professor who created the WeatherCycler kit mentioned under "The Weather School" in the previous section, the Everyday Weather Project includes a series of videotapes and sound filmstrips. Videotape titles include "Hazardous Weather: Hurricanes" and "Hazardous Weather: Thunderstorms." These productions study storm formation and life cycles. Filmstrip titles are "Sensing and Analyzing Weather," "Weather Systems," "Weather Forecasting," "Weather Radar," "Weather Satellites," and the filmstrip version of "Hazardous Weather: Hurricanes." Prices for the 24-minute videotapes are $74.95 each (3/4-inch or 1/2-inch VHS format). Filmstrips are $34.95 each, or $174 for the set of six. Slide set versions are $49.95 each, or $249.95 for the complete set.

Extension Media Center (University of

How to Read a Weather Map

Weather maps represent in condensed form a wealth of information that has been received and interpreted by weather forecasters around the globe. All weather maps use common symbols. Here is a description of what's found on the maps and the symbols used to represent different weather phenomena:

Sky conditions are indicated by small circles (representing key cities) that are completely filled in (overcast skies), partially filled in (partly cloudy conditions), or empty (clear conditions). If it is raining or snowing, the circle may have an *R* or an *S* inside. On professional maps, symbols are used—jagged lines for lightning and snowflakes for snow, for example.

Wind is represented by a line drawn from a sky-condition circle. To determine direction, assume that the top of the circle is north. The line is drawn in the direction from which the wind originates. Barbs representing 10 miles per hour each are drawn horizontally from the wind direction line to indicate wind speed. So a 30-mph wind would have three barbs. (Some maps simply use arrows to indicate wind direction. The arrows point in the direction the wind is blowing.)

Temperature is usually in degrees Fahrenheit, although Celsius may also be used.

Barometric pressure is represented by isobars—solid, curved black lines. *High-pressure* weather systems (clear weather) are drawn as ascending isobars. *Low-pressure* weather systems (cloudy weather) are drawn as descending isobars.

Fronts can be shown in three ways. A *cold front*, the leading edge of a moving mass of cold air, is drawn as a solid black line with small triangles. The points of the triangles face the direction in which the front is moving. A *warm front,* the leading edge of an advancing mass of warm air, is drawn as a solid black line with solid black semicircles. A *stationary front*, the separation of two stationary air masses, is drawn by a solid black line that has alternate triangles and semicircles.

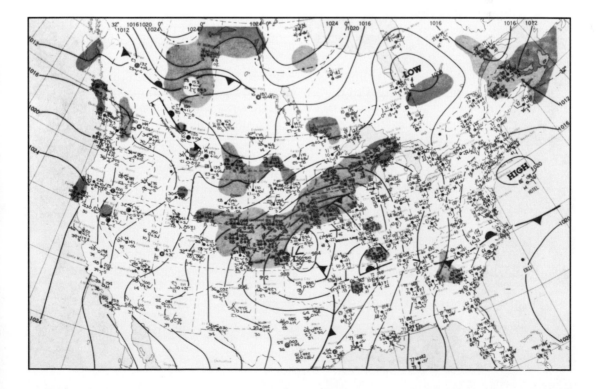

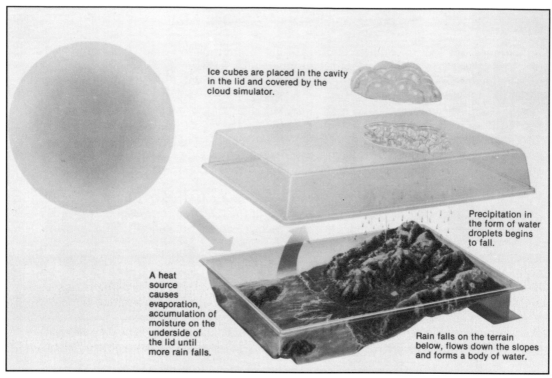

Ice cubes are placed in the cavity in the lid and covered by the cloud simulator.

Precipitation in the form of water droplets begins to fall.

A heat source causes evaporation, accumulation of moisture on the underside of the lid until more rain falls.

Rain falls on the terrain below, flows down the slopes and forms a body of water.

Part of the Water Cycle Model, from Hubbard Scientific Company.

California, 2176 Shattuck Ave., Berkeley, CA 94704; 415-642-0460) has films and videos for rent on the following subjects: acid rain (video, $30), storms (film and video, $29), weather forecasting (film, $29), and a two-part series, "The Weather Machine" (video, $42 for each part), that covers the relationship between climate and the atmosphere, and changes in the global climate.

Gould Media Inc. (44 Parkway W., Mt. Vernon, NY 10552; 914-664-3285) sells overhead transparencies on atmospheric pressures, local climatic influences, and the water cycle. The price is $35 for a set of five overlays.

How the Weatherworks (1522 Baylor Ave., Rockville, MD 20580; 301-762-7669) is the business name of Michael Mogil, a meteorologist who has independently

produced two filmstrips: on tornadoes ($39.50) and on clouds ($35). Also, in conjunction with the National Weather Association, he has designed a set of three 1-by-2-foot cloud charts ($9 each) for use in the classroom and outdoors.

Hubbard Scientific (P.O. Box 104, Northbrook, IL 60065; 800-323-8368, 312-272-7810) produces a 35-by-45-inch vacuum-formed, wall-mountable board that includes a radio receiver with National Oceanic and Atmospheric Administration broadcasts, a set of 14 study prints as a resource for interpretation of observable weather conditions, and a Teacher's Guide ($239). Other weather products include a 12-by-16-inch three-dimensional model that demonstrates air mass structures ($49); a weather map and plotting chart ($30); and six full-color meteorology transparencies ($39.90).

Indiana University (Audio-visual Center, Bloomington, IN 47405; 812-335-2103) has 16-millimeter films for rent on the changing weather ($15.90), climate and seasons ($8.70), clouds ($8.70), and the origins of weather ($11.20).

JLM Visuals (920 7th Ave., Grafton, WI 53024; 414-377-7775) sells slide sets on tools of the meteorologist, clouds, and world climates. The price is $28 each.

MMI Corporation (2950 Wyman Pkwy., P.O. Box 19907, Baltimore, MD 21211; 301-366-1222) manufactures a 16-by-12-by-3-inch weather model that explains basic air mass structures and their interrelationships and a 218-page meteorology manual. Price for the package is $49.

Modern Talking Picture Service (Scheduling Center, 5000 Park St. N., St. Petersburg, FL 33709; 813-541-5763) has films available for free loan on climate, hurricanes, and floods.

National Audiovisual Center (Customer Services PT, 8700 Edgeworth Dr., Capitol Heights, MD 20743; 301-763-1896) has films and videos for rent covering clouds, weather for aviators, and storms. The typical rental fee is $40.

National Geographic Society (17th & M Sts. NW, Washington, DC 20036; 800-368-2728, 301-921-1330) offers weather filmstrips for all ages and a videotape for older children. Filmstrips include a participatory show for very young children (grades K through 2) that explains weather basics (two-filmstrip set, $62.95); an introduction to weather for grades 4 through 9 (three-filmstrip set, $85.95); and a filmstrip for grades 5 through 12 on forecasting weather ($32.95). The video explains how weather works and how to forecast it (22-minute color video; $69.95; 22-minute color film; $279.50).

Ward's Natural Science Establishment, Inc. (5100 W. Henrietta Rd., P.O. Box 92912, Rochester, NY 14692; 11850 East Florence Ave., Los Angeles, CA 90670; 800-962-2660) sells slide sets on subjects ranging from clouds ($37.95) to the water cycle ($28.18). In filmstrips, Ward's has "Weather Awareness and Survival" (two-part set, $79.95) and several single-set packages, including "Hazardous Weather," "Weather Systems," "Weather Satellites," and "Weather Forecasting." Each set is $34.95.

Filmstrip set from National Geographic.

Chasing Tornadoes

by Mike Clary

If the urge to hunt is indeed deep within us, then perhaps those who chase tornadoes give that urge the ultimate expression. There is no bigger game, nor a quarry more capricious, unpredictable, or lethal. For the few who pursue the Big Vortex with the passion of Ahab after the whale, storm chasing is not exactly science, not exactly sport. It's more like pure obsession.

"When that Gulf moisture comes blowing into Texas, I can smell the humidity, and that just makes my adrenaline rise," says Tim Marshall, a chaser who lives outside Dallas. In this, Marshall is typical of the breed; when he dreams he sees himself just a little southeast of a boiling black sky. He sees signs of rotation in the clouds. Looking toward the heavens, he hurls aloft a popular storm chaser's incantation, borrowed from television's "The Price Is Right": Come on down!

Chasers want desperately to stand face-to-face with a howling tornado and take its picture.

Science, of course, is the rationale. Chasers furnish data to researchers trying to solve the mysteries of the earth's strongest surface winds. In recent years photographs and videotapes, along with measurements of atmospheric pressure and wind speed, collected by storm chasers have significantly added to our understanding of how tornadoes form.

But for chasers the immediate payoff is unparalleled excitement. Even scientists such as Robert Davies-Jones—who as director of the tornado intercept project of the National Severe Storms Laboratory (NSSL) is paid to pursue tornadoes—acknowledge the thrills. "It's very exhila-rating seeing a tornado in action," he says. "I remember one in 1979 that formed near Wichita Falls. It had winds of 200 miles an hour, and was coming right at us! It was scary."

Veteran chasers such as Gene Moore insist that a successful tornado hunter is more detective than daredevil. Of course, Moore, a meteorologist, is also well known to his colleagues as the Mad Bomber, a nickname that owes less to science than to relentless derring-do. He has a reputation for meeting twisters head-on. "I have been bashed by hailstones, hit by lightning, and been inside one tornado," says Moore. "But the key to storm chasing is patience."

Patience, however, does not come easily to the men and women who wait all year for spring. The storm season is short, and the odds are long. Divining just where a tornado will form is tough enough. But even tougher is getting in close, getting film, and then getting out alive.

Accidents do happen. Two seasons ago a University of Oklahoma student trying to catch up with a twister was killed when his car overturned on a rain-slicked road. And each year, it seems, more unschooled thrill seekers can be found prowling the plains, sometimes tailing experienced tornado hunters in reckless convoys. "Kamikazes," Marshall calls them. "Just idiots," says Davies-Jones, who adds, "I would be worried if [storm chasing] became a national craze. People who don't know anything about it can get in real trouble."

Experienced chasers often begin each day of hunting with a stop at the local National Weather Service office to

Tornado near Plainview, Texas. Courtesy National Oceanic and Atmospheric Administration.

check the LFM (Limited Fine Mesh), a forecast of vorticity potential. These maps offer, in periods of up to 48 hours, forecasts of the tendency of any thunderstorms to begin rotating. Tornadoes are formed when the air in a thunderstorm's updraft is sent into a cyclonic spin by horizontal winds in the troposphere.

Along with vorticity potential, chasers also pay attention to AC, or the anticipated convention outlook, issued every 12 hours by the National Severe Storms Forecast Center. These bulletins include a "watch" area in which thunderstorms are expected. Other factors considered are early-morning surface conditions and regional changes in the dew point, visibility, and wind flow at 500 millibars (southwesterly is best). Some chasers—Tim Marshall is one—also pay for hookups to the data bases of private weather services that will feed into a home computer forecast maps updated hourly.

From all of the information available, each chaser makes a forecast. "It's like a series of clues," says Gene Moore. "You have to put them all together. And sometimes it looks like angry clouds everywhere."

By midmorning, decisions are due. A chaser starting out in Norman, Oklahoma, for example, may be looking at a dry line that could run from the Texas panhandle into Kansas, a distance of more than 500 miles. Storm hunters who want to arrive in the forecast area by 2 p.m., "to see the first towers go up," as veteran chaser David Hoadley puts it, need to hit the road soon after breakfast.

Says Moore: "My success in the afternoon is related to starting work at 6 to 7 a.m. My mind is made up by 10 a.m., generally speaking, and then I have three to four hours' drive time. Then I live or die by the forecast. I ignore other storms on the way. Over the past ten years, I'd say my average is about 20 percent; I'll catch a tornado once out of every five times out."

Weatherwise magazine, vol. 39, issue 3, June 1986, pp. 137-145. Reprinted with permission of the Helen Dwight Reid Educational Foundation. Published by Heldref Publications, 4000 Albemarle St. NW, Washington, DC 20016. Copyright 1986.

35 KEY WEATHER TERMS

Here are some key weather terms that will help you better understand the ins and outs of the local weather forecast.

Air Mass: A body of air, as large as several states, found in the atmosphere. An air mass has uniform physical characteristics when measured horizontally at any level. It usually takes on the temperature and humidity of the area over which it originated.

Air Pressure: The weight of air on the earth over a given place. A vertical column of air with a 1-inch-square base that reaches from sea level to the top of the atmosphere weighs 14.7 pounds (6.7 kilograms). This average weight fluctuates slightly with high or low pressure. Air pressure is measured by *barometers*, which are read in terms of inches or millibars.

Atmosphere: A blanket of air surrounding the earth. This blanket is kept in place by earth's gravity. The atmosphere is about 78 percent nitrogen, 21 percent oxygen, and 1 percent other gases. Most of earth's weather takes place in the troposphere, the atmosphere's lowest layer (see "Troposphere").

Climate: The characteristic weather conditions of a given region for an extended period of time. Climate descriptions are based on averages of temperature, wind velocity, precipitation, and other weather elements taken over several years.

Cloud Cover: The average amount of clouds in the sky at a given time and place. For example, when the weather newscaster says the sky is *clear*, he or she means that there is 0 to 10 percent

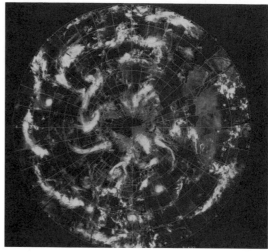

Digital mosaic of cloud pictures taken by ESSA satellite, courtesy National Aeronautics and Space Administration.

coverage; *scattered clouds* means 11 to 30 percent coverage; *partly cloudy* means 31 to 90 percent coverage; and *overcast* means over 90 percent cloud coverage.

Clouds: Condensed water vapor in the sky, usually the result of warm, moist air that has risen and cooled. The condensed droplets or ice crystals inside clouds are much smaller than raindrops.

Cumulonimbus: A thunderstorm cloud. It is dark and has a top shaped like an anvil. Cumulonimbus clouds usually are associated with heavy thunderstorms.

Drizzle: Minute droplets of water, usually between 1/500 and 1/50 of an inch in diameter. Drizzle drops are dispersed haphazardly in the air and resemble fog, except that drizzle falls to the ground.

Easterlies: Winds coming from the east.

Two images of storm clouds from space, combined to form a stereo view. Courtesy National Aeronautics and Space Administration.

The term usually is applied to a broad band of currents or patterns of winds, including the equatorial easterlies, the tropical easterlies, and the polar easterlies.

Fog: A cloud that forms on or near the ground. Radiation fog forms over the land as the air cools at night, usually during cool evenings when there is a slight breeze. *Sea fog* occurs when warm air rushes in over an icy body of water. This occurs most often in the summer along the California coast.

Freezing Rain: Rain that freezes when it strikes the ground.

Front: The area along which two or more air masses of different densities and temperatures interact. A *warm front* is a leading edge of a warm air mass. Warm fronts usually bring hot, humid weather. A *cold front* is the leading edge of a cold air mass. Cold fronts may bring storms. After a cold front passes through, skies are usually clear and temperatures are colder. An *occluded front* is formed when a cold front and a warm front merge. Weather near an occluded front is unpredictable. A *stationary front* has very little movement. Weather on either side of the front will be affected as the front shifts in either direction. Weather is usually stable near a stationary front.

Frost: Small, thin ice crystals that form when a layer of air condenses on the ground, usually when the temperature is below freezing.

Gale: A strong current of wind traveling between 32 and 63 miles per hour.

Hail: Small ice balls that form in thunderstorm clouds. They are carried to the ground in rapidly moving currents of air.

High-Pressure Area: An area where the barometric pressure is higher than in surrounding areas. High-pressure systems usually bring clear weather.

Humidity: The amount of water vapor in the air. Relative humidity is the ratio of water vapor in the air to the maximum amount the air can hold while maintaining the same temperature. *Hygrometers* measure humidity.

Hurricane: A severe tropical cyclone, with winds in excess of 74 miles (119 kilometers) per hour. Hurricanes form in the north Atlantic Ocean, Caribbean Sea, Gulf of Mexico, and eastern north Pacific Ocean. *Typhoon* is the name used to describe similar storms in the Eastern Hemisphere.

Hurricane: A storm with winds spiraling

Hurricane storm surge. Courtesy National Oceanic and Atmospheric Administration.

toward the center of the storm—the eye—at a speed of about 112 miles per hour. The eye is usually between 3.7 and 25 miles in diameter. As much as 45 inches of rain can fall during a three- or four-day hurricane. Hurricanes usually occur in the fall and originate over the Atlantic Ocean or the Caribbean Sea.

Jet stream: A fast-moving belt of winds located in the upper troposphere (see "Troposphere"). These winds can travel more than 200 miles (322 kilometers) per hour. Polar-front jet streams flow in wave-like fashion around the Northern and Southern hemispheres. They change position constantly and move both vertically and horizontally. These jet streams are usually found near the dividing line between cold polar air and warmer tropical air.

Precipitation: All moisture that falls from clouds—rain, snow, sleet, and hail.

Radiosonde: An instrument attached to a weather balloon that measures the temperature, air pressure, and humidity of the upper atmosphere. Data from radiosondes are transmitted back to a ground weather station.

Rain: Water that falls from clouds. Most raindrops are shaped like mushrooms and are between 1/100 and 1/4 of an inch in diameter. Any drop larger than 1/4 of an inch will break into smaller drops when it hits the ground.

Sleet: Ice pellets between 4/100 and 16/100 of an inch in diameter that form when raindrops or partially melted snowflakes freeze while falling through a layer of cold air.

Smog: A combination of car fumes and industrial waste mixed with fog.

Snow: Ice crystals that form deep in

Aftermath of snowfall in Hamburg, N.Y., February 7, 1977. Courtesy National Oceanic and Atmospheric Administration.

clouds at temperatures between 5 and -15 degrees Fahrenheit. If these crystals pass through cold enough layers in the atmosphere, they fall to the ground as snow. Wet, heavy snowflakes have passed through warm, moist layers of air on their descent to earth, whereas dry, feathery flakes have passed through layers of cold, dry air.

Temperature: The degree of heat energy in the atmosphere. Thermometers measure temperature.

Thunderstorm: A heavy rainstorm that develops in cumulonimbus clouds and is accompanied by lightning and thunder. During thunderstorms winds may blow up to 75 miles per hour.

Tornado: The most violent of all storms, a tornado consists of a funnel-shaped cloud with winds blowing as high as 500 miles an hour. Tornadoes travel a path about 16 miles long, with the average length at 400 yards. They move forward at speeds between 25 and 40 miles per hour.

Trade Winds: A group of prevailing winds that were often used for travel during the era of tall sailing ships. Trade winds form when subtropical highs move toward the equator. They fall roughly between the latitudes 25 degrees north and 25 degrees south. They are northeasterly in the Northern Hemisphere and southeasterly in the Southern Hemisphere.

Tropical Cyclone: A storm with strong winds blowing counterclockwise in the Northern Hemisphere and clockwise in the Southern Hemisphere. Tropical cyclones go by different names in different parts of the world: *hurricanes* in the West Indies and *typhoons* in the north Pacific are two examples.

Lightning storm. Courtesy National Oceanic and Atmospheric Administration.

Troposphere: The lowest layer of the earth's atmosphere, rising from the planet's surface to 6 to 12 miles above sea level. Almost all the earth's weather takes place in the troposphere.

Weather: The state of the atmosphere at a given time and place. Weather is measured in terms of temperature, humidity, air pressure, wind speed and direction, precipitation, cloud cover, and other variables.

Westerlies: The dominant North American wind pattern. Air flows from west to east between 35 and 65 degrees north latitude. These winds tend to be stronger in the winter than in the summer.

Wind: The horizontal movement of air over the earth. Wind is caused by the uneven heating of the earth by the sun. Wind *direction* is measured by wind vanes. Wind *speed* is measured by anemometers.

Read All About It

There are many, many books available for weather buffs of all levels of interest and expertise. Here is a selected list of some we've found helpful and easy to read:

Craig F. Bohren: *Clouds in a Glass of Beer* (John Wiley & Sons, 1986) is a collection of simple experiments in atmospheric physics. The experiments are involved enough, however, that they should only be tried by someone with a certain amount of expertise in the field.

Judd Caplovich: *Blizzard! The Great Storm of '88* (VeRo Publishing Company, 1987) is a coffee-table-sized book documenting the severe blizzard that covered the eastern United States in March 1888. It provides an interesting and entertaining view of one of the worst storms in American history.

Frank H. Forrester: *1001 Questions Answered About the Weather* (Dover Publications, Inc., 1981) is a much improved, completely updated version of the book by the same name first published in 1957. This new edition is a wonderful resource book, full of both hard-core scientific information (how storms originate, the water cycle, weather instruments) and fun facts (where the names of storms came from, who invented the thermometer, careers in weather, and lots more). And all this great stuff is put into a question-and-answer format, making it easy to find just what you are looking for. Illustrations are included. This is a must for the amateur weather watcher and a good reference book for the pro.

Ralph Hardy, Peter Wright, John Kingston, and John Gribben: *The Weather Book* (Little, Brown, and Company, 1982) includes basic information about the nuts and bolts of weather: how weather systems are created, how storms are created and travel, and how weather is forecast. Much historical material adds a creative flair to what is basically a science reference book. The book is also enhanced by historical monographs, attractive illustrations, and some color photos.

Patrick Hughes: *American Weather Stories* (U.S. Department of Commerce, 1976) includes charming anecdotes about the ways weather affected important historical events. Did you know that Christopher Columbus encountered a hurricane on his famous voyage to the New World? Or that the Blizzard of '88 brought work to New York's unemployed? Read all about it.

Patrick Hughes: *A Century of Weather Service, 1870-1970* (Gordon and Breach Science Publishers, 1970) presents a comprehensive overview of the history of the National Weather Service.

Albert Lee: *Weather Wisdom* (Doubleday, 1976) is a manual on observational weather forecasting. Sprinkled in are old weather sayings and Lee's explanation of whether they are true or not. Includes some historical anecdotes.

David Ludlum: *The American Weather Book* (Houghton Mifflin, 1982) is one of the most thorough compendiums of weather information available about the United States. Organized by month, the book offers descriptions of region-by-region phenomena interspersed with charts, graphs, and photos.

David Ludlum: *The Weather Factor* (Houghton Mifflin, 1984) is an amazing collection of little-known facts about how weather has influenced the American scene from colonial to modern times, including how weather has affected elections, war, sports, flight, and more.

Louis D. Rubin, and Jim Duncan: *The Weather Wizard's Cloud Book* (Algonquin Books of Chapel Hill, 1984) is a revision of a book called *Forecasting the Weather*, which was a pioneer effort in lay weather forecasting when it came out in the 1960s. This new version is written in very simple language and makes weather both easy and interesting, even for those with little scientific background. It explains key weather terms clearly and has lovely photographs of clouds and simple definitions of their different types. A good sourcebook for the amateur weather watcher.

Ti Sanders: *Weather Is Front Page News* (Icarus Press, P.O. Box 1225, South Bend, IN 46624; $13.45 postpaid) offers a fascinating look at "the greatest American weather disasters." From cold waves to heat waves, floods to droughts, here are the very human stories of natural disasters dating back to 1850. Also by Sanders: *Weather: A User's Guide to the Atmosphere* ($13.45 postpaid), a wide-ranging and highly readable overview of how weather works.

AVIATION

AVIATION

From the moment that humans set foot on the earth's soil, we began looking skyward. The realm of the birds. It was here that we placed the gods we created to worship, and higher still that we looked for our destiny in the stars. From the clouds, we prayed for the rain that fed our crops; from the sun we sought warmth; from the moon, the light that would guide us through darkness. Mystified by the sheerness of air, by the grace of the creatures of the sky, by the swirl of the galaxy at night, we created myths of flight—myths that found logic in our earthbound nature. The Greeks told of Daedalus, the engineer from Crete who created wings of feathers and wax to help him and his son, Icarus, escape from the island where they were held captive. Daedalus escaped, but Icarus flew too close to the sun. His wings melted from the heat, and he fell to his death. Such was the price many believed we would pay for the sin of entering the realm of the gods. Yet our very desire to prove ourselves unworthy of flight is the greatest testament to our fascination with the sky above.

We eventually did learn to fly, of course, but only after we had first learned to walk upright, sow the fields, build civilized societies, sail the oceans, settle new lands, and wage bloody wars. Only after we had abandoned our myths to

Daedalus and Icarus, from a seventeenth-century German print. Courtesy Library of Congress.

plumb the deeper mysteries of science. Only then, with an accumulated history of discovery, exploration, invention, and destruction behind us, did we conquer the air on our own terms. The story of this slow but steady progress toward the skies is, in fact, a mirror of the cultural and scientific evolution of humankind itself.

Our early curiosity about flight was satisfied by the mythology and astrology in which we wrapped the skies and heavens. But as science began to overtake myth, we started to study flight with a more technical curiosity. Natural scientists who had once sought the invisible, spiritual essence of flight in the forms of birds began dissecting them to study their physiology for more tangible explanations. Artists who had once portrayed birds only as representational symbols began making anatomical sketches of their skeletal structures and wingspans. The mystery of flight slowly gave way to the systematic study of its origins. And, as our attitude toward the natural world progressed from one of awe to one of calculation, we began building machines with which to fly.

The simple kite, probably invented at least a millennium ago in Asia, was the first attempt to claim the sky with an object of our own creation. With the knowledge that technological flight was possible, early tinkerers began devising ways to place human beings in the skies. One great inventor, Leonardo Da Vinci, known more for his paintings than for his scientific work, made elaborate sketches of a machine that, had it flown, would have been the world's first helicopter.

The first human to fly may well have been a Brazilian of the early 1700s named Father Laurenco de Gusmao, who, so legend says, built and flew in a winged contraption that sailed through the air like a bird. The raw materials for such an invention—which has been handed down to us as the modern glider—consisted of cloth or thin animal skin, and wood or bone, all of which had certainly been around for centuries. So, although no conclusive evidence has been found to date, it is likely that Father Gusmao, or perhaps some other, earlier ingenious spirit, flew long before the Wright brothers.

Legend aside, and despite the centuries of drawings by would-be aviators, the earliest recorded human flight took place not with the aid of wings, but under a bag of hot air. A Frenchman by the name of J. F. Pilâtre de Rozier was lifted high above the earth on October 15, 1783, the first human balloonist. This was a good year all around for balloons: Within a few summer months, the world's first hot-air balloon, invented by brothers Joseph and Étienne Montgolfier, was introduced to a delighted horde of Parisians; and shortly thereafter a rival inventor, J. A. C. Charles, revealed his own balloon, this one lifted by hydrogen, a lighter-than-air gas Charles proved even more efficient than the Montgolfiers' hot-air method. Both demonstrations were unmanned. In September of that year, the Montgolfiers launched another balloon— this time for the benefit of Marie Antoinette and her husband, King Louis XVI— with the added thrill of live passengers: a sheep, a duck, and a rooster were placed in cages and lifted by a balloon, thus becoming the first known barnyard animals to fly without their own natural apparatus.

The advent of ballooning took the world by storm. Not only did balloons become the fashionable mode of transportation for adventures and sports, they were soon adapted to such uses as carrying mail and cargo—and to warfare. Balloons were the first bombers, dropping their deadly cargo as early as 1794, when the French used them against the Belgians at the Battle of Fleurus. The technology of balloons changed as fast as new uses

The first balloon constructed and flown in North America, by Peter Carnes of Bladensburg, Md., in June 1784. Courtesy National Aeronautics and Space Administration.

could be found for modifications. The most notable development was that of an enormous oblong balloon that was, as the French word that became its name implied, *dirigible*—steerable. The dirigible brought humans one step closer to being able to control our own flight; before balloonists had merely been sailors of the air, but with less control than a ship at sea; their contraptions lacked rudders or other apparatus that allowed change of direction (other than by tossing out ballast to gain greater lift). With the advent of the dirigible, the pilot could steer a course. But the size and dangers of such an enormous balloon made the dirigible impractical for small-scale travel, even if it was useful for bombing missions and other flights requiring a certain level of accuracy. Still, the greatest challenge—that of heavier-than-air, controlled,

powered flight, still lay ahead.

In many ways the balloon was a side trip on the road to modern aviation. As the nineteenth century came and went, ballooning continued to be a popular and useful pastime, but scientists and inventors had again set their sights higher. The problem of human-powered winged flight was back on the drawing board, and the developments in communications and other information technologies during the nineteenth century allowed thinkers and tinkerers around the world to share their discoveries with one another.

In 1890 a German took the stage for some of the most important early flight experiments: Otto Lilienthal had studied the flights of both birds and balloons, and his fascination led him to build a glider large enough to carry his own weight. He began experimenting with wind currents, glider designs, the physics of flight, and the problems of direction control. From 1891 to 1896 Lilienthal accomplished some 2,000 glider flights, many from a special conical platform he had built for his launches. He took copious notes, made careful studies, and published numerous works on his findings. But in 1896, like the mythical Icarus, Lilienthal fell to his death during one of his flights: a sudden gust of wind sent his glider plummeting earthward. The impact of the crash broke his back, ending his life a short time later.

Meanwhile, back in America, a whole spate of eager inventors had been closely watching Lilienthal as they created their own flying contraptions. Foremost among these early aviation engineers was Samuel P. Langley. The second director of the Smithsonian Institution and a renowned scientist, Langley took on the problem of flight in the late nineteenth century. He studied the contemporary body of knowledge and added to it with his own excursions into physics and engineering. In 1896 he published his landmark work *Experiments in Aerodynamics*, which two young brothers who ran a bicycle shop in Dayton, Ohio, received with glee in 1899, when they wrote to the Smithsonian asking for guidance in their own studies of aerodynamics.

Wilbur and Orville Wright had always been a creative, inventive team; even as youths they would take the gimcrack toys given them as gifts and tinker with them to improve design and function. They were born engineers. They developed their fascination for flight early on, when in 1878—Orville was seven and Wilbur eleven—their father gave them a propeller toy made of bamboo, paper, and cork. By 1895 they were feeding their adult curiosity with the studies of flight by Lilienthal and other investigators. By the turn of the century they were deeply engrossed in the writings of Langley, as

On December 17, 1903, this airplane, owned by Orville and Wilbur Wright, arose for a few seconds to make the first heavier-than-air flight in history. Courtesy National Aeronautics and Space Administration.

well as works such as *Progress in the Flying Machine* by the renowned engineer Octave Chanute. By now the Wrights' fascination had become an obsession, and their bicycle business became a workshop for airplanes.

But long before the Wrights made history above the sand dunes of North Carolina, they engaged in a rigorous study of the elements and physics of flight, learning about technologies such as a wind machine and the internal combustion engine in their quest to create the world's first heavier-than-air flying machine. Any number of their achievements would be proof of their genius, but certainly one of the greatest examples is the way (and speed) with which they acknowledged and then dispatched some of the key problems earlier scientists had failed to solve (much less identify). Through basic observations of birds in flight and a careful study of the existing aerodynamic body of knowledge, the Wrights developed the theory and practical application of wing warping and also designed and built functional propellers.

Eventually, after long hours of hard work and painstaking calculations, Wilbur and Orville Wright began building their airplanes. The first versions were, in reality, oversized kites built to test theories such as wing warping in an actual flight situation. The Wrights wrote to the National Weather Service, requesting information on the where they might find wind conditions suitable for their experiment; Kitty Hawk, North Carolina, was one of the answers. In 1900 the Wrights came to the beaches of Kitty Hawk, flying their giant kites from tethers and refining their engineering designs while living and working in a one-room wooden shack. Because of high winds or design flaws, not all of their experiments were successful; but for the next three years they returned again and again to Kitty Hawk, bringing with them improved kites and gliders to test and refine. By now they had completed successful manned flights of the kites and controlled manned glider flights; all that was left was the addition of power. In 1903 they completed work on the *Wright Flyer* that would carry them into the history books; it was similar to their gliders but featured propellers and a little combustion engine of their own making.

From September through December the Wrights made a series of failed flights. Some failures were because the winds were too strong; the craft was damaged several times. Other mishaps occurred because of minor design flaws. But December 17 was different. With little pomp albeit great circumstance, the Wrights brought their flyer to Kill Devil Hill, near Kitty Hawk. Orville climbed aboard the rickety-looking contraption, and at 10:35 a.m. the plane lifted off. For 12 seconds Orville managed to fly that wondrous machine. The flight went neither high nor far. But it did take place, thus at last heralding the age of flight.

A simple telegram to their father announcing the achievement of flight soon sent the news around the globe. Many greeted it with skepticism, largely because there had been so many earlier, false claims. And there were a few disappointed inventors—notably Samuel Langley himself, who, as recently as December 8, 1903—only nine days before the Wright brothers' success—had made an elaborate but failed attempt at powered flight. The fact that the Wrights spent a good deal of their time thereafter defending themselves against patent disputes and the angry denouncement of inventors who claimed to have flown first is testament to the number of participants in the largely secretive race for flight that had been taking place.

The twentieth century witnessed the birth and explosion of aviation technology, taking it from that simple little

Wright Flyer of 1903 (which now hangs proudly in the Smithsonian's National Air and Space Museum, along with other early artifacts such as an original Lilienthal glider) to the ultimate in aviation engineering: the space shuttle. And, in less than 75 years from the birth of the airplane, the greatest challenge of global flight was met in 1986 when Jeana Yeager and Dick Rutan flew nonstop around the world on a single tank of gas. During the decades between planes proved capable of dogfighting, surpassing the speed of sound, and dropping atomic bombs. And the space program took us to the moon.

And with this new technology came a new breed of hero and heroine, personified in the daring flights of legends such as Charles Lindbergh, Amelia Earhart, Chuck Yeager, Neil Armstrong, and Sally Ride. They created the myths of the twentieth century with their amazing feats of flight (and in Earhart's case, mysterious disappearance).

But the one thing shared by all kinds of aircraft and all breeds of aviator alike is the simple act of flight. It may have taken humans millions of years to breach that final barrier, but when we finally did the echoes of our ancestors could be heard in the roar of the engines, cheering us on into the open sky.

FLIGHTS OF FANCY: KITING

At one time or another all of us have been told by an exasperated friend to "go fly a kite." The assumption underneath the demand is that kite flying will keep a person busy for quite a while. And this is very true. Not only is kite flying a time-consuming activity but also it is an important scientific enterprise, recognized as responsible for many key discoveries and still not fully understood by the experts.

Kites have been around for a long time. Most historians agree that the first kites were flown in China about 3,000 years ago. Kites reached Europe around the fourteenth century through trade routes. As early as 196 B.C., kites were employed for scientific experiments. In that year General Han Hsin used kites to measure the distance his forces had to travel to reach the enemy's stronghold. Perhaps the most famous kite experimenter was Benjamin Franklin, who fearlessly used a kite to show that lightning is electricity. Scientists still marvel that he didn't get electrocuted in the process.

But it has been in the history of astronautics that kites have played the most dominant role. Orville and Wilbur Wright used box kites to test wing performance and adapted the principles they learned to the airplane. Alexander Graham Bell went on to construct enormous tetrahedral box kites that were strong enough to carry people.

Today's kites are far different from Franklin's model. Many are made of nearly indestructible ripstop nylon. They use ultralight graphite or boron components, and high-strength, ultra-thin line made of high-tech materials such as Kevlar and Spectra. There are kites big enough to pull water-skiers, and kites that can be joined together to do tricks in tandem; as of this writing, the record is 253 kites at once, held together on a single line. Stunt kiting has become a recreational sport, with regional and national contest—including individual and team events—held around the country.

What's more, kites have become big business. No longer the playthings of tots, they are being used as advertising vehicles, hawking every from cars to Coke.

All kites, from simple ones children enjoy to the complicated ones built by Bell, have five basic parts. The *flying line* keeps the kite in the wind. The *bridle* connects the main body of the kite to the flying line. The *spine* is the kite's main structure, and the *struts* are the supports that keep the kite open. The *frame* includes both the spine and the struts.

The shape of the kite will determine how effectively it soars through the air. Flat kites, probably the most common among hobbyists, come in diamond and

The annual kite festival sponsored by the Smithsonian Institution, held on the grounds of the Washington Monument in Washington, D.C., is a harbinger of spring in the Nation's Capital. Photo by Jeff Tinsley.

hexagonal shapes. They fly at low angles and need a tail. More sophisticated kites— eddy and bowed kites, delta kites, and the elegant fighter kite, to name a few—can be flown without tails. But no matter what kind of kite you are flying, the force of the wind against the kite's surface must be strong enough to carry it upward.

So now that it's clear that kite flying is a bit more complicated than you had thought, the next question is where to go if you are interested in flying a kite. The largest manufacturer of kites in the world is **Gayla Industries** (6401 Antoine St., P.O. Box 920800, Houston, TX 77292; 713-681-2411). It makes every kind of kite imaginable, from simple diamond kites to complex pterodactyl and shark three-dimensional kites. Prices begin at $4.35. Perhaps the company's most innovative

new product is the Skylab Kite kit, which is sold to both retail markets and educational institutions. The kit comes with two types of kites. The classic Diamond Eddy kite comes with an illustration of the Wright brothers' historic flight. The sled kite is printed with an illustration of the space shuttle. In assembling both kits one learns about the basic principles of aerodynamics, and has a good time. The retail model comes with twine and twine winders and sells for $49.20. The institutional model does not include twine and sells for $39.60. (The institutional model also comes with a lesson plan with additional activities.)

Here is a list of several other companies that manufacture kite-making supplies. Contact each company for a detailed catalog and price list.

Great Winds Kites
402 Occidental Ave.
South Seattle, WA 98134
206-624-6886

High Fly Kite Co.
30 West End Ave.
Haddonfield, NJ 08033
609-429-6260

Into the Wind
1729 Spruce St.
Boulder, CO 80302
303-449-5356

Kite Kompany
33 W. Orange
Chagrin Falls, OH 44022
216-247-4223

Kite Kraft
School Haus Sq.
Frankenmuth, MI 48734
517-652-2961

Kite Site
3101 M St. NW
Washington, DC 20007
202-965-4230

Kitty Hawk Kites
P.O. Box 340
Nags Head, NC 27959
919-441-4124

The Unique Place
525 S. Washington
Royal Oak, MI 48061
313-398-5900

Finally, for accessible, easy-to-read books about kite making, be sure to look for the many works of Wayne Hosking. One of the world's experts on kite making, Hosking writes books that even young children can understand and enjoy. The most comprehensive is *Flights of Imagination*, published by the **National Science Teachers Association** (1742 Connecticut Ave. NW, Washington, DC 20009; 202-328-5800). The book includes a simple discussion of aerodynamics as well as detailed instructions for assembling kites of all shapes and sizes. Discussion questions follow each activity. Price is $7 plus shipping costs.

FLIGHTS OF FANCY: BOOMERANGS

"Consider the boomerang," writes John Calderazzo in *Marathon World Magazine*, "a slim, crooked stick, sanded and polished to a shiny finish, it is all wing. Thrown overhand like a peg to second base, it flies end over end toward a distant line of trees, then curves, flattens out, spins, swoops, and all the while traces a serene and birdlike arc through the air. Riding the breeze back home, it slows, hovers for a moment above an outstretched hand, and drops gently down. Beautiful. At once a baseball, helicopter, glider, hawk, and feather, the boomerang seems the most complicated and the simplest of miracles—a flight of fancy come to life."

Most boomerang aficionados share Calderazzo's love for those two-armed (mostly) objects that can fly great distances and then find their way back to the starting point—all within seconds. Because of their elegance and efficiency of flight, boomerangs have garnered a small cult following that sponsors competitions and seeks to spread the word through the **United States Boomerang Association** (Box 182, Delaware, OH 43015). The USBA plays an important role in organizing the sport by regulating player rules at competitions and maintaining a player rating system.

So how do you play with this newly rediscovered object? That depends on whether you want to play alone or on a team, and whether you want to test your skill or your endurance. A common competition event is throwing for accuracy. The object of the stunt is to throw the boomerang and see if comes back to your feet. For that event you would probably use a standard "hook" boomerang, with a small angle between the two arms. To test distance competitors use a special boomerang called maximum time aloft. The world record for distance is 150 yards, the equivalent of one and a half football fields—quite an impressive length, especially when you realize that the boomerang must return to the thrower. Each of these events requires a boomerang of special design that conforms properly with principles of aerodynamics.

Other popular events include consecutive catching—seeing how many times you can throw and catch one or more boomerangs in five minutes (the record is 70)—and juggling two boomerangs in the air alternately, catching one seconds after the other leaves your hands. There are innumerable other catching feats, and all are played on a course arranged around a 50-meter circle, with bull's-eye-like circles of 20, 10, 8, 6, 4, and 2 meters also clearly marked. And all the events are played until the competitor drops the boomerang.

The USBA is the centerpiece of the sport and provides a variety of services for its $10 annual membership fee. In addition to the quarterly newsletter, *Many Happy Returns,* the USBA offers a wide array of information services. If you send a self-addressed envelope, a USBA representative will send you a listing of manufacturers and retailers, local clubs and organizations, and materials needed to make boomerangs. For $1 you can receive copies of USBA rules, rating systems, and bylaws. And for $2 you can receive a collection of boomerang catalogs and product information sheets.

There are between 20 and 30 boomerang manufacturers. Most are mail-order and have catalogs showing their wares. Overall, boomerangs range in price from about $3 for plastic ones to $30 for

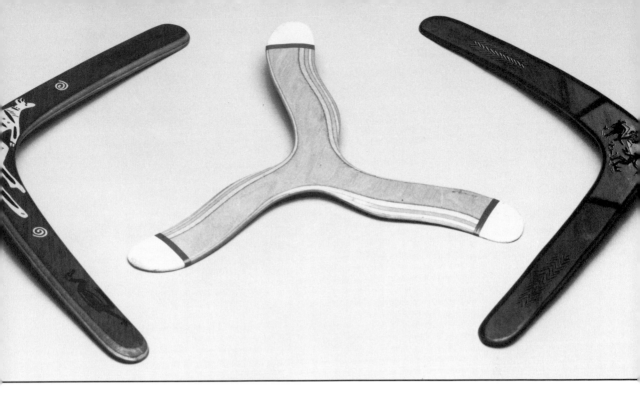

polished, sleek wood models. **Outback Boomerangs** (P.O. Box 25577, Portland, OR 97225; 513-292-4316) offers a wide range of wood boomerangs. The tri-blader ($15), a beginner's boomerang, travels well in 0-to-5-mile-per-hour breezes and can go as far as 27 yards. The Chinook ($18), which can move as fast as 25 miles per hour and go as far as 54 yards, is used mostly for competitions. Fast Catch II ($20) is very light and unforgiving when thrown hard: it starts to return within three seconds. Clearly, only a skilled player dare try to use this model.

Here is a list of other boomerang manufacturers and distributors. All the organizations listed have catalogs and price lists, free for the asking unless otherwise indicated. Because many of these distributors are individuals providing mail-order services, not all have listed telephone numbers.

American Boomerang Co.
33 S. 10th St.
Allentown, PA 18102
215-433-2200

BEMCO
3415 E. Skinner
Wichita, KS 67218
316-682-9535

Boomerang World
P.O. Box 187
Agawam, MA 01001 (catalog $1)

The Boomerang Man
1806 N. 3rd St.
Monroe, LA 71202
318-323-2356 or 323-8157

Boomerangs
c/o Col. John M. Gerrish
4885 S.W. 78th Ave.
Portland, OR 97225

The Cleveland Boomerang School
P.O. Box 17385
Euclid, OH 44117
216-442-6024

Colorado Boomerangs
204 N. Main
Gunnison, CO 81230
303-641-3539

Comeback Press
277 Barkley Pl. W
Columbus, OH 43213
614-868-8898

Ben Dehner Boomerangs
1128 Kearney
Atchison, KS 66002

Flying Trees Boomerangs
3804 Greenly St.
Wheaton, MD 20906

Koehlerangs
37 Dufief Ct.
Gaithersburg, MD 20878
301-340-1538

Leading Edge Boomerangs
51 Troy Rd.
Delaware, OH 43613
614-363-8332

MTA-Sticks
2967 Gracewood Rd.
Toledo, OH 43613
419-471-9989

M. J. O'Brien Inc.
P.O. Box 6091
Denver, CO 80206

Outback Boomerangs
P.O. Box 25577
Portland, OR 97225

Owl Boomerangs
1435 Burney Sq. N
Columbus, OH 43229
614-436-0219

Rangslinger
1414 Airline N
Rosharon, TX 77583

Rose City Boomerangs
2812 S.E. 37th Ave.
Portland, OR 97202
503-233-0836

Ruhe-Rangs
Box 21181, Kalorama Sta.
Washington, DC 20009
202-234-9208

Ruhf Boomerangs
P.O. Box 112
Emmaus, PA 18049
215-432-0724

Dan Russell
Box 84895
San Diego, CA 92138
619-296-4243

Stick Around Boomerangs
123 Cimarron St.
Richland, WA 99352
509-627-4914

Texas Boomerang Works
13410 Maxwell Rd.
Cypress, TX 77429

Turning Point
Star Rte.
South Strafford, VT 05070
802-765-4066

USBA Store
P.O. Box 2996
Newport News, VA 23602

USBA Video Archives
18 St. James Ave.
Easthampton, MA 01027
413-527-9956

Vor-Tec Sports
19323 Dalby
Detroit, MI 48240
313-534-2522

Steve Wood Boomerangs
9210 Central Ave. NW
Albuquerque, NM 07105.

The best book on boomerangs was written by Ben Ruhe. Called simply *Boomerang*, it offers a range of information: the history of boomerangs, how to throw them, where to learn more about them. The book reflects Ruhe's expertise as honorary consultant on 'rangs to the National Air and Space Museum and captain of the United States boomerang team, which has challenged —and beaten—the Australian team. To obtain a copy, send $6 to **Minner Press**, 1882 Columbia Rd. NW, Washington, DC 20009.

FLIGHTS OF FANCY: BALLOONING

"Up, up, and away," the song goes, and for good reason. Imagine ascending to the heavens in a finely woven basket, protected by a rainbow-colored gas-filled envelope that lifts you ever higher into the skies. What's more, this wonderful journey is in the fine tradition of Dorothy, who tried to leave Oz in a hot-air balloon, and of the brave folks from England who traveled partway around the world in 80 days in the comfort and luxury of a balloon.

Balloons have the distinction of being the first device used to carry people through the skies; balloons predate parachutes and the Wright brothers' first airplane ride from Kitty Hawk. After airplanes took hold, however, the passion for balloons deflated somewhat. But the sport was revived in the early 1960s with the development of synthetic materials and propane fuel systems. Today's hot-air balloons are made of nylon or Dacron and fueled by propane. Gas balloons are made of airtight material and are inflated with lighter-than-air gases, such as helium.

Most balloon envelopes range in size from 60,000 to 85,000 cubic feet and carry between two and ten people. The passengers have their work cut out for them, too; it takes almost that many people to help inflate, and launch, the balloon and prepare it for landing.

Right after sunrise or shortly before sunset (the safest times to fly), when the winds are blowing at 10 miles per hour or less, you might see a fleet of balloons gracefully gliding through the air. The wind dictates the balloon's direction, but by flying higher the pilot can promptly change the course of the trip. Although balloons usually travel at treetop level, they can go much higher—as proven by the world records of 53,000 feet for hot-air balloons and more than 90,000 feet for gas balloons.

Today there are 7,000 Federal Aviation Administration-licensed balloonists in the country, and 6,000 FAA-licensed hot-air balloons. For the safety and well-being of everyone, the government requires that balloon pilots pass a written test and log in at least 35 hours of flight time. Balloons also must be maintained according to FAA requirements. Many have been purchased for promotional or recreational purposes, by companies, from financial institutions to industrial manufacturers, amusement parks to hotels. Because the balloons are being used as advertising ploys, they tend to be wonderfully creative. They are as elaborate as the Spider Man balloon designed by comic-book publisher Marvel Entertainment Group, or as whimsical as Macy's Raggedy Ann doll.

But ordinary folks can get in on the action, too. There are several easy ways to get involved. You might pick up a copy of *Taming the Gentle Giant: A Guide to Hot Air Ballooning* ($15.95, from **Land O'Sky Aeronautics**, P.O. Box 636, Skyland, NC 28776; 704-684-2092), the only comprehensive book written for the fledgling pilot. The manual includes information about the design and construction of balloons, flight instruments, meteorology, and aviation weather forecasts. Amogene Norwood, the author, is co-owner of Land O'Sky Aeronautics (see their listing later in this section), one of the companies that will take you up in a balloon to feel for yourself the glory of floating.

If you find that your interest continues to soar, the next logical step would be to join the **Balloon Federation of America** (P.O. Box 400, Indianola, IA 50125; 515-961-8809), the national organization

for balloonists and balloon enthusiasts. Membership is open to any pilot, crew, or interested individual. Fees are $100 a year for corporate members, $30 a year for associate members, $36 a year for crew members, and $15 a year for students. Each new member receives a pin, patch, decal, and membership certificate. Other benefits include *Pilot News*, the monthly newsletter, which provides briefings on technical developments, and changes in FAA regulations, listings of competitive events, board meeting notes, and committee reports; *Ballooning*, the full-color, high-quality quarterly magazine, which includes feature articles by members, coverage of events, and full-color photographs that capture the beauty of the sport; seminars on fire safety, weather, crew techniques, and more; and borrowing privileges from the film-video and reference library.

The Balloon Federation of America works with the FAA to ensure the safe operation of balloons. The organization has ties to the National Aeronautic Association and supports the National Balloon Museum. (See "Aviation Museums.")

Like all serious hobbyists, balloonists love to gather and display their prized possessions. The major annual event for balloonists is the **Albuquerque International Balloon Fiesta**, held each year in New Mexico. This event is intended mostly for fun—there is little serious business accomplished—and features some notable balloons, with names such as *Air Force I* and *Tony the Tiger*. For more information, contact Albuquerque International Balloon Fiesta, 8309 Washington Pl. NE, Albuquerque, NM 87113; 505-821-1000.

Finally, if you want to take the big step of designing and buying your own balloon, there are several companies that specialize in just that. Be forewarned, though, balloons are very expensive: A moderately priced one begins at about $500 and can go much higher. Even if that price is a bit steep, it might be fun to browse a little. Here are few places to begin your search:

Aerostar International, Inc. (1813 E Ave., P.O. Box 5057, Sioux Falls, SD 57117; 605-331-3500), one of the oldest balloon companies around, has standard helium models that start at about $495. These fly best in light and moderate winds and hold up well. Custom helium shapes, which begin at $5,000, require very light winds. Aerostar has a long list of commercial clients and has designed an array of spectacular balloons, including a balloon shaped like the Liberty Bell and one with a map of the world printed on its massive envelope.

The Balloon Works (810 Salisbury Rd., Statesville, NC 28677; 704-878-9501) specializes in two systems. Dragonfly has a vertically woven carriage that is upholstered in dark brown suede. Its envelope is made of polyester and comes in 15 colors. Firefly, Balloon Works's top-of-the-line model, has a luxurious carriage; its envelope comes in 20 colors. Both come in different volumes and heights, some small enough for three to four people or large enough for nine. Prices range from $10,500 for a 56,000-cubic-foot Dragonfly to $18,000 for the deluxe model.

Cameron Balloons (P.O. Box 3672, Ann Arbor, MI 48106; 313-426-5525) manufactures a whole range of balloons, including the Sport, which is perfect for beginners. Cameron also makes unique shapes for companies (Mickey Mouse, for example)

Left: Courtesy Albuquerque International Balloon Fiesta. Photo by Thomas McConnell.

and has deluxe models for more experienced pilots. Prices range from $13,200 for the Sport balloon to nearly $20,000 for a top-of-the-line model.

Galaxy Balloons (820 Salisbury Rd., Statesville, NC 28677; 704-878-9147), a subsidiary of The Balloon Works, offers the Galaxy 7 balloon with two different-sized carriages. The balloons come in ten colors and can carry up to 1,300 pounds. Prices range from $10,000 to $24,000.

Land O'Sky Aeronautics, Inc. (P.O. Box 636, Skyland, NC 28776; 704-684-2092) wears two different hats: it sells balloons, but it also offers hour-long recreation flights. Trips are either in the early morning or at sunset. Flights provide a wonderful opportunity to take aerial photographs. After landing in a beautiful green meadow, the group returns to the "balloonport," where they share a bottle of champagne. Cost is $100 per person.

Children must be 6 or older. Land O'Sky sells balloons from The Balloon Works, but they are much more expensive than they are if you buy them direct from the manufacturer. Land O'Sky balloons cost $10,000—or more. One more feature of this company: flight instruction, using the company's balloons and equipment, is available for $150 an hour.

Southwest Balloon Adventures (3815 Academy Pkwy. North NE, Albuquerque, NM 87109; 505-345-2521) sells pins and patches for those who like ballooning in theory more than in practice. It has pins shaped like unicorns, Icarus, dragons, pumpkins, cars, and the planets. Patches, shaped like fantastic balloons, include those with sayings such as "I love ballooning" and "Follow your dreams," and one of the father of it all, Montgolfier. Prices range from $3.50 each for a group of 11 to $1.35 each for quantities of 500 or more. Send for a free catalog.

Flights of Fancy:
Skydiving, Soaring, and Hang Gliding

"To fly like the birds" has always been one of the great human quests. And we *have* learned to fly, thanks primarily to a wide range of technology. But what about the way birds *really* fly—with no sound save the wind? Here are three ways to do that.

Skydiving

Skydiving is a euphemism for falling through the air with nothing more than a piece of nylon as protection against the elements—in this case, the hard ground below. For many the prospect of flinging oneself from an airplane is terrifying. For a few it is the thrill of a lifetime, an exhilarating way to experience sheer freedom.

If this sport turns you on, where's a good place to begin exploring it? Probably the best is the **United States Parachute Association** (1440 Duke St., Alexandria, VA 22314; 703-836-3495). A division of the National Aeronautic Association, USPA promotes safety standards for skydivers; issues licenses, ratings, and awards; and sponsors national competitions. Membership costs $32.50 a year and includes the organization's monthly magazine, *Parachutist*; eligibility in USPA-sanctioned competitions; and eligibility for membership in USPA-affiliated clubs. For an additional $3.50, members receive copies of the USPA list of skydiving centers throughout the country.

One of those many schools, **Sky Dance Sky Diving** (Rte. 2, Box 2410-A, Yolo County Airport, Davis, CA 95616; 800-752-3262; 916-753-2651) offers an innovative way to teach the sport: tandem skydiving, or the buddy system in the air. Harnessed together, student and teacher make the big leap. Using this system, ground training is limited to only 20 minutes. Price for the skydive is $135;

rates for more advanced training range from $150 for each level of training to a package deal of $1,030 for all eight levels.

To get the supplies you need for skydiving, try either of these distributors:

National Parachute Industries (P.O. Box 1000, 47 E. Main St., Flemington, NJ 08822; 800-526-5946; 201-782-1646) sells parachutes of different sizes, ranging in price from $755 to $1,225. This company also offers the full range of parachute paraphernalia, including items sold specifically to the military. Check the free catalog for details.

Para-Gear Equipment Co. (3839 Oakton St., Skokie, IL 60076; 800-323-0437; 312-679-5905) offers a wide selection of parachutes for people weighing between 93 and 274 pounds. Prices range from $828 to $1,028. Other offerings in the free catalog include tandems (ranging between $525 and $640); helmets ($30 to $40); pilot chutes ($30 to $46); and aeronautical instruments ($100 to $130). On the more whimsical side of things, the catalog also includes T-shirts ($8), bumper stickers ($1), and decals ($2.75 to $4) especially designed for skydivers.

Soaring

Imagine gliding through the air in a motorless vehicle, effortlessly exploiting the power of the wind and the sun. That's what soaring is all about, and, according to some, it's flying the way nature intended it. Today the hobby has quite a following: there are 20,000 licensed glider pilots in the United States, more than 180 soaring clubs, and more than 150 commercial gliderports and soaring supply businesses.

Hang gliding over the hills of southern California. Photo by John Heiney.

The backbone of the sport is the **Soaring Society of America** (P.O. Box E, Hobbs, NM 88240; 505-392-1177), which oversees state and national records and awards soaring proficiency badges. For the $35 membership fee, participants receive *Soaring*, the official journal for avid soarers; special rates for workshops and seminars; the *SSA Membership Handbook*; and the *Directory of U.S. Soaring Sites and Organizations*, a state-by-state guide to all soaring clubs, schools, and gliderports. The SSA also manages the National Soaring Museum, the official repository for all motorless flight memorabilia and artifacts. The museum has the largest exhibit of classic and contemporary sailplanes in the world (See "Aviation Museums").

For those who want to invest in the thrill of soaring without the expense, there are companies that give rides. Here are two; contact them for information:

Harris Hill Soaring Corporation
R.D. 3
Elmira, NY 14903
607-734-3128

Soaring Adventures of America
Box 541, Wilton Ctr.
Wilton, CT 06897
800-762-7464; 203-762-9583

HANG GLIDING

Hang gliding is one of the oldest forms of flying, invented by Otto Lilienthal in the late nineteenth century. Flying close to the clouds, most experts of this craft speak of the freedom they feel and the release gliding offers from the tensions of everyday life.

The **United States Hang Gliding Association** (USHGA, P.O. Box 500,

Pearblossom, CA 93553; 805-944-5333) monitors the sport and stresses that its main mission is to promote and perfect flying systems launched and flown by human power alone. The organization also charters hang-gliding clubs across the country, sanctions hang-gliding competitions, certifies official national and world records for hang gliding, and certifies instructors. The membership fee is $39 in the United States ($42 elsewhere) and includes the monthly magazine *Hang Gliding*.

There are several schools throughout the country that give hang-gliding lessons at reasonable prices. Here is a list of a few that are USHGA certified. Contact them directly for more information about products and services.

Arizona Windsports
1114 W. Cornell Dr.
Tempe, AZ 85283
602-897-7121

Colorado Hang Gliding
P.O. Box 1423
Golden, CO 80402
303-278-9566

Fly High Hang Gliding
R.D. 2, Box 561
Pine Bush, NY 12566
914-744-3317

Freedom Wings
9173 Falcon Cir.
Sandy, UT 84092
801-943-1005 or 801-561-5708

Hang Flight Systems
1202 E. Walnut, Unit M
Santa Ana, CA 92701
714-542-7444

Mission Soaring Center
1116 Wrigley Way
Milpitas, CA 95035
408-262-1055

One good source of information: **Sport Aviation Publications** (Dept. R, P.O. Box 601, State College, PA 16801; 814-383-2569) offers a series of books about hang gliding. Written by Dennis Pagan, author of the *USHGA Instructors Manual*, the books are considered standard texts on hang gliding. Prices are $8.95 for *Hang Gliding Flying Skills* and $6.95 for *Hang Gliding Techniques*.

MODEL AIRPLANES AND ROCKETS

Are you a model citizen? No, not the type who votes in every election and keeps the lawn neatly trimmed. We're talking about model aircraft builders, the happy craftspeople who build, and sometimes fly, their own miniature airplanes, rockets, or gliders.

Model builders seem to fall into three categories. The first type does not consider model building a hobby. For them it is serious business. These are the people who build scale models during the planning stages of a larger project, such as an airplane or a rocket. They are often engineers who plan to test the model in a wind tunnel, or feel it's important to have a good look at the design before putting a craft into production.

The second type of model builder is part hobbyist and part historian. These people enjoy building detailed scale models of plastic, not for testing but to preserve a piece of history as art and as a learning tool for future generations. They range from the kid with a snap-together kit to the skilled craftspeople who combine epoxy resins, Fiberglas, polyfoam, and sheet materials into museum-quality replicas. To them, the building of a model is a reward unto itself.

The third type of modeler may also strive for historical accuracy but usually wants to do something with the model after it's built. Rather than just set them on a shelf, these folks like to play with their creations. They may take their models out and fly them. They may end up crashing their planes or rockets, but they're willing to take that chance. After all, they reason, if they built it once they can always take the wrecked plane home and build it again.

If flight simulation in front of a computer isn't exciting enough for you (see "Flight Simulators"), this third category of model building may be your cup of tea. Flying a model is about as close as you can get to flying a real plane without actually strapping on a seat belt and yelling "Contact!"

Propulsion for these small aircraft usually comes from a single-cylinder engine than burns an alcohol-based fuel. The models are often controlled by a radio transmitter, which can send instructions (on over a dozen frequencies) to control flaps, speed, landing gear, and more. Other people build models that are propelled by rubber bands, carbon dioxide, or electric motors.

Be aware, however, that it takes a good deal of open space to fly a model plane: several hundred feet in every direction, along with a smooth landing area. And modelers also need to check local regulations about flying models in their area. Not only can these flying toys be a hazard to commercial air traffic but their use may be against the law in some neighborhoods. That's because some compact engines generate enough noise to sound a bit like a flying chain saw.

Because some of these models can weigh as much as a small person, it's also a good idea for flyers to carry some sort of insurance, in case a model plane comes down in the wrong place—like through someone's roof or window.

But in spite of these safety matters, if you have the time to build a model, and the unrestricted space in which to fly it, model airplane flying or rocket launching can be a very rewarding hobby. And you're sure to attract a crowd of kids—old and young—wherever you go. Keep in mind that even Neil Armstrong started out this way: He was a model airplane flyer in the 1940s.

Two modified deHaviland "Chipmunks." Courtesy Academy of Model Aeronautics.

Here are some of the more popular model aircraft companies. Others can be found in model airplane magazines; see "Read All About It" (page 207):

Aerodrome Models, Ltd. (2623 S. Miller Rd., Saginaw, MI 48603; 517-781-3000) offers hand-cut, prepackaged kits that are designed and manufactured at the company's headquarters. The company takes pride in making assembly easy for the "Sunday flyer," which means each piece is stamped with an identification number. Besides the kits, Aerodrome also sells sections of planes or individual parts for replacement from crash damage. Popular models include the Curtiss Jenny biplane (RC 110; $139), the Jester, an easy-to-

build trainer (RC 109; $69), and the Baby-Pacer ($59), a scaled-down version of the Aero-Pacer ($98), which weighs less than 4 pounds and has a 50-inch wingspan. Engines must be ordered separately.

Byron Originals (P.O. Box 279, Ida Grove, IA 51445; 612-364-3165) offers a 92-page catalog that's full of information and parts for model airplane building. Choose from simple-assembly plastic models such as the F6F-3 Hellcat, which snaps together in minutes, or any number of complex balsa-wood models that take a craftsperson's touch to put together. The catalog will give you hints on which planes are best for training, stunt flying, and other feats. You can get a basic model

PAPER AIRPLANES

Most of us probably remember paper airplanes as those primitive objects we constructed out of thin white paper during boring classes to be used as weapons against friends, foes, or a defenseless teacher. After serving their purpose, most of them found their way to the nearest trash can. But like just about everything else, making paper airplanes can be an art, practiced avidly by a handful of hobbyists. Two big manufacturing companies—AG Industries and Paper Airplanes International—sell sophisticated kits to mail order houses, museum gift shops, and specialty shops catering to the needs of this clientele.

AG Industries, Inc. (3832 148th Ave. NE, Redmond, WA 98052; 206-885-4599) sells a 15-model kit featuring Whitewings, its own model airplane. The kit comes with an instruction manual that describes in glorious detail how to make realistic replicas of airplanes. It sells for $15. Every two years AG Indus-

tries sponsors a World Paper Airplane Contest in Seattle. Participants must design, build, and ship a plane that can be made only of paper and adhesive. Instructions for flying the plane must be included. Categories judged include distance, time aloft, stunt, and aesthetics. You can buy a book describing the second contest, aptly called *Second International Airplane Contest*, for $10.

Paper Airplanes International (1521 Morningside Dr., Burbank, CA 91506; 818-842-3455 or 213-822-9185) has a catalog with more than a thousand planes to choose from. It offers paper planes that are solar- or rubber-powered, gliders, rockets, and planes created from origami, the Japanese paper-folding art. Some planes have wingspans as wide as 6 feet. Try your hand at modeling Boeing 727 airliners, a U.S. Air Force F100 Super Sabre, spacecraft, and helicopters. The catalog is $7.50; its cost may be applied to your first order over $25. Prices vary, from $4.50 on up.

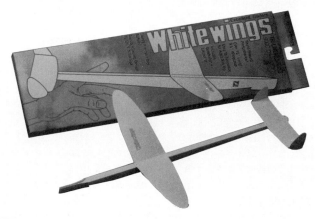

Four radio-controlled aerobatic airplanes. Courtesy Academy of Model Aeronautics.

for around $300, plus a few dollars for extra propellers, fuel pumps, decals, and the like. A look at the Byron price list shows that a serious modeler can spend well over $1,000 on a good model plane. Byron also has its own "International Airport" in Ida Grove, where it sponsors air shows.

Cleveland Model & Supply Co./Cleveland Designed Models (10307 Detroit Ave., Cleveland, OH 44102; 216-961-3600), founded in 1919, has attracted the interest of the Smithsonian Institution for its work in preserving the art of precisely detailed model building. The head of the company, octogenarian Edward Packard, crams every square inch of his newsletter with information about model building and the history of his company. The company specializes in scale plans for historic planes. You can order detailed plans for a 1916 Sopwith Camel, a 1928 Boeing Mail Plane, or a 1947 Bell X1, the first supersonic jet. Over 100 sets of plans are available, at prices from $4 to about $50; most are under $20. A price list is available for $1; a catalog (including price list) costs $2.

Carl Goldberg Models, Inc. (4734 W. Chicago Ave., Chicago, IL 60651; 312-626-9550) sells easy-to-build models with full-size plans. Popular models include the Eagle 63 and Eaglet 50 "sport trainer," which are great for both learning and accomplishing difficult maneuvers. Prices range from $49 to $159 for basic airplanes. Accessories such as landing gear and controllers are extra. Goldberg also has a good supply of adhesives, striping tapes, and covering materials.

Lone Star Models (1623 57th St., Lubbock, TX 79412; 806-745-6394) offers bulk balsa wood at rock-bottom prices. You can order tapered sheets, 36-by-36-inch sheets, planks, sticks, and special bulk-bundle deals. Prices range from a few cents for small pieces to $10.35 for a large bundle. Lone Star also keeps a good supply of hardware, such as special screw nuts, nylon snap links, and straps. Check out their Fiberglas, steel cables, propellers, glue, and spark plugs.

If you find that you are becoming very serious about model airplane building, you might consider joining the **Academy of Model Aeronautics**, a subsidiary of the National Aeronautics Association (1810 Samuel Morse Dr., Reston, VA 22090; 703-435-0750). The group has more than 2,000 charter clubs across the country. It sponsors model competitions, has an annual week-long National Model Airplane Championship meet, and works with the Federal Communications Commission, local governments, and zoning commissions to promote safe model flying. It also publishes a slick, colorful monthly magazine to keep members up to date on club news, new products, noise-abatement techniques, and local club doings. Single copies of the magazine are $1.75. Subscriptions are $18 a year for non-members and $9 for members (as part of membership dues). Special-rate insurance is also available from the organization. Membership is $40 for a full, open membership, including insurance and a magazine subscription; $36 for an open limited membership, which is the same as an open membership but includes only the "AMA News" section of the monthly magazine; and $21 for senior citizens. Family and partial-year rates are also available.

Aviation Libraries and Archives

The history of aviation has left a paper trail that anyone with a bit of time and a lot of fascination can trace, using the libraries, archives, and research collections around the country. Imagine the breadth of the story of flight and the volume of records it produced soon becomes apparent—the rudimentary drawings and engineering blueprints left by early designers, the official military reports filed by flying aces and transport captains alike, the flight logs, journals, diaries, letters, and all the other ephemera surrounding, supporting, and recalling the history of aviation. Libraries and archives become the repositories not only for these materials but also for the wealth of technical manuals, training records, historical treatises, and other published reference and research works related to aviation.

There are some libraries and archives, such as the extensive collection affiliated with the National Air and Space Museum, that are utterly devoted to the preservation of materials on the whole history of aviation and aerospace technology; but there are other, less well-known collections that concentrate on a single aspect of flying, or on the personalities and cultural influences that helped build the aviation industry. Most aviation museums (see the section on these) have affiliated research facilities, although use of their materials is often restricted to official personnel or authorized researchers. Nevertheless, there are enough libraries and archives for everyone—and, given the vast amount of literature on the subject, a good public or university library is as good a place as any to seek out general research materials. Many have computer terminals that can be connected to on-line information services such as Dialog and NEXIS. In addition, many libraries are depositories of the publications and documents of the federal government, including materials from the FAA, NASA, and the air force.

For those looking for the "real" things—rare records, letters, and so on, or the most complete set of aviation reference materials available—the Library of Congress and the National Archives in Washington, D.C. are the obvious places to begin. These repositories of practically all knowledge have such a wealth of materials on every conceivable topic (including aviation) that it would probably take a researcher years just to read all the literature preserved in them.

For those seeking a happy median between a general library and the voluminous holdings in Washington, there are a number of good aviation history collections around the country; some, especially those held by universities, are readily accessible to the general public. Others, including those at military research centers, and in the offices of aviation industry associations, are often harder to gain access to, although many will provide research services or allow limited access to some researchers.

Whether you're researching a high school term paper on aerodynamics or a biographical treatise on great flying aces, the written record of aviation history is there for the studying. Listed here are a sampling of the libraries, archives, and other collections where the history of flight is a specialty. Although some institutions indicate they are available for use only by members or related professionals, many will make exceptions for serious, qualified researchers.

B-29 Super Fortress. Photo by Nancy Engebretson. Courtesy Pima Air Museum.

Aeronautical Library (101 Guggenheim, California Institute of Technology, Pasadena, CA 91125; 818-356-6811). This academic library is a major resource center for the aerospace industry. It has a vast collection of technical books and journals.

Air Force Association Research Library (1750 Pennsylvania Ave. NW, Washington, DC 20006; 202-637-3300). This relatively small association library holds approximately 2,000 volumes on the history of military aviation. Open to qualified researchers.

Air Force, Office of Air Force History Library (Bldg. 5681, Bolling AFB, Washington, DC 20332; 202-767-5089). This office maintains the historical records of the air force, along with related publications and materials. Use of the library is limited to those with prior permission, but the staff will perform research services within reason.

Air Force, Office of Scientific Research Library (Bldg. 410, Bolling AFB, Washington, DC 20332; 202-767-4910). This branch of the air force is devoted to research and development; its library has approximately 16,000 volumes (including periodicals and other bound publications) on scientific matters related to aviation technology, including aeronautics, physics, astronomy, astronomics, solid-state science, and other fields. Online services: Dialog and DTIC. Closed to the public, except by prior arrangement.

Air Line Pilots Association Engineering and Air Safety Resource Center (535 Herndon Pkwy., Herndon, VA 22070; 703-689-4204). This association's technical library maintains a collection on aviation safety and related topics. Multimedia holdings include films, audio- and video-tapes, and slides. Open only to association members and support staff.

Air Transport Association of America Library (1709 New York Ave. NW, Washington, DC 20006; 202-626-4184, ext. 4185). This large association museum has approximately 14,000 volumes, as well as most periodicals, journals, and other publications related to the air transportation industry. The collection also includes statistical and technical reports and a complete set of the *Official Airlines Guides*, dating back to 1929. Online service: Westlaw. Open to the public, by appointment.

American Heritage Center (University of Wyoming, P.O. Box 3924, Laramie, WY 82071; 307-766-4114). This academic center has extensive collections on

There are many different aviation magazines, many of them published under the auspices of organizations; see "Aviation Organizations." But there are enough other aviation-related publications to fulfill any enthusiast's interest. Rates shown are for an annual subscription unless otherwise indicated.

❏ *Air Combat* (Challenge Publications, 7950 Deering Ave., Canoga Park, CA 91304; 818-887-0550). 9 times/year. $23.50 U.S., $28.50 elsewhere.

❏ *Air Progress* (Challenge Publications, 7950 Deering Ave., Canoga Park, CA 91304; 818-887-0550). Monthly. $26.50 U.S., $32.50 elsewhere.

❏ *Airpower* (Sentry Books Inc., 10718 White Oak Ave., Granada Hills, CA 91344; 818-368-2012). Bimonthly. $15.

❏ *Aviation Week & Space Technology* (McGraw-Hill, 1221 Avenue of the Americas, New York, NY 10020; 212-512-2000). Weekly. $64 for people in aviation, $80 for others.

❏ *Flying* (CBS Magazines, One Park Ave., New York, NY 10016; 212-503-4200). Monthly. $18.98 U.S. and Canada, $23.98 elsewhere.

❏ *Flying Models*, (Carstens Publications, P.O. Box 700, Newton, NJ 07860; 201-383-3355). Monthly. $21 U.S., $25 elsewhere.

❏ *Kitplanes*, (Fancy Publications Inc., 3 Burroughs, Irvine, CA 02718; 714-855-8822). Monthly. $24 U.S., $32 elsewhere.

❏ *Model Airplane* (Air Age Inc., 251 Danbury Rd., Wilton, CT 06897; 203-834-2900). Monthly. $25.

❏ *Plane & Pilot* (Werner Publishing Corp., 16000 Ventura Blvd., Ste. 800, Encino, CA 01436; 818-986-8400). Monthly. $16.95 U.S., $23.95 elsewhere.

❏ *Private Pilot* (Fancy Publications Inc., 3 Burroughs, Irvine, CA 02718; 714-855-8822). Monthly. $21.97 U.S., $29.97 elsewhere.

❏ *Sport Pilot's Hot Kits* (Challenge Publications, 7950 Deering Ave., Canoga Park, CA 91304; 818-887-0550). Monthly. $31.50 U.S., $37.50 elsewhere.

aircraft and aviation history, with less extensive collections on aeronautics and space.

American Institute of Aeronautics and Astronautics Library (555 W. 57th St., New York, NY 10019; 212-247-6500). This library, part of the association's Technical Information Service, contains one of the world's largest private collections of aerospace materials. It also has an extensive data base of technical abstracts from NASA and other sources. For use by members only.

A 1922 parasol wing Farman Sport. Photo by Dale Hrabak. Courtesy World War I Aeroplanes and National Air and Space Musuem.

James Carruthers Aviation Collection (Norman F. Sprague Memorial Library, Claremont, CA 91711; 714-621-8000). This collection, housed at the library on the Harvey Mudd College campus, was donated to Claremont-McKenna College in 1950. It now includes approximately 3,500 volumes, with an emphasis on World War I aviation, notably as it was reported in American, British, French, and Italian publications. Other specialties include materials on the history of ballooning and a collection of children's literature on aviation. Open to scholars and researchers.

Department of Transportation, Aviation Reference Room (400 7th St. SW, Rm. 4125, Washington, DC 20590; 202-426-7888). This reference room maintains a collection of all board orders and reports, as well as some technical, statistical, financial, and other records filed by commercial airlines and air carriers. Open to the public.

Department of Transportation FAA Legal Library (800 Independence Ave. SW, Washington, DC 20591; 202-426-3604). This library maintains a collection of specifications, findings, and other legal documents and materials produced by the Federal Aviation Administration. Some of these materials can also be found at regional depository libraries and other federal depository libraries, including many public and university libraries. Materials in the library may be examined by the public, although the facility is primarily for the use of department employees.

History of Aviation Collection (University of Texas at Dallas, P.O. Box 643, Richardson, TX 75080; 214-690-2996). This extensive collection on the history of aviation is internationally recognized for its scope and diversity. Officially established in 1963, the collection includes a library, archive, and the Business Aviation Historical Collection, which preserves the contributions aviation has made to industry. Aviation artifacts are also displayed. The library includes 20,000 volumes, 200,000 journals, and 250,000 photographs, as well as thousands of audiovisual and technical reference materials. Special collections of materials on famed aviators include items relating to the flights and lives of the Wright brothers, Charles Lindbergh, Amelia Earhart, Santos Dumont, and other great flyers. Open to the public.

Library of Congress, Manuscript Division (Library of Congress, James Madison Bldg., Rm. 102, Washington, DC 20540; 202-287-5383). This division holds various collections of manuscripts and other documents totaling more than 35 million pieces, including many items related to the history of aviation. Materials may be studied by the public under the supervision of an attendant in the adjacent reading room.

Library of Congress, Science and Technology Division (Library of Congress, John Adams Bldg., 5th fl., Science Reading Rm., Washington, DC 20540; 202-287-5639). This division maintains the library's extensive collection of general reference materials on science and tech-

nology, including those on aviation and related sciences. It also has microfilms of the records of government scientific organizations, including those of the Atomic Energy Commission, NASA, and others. Open to the public, although some materials may require supervision by an attendant.

Library of the Ninety-Nines (Will Rogers Airport, P.O. Box 59965, Oklahoma City, OK 73159; 405-685-7969). This limited library has about 600 volumes dealing with women in aviation. It also holds the archives of the Ninety-Nines and the records of the Powder Puff Derby, the most famous women's air race.

National Air and Space Museum Branch Library (7th St. & Independence Ave. SW, Rm. 3100, Washington, DC 20560; 202-357-3133). The quintessential aviation museum has an exhaustive collection of reference materials on the history of flight and space exploration. The library holds

Flight deck of Howard Hughes' H-4 Flying Boat, *later named the "*Spruce Goose.*" Inset: Hughes at the cockpit prior to the plane's first and only flight.*

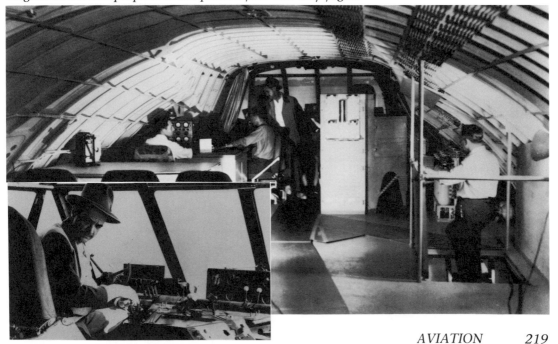

B-25 North American Mitchell fighter. Courtesy Canadian Warplane Heritage Museum.

35,000 volumes, 7,000 bound journals, and an extensive microform collection of other publications and technical materials. Special features include William A. Burden's collection of early works on ballooning, autographed first editions of classic aviation works, and the aerodromic workbooks of the Wright brothers and Charles Lindbergh. Collections of children's literature, multimedia materials, and other educational materials are also held. Open to the public.

National Archives and Records Administration (8th St. & Pennsylvania Ave. NW, Washington, DC 20408; 202-523-3286). This is the central repository for all documents of the federal government, including those by its aviation-related agencies (including NASA). The archives also holds voluminous collections of personal papers, business records, and so on of thousands of famous Ameri-cans, industries, and other organizations, including many in the aviation field. Open to the public, although access to some material is restricted.

Naval Aviation History Office (Washington Naval Yard, Washington DC 20374; 202-433-2005). This historical center has studied and preserved the history of U.S. naval aviation since it was first established in 1942. The office maintains naval aviation records and other related papers, and produces monographs on aspects of naval aviation such as naval aviation training, pistons to jets, and the U.S. Naval Air Reserve. The majority of records available to the public through this office cover the unit history reports for aviation commands from June 1957 to the present.

New York Public Library, Science and Technology Research Center (5th Ave. & 42nd St., New York, NY 10018; 212-930-

0573). The New York Public Library has an extensive aviation and astronomy collection, with emphasis on military aviation of World Wars I and II.

Ross-Barrett Historical Aeronautics Collection (Denver Public Library, Special Collections, 1357 Broadway, Denver, CO 80203; 303-571-2010). This special collection of materials on the history of aeronautics concentrates more on the social and cultural aspects of the field than on the military (the collection stopped gathering materials on post-World War II aeronautics in 1975). It includes approximately 12,200 books, 950 volumes of bound periodicals, 600 photographs and prints, 12 linear feet of manuscripts, 50 films, and 100 World War I and II posters. Fiction, poetry, and other humanities materials relating to aviation are included in this eclectic collection, as are materials on topics as diverse as paper and model airplane building, kites, and space medicine. Open to the public, with some restrictions.

Schlesinger Library on the History of Women in America (Radcliffe College, 10 Garden St., Cambridge, MA 02138; 617-495-8647). This library of historical materials on American women includes special collections on famous individuals. Amelia Earhart is well represented with archival and published materials, as are a few other female aviators. Open to the public.

Technical Libraries of Boeing Aircraft Co. (Box 3707, MS 74-60, Seattle, WA 98124; 206-237-8314). Boeing has a collection of 73,000 books, 18,000 bound periodicals, and 150,000 reports dealing with aeronautics and astronautics. Boeing also holds collections of thousands of photos and a million microfilmed reports.

United States Air Force Historical Research Center (Maxwell AFB, AL 36112; 205-293-5958). Maxwell Air Force Base holds some 3 million documents, including air force histories. This collection is considered the basic source for air force history.

United States Air Force Museum Research Division Library (Bldg. 489, Area B, Wright-Patterson AFB, OH 45433; 513-255-3284). This air force collection has some 200,000 documents, manuscripts, and technical papers covering the history and technology of the air force.

Aviation Museums

Trying to capture the history of aviation in a museum is a bit like collecting butterflies: You can net and mount all the rare species in the world, but those who look through your collection with polite "oohs" and "ahhs" will never sense the grace these creatures possessed as they glided through the air. This aesthetic problem of how to make display imitate the life of the objects exhibited is inherent to the concept of aviation museums: How do you turn a building filled with machines into an experience that conjures up the exhilarating feeling of flight, the wondrous ingenuity of technology, and the still-reverberating echoes of history?

One way is to fly above the flock of science and technology museums, leading the way in exhibition designs, interactive displays, and delightful galleries illustrating thematic concepts. Given the seeming similarity of the subject matter, it is quite amazing that there are probably more diverse museums devoted to the history of flight than there are to any other accomplishment of humankind. But the sheer versatility of the history of flight lends itself to an expansive creativity that can be found in the variety and vastness of collections across the United States and in Canada.

Certainly one of the biggest problems any would-be aviation museum faces is size—the sheer acreage and tonnage of a collection of aircraft, even a small one, requires a facility of enormous proportions. The soaring, sunlight-filled exhibition halls of the National Air and Space Museum in Washington, D.C., are a perfect example

of the ways in which enclosed aviation museums have benefited from the challenges of size, which dictate an architectural environment on a scale with their collections. For many museums with fewer resources than the Smithsonian, the size problem has been addressed by an organic solution that actually adds to the vitality of the museum-going experience: airports, military aviation bases, and old airfields are often used as exhibit spaces. Thus, rather than being made to conform to the tradition of indoor display favored by most museums, the holdings of many aviation collections are shown in their natural settings.

Such disarming museums can be found in all climates and regions, from Mesa, Arizona's Champlin Fighter Museum to the Old Rhinebeck Aerodrome in New York. There are even some exhibitors who have taken the idea of organics a step further, by making a museum out of the artifact itself: the USS *Intrepid*, a battle-tested aircraft carrier that has been turned into a floating museum, docked at the edge of Manhattan in the Hudson River. And, in the case of Kill Devil Hill, North Carolina, the site of the Wright brothers' historic feat, the location itself has been preserved as a memorial to that event.

Variations on the theme of display are only the tip of the nose cone when it comes to the ways aviation collections differ from one another. They do in fact come in all shades and plumages. For flight fans turned on by propellers, museums such as the Reynolds Aviation Museum in Wetaskiwin, Alberta, and the New England Air Museum in Windsor Locks, Connecticut, sport collections devoted to antique planes; those who

AIR SHOWS

Part of the aircraft camping area at the EAA Oshkosh '88 air show. Photo by Jeffrey Isom. EAA photo by Jim Koepnick.

Imagine the sky teeming with planes, from refurbished Confederate aircraft to tottering homebuilts, B-29s to the elegant Concorde. This is the scene each year at the **Experimental Aircraft Association (EAA) Fly-in** held at Wittman Airfield in Oshkosh, Wisconsin. Pilots literally fly in from all over the country to have their planes judged in a variety of categories. But all planes must be flown to and from Oshkosh, and each must reflect the era from which it came. What's valued the most at Oshkosh is a plane that does what it was built to do well.

During fly-in week, participants have a chance to view some exceptional planes that once cruised the skies. Such notables include the Federal Aviation Administration's DC-

3 aircraft, known as N-34, which performed inspection flights across the country between 1945 and 1985. And you can witness some renowned aircraft swooping down, such as the Concorde, British Airways' supersonic jet that flies at twice the speed of sound, and the Goodyear blimp, an airship that remains a colorful link to aviation's past.

The Oshkosh event is held every year in the summer, usually in late July or early August. For more information about aviation's biggest fly-in, contact EAA, Wittman Airfield, Oshkosh, WI 54903; 414-426-4800.

Although the Oshkosh event is
(continued on next page)

(continued from previous page)
the biggest and most famous in the country, there are many others. One newer show is one sponsored by **Air/Space America** (6110 Friars Rd., Ste. 204, San Diego, CA 92108; 619-293-3788), an exposition designed to show off the latest aviation and aerospace equipment from around the world. Held at Brown Field in San Diego, the event includes displays of the latest technology from leading aviation and aerospace companies and from NASA, as well as 100 military and civilian aircraft, including antiques and experimental aircraft. This event was held for the first time in the spring of 1988.

Most other air shows are sponsored by local chapters of aviation organizations, including the EAA. Here are a few of the more prominent ones. Because they are organized informally, not all information is available about all shows.

EAA Events
• Arlington, WA, Annual Northwest Fly-in (206-435-5857). Summer.
• Lakeland, FL, EAA Chapter (PO Box 6750, Lakeland, FL 33807; 813-644-2431). Spring.
• Marion, OH, Annual Marion EAA Fly-in (513-849-9455). Early fall.
• Orange, MA, EAA Chapter, Annual New England Regional EAA Fly-in (c/o Dick Walsh, Municipal Airport, Orange, MA 01364). Early summer.
• Winchester, VA, EAA Chapter, Spring Fly-in (George Lutz, Municipal Airport; 703-256-7873). Spring.

Other Events
• Bartlesville, OK, National Biplane Fly-in, Frank Phillips Field (918-742-7311 or 299-2532). Early summer.
• Breckenridge, TX, Annual Airshow (featuring classics, homebuilts, and warbirds). Sponsored by the West Texas CAF Wing (817-559-9129). Late spring.
• Casa Grande, AZ, Annual Copperstate Fly-in (602-298-3522 or 744-1487). Fall.
• Dayton, OH, Wright Brothers Invitational, Dayton Air and Trade Show (513-836-4281). Summer.
• Hamilton, ON, International Airshow (416-528-4425 or 416-679-4183). Early summer.
• Merced, CA, Annual Merced West Coast Antique Fly-in (209-722-6666). Early summer.
• North Bend, OR, Airshow (800-255-0439). Summer.
• Reno, NV, National Championships Air Races (P.O. Box 1429, Reno, NV 89505). Fall.
• Rome, GA, Ole South Annual Fly-in (404-235-5530). Fall.
• Tahlequah, OK, Annual Tulsa Fly-in (817-853-2008). Fall.

prefer less-tested machines can make a beeline for the Air Adventure Museum in Oshkosh, Wisconsin. Meanwhile, those with stellar visions can set their sights on the likes of Howard Hughes's enormous *Spruce Goose* plane in Long Beach, California, or visit a host of star vehicles at the aptly named Planes of Fame Air Museum in Chino, California. There are also museums devoted to kindred spirits, such as soaring and ballooning; there's even a collection in Kalamazoo, Michigan, with so many "animal" planes (whose noses have been painted to resemble the faces and fangs of growling beasts) it's been nicknamed the "Air Zoo."

When aviation museums succeed in bringing their subject to life, they capture the imaginations of visitors in a profound and exciting way. It is no wonder then that the finest aviation collection in the world, the National Air and Space Museum, is also the most popular museum in the country. When its doors opened, four days before the nation's bicentennial in 1976, President Gerald Ford proclaimed it "a perfect birthday present from Americans to themselves." Visited by approximately 10 million people a year, the museum soon became the crown jewel in the treasure trove of Smithsonian museums.

Equally impressive is the Air Force Museum, five miles outside of Dayton, Ohio, at Wright-Patterson Air Force Base. The world's oldest and largest aviation museum, this institution holds an astounding assemblage of military machines and artifacts that traces the heritage of air power in times of war and peace, and reveals how air force technology and advances have played a role in the evolution of America's flight and space industries.

The success of museums like these lies in their explicit commitment not only to the preservation of America's airborne heritage but also to the education of future generations. At these and other great aviation museums, the power to interpret and disseminate the technological legacy of humankind is exercised in a partnership among those who make history and those who preserve it.

Here are a few of the more unusual or extensive aviation museums in the United States:

National Air and Space Museum (Washington, DC 20560; 202-357-2700). The Air and Space Museum opened its doors in 1976, the grand finale of a century of aviation history collecting. In 1876 the Smithsonian acquired its first flight-related artifacts, a group of Chinese kites that had been brought to America for the Philadelphia Centennial Exhibition. In 1946 Congress chartered the museum, but the collection wasn't displayed in all its glory until the opening of the present building.

There is so much to see at the National Air and Space Museum that many visitors come back time and again to take in a bit more of the nation's aviation and aerospace history. From the moment you enter and look up to see the airplanes and space capsules that dangle like giant marionettes from the ceilings of the museum's cavernous exhibition halls, you know that this is a place of giants. The main entry hall, the Milestones of Flight Gallery, dedicated to histories of early flight and space exploration, is a treasure trove of true history—here is the *Spirit of St. Louis*, in which Charles Lindbergh made his historic transatlantic crossing, and over there hangs the actual *Wright Flyer* that gave Orville Wright the ride of his life. In the Space Hall the *Mercury 7* capsule in which John Glenn became the first American to orbit the earth is on display, as is Glenn's space suit (including his pressure garment and underwear). The mix, especially of aerospace artifacts, is eclectic and imaginative—space suits are well represented (Sally Ride's is here)—as are such oddities as freeze-dried space food, Buck Rogers toys and memorabilia, and a model of a Walt Disney Productions space station. But early aviation is equally well represented. Aside from what may be the two most famous planes of all time (the *Wright Flyer* and Lindbergh's Spirit), there are even earlier rarities, such as an 1894 Lilienthal glider.

Rooms that jut off from the two-level main halls offer exhibits such as a realistic sea-air operations display, a collection on balloons and airships, and a gallery featuring flight-inspired artworks. Visitors can reach out and touch the craggy surface of a moon rock, design an airplane using the latest computer technology, or just gaze in awe at a giant-screen film on flying or a dramatic planetarium presentation.

For those who want to see even more of the collection than the museum has room to display, a visit to the Smithsonian's Paul Garber Preservation, Restoration and Storage Facility in Suitland, Maryland, is in order. The Garber Facility could well be called the attic of the "Nation's Attic" (as the Smithsonian is often described). Here aircraft and other artifacts are stored and restored, among them the world's most infamous airplane: the *Enola Gay*, which dropped an atomic bomb on Hiroshima, Japan, in 1945. Tours of the facility can be arranged by contacting the Air and Space Museum. The Air and Space Museum itself is open daily from 10 a.m. to 5:30 p.m. (evening hours between Memorial Day and Labor Day). No admission is charged.

Pima Air Museum (6000 E. Valencia Rd., Tucson, AZ 85706; 602-574-9658). Out on a flat, desert landscape of dust and green brush, the Pima Air Museum sits like a mirage. From high above it could be any airport with its prefab hangar buildings and willy-nilly gathering of aircraft. But come closer and the airfield reveals a stunning diversity of planes ancient and modern, domestic and military, while the utilitarian hangars conceal a wealth of historic air artifacts. The museum opened its doors in 1976, the product of ten years of fund-raising and planning by the people of Tucson and other supporters. Now the third largest in the United States and the largest privately funded aviation museum in the world, the museum currently owns some 200 aircraft, about 150 of which are on display on the airfield or in one of the hangar buildings.

The holdings range from a full-scale replica of the historic 1903 *Wright Flyer* to an extensive collection of World War II bombers. Among the rarities to be found here are a Consolidated B-24J Liberator, the likes of which flew more missions than any other bomber during World War II, and a Northrop YC-125A Raider, one of 23 built, which became obsolete so fast it ended up being used only as a mechanic trainer and later as civilian transport. In the one-of-a-kind category, the Pima Air Museum also has a few bragging rights: On display here are a Martin PBM-5A Mariner, the only surviving postwar amphibian version of this antisubmarine PBM; a Boeing S-307 Stratoliner, used by the Army Air Corps during World War II (and the first airliner with a pressurized passenger compartment); and one of only two Columbia XJL-1s ever made, a monoplane that first flew in 1946. The museum also has a variety of related artifacts and exhibits, including a replicated World War II barracks; the 390th Memorial Museum, which features a B-17 bomber and memorabilia from the 390th Bomb Group (World War II) and the 390th Strategic Missile Wing; and displays on topics such as black flyers, trainers, and engines. The Arizona Aviation Hall of Fame is set to open here in the near future, along with an extensive research library.

But to see what is perhaps the museum's most unique holding, you have to drive some 30 miles outside Tucson, to Green Valley. Here the Pima Air Museum's Titan Missile Museum preserves an actual Titan II missile site (complete with semidismantled missile) for the edification and terror of tourists. The ultimate lesson in the power of technology, this museum is not to be missed—not only because it is the only remaining Titan site in the United States (not to mention the only nuclear missile launch site open to the public)—but also for the sheer force of

With a wingspan longer than a football field, Howard Hughes' Spruce Goose *perches in its permanent resting place in Long Beach, California.*

coming face-to-face with the nuclear age. Information on the museum's hours and admission prices can be obtained from the Pima Air Museum, which is open daily and charges admission.

Spruce Goose (far end of the Long Beach Freeway; mail: P.O. Box 8, Long Beach, CA 90801; 213-435-3511). Famed as the largest plane in the world, the Spruce Goose was designed as a "flying boat" to serve as a long-range troop and equipment transport. The time was 1942, and German U-boats were sinking so many ships that the military decided to move forward on efforts to find alternative ways to get troops to Europe. In stepped industrialist Henry J. Kaiser and millionaire aviator Howard Hughes, who set to work building the world's largest plane. By the time the project was nearing completion, the military no longer needed the plane, but it gave Hughes the go-ahead to turn out one model of the already obsolete craft. The *Goose* soon became a sitting duck—weighing in at 400,000 pounds,

the heavy wooden plane made only one flight (in 1947 Hughes flew it for about a mile across Long Beach Harbor) before being grounded permanently. Now it rests beneath "the world's largest clear-span aluminum dome" near the docks at Long Beach, sharing the spotlight with the majestic old *Queen Mary* ocean liner, which herself has been put out to pasture as a luxury hotel and tourist attraction. Visitors can see the *Goose* from a walkway that gives a full view of the flying behemoth, with its football-field-length (320-foot) wingspan. The more curious can walk inside through the cargo hold to get a load of the no-nonsense interior that was designed to carry 750 troops or two 30-ton Sherman tanks.

Displays surrounding the plane include collections of artifacts such as Hughes's flight jacket and golf shoes, an actual Sherman tank, and a life-sized replica of Hughes's first racing plane, the H-1. Two audiovisual presentations—a 30-minute film and a 7-minute slide show—put the life of the millionaire adventurer,

The carrier USS Intrepid, *at its permanent home on the Hudson River in New York City.*

movie mogul, and recluse into perspective. But the *Spruce Goose* is the star of this megatourist attraction, and, by virtue of size alone, it lives up to its billing. The Spruce Goose and Queen Mary Entertainment Complex is open daily; admission is charged.

U.S. Air Force Museum (Wright-Patterson AFB, OH, 45433; 513-255-3284). The U.S. Air Force Museum has been around, in one form or another, since 1923. Its longevity gives it the honor of being the oldest such museum in the world, though unfortunately most of the original collection no longer exists. And by the sheer size of its aircraft holdings—more than 200 are on display here, and another 1,200 are on loan to other museums worldwide—it can also claim the title of world's largest aviation collection. But, never one to rest on its laurels, this grandparent of flight exhibition recently opened its Modern Flight Gallery, which nearly doubled the display area of the museum as a whole. Among the stars of the newest addition are a Boeing B-52 Stratofortress used for long-range heavy

bombing missions during the Vietnam War and by the Strategic Air Command; the only known Curtiss AT-9 still in existence; a North American F-100D used during the 1970s by the Thunderbirds, the air force's daring aerial demonstration team; and a Convair B-58A Hustler, the air force's first operational supersonic bomber. Examples of early spacecraft and other experimental vehicles are also on display in the new wing. Meanwhile, the rest of the museum continues to exhibit its lively collection of vintage military aircraft and historical air force artifacts, including uniforms, medals, and other related memorabilia. The Air Force Museum is open daily, and there is no admission charge.

USS Intrepid (One Intrepid Sq., W. 46th St. & 12th Ave., New York, NY 10036; 212-245-0072). The history of the aircraft carrier USS *Intrepid* is in many ways a mirror of the twentieth century's greatest accomplishments and most infamous conflicts. During its 31 years of active duty, the *Intrepid* served in both World War II and the Vietnam War, surviving

The colorful scene at the Albuquerque International Balloon Fiesta. Photo by Steve Vidler. See "Flights of Fancy: Ballooning," page 203.

Portion of an aeronautical chart of western Washington, including Seattle, the San Juan Islands, and part of Vancouver, B.C. See "Aeronautical Charts," page 256.

View of Mercury obtained by the Mariner 10 spacecraft in 1985. This photomosaic has been tinted to approximate the visual appearance of the planet. Courtesy National Aeronautics and Space Administration. See "The View From Up: Aerial and Space Imagery," page 309.

View of Venus taken by the Mariner 10's video cameras in 1974. Individual TV frames were computer-enhanced, mosaicked, and retouched. The blue tint does not represent the planet's true color. Courtesy National Aeronautics and Space Administration. See "The View From Up: Aerial and Space Imagery," page 309.

Two views of earth photographed by Apollo astronauts: from 250,000 miles away (top) and 100,000 miles away. Courtesy National Aeronautics and Space Administration. See "The View From Up: Aerial and Space Imagery," page 309.

Top: Jupiter and three of its four largest satellites, as photographed by Voyager 1 in 1979. Bottom: Four photographs of Mars taken in 1967. Courtesy National Aeronautics and Space Administration. See "The View From Up: Aerial and Space Imagery," page 309.

Top: Montage of images for Voyager 1 during its 1980 flight through the Saturnian system.
Bottom: A montage of Voyager 2 images of Uranus overlaid with an artist's conception of the
planet's dark rings. Courtesy National Aeronautics and Space Administration. See "The View
From Up: Aerial and Space Imagery," page 309.

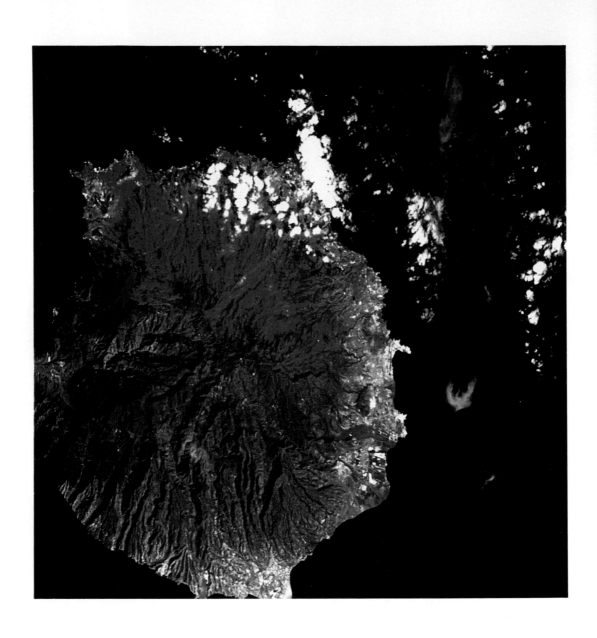

Grand Canary Island, as seen by the French satellite Spot. *Copyright 1988 CNES. Provided courtesy Spot Image Corporation, Reston, Virginia. See "The View From Up: Aerial and Space Imagery," page 309.*

Grumman F6F-3 fighter. Courtesy Champlain Fighter Museum, Mesa, Arizona.

kamikaze and torpedo attacks, was the Prime Recovery Vessel for early NASA splashdowns, and sailed proudly as the U.S. Navy and Marine Corps Bicentennial Exposition Vessel. Today it is docked in mid-Manhattan as a museum. Visitors can come aboard to explore the ship's five major theme halls, see the world's largest collection of Congressional Medals of Honor, and wander the deck, where 42 original or replicated military air- and spacecraft hold court. Among the craft on display are the last Grumman F11F-1 Tiger made, the second Chance-Vought F-8J Crusader built, and a full-size replica of an Apollo Lunar Lander. The *Intrepid* is open Wednesday through Sunday all year; admission is charged.

The Charles Lindbergh exhibit at the Experimental Aircraft Association's Air Adventure Museum, Oshkosh, Wisconsin. Photo by Jim Koepnick.

Grumman F7F-3P Tigercat. Courtesy Kalamazoo Aviation History Museum, Kalamazoo, Michigan. Photo by Warren Pridgeon.

OTHER NOTABLE MUSEUMS AND COLLECTIONS

UNITED STATES

Airpower Museum (Antique Airfield, Rte. 2, Box 172, Ottumwa, IA 52501; 515-938-2773). Exhibits a large, impressive collection of early and modern aircraft, and promotes the study and history of aviation. The museum is open Monday through Friday, 9 a.m. to 5 p.m.; Saturday, 10 a.m. to 5 p.m.; Sunday, 1 to 5 p.m. No admission fee, but donations accepted.

Castle Air Museum (Castle AFB, CA 95342; mail: P.O. Box 488, Atwater, CA 95301; 209-723-2178 or 723-2177). Exhibits 32 vintage military aircraft and related artifacts. Open daily. No admission fee.

Champlain Fighter Museum (4636 Fighter Aces Dr., Mesa, AZ 85205; 602-830-4540). Exhibits a collection of 30 restored fighter planes dating from pre-World War I to post-World War II; special artifact collections and exhibits focus on ace pilots. Located at an active airfield. Open daily. Admission fee.

Cradle of Aviation Museum (Davis Ave., Hempstead, NY; 516-222-1190). Displays more than 40 original or replica aircraft of all vintages, dating from 1903 to 1983, as well as more than a dozen space and lunar vehicles. Open from the first full weekend in April to the last weekend in October, noon to 5 p.m. No admission fee, but donations accepted.

Right: The Great Gallery exhibit hall at the Museum of Flight, Seattle, Washington.

The main exhibit building of the New England Air Museum, Windsor Locks, Connecticut.

Experimental Aircraft Association's Air Adventure Museum (Wittman Airfield, Oshkosh, WI 54903; 414-426-4818). Displays more than 80 aircraft and related exhibits on aerodynamics and other topics. Open daily. Admission fee.

Franklin Institute (20th St. & the Parkway, Philadelphia, PA 19103; 215-448-1200). Aviation exhibit includes flight simulator, wind tunnel, airplane models, and unique collections of Wright brothers' artifacts. Open Monday through Friday, 9:30 a.m. to 4:30 p.m.; 10 a.m. to 5 p.m. on weekends. Admission $5 for adults, $4 for children 4 through 11, free for children under 4.

Harold Warp's Pioneer Village (Minden, NE 68959; 800-445-4447). Exhibits 20 historic aircraft, early aviation engines and artifacts, and extensive collections of Americana. Open daily. Admission fee.

Kalamazoo Aviation History Museum (3901 E. Milham Rd., Kalamazoo, MI 49002; 616-382-6555). Exhibits 20 vintage military aircraft, a large collection of model planes, and other related artifacts. Known as the "Air Zoo" because of its large collection of fiercely painted "animal" planes. Sponsors demonstrations and air shows. Open daily. Admission fee.

Museum of Flight (9404 E. Marginal Way S, Seattle, WA 98108; 206-764-5720). Displays an extensive collection of early and modern air- and spacecraft, as well as related artifacts. Highlights include exhibits tracing the history of "The Red Barn" (the museum's first building, which also served as Boeing's first manufacturing plant) and a working replica of the wind tunnel used by the Wright brothers. Open daily. Admission fee.

National Balloon Museum (711 N.E. St., Indianola, IA 50125; 515-961-8415). Displays a collection of hot-air balloons

(continued on page 242)

A 1916 Jenny Biplane, courtesy The Owls Head Transportation Museum.

Aircraft on display at the Canadian Museum of Flight and Transportation, Surrey, British Columbia. Photo by S. Senaratne.

and related artifacts, including pilots' lapel pins, baskets, and various items tracing the history of ballooning from the early nineteenth century to the present. Open weekdays. No admission fee, but donations accepted.

National Soaring Museum (R.D. 3, Hams Hill, Elmira, NY 14903; 607-734-3128). Exhibits gliders and other lighter-than-air craft. Displays also include a cockpit flight simulator and collections on soaring history and related subjects. Open daily. Admission fee.

New England Air Museum (Bradley International Airport, Windsor Locks, CT 06096; 203-623-3305). Displays extensive permanent and changing exhibits of early aircraft, engines, propellers, and related artifacts. Open daily. Admission fee.

Old Rhinebeck Aerodrome (42 Stone Church Rd., Rhinebeck, NY 12572; 914-758-8610). Exhibits a large collection of antique aircraft and related memorabilia, with emphasis on early U.S. airmail service, barnstorming, and World War I fighter aviation. A "museum of the air," on summer weekends the aerodrome features air shows starring its own re-

stored planes and offers open-cockpit biplane barnstorming rides. Open spring and summer only. Admission fee.

Owls Head Transportation Museum (Knox County Airport, P.O. Box 277, Owls Head, ME 04854; 207-594-4418). Exhibits antique aircraft and other restored vehicles. Often sponsors air shows of vintage planes. Open daily, May through October; weekdays only, November through April. Admission fee.

Planes of Fame Air Museum (7000 Merrill Ave., Box 17, Chino Airport, Chino, CA 91710; 714-597-3722). Exhibits famous aircraft, with specialties in American, German, and Japanese military vehicles. Sponsors air shows and offers rides. Open daily. Admission fee.

U.S. Army Aviation Museum (Ft. Rucker, AL 36362; 205-255-4507). Displays an extensive collection of historic and modern U.S. military aircraft, including "the largest collection of helicopters in the free world." Related memorabilia also exhibited. Open daily. No admission fee.

U.S. Naval Aviation Museum (Naval Air Station, Pensacola, FL 32508; 904-452-

1918 Curtiss Jenny JN-4H on display at the Old Rhinebeck Aerodrome, Rhinebeck, New York.

3604). Exhibits an extensive collection of early and modern military aircraft, space vehicles, and related artifacts. Special exhibits on aircraft carriers, Medal of Honor recipients, Skylab; and U.S. Coast Guard. Open daily. No admission fee.

Wright Brothers National Memorial
(U.S. Bypass 158, between Nags Head and Kitty Hawk; Mail: U.S. Dept. of the Interior, Rte. 1, Box 675, Manteo, NC 27954). On Kill Devil Hill a shaft of gray granite marks the spot where the Wrights carried out various test flights, and a large granite boulder designates the place where the *Wright Flyer* lifted off the ground for the first time. A nearby visitors' center tells the story of the Wright brothers' historic work and displays artifacts from their lives and full-scale replicas of their vehicles. Open daily. No admission fee.

CANADA
Canadian Museum of Flight and Transportation (13527 Crescent Rd., Surrey, BC V4A 2W1; 604-531-2465 or 531-3744). Exhibits an extensive collection of vintage and modern civilian and military aircraft and related artifacts. Other transportation history is also displayed. Open daily May through October. Admission fee.

Canadian Warplane Heritage Museum
(Hamilton Civic Airport, Box 35, Mt. Hope, ON L0R 1W0; 416-679-4183). Exhibits more than 20 Canadian military aircraft flown during World War II and the Korean conflict, and related artifacts. Open daily. Admission fee.

National Aviation Museum of Canada
(Rockliffe Airport, Ottawa, ON K1A 0M8; 613-993-2010). Displays an extensive collection of aircraft with historic importance to Canadian military and civilian aviation. Includes a collection of bush planes used for forestry patrols and other rugged-terrain flying. The museum is open Tuesday through Sunday, 9 a.m. to 5 p.m. (Thursday, until 8 p.m.). Admission is $3.50 for adults, $2.50 for students and senior citizens, and $1.50 for children 6 through 15; free on Thursdays.

Reynolds Aviation Museum (4110 57th St., Wetaskiwin, AB T9A 2B6; 403-352-6201). Exhibits more than 35 antique and rare military aircraft and related artifacts. Specializes in World War II and earlier aviation, and also displays various amphibious and other military vehicles. Open summers, or by appointment. No admission fee, but donations accepted.

Aviation Organizations

The federal government plays a major role in the world of aviation, but so do a number of private groups.

Government Organizations

Federal Aviation Administration

Ever since the Wright brothers first flew, the federal government has been concerned with the safe management and growth of this new technology. Although Uncle Sam waited about 20 years before getting involved, it did have an Aeronautics Branch in the Department of Commerce in 1926, charged with the authority to certify pilots and aircraft, develop air navigation facilities, promote flying safety regulations, and issue flight information. The new branch was fully functional by the time Charles Lindbergh took his famous north Atlantic solo flight in 1927.

Over the next 40 years, the government restructured the Aeronautics Branch several times, leading in 1967 to creation of the Federal Aviation Administration (FAA), which was made part of the new Department of Transportation. The FAA's responsibilities have changed little over the years. Here are some of them:

Air Traffic Control: The agency manages one of the world's largest and most advanced air-traffic-control and navigation systems. About 25,000 people are involved in this system, including staff for 400 airport control towers, 23 air-route-traffic control centers, and more than 300 flight service stations. An additional 10,000 technicians and engineers maintain radars, communication sites, and ground navigation systems.

Almost all airline flights operate under what are called *instrument flight rules* (IFR). This means that air-traffic-control personnel monitor their flight from takeoff to touchdown. To give you an idea of how involved this system is, a flight from Los Angeles to New York involves almost a dozen air-traffic-control facilities.

If the weather is clear, noncommercial pilots may follow *visual flight rules* (VFR), which are outside the air-traffic-control system. But VFR pilots rely on the FAA's network of flight stations, which provide preflight and in-flight briefings, weather information, suggested routes, and other pertinent information. The flight service station also provides emergency services to pilots in trouble.

As air traffic continues to increase the FAA has been under greater pressure to upgrade its systems to ensure maximum safety. To help keep pace with changing needs the FAA in 1982 devised a 20-year plan, called the National Airspace System, which calls for replacement of the current system with state-of-the-art equipment. Other provisions include automation and consolidation of the flight service station network, installation of advanced new landing systems, and upgrading of weather services available to pilots.

Air Certification: The FAA is responsible for establishing standards, training, and testing for pilots, and for determining the airworthiness of aircraft. This is no small feat, considering that there are more than 200,000 civilian aircraft in the United States, and some 800,000 certified pilots.

To earn an FAA pilot's certificate, an applicant must meet carefully prescribed tests in the air and pass a written exam as well. There are four main pilot categories:

How to Become a Pilot

The boom in air travel since airline deregulation has sharply increased the need for seasoned pilots. In fact, the need has grown so much that the airlines will be hiring about 52,000 new pilots during the 1990s, according to estimates from Future Aviation Professionals of America (FAPA, 4291-J Memorial Dr., Atlanta, GA 30032; 404-294-0226). So, how do you get your wings? Here are some guidelines:

❑ **Education.** Most commercial pilots attend college and receive an undergraduate degree. To combat pilot shortages, some universities are now teaming up with aerospace centers to start pilot training during college. These programs allow first-year college students to begin training in the cockpit. Someone with this kind of background will be much better equipped to start flying shortly after graduation.

❑ **Experience.** The number of flight hours needed to qualify varies greatly from airline to airline. The requirement for captain is 2,000 hours, 500 of which are spent in a multiengine craft and 200 using flight instruments correctly. Half of these last hours may be accrued by using a flight simulator. The requirement for copilot is a minimum of 1,500 hours.

❑ **Age.** If you are older, don't be discouraged. Many airlines are now hiring older people with sound experience, either from another carrier or from the military.

❑ **Vision.** Airlines no longer require that pilots have 20/20 vision. Good vision is sufficient.

❑ **Training.** Most airlines require that a pilot have a flight engineer certificate. Often newly hired pilots must complete a training program offered by the airline.

Pilots looking for work should take advantage of the services offered by FAPA. It provides information about what the airlines are looking for and even has a job bank. See "Aviation Organizations" for more information.

---

student, private, commercial, and airline transport. There are different ratings systems for pilots who fly different kinds of planes, and an additional rating system for instrument flight rules. All pilots must pass periodic medical examinations to maintain a valid certificate.

For an aircraft to pass muster the design and construction of each of its parts must be approved by the FAA. When the new aircraft is finished, it must pass a series of ground and flight tests. If the aircraft passes it receives a type certificate.

The manufacturer receives a production certificate, and the aircraft receives an overall airworthiness certificate guaranteeing that it is safe to fly.

Environmental Protection: The FAA issues noise standards, limitations on undesirable exhaust gases, and restrictions on smoke allowed from aircraft engines. The agency also encourages energy conservation and fuel efficiency.

Other Programs: The FAA is responsible

for keeping the airways safe from criminals. As part of this effort, the agency requires screening of all airline passengers and a search of all carry-on luggage. The FAA also works with the International Civil Aviation Organization in establishing worldwide safety and security procedures, providing technical advice on the export and import of aviation products, and handling certification of foreign-made aircraft. Working with the National Transportation Safety Board, the FAA investigates aircraft accidents and decides what kinds of actions should be taken.

PRIVATE ORGANIZATIONS

What separates aviation buffs from the rest of the world is very simple: They all share a deep love of airplanes and the art and science of flying. Aviation enthusiasts describe in glowing terms the exhilaration of flying, the rush that comes with soaring in the sky. Given the intensity of their feelings, it's not surprising that there is a large number of organizations documenting just about every aspect of the flying experience.

There are professional organizations representing technicians and engineers, pilots and flight attendants. Many of the most reputable organizations date back to the early days of flight. The **National Aeronautic Association** (NAA) includes among its past members such aviation greats as the Wright brothers, Glenn Curtiss, Wiley Post, Charles Lindbergh, and Amelia Earhart. Today the NAA is mandated to promote the development of both civil and military aviation in this country. The American Institute of Aeronautics and Astronautics, the oldest and largest technical society in these fields, offers engineers, scientists, managers, policy-

makers, and educators numerous opportunities to stay up to date in a rapidly changing profession.

But perhaps the most diverse organizations are those formed by recreational pilots coming from all walks of life. Farmers, lawyers, and women, among others, have formed organizations promoting their great passion. Numbering in the thousands, pilots from these various groups participate in "fly-ins"—events in which people fly to their destinations and enjoy a raucous weekend sharing aviation anecdotes—among other activities. Most of these organizations also publish newsletters or magazines and hold annual conventions, many at Oshkosh, Wisconsin, the site of the world's largest air show (see "Air Shows").

Aviation buffs with a love of flying but without the means to own a plane can still get involved in the action without great expense. For example, there are organizations for collectors of aviation stamps, airmail covers, and military insignia. And those with a historical bent can peruse the history of air racing, World War I flight, or female aviators.

Here are some of the principal aviation organizations around the country. They are divided into recreational clubs, collectors' organizations, and professional organizations.

RECREATIONAL CLUBS

Antique Airplane Association (AAA, Rte. 2, Box 172, Ottumwa, IA 52501; 515-938-2773) was formed in 1953 by a group of people deeply interested in antique airplanes and committed to keeping them flying. At the time there were no aviation historical societies. Today the organization has expanded to include 42 affiliated chapters. Two publications, *AAA Digest* and *AAA News*, feature the latest restorations and their relationship to aviation history. The association is located at Antique Airfield near Blakesburg, Iowa,

Experimental Aircraft Association headquarters in Oshkosh, Wisconsin. Photo by Jeffrey Isom.

next to the Airpower Museum. The museum has over 20,000 square feet of display and storage space plus tons of spare engine and aircraft parts being made available to AAA members to assist in their renovations. Membership is open to anyone and costs $35 a year for full membership, $20 for associate membership, and $500 for life membership.

Cessna Pilots Association (P.O. Box 12948, Wichita, KS 67277; 316-946-4777) is for individuals who own, operate, or have an interest in Cessna aircraft. The organization has a technical staff and provides support to Cessna owners.

Membership is $30 a year and includes the monthly *CPA Magazine*. Every year at the fly-in at Oshkosh, the Cessna Pilots Association holds its annual meeting. Other fly-ins take place during the year.

Experimental Aircraft Association (EAA, Wittman Airfield, Oshkosh, WI 54903; 414-426-4800), perhaps best known for sponsoring the world-famous annual fly-in at Oshkosh, plays a crucial role in the aviation community. It is involved in every aspect of the flying experience: preserving antique planes, sponsoring competitive events, encouraging members to build their own planes. Through its

First meeting of licensed women pilots, November 2, 1929. Courtesy The Ninety-Nines.

publications, *Sport Aviation* and *The EAA Experimenter*, the organization keeps members up to date about events, research, and changes in sport aviation. Working with more than 700 chapters nationwide, EAA encourages groups to communicate. Three subgroups—Antique/Classic Division, International Aerobatic Club, and Warbirds of America—encourage members to pick an area in which to specialize. Membership dues are $30 for full members, $18 for junior members, and $40 for family members. (See "Air shows" for more information about EAA's famous event.)

International Flying Farmers (P.O. Box 9124, Mid-Continent Airport, Wichita, KS; 316-943-4234) was begun in the 1940s by a group of farmers who used airplanes to haul supplies. Today members mostly gather to share aviation anecdotes and to participate in periodic fly-ins. But the organization has grown tremendously and now has 35 chapters in the United States and Canada. Membership is $45 a year and includes the monthly magazine *International Flying Farmer*.

Lawyer-Pilots Bar Association (c/o Yodice Associates, 600 Maryland Ave. NW No. 701, Washington, DC 20024; 202-863-1000) is a group of lawyers who are also licensed pilots. Many practice aviation law. Membership is $20 a year and includes a quarterly newsletter.

The Ninety-Nines (Will Rogers World Airport, P.O. Box 59965, Oklahoma City, OK 73159; 405-685-7969) is an organization of licensed women pilots from 33 countries. Mostly philanthropic, the group sponsors educational programs, including aerospace education workshops for teachers, airport tours for schoolchildren, aviation talks to service clubs, fear of flying clinics, and flight instructor revalidation courses. The Ninety-Nines are

concerned about flight safety and sponsor more than 75 percent of the FAA pilot safety programs. In addition, members arrange transportation for cancer patients through CAN, the Corporate Angel Network; transport blood for the Red Cross; give airplane rides to Boy and Girl Scout troops; and fly donated supplies to Mexico and other countries. Each year at the international convention, club members present the Amelia Earhart Memorial Scholarship to qualified members for advanced flight training in a specialized area. Membership dues are $45 each year and include a subscription to the monthly magazine *The 99 News*.

Order of Daedalians (Kelly AFB, Bldg. 1635, San Antonio, TX 78241; 512-924-9485) is an association of military aviators started by World War I aviators, the first to fly our country's airplanes in time of war. Today's members include World War I pilots, those nominated by members, and descendants of founding members. The organization publishes the *Daedalus Flyer* quarterly and has an active awards program. Membership is $35, $15 a year to renew. The magazine comes with membership dues.

Pilots International Association (4000 Olson Memorial Highway., Minneapolis, MN 55422; 612-588-5175) is committed to offering pilots interesting places to go and equally interesting places to stay during their journeys. The organization publishes a directory highlighting bed-and-breakfast inns and private homes particularly receptive to pilots and their families. The directory lists places throughout the country and describes them in a friendly, anecdotal style. Reading the group's materials makes you want to become a pilot to get involved in the action. Associate members, who must be pilots, pay a $15 membership fee, with $12.50 renewals. General members, who

Order of Daedalians, circa 1921. Courtesy Order of Daedalians.

are pilots offering their private homes as accommodations, have a $7.50 membership fee. All members receive the monthly newsletter.

Seaplane's Pilot Association (421 Aviation Way, Frederick, MD 21701; 301-695-2083) is committed to promoting water flying through educational programs, seminars, and annual meetings. Seaplanes, many of which can land on both land and water, are particularly popular in Alaska and in "oil country," because they can land close to the rigs. The organization publishes a quarterly magazine, *Water Flying,* and a comprehensive annual report with detailed descriptions of seaplane activities and award-winning photographs. Membership is $28 a year.

Silver Wings Fraternity (P.O. Box 11970, Harrisburg, PA 17108; 717-232-9529) accepts as members only individuals who made a solo flight in a powered aircraft at least 25 years ago. An organization of distinguished old-timers, it includes in its rosters a host of public figures, from Arthur Godfrey to Barry Goldwater. Some women have met the challenge and are

also members. The group sponsors air shows and publishes a bimonthly newsletter, *Slipstream.* Membership dues are $10 a year.

Society of Air Racing Historians (1201 S. Washington St., Apt. 227, Alexandria, VA 22314; 703-548-0405) was organized in 1984 to bring together people with a serious interest in the history of pylon and long-distance air racing. The organization publishes a six-page newsletter semimonthly, which includes news of old race planes and pilots, reproductions and replicas of old racers, research aids, news of personalities, a calendar of current events, ads, and book reviews. The highlight of the year is the group's Air Racing History Symposium, held in early May near Cleveland, Ohio, the site of the great 1930s races. The symposium lasts for a weekend. The society is open to anyone with an interest in air racing history and costs $10 to join.

Twin Bonanza Association (19684 Lakeshore Dr., Three Rivers, MI 49093; 616-279-2540) promotes the exchange of information among pilots who own Twin

Bonanza aircraft. The group encourages flight safety through training programs for pilots and instructors. Annual membership dues are $25 in the United States and $35 elsewhere. The organization publishes a quarterly newsletter and holds an annual convention.

United States Air Racing Association (USARA, 26726 Henry Rd., Bay Village, OH 44140; 216-871-3781 or 961-9010) is a national organization of air race pilots, race plane owners, officials, and enthusiasts whose mission is to organize and conduct air-racing events in the United States. The organization assists in sponsoring events, supplies FAA-approved race-course layouts, provides staff for each event, and works with the National Aeronautic Association in keeping records at events. The USARA publishes a periodic newsletter that lists upcoming events. Membership is $10 a year.

World War I Aeroplanes (15 Crescent Rd., Poughkeepsie, NY 12601; 914-473-3679) caters to aviation history buffs who have a particular fondness for planes built between 1900 and 1919, and 1920 and 1940. These folks include builders, historians, museums, modelers, and collectors. The group publishes two journals—*World War I Aero* and *Skyways*. Both have information about historical research, modeling, museum displays and air shows, and new publications. Membership fees vary, depending on whether you want both publications, from $25 to $100.

COLLECTORS' ORGANIZATIONS

American Air Mail Society (102 Arbor Rd., Cinnaminson, NJ 08077) is one of the oldest and largest aerophilatelic societies around. Its members collect postal covers of all kinds, including the balloon posts of the Siege of Paris, jet and rocket mail, U.S. first flight covers, and transoceanic and foreign flight covers. People who belong to this society are serious collectors, usually specialists in a particular kind of cover. Some might collect only covers of types of flights;

Restoration in progress of Fokker C-IV. Courtesy World War I Aeroplanes and National Air and Space Museum.

others might focus on postal markings. Still others might select air events. To alert members to what's out there, the organization publishes the *American Air Mail Catalogue*, consisting of five volumes, which includes all newly discovered items as well as covers included in previous editions. The volumes are organized chronologically. The society also puts out a monthly bulletin. Dues are $12 a year; life membership is $240.

American Society of Military Insignia Collectors (5443 Fox Rd., Cincinnati, OH 45239) helps collectors of both military and naval insignia pursue their hobbies. The organization's newsletter and journal both list new insignia available for purchase. The journal, *Trading Post*, also includes military history. Both newsletter and journal are published quarterly. Every Labor Day the group holds its national convention, and smaller meetings take place throughout the year. Membership is $25 a year.

Association of American Military Uniform Collectors (P.O. Box 1876, Elyria, OH 44036; 216-365-5321) provides a forum for collectors of military uniforms to exchange ideas and products. The quarterly newsletter *Footlocker* is chock-full of ads on where to buy different kinds of uniforms. Articles about preservation and restoration also abound. Membership dues are $12.50 a year in the United States, Canada, and Mexico; $17.50 elsewhere.

Professional Organizations
Aerospace Industries Association of America (1250 Eye St. NW, Washington, DC 20005; 202-371-8400) is the professional organization representing U.S. companies involved in research, development, and manufacture of systems such as aircraft, missiles, spacecraft, and space launch vehicles. The association deals with issues of concern to these professionals. These include the financial health of the industry, relationships to the Department of Defense, research developments, space exploration, and competitiveness in the world market. The organization is dedicated to fostering economical commercial and private air transportation and to achieving the peaceful conquest of space. Information about the organization can be found in the newsletter, which is published ten times a year. Membership dues, which include copies of the newsletter, are $500 a year in the United States and $520 elsewhere.

Aerospace Medical Association (Washington National Airport, Washington, DC 20001; 703-739-2240) has a membership of aerospace physicians, physiologists, and nurses. These professionals are dedicated to studying the effects of space travel on people and pursuing other research endeavors related to medicine and aviation and space. The association publishes a monthly magazine, *Aviation, Space, and Environmental Medicine*, a subscription to which is part of the annual membership fee of $95. It also holds an annual meeting.

Aircraft Owners & Pilots Association (AOPA, 421 Aviation Way, Frederick, MD 21701; 301-695-2000) is the world's largest pilot organization, respected internationally and known for a wide variety of services. High points of membership include two publications—the magazine *AOPA Pilot* and the AOPA newsletter—free flight planning assistance, legal services, educational programs, and insurance options. The magazine has stories about flight safety, equipment, weather, and aviation history. The newsletter keep pilots up to date on changes in federal, state, or local regulations, airport access, airspace requirements, and other crucial issues.

Biplane used in flight research program by federal government in the early 1920s. Courtesy National Aeronautics and Space Administration.

The AOPA Safety Foundation is the branch of the organization that prepares education programs and seminars throughout the country. Courses include weekend ground schools, flight training clinics, flight instruction refresher courses, and weather radar seminars. AOPA also prepares two practical guides a year. *Airports USA* lists facilities and services at more than 9,000 airports, heliports, and seaplane bases. *Handbook for Pilots* includes information on operational techniques, aircraft performance tables and charts, weather, and customs regulations. The organization also sponsors an annual convention offering workshops, seminars, and aviation products. Membership dues are $35 a year; $15 a year more covers each additional pilot in the family.

Air Line Pilots Association (ALPA, 1625 Massachusetts Ave. NW, Washington, DC 20036; 202-797-4074. Also: 535 Herndon Pkwy., Herndon, VA 22070; 703-689-2270) is the labor union for commercial pilots. It represents 41,000 pilots from 43 airlines. The association is concerned with collective bargaining, air safety and health, lobbying the FAA and Congress, and addressing grievances. ALPA publishes a monthly, *Airline Pilot Magazine*, which comes with the *monthly* membership dues of $34.

American Helicopter Society (AHS, 217 North Washington St., Alexandria, VA 22314; 703-684-6777) represents the designers, developers, and manufacturers of vertical flight aircraft, better known as helicopters. Its members include 8,000 aerospace professionals and 165 corporations involved in every aspect of vertical flight, including users and operators. AHS maintains one of the largest collections of vertical flight technical documents in its library and technical services center. The technical services center houses more than 4,000 documents, as well as 300 books. The library has films, videotapes, and audiocassettes. The society puts out three publications. *Vertiflite* is a bimonthly magazine that aims to bridge the gap between the designer-engineer and the user-operator in both the private and public sectors. *The Journal of the American Helicopter Society* is a quarterly technical publication that publishes research papers pertinent to the industry. *Membergram* is the bimonthly newsletter, which keeps members up to date on industry developments and special events. AHS holds a yearly meeting—Annual Forum and Technology Display—to display the latest technological developments and to honor outstanding achievements. The forum attracts as many as 2,500 participants and displays the work of as many as 130 companies.

American Institute of Aeronautics and Astronautics (AIAA, The Aerospace Center, 370 L'Enfant Promenade SW, Washington, DC 20024; 202-646-7400) is the nation's oldest and largest professional society specializing in aeronautics and astronautics. Engineers, scientists, managers, policymakers, and educators all make up its membership, which totals about 40,000. Benefits of membership include the monthly *Aerospace America Magazine*, which covers international aviation, research advances, and technological developments; more than 20 national and international conferences a year; technical journals; and educational programs. AIAA also has an active publishing program, offering a wide range of technical books covering subjects such as

aerodynamics, aircraft engine design, and aircraft structure. Annual dues of $60 include the magazine and journals. Members receive a discount on AIAA books.

Association of Flight Attendants (1625 Massachusetts Ave. NW, Washington, DC 20036; 202-328-5400) is the labor union for flight attendants. It has 23,000 members representing 18 airlines. The union stresses that the main responsibility of flight attendants is to promote flight safety and to save lives, if necessary, aboard the aircraft. The union publishes a quarterly magazine, *Flightlog*. Membership dues are $34 a *month*.

Aviation/Space Writers Association (17 S. High St., Ste. 1200, Columbus, OH 43215; 614-221-1900) works with writers, editors, and photographers to help maintain high standards in the reporting of aeronautical information. The association provides expert advice on covering aviation and space events through individual contacts, referrals, seminars, meetings, booklets, and newsletters. By publishing a directory of members, the organization serves as a network for aviation and space journalists. Membership dues are $75 for active members, $25 for retired members and military, and $10 for students. There is also a $20 initiation fee for all but student members. Membership includes the monthly newsletter.

Future Aviation Professionals of America (4291-J Memorial Dr., Atlanta, GA 30032; 404-294-0226) offers a wide assortment of information about aviation careers. Membership brings a range of information pieces. The monthly newsletter, *The Career Pilot Job Report*, outlines past, present, and projected hiring activity of major, national, turbojet, and regional airlines; helicopter operators; and some non-U.S. airlines. *Piloting Careers Magazine* focuses on a different airline or corporation each month, giving information about its routes, personnel, equipment, history, financial status, and working conditions. The *Pilot Employment Guide* is a 60-page guide to career planning. The *Directory of Employers* includes addresses for major airlines, as well as a contact name, minimum qualifications, and starting salary. The *Pilot Salary Survey* is an annual study of each airline's salary system, including minimum to maximum pay. The Jet Jobs computer referral system provides access to hundreds of unpublished jobs. Finally, the organization's Information Center, open from 9 a.m. to 5 p.m. weekdays, offers job candidates the chance to talk with professional pilots about career options. All these services cost $144 a year. Additional services include an airline testing study kit (member: $27.95; non-member: $32.95); Career Pilot Starter Kit ($49.95); aviation résumé kits (member: $25; nonmember: $30); and aviation maintenance information ($66).

ISA + 21: International Society of Women Airline Pilots (P.O. Box 38644, Denver, CO 80238) is made up of more than 200 women involved in the airline industry worldwide. The society's goal is to bring together women pilots with a wide range of backgrounds to discuss new ideas and recurring problems. The organization holds an annual convention and sponsors an Information Bank, where questions about the profession are received and channeled to an appropriate person for response. Membership dues are $35 a year, $10 for those on furlough.

National Aeronautic Association (NAA, 1763 R St. NW, Washington, DC 20009; 202-265-8720) is our oldest national aviation organization. The NAA is the official record keeper for private, commercial, and military aviation and publishes *U.S. & World Aviation & Space Records* documenting this information. The association is the only U.S. representative to the Fédération Aéronautique Internationale, which has jurisdiction over all world aviation and space records as well as sport aviation. It also publishes a newsletter, *For the Record*, which comes out quarterly. Membership is $10 a year. NAA members also receive a discount on *Flying* magazine. *Aviation Warehouse* is available to members for $15 a year. This magazine includes updates on FAA alerts affecting all aircraft, current airworthiness directives, and a monthly aircraft and parts report on theft.

National Association of Flight Instructors (Ohio State University Airport, P.O. Box 793, Dublin, OH 43017; 614-889-6148) includes both full-time and part-time flight instructors. The organization promotes flight education and disseminates new information on flight instruction. Its major publication is *Safety Bulletin & Guidelines for the Conduct of Biennial Flight Reviews*, which comes out annually. Membership dues are $35, with an annual renewal rate of $30.

Tailhook Association (P.O. Box 45308, Naval Air Station, Miramar, San Diego, CA 92145; 619-279-2010) includes among its 14,000 members naval aviators or naval flight officers who have made a landing on an aircraft carrier. The organization is designed to keep naval flight officers abreast of both the history of carriers and the latest developments affecting carrier aviation. Membership for one year costs $30; for three years, $50; for foreign subscribers, $40; and for life members, $300. Membership includes copies of *The Hook*, the association's quarterly journal. The organization also holds an annual meeting in Las Vegas in the fall.

FEAR OF FLYING

More than 25 million people in the United States have a flying phobia, according to recent surveys. Because of these high numbers, phobia experts have emerged to offer sound tips to help people conquer their fears. These professionals even offer workshops that give people a chance to air their fears while educating them about the ins and outs of aviation. Here are a few tips culled from their findings:

❏ Learn about airplanes by reading about flight and even wandering around your local airport.
❏ When thinking about flying, practice a relaxation technique, such as yoga or relaxation exercises.
❏ Stay away from movies showing plane crashes and other disasters.
❏ If you are planning a trip, arrive at the airport on time and calm yourself by walking around and observing the activity. Don't buy flight insurance.
❏ When you board the aircraft, tell the flight attendants that you are afraid of flying. Ask for support during the trip if you feel you need it.
❏ Don't sit idly during the flight. Bring games, books, and magazines to fill up the time. Don't clock watch, either. That always makes the time go slower.
❏ At the end of the trip, pat yourself on the back for a job well done. If possible, schedule another flight soon.

If you think your phobia requires more attention, contact one of these clinics for more extensive treatment:

Freedom from Fear of Flying (2021 Country Club Prado, Coral Gables, FL 33134; 305-261-7042) offers seminars about fear of flying and a tape that sells for $25. The tape takes the listener on a realistic audio flight. The organization's founder, a former Pan Am pilot, wrote a book, aptly called *Freedom from Fear of Flying* (Simon & Schuster, 1987), which describes other ways to combat fears.

Travel & Fly Without Fear (310 Madison Ave., New York, NY 10017; 212-697-7666 or 516-368-4244) sponsors education seminars, counseling programs, and support groups. This was the first group of its kind and was founded by former phobic Nate Cott. With his death in 1973, his daughter, Carol Cott Gross, took up the cockpit and in the process conquered her own flying fears. Programs include a "conditioning flight"—a short hop from La Guardia Airport to Kennedy Airport in New York, or a shuttle between New York and Boston or New York and Washington, D.C. The flights are held about every eight weeks.

And remember that when your plane lands safely at your destination airport, the *real* danger begins—statistically, at least: driving home.

University Aviation Association (690 Airport Rd., Auburn, IL 36830; 205-826-2308) promotes high-quality aviation education. Institutional members reap the benefits of this mandate by receiving reports about surveys and studies and being invited to participate in workshops. For this, dues for institutions are higher than for others: $100 a year, compared with $70 a year for corporations and $30 for individuals. Dues cover a monthly newsletter and two annual meetings.

Aeronautical Charts

Aeronautical charts provide a wealth of fascinating information, regardless of whether you intend to take over a Piper Cub or a DC-10. Granted, these are not simple maps to read. At first glance, they seem filled with colorful circles, arrows, and other strange markings, and the little text that exists consists primarily of cryptic letters and numbers—"Picket 3 MOA 4000' to and incl. 10,000'" is one example.

But with a bit of patience, you can spot areas that are prohibited or restricted to fly over—usually military bases and other high-security locations. And you are likely to find dozens of heretofore unknown landing strips in your region—possibly belonging to some tycoon who may have quietly constructed a runway capable of handling a jumbo jet. You'll find out exactly where low-flying aircraft are permitted and where they're banned, perhaps giving you the informational ammunition to inform the authorities about some commercial airliner that has been repeatedly flying over your home at an altitude a bit too close for comfort. It's all there, if you know how and where to look.

Aeronautical charts are published by both the federal government and private publishers. Both sources create charts covering the skies over the United States as well as the rest of the world.

Government Charts

The **National Ocean Service** (NOS), part of the Commerce Department's National Oceanic and Atmospheric Administration, publishes and distributes U.S. aeronautical charts. Charts of foreign areas are published by the Defense Mapping Agency, which makes them available through the NOS. In addition to the NOS's five distribution centers, both domestic and foreign aeronautical charts and related publications are available through a network of several hundred sales agents, usually located at or near airports. A free publication, *Catalog of Aeronautical Charts and Related Publications*, includes a list of such dealers, as well as detailed descriptions of the various charts and publications distributed by the NOS.

According to the NOS, the date of an aeronautical chart is important if you are using it for aviation purposes. The agency notes that when charted information becomes obsolete, *using the chart or publication for navigation may be dangerous*. Critical changes occur constantly, and it is important for pilots to purchase up-to-date charts. To ensure that only the latest charts are used, NOS publishes *Dates of Latest Edition*, available free from NOS distribution centers.

Available NOS charts include:

Aeronautical planning charts, used for preflight planning of long flights. Portions of the flight route can then be transferred to more detailed charts for actual flight use. NOS publishes two types of flight-planning charts: "VFR/IFR Wall Planning Charts," at a scale of 1:2,333,232, a large (82-by-56-inch) chart in two pieces, which can be assembled to form a composite Visual flight rules (VFR) planning chart on one side and an Instrument flight rules (IFR) chart on the other. The chart is revised every 56 days. A one-year subscription is $45.50; single copies are $6.50. Another planning chart, the Flight Case Planning Chart, is a somewhat smaller (30-by-50-inch), folded chart (scale 1:4,374,803) designed for pre- and

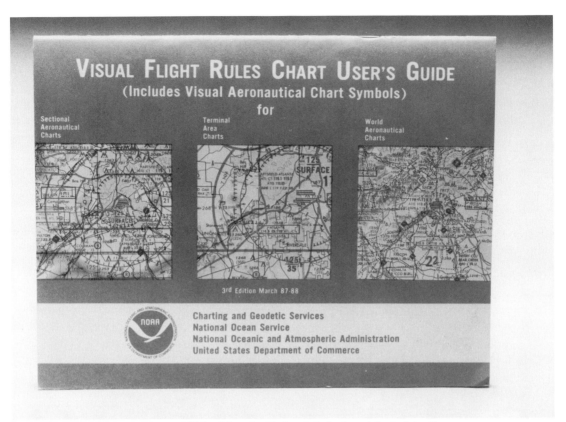

VFR Chart User's Guide, *published by the Federal Aviation Administration.*

in-flight use. It contains the same information as the VFR/IFR chart, with the addition of selected flight services stations and National Weather Service offices at airports, parachute jumping areas, a tabulation of special-use airspace areas, a mileage table listing distances between 174 major airports, and a city-airport location index. This chart is revised every 24 weeks. A two-year subscription is $15; single copies are $3.60.

Visual aeronautical charts, multicolored charts designed for visual navigation of slow- to medium-speed planes. The information featured includes selected visual checkpoints, including populated places, roads, railroads, and other distinctive landmarks. There are three types of these charts: Sectional Aeronautical Charts (1:500,000; 20-by-60 inches) show the airspace for a large region of several hundred square miles; Terminal Area Charts (1:250,000; 20-by-25 inches) show the airspace designated as Terminal Control Areas around airports; and World Aeronautical Charts (1:1,000,000; 20-by-60 inches) cover much larger areas with much less detail. Single-copy prices are $2.75. One helpful publication is *VFR Chart User's Guide* ($3), a 36-page multicolored booklet intended as a learning document for all three types of charts. It includes detailed definitions of the dozens of symbols used on these charts.

Instrument navigation charts, providing information for navigation under instrument flight rules. There are different series for low-altitude flights (below 18,000

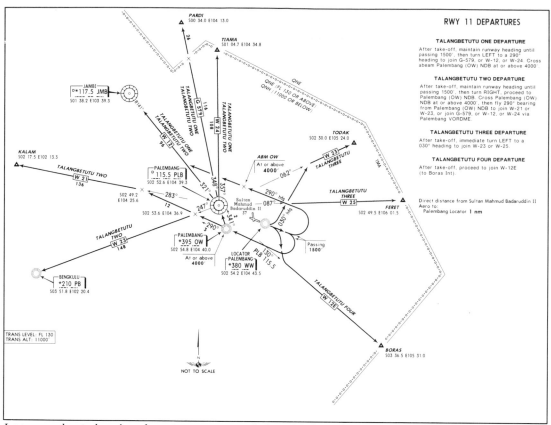

Jeppesen chart showing departure routes at Sultan Mahmud Badaruddin II airport, Palembang, Indonesia. Copyright 1989 Jeppesen Sanderson, Inc.

feet), high-altitude flights, and instrument approach procedure (IAP) charts.

The **Defense Department** also publishes aeronautical charts, which are distributed by NOS and primarily provide information about flying over airspace outside the United States. These can be ordered through Defense Mapping Agency Distribution Services (Washington, DC 20315; 202-227-2495). Defense maps include:

❏ **FLIP (Flight Information Publications) charts** are available for most of the world, including Africa, Asia, and Antarctica. Each map set provides the information needed for flying in foreign airspace.

❏ **Operational navigation charts** provide information on high-speed navigation requirements at medium altitudes.

❏ **Tactical pilotage charts** provide information on high-speed, low-altitude, radar, and visual navigation of high-performance tactical and reconnaissance aircraft at very low through medium altitudes.

❏ **Jet navigation charts** are used for long-range, high-altitude, high-speed navigation.

❏ **Global navigation and planning charts** are suitable for flight planning, operations over long distances, and en

Right: Page from Jeppesen airport directory showing detailed runway information for nine airports in Michigan. Copyright 1989 Jeppesen Sanderson, Inc.

(Delta Co) **see ESCANABA**

CRYSTAL FALLS (Iron)   50D
1340'. 46°01'N 88°16'W.
Lights: Activate RL-121.7.
Mgr: E. Jackson, (906) 265-5525.
Hrs. of opn: Unattended, closed ngts.
Accom: L. Iron Traffic CTAF 122.9.
330°/13.8 NM-Iron Mountain VORTAC.

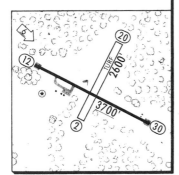

(Custer) **see MONROE**
(Dalton's) **see FLUSHING**
(David's) **see ATHENS**
(Davis) **see EAST LANSING**

DECKERVILLE (Lamont)   56G
745'. 43°35'N 82°39'W.
Mgr: G.H. Lamont, (313) 372-8833.
Hrs. of opn: Irregular. Fuel: 2,4. Lndg
length rwy 9--4955', rwy 18--2005',
rwy 27--4492', rwy 36--2005'.
Accom: T,L. UNICOM CTAF 122.8.
At field-Deckerville NDB.

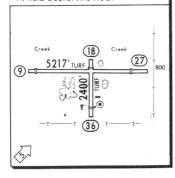

DAVISON (-Genova)   6G0
780'. 43°02'N 83°32'W.
Mgr: D.L. Parks, (313) 653-4443.
Hrs. of opn: Unattended. Lndg length
rwy 8--3351', rwy 26--3186'.
Accom: T,L. Traffic CTAF 122.9.
071°/10.1 NM-Flint VORTAC.

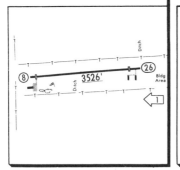

DETROIT (-City)   KDET
626'. 42°25'N 83°01'W. Lights: REIL
15,33. VASI 15,25. RAIL 15. Mgr: L.
Snyder, (313) 267-6400. Fuel: 2,4,JetA.
Ox 3,4. Repairs: MAME. Apt of entry.
Lndg Fee. Lndg length rwy 7--3301', rwy
25--3298, rwy 33--4848'. Accom: All.
ATIS 120.75. APP 126.85. TWR 121.3.
GND 121.9. UNICOM 122.95.
326°/12.5 NM-Windsor VORDME.

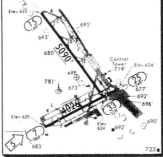

DETROIT/GROSSE ILE   2G5
(Grosse Ile)
590'. 42°06'N 83°10'W. Lights:
Activate MIRL, REIL, VASI 3-123.0.
Mgr: R. Quinn, (313) 675-0155. Hrs. of
opn: 0700-Dusk. Fuel: 3,4. Repairs:
MAME. CAUTION: Birds. Lndg length
rwy 3--4400', rwy 21--4129'. Rgt tfc
rwys 3,35. Accom: All. APP Detroit
120.15. UNICOM CTAF 123.0.
At field-Grosse Ile NDB.

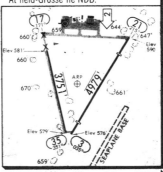

DETROIT (-Metro Wayne Co)   KDTW
639'. 42°13'N 83°21'W. TCA II. Lights:
CL 3L/R, 21L/R. REIL VASI 9, 3C, 21C.
TDZ 3L/R. Rwy 3R ALSF-II ops as SSALR
above RVR 6000'. Mgr: T. Ward, (313)
942-3550. Fuel: 2,4,JetA,JetA-1. Ox 1,3.
Repairs: MAME. LLWAS. Apt. of entry.
Lndg Fee. Accom: All. ATIS 124.55. TCA
Detroit 124.9 (NW/NE), 120.15
(SE), 118.95 (SW). APP Detroit 124.05.
TWR Metro 118.4 (E), 135.0 (W). GND
121.8. UNICOM 122.95.
102°/8.0 NM-Willow Run VORDME.

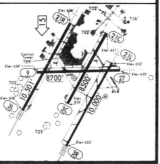

DETROIT (Willow Run)   YIP
716'. 42°14'N 83°32'W.
Lights: VASI 23L, 27L. REIL 27L. Mgr:
T. Ward, (313) 482-2943. Fuel:
2,4,JetA. Ox 1,3. Repairs: MAME.
Accom: All. ATIS 127.45. APP Detroit
124.05. TWR Willow Run 120.0. GND
121.9. UNICOM 122.95.
At field-Willow Run VORDME.

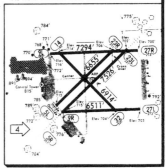

DEXTER (Cackleberry)   2MI9
890'. 42°26'N 83°52'W.
Mgr: J. Wiltse, (313) 426-4493.
Hrs. of opn: Irregular.
Apt gate locked, PPR. Limited snow
removal winter months. Rwy cond
PR. Lndg length rwy 24--1820' days.
Cackleberry Traffic CTAF 122.9.
278°/12.3 NM-Salem

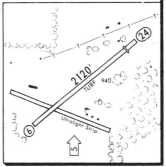

DOWAGIAC (Cass Co Mem'l)   C91
748'. 42°00'N 86°08'W. Lights: After
2330 activate MIRL, VASI, REIL 9,27-
122.8. Mgr: D. LaPointe, (616) 782-
8530. Hrs. of opn: 0900-1900 Apr-Oct,
0900-1700 Nov-Mar. Fuel: JetA.
Repairs: AE. Accom: T,L. APP South
Bend 118.55. UNICOM CTAF 122.8.
181°/9.2 NM-Keeler VORTAC.

route navigation in long-range, high-altitude, high-speed aircraft.

NONGOVERNMENT CHARTS

One of the oldest and largest producers of aeronautical charts is **Jeppesen Sanderson** (55 Inverness Dr. E, Englewood, CO 80112; 303-799-9090), which creates a wide range of charts and other publications for pilots. "Jeppesens," as they are known among pilots, are available only by subscription, which includes the initial charts for a particular area plus updates (biweekly for the United States and Canada, weekly for other areas). In addition to the navigation charts, Jeppesen manuals include a rich lode of additional information pages covering topics such as chart terminology, a glossary, and standard abbreviations. Another Jeppesen publication is its *Bottlang Airfield Manual, offering detailed charts of airports* large and small throughout Europe. There are ten editions, each updated monthly, covering different European countries.

Jeppesen offers a variety of subscription services, described in a free catalog available by writing or calling the company. Also available is a set of sample charts— a U.S. Low Flight Planning Chart, an Enroute Chart, an Area Chart, and the Terminal Charts for an airport in your local area that has a published approach. To obtain the samples, send $1 to cover postage and handling.

WHERE TO BUY CHARTS

The best place to purchase government and nongovernment aeronautical charts is at almost any general aviation airport— that is, an airport, or portions of an airport, that serves private, noncommercial flights. The "fixed-base operators" (or FBOs) that run these private airport facilities typically sell charts covering the immediate region surrounding the airport; some also sell other domestic or international charts. In addition, there are many other retailers of the charts, including many map stores; a list of select retailers is included below.

Government-produced charts, besides being available at many airports and the dealers listed below, also may be purchased through three NOS offices:

❏ 439 W. York St., Norfolk, VA 23510; 804-441-6616.

❏ 1801 Fairview Ave. E, Seattle, WA 98102; 206-442-7657.

❏ Federal Bldg. and Courthouse, 701 C. St., Box 38, Anchorage, AK 99513; 907-271-5040.

These offices also can send you NOS's free *Catalog of Aeronautical Charts and Related Publications.*

Here are a few of the many aeronautical chart dealers:

Aero Supply Inc.
1624 Aviation Center Pkwy.
Daytona Beach, FL 32014

Air Delphia
1834 E. High Ave.
New Philadelphia, OH 44663

Atlanta Pilot Center
1954 Airport Rd., Ste. 66
Atlanta, GA 30341

Aviation International Corp.
5555 N.W. 36th St.
Miami, FL 33166

Aviation Management
195th & Bernham
P.O. Box 553
Lansing, IL 60438

Bodas Aero Mart
3930 Campus Dr.
Newport Beach, CA 92660

Cableair Inc.
Cable Airport
1749 W. 13th St.
Upland, CA 91786

Centerline Flight
P.O. Box 328
Valley City, ND 58072

Chief Aircraft Parts
345 Whispering Pines
Grants Pass, OR 97527

D & M Pilot Supply
4N 116 Wyant Rd.
West Chicago, IL 60185

El Cajon Flying Service Inc.
1825 N. Marshall Ave.
El Cajon, CA 92020

Farmers Flying
2915 Rutger
St. Louis, MO 63104

International Aviation
4135 Donald Douglas Dr.
Long Beach, CA 90808

J-Mar Aero Service
R.R. 2, Box 6C
Litchfield, IL 62056

J. C. Air
400 Industrial Pkwy.
Industrial Airport, KS 66031

Jem Aero
2003 Quail St.
Newport Beach, CA 92660

Kimco Flight Crew
107 Millwood Dr.
Warner Robbins, GA 31088

Marv Golden Discount Store
8690 Aero Dr., Ste. 102
San Diego, CA 92123

The Pilot Shop
106 Access Rd.
Norwood, MA 02062

Plane Things
1875 W. Commercial Blvd., Ste. 180
Ft. Lauderdale, FL 33304

Prescott Pilot Shoppe Inc.
2054 Old Kettle Dr.
Prescott, AZ 86301

San-Val Aircraft Parts
7456 Valjean Ave.
Van Nuys, CA 91406

Sportsman Market
Clermont County Airport
Batavia, OH 45103

Sporty's Pilot Shop
Clermont Airport
Batavia, OH 45103

Wings Inc.
501 N. Dalevill Ave.
Daleville, AL 36322

FLIGHT SIMULATORS

You've probably heard of armchair quarterbacks, but what about desktop pilots? Just as someone enjoying a Sunday-afternoon six pack and a bowl of popcorn can imagine leading a football team to victory, someone else with a personal computer and the proper software can imagine sitting at the controls of a vintage World War I dogfighter, or an F-14 fighter plane.

The catalyst for these flights of imagination are programs called flight simulators. By simply inserting a floppy disk into a personal (or office!) computer, you can become a jet jockey, leaving terra firma behind for a few minutes. After pressing a few buttons, you can soar out over the hills, race against the clock, or hunt down and fight an enemy plane. Keys on the keyboard become controls for the throttle and flaps. A mouse or joystick device can become a flight stick. After a few minutes in front of the screen, it takes only a bit of imagination to lose yourself in the fantasy.

Flight simulators have actually been around for years. But until the age of the personal computer, they were much too expensive for the average person to play with. From the very beginning, the goal of flight simulators was to make the ride as realistic as possible, with moving platforms, multiple projections, and realistic instruments and controls. Even today the most sophisticated home-computer flight simulators are merely pale imitations of state-of-the-art professional versions.

The flight simulation business got off the ground, so to speak, with the formation of the Link Flight Simulation company. The company was established in the late 1920s, when Edwin A. Link began tinkering with spare parts in the basement of his father's pipe organ factory. Using a pneumatic bellows, he found that he could simulate flight motion. Link built his first pilot trainer in 1929, when he was 25 years old. It was a stubby fuselage that looked like a mini-plane with tiny wings. But the simulator was used as little more than a carnival ride until 1934, when the army bought several to train pilots for mail delivery. By the time World War II began, the trainers had become an important tool.

The Link company grew steadily, but its most significant advances came in the computer age. By the 1960s, computers attached to simulators could provide enough computing power to give realistic in-the-air views, but it was another ten years before simulators could process enough data fast enough to provide realistic "real-time" takeoffs and landings.

Today advances in computer graphics have helped simulator engineers create incredibly realistic scenes outside cockpit windows. Link's helicopter trainers feature sunsets, farm fields and villages, and extremely detailed images of other helicopters that may come in for an attack. These simulators sit on hydraulic legs that can raise the platform up to 20 feet. Controllers sit at computerized panels near the simulators, where they can determine what the training pilots see, from weather conditions to other aircraft.

But all this realism does not come cheap. The Apache attack helicopter simulator goes for a cool $30 million. Simulators are not cheap to operate either. A simulator for a Boeing 737 can rent for about $400 an hour.

Yet commercial airliners and the military have known for years that it is cheaper to train pilots, at least some of the time, in front of a computer than inside an airborne plane. Highly elaborate flight simulators have been built, using real-life films combined with computer-graphic images, and full-sized fully equipped cockpits that buzz and blink and tilt and even crash—just like the real thing, but safer. Some simulators are so realistic that pilots who pass their tests in the trainers can go out and fly the actual airplane, with passengers, without ever having taken off in that plane before, although this may not be actual airline policy.

Once the domain of professional pilots, flight simulators moved into the home and office as personal computers became faster and more graphically sophisticated. The simulation software has also kept pace with the expanding capacity of desktop computers. A few years ago it took much more imagination to pretend you were flying a computer-screen airplane. The cockpit instruments appeared only as a series of dots and letters against a dark background, and what little horizon could be seen out of the supposed airplane window was, at best, a meek collection of broken lines.

But no more. Now full-color, highly detailed cockpits are readily available at software stores and by mail order. And you can buy additional software picturing specific areas around the country. This allows you to take off and land at your home airport, and to keep an eye out for familiar landmarks while "in the air."

If all this sounds kind of neat, it is. But unfortunately even in the most recent personal computer versions the picture of what you can see out of a cockpit window is no match for the huge professional simulators. At best the desktop versions look like sparsely detailed cartoons of the real thing. But programmers are great tinkerers, and it's a safe bet that the quality of flight simulators will continue to improve.

The commercial software packages listed here are some of the most popular flight simulators available for personal computers. Most are sold in stores selling computer software, and by mail from companies listed in the back of popular computer magazines. Also listed are helicopter simulators and more sophisticated—and expensive—programs for professionals.

PERSONAL COMPUTER MODELS

Dive Bomber, by Epyx (600 Galveston Dr., Redwood City, CA 94063; 415-366-0606). For IBM PC and compatibles. Set in 1941 at the onset of U.S. involvement in World War II, this program gives you a plane armed with torpedoes and machine gun, and a mission: sink the *Bismarck*, the great German battleship. However, you need to protect your own aircraft carrier at the same time. How can you be in two places at once? It all depends on how good you are. List price: $39.99.

F-19 Stealth Fighter, by Micro Prose (180 Lakefront Dr., Hunt Valley, MD 21030; 301-771-1151). For IBM PC and compatibles, and Apple II. Fly a mission into Southeast Asia, tackle Europe and the Middle East. Seven combat missions let you try your hand at bombing, machine gunning, and surface-to-air missiles. List prices: $34.95 (IBM); $39.95 (Apple).

Falcon AT, by Spectrum Holobyte (2061 Challenger Dr., Alameda, CA 94501; 415-522-3584). For IBM AT or PS/2, model 50 or above, and compatibles. This is an advanced F-16 fighter jet simulator, with high-quality graphics. Fly a mission on your own, or fly against a friend via direct computer hookup. Cartoon figures help you tune in to the action. List price: $59.95.

Flight Simulator II, by Bruce Atwick, Sublogic Corp. (713 Edgebrook Dr.,

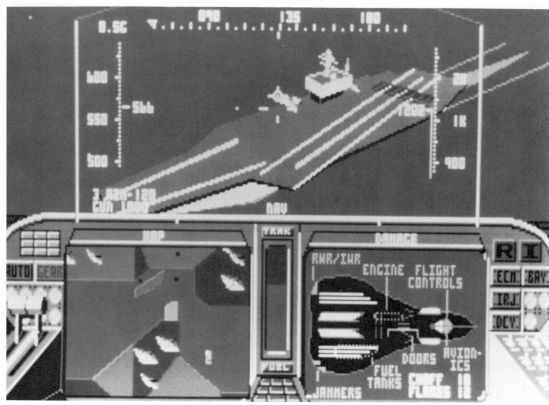

Screen image from F-19 Stealth Fighter, *from Micro Prose. Photo by Gary T. Almes.*

Champaign, IL 61820; 217-359-8482). For Apple II, II plus, IIe, and Macintosh; Atari 800, 800XL/XE, 1400XL, 1450XLD; and Commodore 64/128. Produced by the father of simulation software, *Flight Simulator II* is perhaps the most realistic product around. It has a fully operational instrument panel, and airports come equipped with fuel stops and are at the correct elevation and location. Because this is a basic program, flyers are given background information about aviation principles and skills. Pilots are encouraged to plot courses, keep track of positions, and try fancy maneuvers, such as loops, spins, and figure 8s. List price: $49.95.

General Electric Computer Network (GENIE) (401 N. Washington St., Rockville, MD 20850; voice: 800-638-9636, modem: 800-638-8369). A few years

ago, General Electric decided it wanted to make use of its vast computer resources during the evening, when few employees needed to be on-line. It started GENIE and allowed home computer buffs to tap into its network for $5 an hour ($35 an hour during work hours). The network has a flight simulation section, giving users the ability to allow dozens of airplanes to fly at the same time. Users can "join" a country or take up a plane to "join" a battle. These are usually propeller planes, but the network does organize an occasional jet night. Users can download programs for a variety of cockpits and shoot down other users as they see fit.

Harrier Combat Simulator, by Mindscape, Inc. (2444 Dundee Rd., Northbrook, IL 60062; 312-480-7667). For IBM PC, XT, AT, and compatibles; and Tandy

1000. Learn to fly a Harrier Jump Jet, which has the unique ability to take off and land vertically. Your mission: to attack a desert command post, complete with oil reserves. Blow it up, and get out safely—if you can. List price: $34.95.

Jet, by Sublogic Corp. (713 Edgebrook Dr., Champaign, IL 61820; 217-359-8482). For IBM PC, AT, and compatibles, and PCjr. Take off and land on a bobbing aircraft carrier. *Jet* lets you try your hand at an F-16 fighter jet, running missions for the navy. List price: $49.95.

Microsoft Flight Simulator III by Bruce Atwick (16011 N.E. 36th Way, Box 97017, Redmond, WA 98073; 800-426-9400, 206-882-8080). For IBM PC, XT, AT, and PS/2, or compatibles. Supplemental Microsoft scenery disks included. This is a newer version of *Flight Simulator II* (see earlier listing). This simulator is state of the art, by the father of simulation software. It uses two types of aircraft—a single-engine Cessna 182 light plane and a Learjet 25G business jet. But they are completely instrumented and fly in a highly realistic environment, with cloud layers, winds, thunderstorms, and even stars at night. Twelve different scenery disks cover the United States from coast to coast and include recognizable landmarks and known airports. This software too offers a unique feature: You can connect your computer with a modem and fly against a friend. You also get 10,000 square miles of airspace to play in. The simulator follows FAA visual flight rules. List price: $49.95.

Chuck Yeager's Advanced Flight Trainer, by Electronic Arts (1820 Gateway Dr., San Mateo, CA 94404; 415-571-7171). For IBM PC and compatibles, and Apple. With this software you can sit in the cockpits of 14 different aircraft as you race the clock, or you can perform four formation acts, with legendary pilot Yeager

flying the lead plane. Follow him through the "Dead Man's Slalom" course, for example. If you crash, Yeager's own face will demand "You call yourself a pilot?" Or try pushing the SR-71 jet to the outer limits of the atmosphere. Can you bring it down in one piece? List price: $39.95.

To give your computer an added dose of realism when using flight simulator software, you might want to buy a special attachment that lets you take your controls in hand rather than pretend that your keyboard or mouse is part of an airplane. **Cockpit/Novel Twist** (P.O. Box 2046, Melbourne, FL 32902; 407-254-6484) offers you just such an attachment. The device lets your put your hands on a real yoke, look at real printouts, and play with a variety of instruments. List price: $625 plus shipping.

HELICOPTER SIMULATORS

Gunship, by Micro Prose (180 Lakefront Dr. , Hunt Valley, MD 21030; 301-771-1151). For IBM PC, XT, and AT and compatibles. Jump aboard an Apache attack helicopter and expand your flight experience. Unlike airplanes, helicopters can hover, go backward, fly sideways, and rotate 360 degrees. *Gunship* lets you make combat decisions based on maps, cockpit damage displays, and more. List price: $49.95.

Infiltrator, by Mindscape, Inc. (2444 Dundee Rd., Northbrook, IL 60062; 312-480-7667). For most IBM and Apple computers. Your mission is to attack a military base and eliminate a "mad leader." This tongue-in-cheek game allows you to use a helicopter to infiltrate the enemy's defenses. Has good graphics and a good sense of humor. List price: $29.95.

3-D Helicopter Simulator, by Sierra On-Line (**address tk**). For most IBM computers and compatibles. A good, basic learn-

Cockpit of a general aviation simulator from Aviation Simulation Technology.

to-fly helicopter program that also let you look at your craft from outside the pilot's perspective, such as from a radar tower. List price: $49.95.

PROFESSIONAL FLIGHT SIMULATORS

Aviation Simulation Technology (AST, Hanscom Field East, Bedford, MA 01730; 617-274-6600). Keeping price in mind, AST has put together a sampling of generic simulators that can be used for basic training in a specific environment. The company's three big sellers are the model 201 Single Engine simulator ($67,250), the model 300 Multi Engine simulator ($69,750), and the model 300 Turboprop ($124,750). These units can be customized with a wide range of optional equipment. AST also has ventured into color visual displays. Like their black-and-white predecessors, the new displays automatically create a scene of the horizon, sky, ground track, and speed, allowing the instructor to select weather conditions and airport configuration.

Over the past few years a flight school in New Jersey has relied solely on flight simulators, especially AST simulators, to train its students. This school does not even own an airplane!

Frasca International (606 S. Neil St., Champaign, IL 61820; 217-359-3951). Founded in 1958, Frasca makes machines that are real workhorses in the flight-simulation industry. Its 140 and 240 series are very popular with flight schools, and Frasca's stated goal is to keep the cost of flight simulation within reach of major private training schools. Frasca's 142-T trainer, which can simulate any category of aircraft up to the light twin-turboprop class, can be delivered for around $100,000. Most of Frasca's designs feature a working cockpit and an instructor's computer station. Images are generated on a screen in front of the cockpit window.

CAE Link Corp., Flight Simulation Division (Binghamton, NY 13902; 607-

721-6646). The military end of Link Flight Simulation is now part of CAE Link Corporation. It has built some of the biggest flight simulators in the business, including advanced spacecraft simulators for NASA for the Gemini, Apollo, Skylab, and space shuttle programs. As the oldest flight simulator company in the business, Link has the most experience and makes the widest variety of simulators. Its helicopter flight and weapons systems trainers are among the most advanced in the world and take a whole roomful of computers to feed information to the interactive visual systems.

An advanced Link simulator costs far more than most people can afford. To operate the AH-64A Apache helicopter simulator, for example, the U.S. Army spends $625 an hour. But that's quite a bargain, considering that operating the real aircraft can cost $1,820 an hour, plus thousands of dollars for ammunition. A more realistic alternative for the average pilot might be Link's Microflight System. This system comes in two parts: a cockpit and an instructor station. Its visual effects are nice, but not nearly as stunning as those of the bigger models. And the price is a relatively cheap $250 an hour.

Singer Link Miles Corporation (Binghampton, NY 13902; 607-721-6646). This offshoot of the Link organization supplies commercial airlines with the Link Microflight System, an alternative to the CAE Flight Simulators. This system comes in two parts: a cockpit and an instructor station. Its visual effects are nice, but not nearly as stunning as those of the bigger models. Microflight prices begin at a half-million dollars.

Flight Planners

A fairly new addition in flight software, flight planners offer pilots an alternative way to familiarize themselves with basic flight information. This includes weather reports and forecasts, fuel requirements, alternative landing sites, air traffic, and designated runway lengths. Although relatively few pilots have turned to computer software to find out this information, computers do offer some advantages. They are a quick, efficient, and relatively inexpensive way to find out important details pilots must be aware of before climbing into that cockpit. Here is a list, by company, of popular flight planners and a description of the services they provide.

Creative Business Computers (P.O. Box 62197, Sunnyvale, CA 94088; 408-730-9330) offers a relatively simple software package, *Flight Planning System*, with only very basic flight information. It supplies data about altitudes, wind speeds, takeoff fuel consumption, and en route descents and descent rates. The software makes important computations and then provides a detailed printout outlining the flight plan. Unfortunately, its data base is limited to western states. The data base also includes basic information needed for filling out FAA flight plans. The annual subscription is $99, and the data base can be updated every 56 days through a subscription with the publisher. One free update is included with the subscription. List price: $99.

EZ-Flight Software (12021 Wilshire Blvd., Ste. 172, Los Angeles, CA 90025; 818-997-7444) offers simple charts and logs to help a pilot plan a trip with up to 29 legs. You can store common routes and customize routes as needed for any aircraft. The software even gives a graphic routing display and a cost-performance analysis to compare different aircraft, winds, and altitudes for a given flight. Its data base includes descriptions of 20 popular aircraft, airports, routes, and intersections. Annual updates are $30. List price: $99.95.

FltGuide/RSE (Auburn, WA 98071; 800-445-8170) offers the *FltGuideEX* flight planner system, which has the advantage of extreme portability. Another advantage is that the *EX* asks for all the information it needs, so there are no formulas to remember. The *EX* performs 24 calculations, ranging from distance, bearing, and projected position to fuel flow, ground speed, and point of no return. It also features nine-leg flight planning, direct "great circle" navigation calculations, customized weight and balance, and a 16K RAM computer. List price: $239.

IGS International (130 Redwood Pl., Scotts Valley, CA 95066; 408-438-2276) is the only flight planner available that includes complete data bases for other parts of the world. It offers characteristics of airspaces over Australia, Central America, and South America. The data base also has a directory of aircraft and a summary giving information about departure times, enroute, and destination segments. A step-by-step navigational log is part of the package. List price: $99.95 for western, central, or eastern regional data bases. Additional data bases are $29.95 for one and $49.95 for two. Foreign data bases are $34.95 each. Directory updates (three a year) are $49.95 for one region, $69.95 for two regions, and $89.95 for the entire United States.

The Flight Planner, from EZ-Flight Software.

RMS Technology (9680 S. Gribble Rd., Canby, OR 97013; 800-533-3211; 503-266-7688) is the maker of *Flitesoft Personal Flight Planner* and *Flitesoft Professional Flight Planner*, two of the first and most popular programs. Easy planning techniques, an extensive data base with a comprehensive airport directory, and exciting graphics are just a few of the software's unique features. The package for professional pilots includes information to make a complete cost-accounting evaluation, printouts, and telephone support if a problem comes up. List price: $125 for the personal package; $245 for the professional package.

AVIATION STUFF

Whether you're an armchair ace or a toughened test pilot, there are stores and mail-order outlets around the country with aviation products galore to please you. Many such stores are located at or near airports, and here you will find local pilots stocking up on logbooks and flight suits. Other stores specialize in vintage or collectible aviation and military artifacts; there's even an auction and collectors' clearinghouse for such rarities of flight, called **Air Cargo Aviation Auction** (c/o House of History, 4635 Woodsorrel Ct., Colorado Springs, CO 80917; 719-574-4382), which helps collectors and sellers of aviation artifacts connect with one another. For the more erudite of flight, signed lithographs and oil paintings can be found at specialty galleries such as Heritage Aviation Art. But for those seeking cheaper thrills, good old Army-Navy surplus stores, such as Kaufman's, often stock inexpensive aviation clothing and even a few collectibles. For those who want a little bit of everything, there are the giant aviation stores, such as Wings and The Cockpit; they feature thousands of aviation-related items, from profes-

Illustrations by Hank Caruso, from Heritage Aviation Art. Clockwise from upper left: "Delivering the Hornets Sting," "Harrier's in Hot," "Trapping the Phantom," and "Speed of Heat at 80,000 Feet."

sional flight calculators to T-shirts and insignia.

There are also entire bookstores devoted to aviation publications, training manuals, and historical studies; there's even a book club for aviators. And, for those who prefer watching to reading, there are a number of aviation video distributors and rental clubs.

Here is a sampling of available "stuff." You are advised to contact each organization directly to obtain its latest catalog and price list.

AVIATION ART

Heritage Aviation Art (8500 Perimeter Rd. S, Boeing Field, Seattle, WA 98108; 206-767-4170), a gallery dedicated to displaying and selling works of fine art depicting aviation. It offers a variety of lithographs, prints, and paintings. Recent offerings have included Harley Copic's limited-edition print *Into the Unknown*, autographed by Chuck Yeager (1,000 prints, $120 each); and John Young's oil painting *Two Majesties*, depicting a Boeing flying boat ($4,000).

Wings (P.O. Box 430, Daleville, AL 36322; 205-598-4270), a mail-order source for all things aviational, has a large selection of posters, lithographs, statuettes, carvings, and other art depicting flight, aircraft, and great aviators. Among the recent offerings are a collection of signed prints of classic helicopters (16 by 20 inches for $8.50, 11 by 14 inches for $6.50) and note cards of the same prints (75 cents each); bronze-stone renditions of military aviators by sculptor Terrance Patterson ($69); and limited-edition prints of Jim Stovall's detailed sketches of military helicopters, training aircraft, and other vehicles ($20).

CLOTHING AND GEAR

The Aviator's Store (7201 Perimeter Rd., Boeing Field International, Seattle, WA 98101; 206-763-0666) stocks a large

Aviator's jacket from The Cockpit.

selection of jumpsuits ($49 to $110), pilot shirts ($19.95 to $29.95), and leather bomber jackets ($79 to $279) by makers such as Avirex, Schott Brothers, and Mirage. The store also stocks aviation books and supplies, gift items, and other related materials at a wide range of prices.

The Cockpit (33-00 47th Ave., Long Island City, NY 11101; 718-482-1860) is a mail-order store (with a retail outlet at 595 Broadway, New York City; 212-925-5455) offering a variety of flight clothing and related gear. Among the items available are an Avirex current-issue U.S. Air Force goatskin aviator's jacket ($300); World War II-styled fighter pilot's coveralls made of cotton poplin, with plenty of pockets and pouches ($99); a Flying Tigers "bail out" bag, a roomy knapsack made from antiqued leather and sewn with Flying Tigers insignia ($195); and a classic white silk aviator's scarf ($22.50).

Flight Suits Ltd. (1675-D Pioneer Way, El Cajon, CA 92020; 619-440-6976) sells uniforms, flight suits, custom-made helmets, aviation gear, and gift items. Products include airline crew and emergency medical flight uniforms (starting at $112), various military white and designer helmets (starting at $175), test pilot's boots ($115), and flight jackets (starting at $195 for a lady's goatskin model and ranging up to $435 for a Royal Air Force sheepskin version).

Kaufman's West Army and Navy Goods (1660 Eubank St. NE, Albuquerque, NM 87112; 505-293-2300) stocks a wide variety of military surplus clothing and gear, including many aviation-related items. Products include an insulated NASA nylon jumpsuit ($70), a heavy-weight U.S. Air Force flight jacket ($95), and an Israeli canvas paratrooper shoulder bag ($28).

Watkins Aviation (15770 Midway Rd., Hangar 6, Dallas, TX 75244; 214-934-0033) sells a variety of flying clothing and gear, including flight suits similar to those currently issued in the military, patches, wings, and insignia from the U.S. armed forces, aviator's glasses, compasses, and other gear. Prices range from $3.50 for an embroidered U.S. Air Force World War II insignia, to $350 for a single-visor military white flight helmet.

Wings (P.O. Box 430, Daleville, AL 36322; 205-598-4270) sells a broad range of aviation clothing and flight gear for adults and children. Products include a military-issue mesh survival vest with pockets for gear ($59), a nylon child's flight jacket styled to resemble a classic World War II leather bomber jacket ($39), a leather flight case for carrying charts and other necessary aviation gear ($179), and a quilted nylon bag for stowing one's helmet ($24).

Jump suit from Flight Suits Ltd.

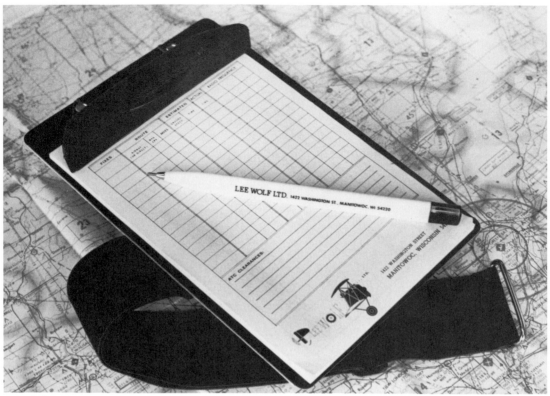

Pilot's log from Aviation Book Company.

INSTRUMENTS AND SUPPLIES

Aviation Book Company (1640 Victory Blvd., Glendale, CA 91201; 818-240-1771) sells a variety of instruments, maps and charts, record books, and related items. Offerings include a pilot master logbook ($24.95), aircraft expense record ($9.95), a rotating azimuth plotter ($7.95), and Los Angeles helicopter charts ($2.25).

AWK Aviation Checklists (5539 W. 142nd Pl., Hawthorne, CA 90250; 213-643-8386) sells pilot checklists and related flight supplies. Items include checklist cards for a variety of planes, as well as a set of cards adaptable to any vehicle ($12.50 each), IFR and VFR flight management logs ($8.50), and a time/distance/speed table ($2.75).

Watkins Aviation (15770 Midway Rd., Hangar 6, Dallas, TX 75244; 214-934-0033) sells a selection of U.S. military issue plotters and computers. Items available include an MB-4A slide computer, navigator-sized ($33.50), a PLU-1A/C plotter, for air navigation for world aeronautical charts and sectional charts ($5), and a PT-2 computer for high-altitude air navigation ($23).

Wings (P.O. Box 430, Daleville, AL 36322; 205-598-4270) sells a variety of aviation supplies, flight instruments, and related items. Inventory includes a pilot-sized etched-aluminum "dead reckoning" computer for accurate navigational calculations ($27.95), a holding-pattern computer ($7.95), and a ProStar electronic flight computer for fast calculations of altitude, airspeed, crosswind components, and other important flight factors ($195).

Flight patches from The Cockpit.

PATCHES, MEDALS AND INSIGNIA

The Cockpit (33-00 47th Ave., Long Island City, NY 11101; 718-482-1860) sells numerous aviation-related insignia, wings, patches, and medals, including "blood chit" identification patches like those worn by the Flying Tigers during the World War II South Pacific campaign ($13 to $24); Royal Air Force button and blazer crest set in a presentation case ($89); and various World War II cloisonné insignia, made by the original supplier ($8.95).

Queen City Military Sales (5443 Fox Rd., Cincinnati, OH 45239; 513-681-5233) distributes a large selection of aviation-related patches and insignia and some international military aviation wings. Recent offerings have included U.S. Navy VXE-6 (Antarctic) Search and Rescue Team patches ($9 each), U.S. Air Force Air Weather Service patches ($1.50 each), and a Royal Air Force Chaplain air marshal hat badge from World War II, in mint condition ($40). Some surplus and vintage uniforms are also sold. Some items, particularly foreign ones, are rare, so the stock changes frequently.

Watkins Aviation (15770 Midway Rd., Hangar 6, Dallas, TX 75244; 214-934-0033) sells U.S. Air Force and other armed forces embroidered patches, ribbon decorations, insignia, and wings, including many from World War II. Prices range from $3.50 for an embroidered insignia from the Far East Air Force of World War II to $8 for a pair of Air Force command pilot regulation metal wings.

Wings (P.O. Box 430, Daleville, AL 36322; 205-598-4270) sells a large selection of pilot's wings, insignia, and patches. Recent offerings include brass army aviator wings ($11.95), miniature medals such as those for the Purple Heart ($7.95), and the Air Medal ($7.50) and a variety of military/aviation ribbons (75 cents), rank insignia (60 cents a pair), and qualification badges for everything from parachutist ($4.50) to flight surgeon ($5.50).

PUBLICATIONS

Aircraft Designs (11082 Bel Aire Ct., Cupertino, CA 95014; 408-255-8688) publishes and distributes several books on aircraft design, gyrocopter flight, and related topics. Works available include *Composite Aircraft Design* ($20), *Gyrocopter Pilot's Manual* ($50), and *Modern Subsonic Aerodynamics* ($28). This company also produces and distributes manuals and software programs for computer airplane design, with prices running about $35 for the software disks and $36 for the manuals.

American Institute of Aeronautics and Astronautics (The Aerospace Center, 370 L'Enfant Promenade, SW, Washington, DC 20024; 202-646-7400) publishes a variety of aeronautic and astronautic manuals, case studies, textbooks, and journals. Publications include *Radar Electronic Warfare* ($49.95 to nonmembers), *AIAA Aerospace Design Engineers Guide* ($32 to nonmembers), and the *Journal of Propulsion and Power* (bimonthly; $180 to nonmembers). Discounts for members (see "Aviation Organizations").

Aviation Book Company (1640 Victory Blvd., Glendale, CA 91201; 818-240-1771) publishes and distributes its own and other publishers' products, including a vast array of aviation books and related items in areas from popular culture to technical manuals. Biographies, memoirs,

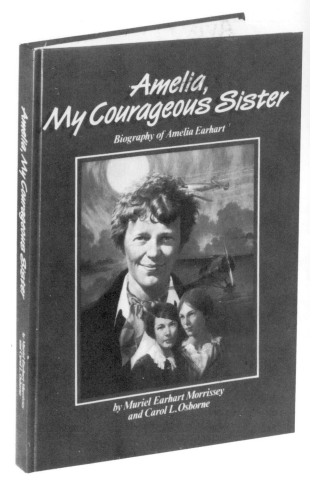

military histories, and training materials are highlights of the company's offerings. Titles available include *Amelia, My Courageous Sister* by Muriel Earhart Morrissey and Carol Osborne ($23.95), *The Complete Private Pilot* by Bob Gardner ($15.95), and *Ghosts: Vintage Aircraft of World War II* by Philip Markanna ($36). The company also offers a variety of videos and gift items (see following sections).

Aviation Publishers (One Aviation Way, Dept. D, Lock Box 234, Hummelstown, PA 17036) publishes and distributes books and training and construction manuals. Recent offerings include *Canard—A Revolution in Flight* ($17.95), *Ultralight Airmanship* ($10.95), and *Composite Construction* ($17.95).

Aviators Guild Book Club (c/o Tab Books Inc., Blue Ridge Summit, PA 17294; 717-794-2191) distributes a variety of books and manuals on aviation history, technology, culture, and related topics. Members receive 14 club bulletins a year, detailing a main and alternate selections, offered at a discount from the publisher's price.

Federal Aviation Administration (U.S. Department of Transportation, Utilization and Storage Section, M-443.2, Washington, DC 20590; 202-783-3238) publishes and distributes a regular series of free advisory circulars outlining FAA regulations and findings on a wide range of commercial and private aviation subjects, including pilot and flight certification, airworthiness of aviation vehicles, computer software, and flight safety. A catalog of available circulars, *Advisory Circular Checklist and Status of Other FAA Publications*, is available. In addition to its free circulars, the FAA also produces a number of other publications, including books, tests, manuals, and technical specifications, which may be purchased at GPO bookstores, or by writing Superintendent of Documents, U.S. Government Printing Office, Washington, DC 20402. FAA publications available through the GPO include *Bilateral Airworthiness Agreements* ($7), *Utility Airports—Air Access to National Transportation* ($5.50), and *Guide to Drug Hazards in Aviation Medicine* ($5.50). FAA flight charts are also available from GPO.

House of History (4635 Woodsorrel Ct., Colorado Springs, CO 80917; 719-574-4382), which also runs Air Cargo Aviation, an auction and distribution clearinghouse for aviation items, offers a series of reference books and booklets on military insignia and badges, including many from aviation forces. Among the works available are *Wings of the Nationalist Chinese Armed Forces* ($7) and *Wings of the Canadian Armed Forces, 1913-1972* ($7).

Smithsonian Institution Press (Dept. 900, Blue Ridge Summit, PA 17214; 717-794-2148) publishes books on the history and technology of aviation and space travel. Among the press's offerings are *The Wright Brothers, Heirs of Prometheus*, edited by Richard Hallion ($9.95); *Famous Personalities of Flight Cookbook* by Mary Henderson ($5.95); *Black Wings, The American Black in Aviation* by Von Hardesty and Dominick Pisano ($6.95); and *Air Warfare in the Missile Age* by Lon O. Nordeen, Jr. ($24.95). Also available through the press are three archival videodisks ($45 each) that combined reproduce the entire photographic collection of the National Air and Space Museum.

Wings (P.O. Box 430, Daleville, AL 36322; 205-598-4270) sells a variety of training manuals, vehicle guides, and exam books. Offerings include publications such as *Aerobic Flight Training Manual* ($9.95), *Aviation College Directory* ($12.95), and *World Encyclopedia of Aero Engines* (24.95).

SOUVENIR AND GIFT ITEMS

The Cockpit (33-00 47th Ave., Long Island City, NY 11101; 718-482-1860) sells a variety of aviation gifts and accessories. Among the items offered are T-shirts with renditions of 1940s "pinup" girls for flyers ($18.50); baseball caps emblazoned with command insignia ($9.95 to $15.50); and a brightly painted kid's airplane desk for ages 2 through 6 that measures almost 4 feet long ($125).

Flight Suits Ltd. (1675-D Pioneer Way, El Cajon, CA 92020; 619-440-6976) offers a selection of aviation-related gift items, including a 5-foot replica of a propeller embedded with a quartz-movement clock ($250) and a variety of aviation-related desk accessories featuring statues of aviators ($40 to $110).

Wings (P.O. Box 430, Daleville, AL 36322;

205-598-4270) offers an extensive collection of flight-related gift and commemorative items. Products include a plush stuffed "Aviator Bear," complete with his own flight jacket ($39.95); coffee mugs emblazoned with slogans ("Helicopters Don't Fly . . . They Beat the Air into Submission") or with the names and logos of aircraft manufacturers ($4.50 each); a wine cork adorned with a tiny ceramic bust of a pilot ($9.95); an T-shirts illustrated with various brightly colored electronic graphics of airplanes and helicopters ($15).

VIDEOS

ARP Videos Inc. (P.O. Box 4617, North Hollywood, CA 91607; 818-506-4081) distributes a wide variety of entertainment and training videos on aviation, military history, and motor sports. Titles include *Flying the B-17* ($49.95), *Kamikaze* ($39.95), and *Project X-15* ($49.95).

Aviation Action Videos (3960 Laurel Canyon Blvd., Ste. 244, Studio City, CA 91604; 818-980-9049) distributes classic aviation documentaries, training films, and other flight-related videotapes. Titles include FAA safety programs such as *Warm Front, Cold Front, Tips on Winter Flying* ($19.95); a collection of four World War II aviation films and propaganda dramas: *To the Gates of Japan, Handing It Back, My Japan*, and *Freedom Comes High* ($39.95 for the four); and *History of the Air Force (1931-1953)* ($39.95).

Aviation Book Company (1640 Victory Blvd., Glendale, CA 91201; 818-240-1771) sells a variety of aviation videos, including six tapes in the Modern Combat Aircraft series ($29.95 each), and *U.S. Military Aviation, 1903-1945* ($29.95).

Aviation Video Rentals (1111 W. El Camino Real, Ste. 109-347, Sunnyvale, CA 94087; 408-224-1654) is a membership video club that rents videos on topics such as visualized flight, safety, flight instruction, and instrument flying. Rental is $10 per tape, including postage and handling; membership fee is $35.

VINTAGE AND COLLECTOR'S ITEMS

Aviator's World (Mojave Airport, Tower Bldg. 58, Mojave, CA 93501; 805-824-2424) sells vintage, collectible, and surplus aviation and military clothing, gear, and instruments. Typical offerings include Jet Aircrew helmets with bayonet receivers ($350), a World War II "Lollipop" Signal Corps microphone ($39.50), a Royal Air Force Survival Fishing Kit ($25), and an A-5 Auto Pilot control box from the U.S. Army Air Corps ($55). Old flight-training and service manuals and handbooks from U.S. Air Force and Royal Air Force are also sold at prices ranging from $35 to $250. Many of the items offered are quite rare, so the stock changes rapidly. A yearly subscription to *Collectors Paper*, Aviator's World's catalog, is available for $5, or free with a $25 purchase.

The Cockpit (33-00 47th Ave., Long Island City, NY 11101; 718-482-1860) sells a selection of authentic aviation items and collectibles. Among recent offerings are original-issue U.S. Air Force oxygen bailout bottles ($20); rare original World War II escape maps printed on cloth or nylon by the Army Map Service ($50); Royal Flying Corps Sopwith bags dating to before World War I ($50); and AN-6530 World War II flight goggles ($200).

Kaufman's West Army and Navy Goods (1660 Eubank NE, Albuquerque, NM 87112; 505-293-2300) sells military and aviation surplus, including some rare early items and reproductions, such as flight goggles made in 1942 by the Foster Grant company ($35 each), silk aviator's scarves ($19.50 each), and "Snoopy" calfskin flight helmets ($35 each).

SPACE FLIGHT

SPACE FLIGHT

We humans have always wanted to fly. And once we learned how, we wanted to fly far, far away.

In scarcely more than a quarter of a century we have flown far indeed. Although we have not fulfilled the futuristic visions of science-fiction writers—who would have us by now living comfortable lives in distant galaxies, commuting with ease to and from our home planet—our accomplishments have been nothing short of remarkable.

Unlike most other ongoing high-tech developments, the space program, as it has come to be called, has been fiercely monitored at nearly every step by citizens of all ages, from schoolchildren on up. Who cannot remember at least one awe-inspiring space-related event that kept us glued to televisions and radios, sometimes for days? From the first trip by a monkey in space—Ham, a 37-pound chimpanzee, who took an 18-minute, 420-mile ride over the Caribbean on January 31, 1961—through the death and rebirth of the space shuttle in the mid-1980s, our adventures in space have been part and parcel of American culture. Almost as a family we have shared the joys and sorrows, the trials and tribulations that have accompanied our pioneering and often heroic efforts.

Those efforts did not come without dreams. For centuries a host of dreamers around the world wondered what it would be like to soar high into the heavens—and how it could be done. In the 1866 book *From the Earth to the Moon*, Jules Verne's hero Michael Ardan explains quite matter-of-factly how simple it would be to travel to the moon—the distance from the earth to the moon being less than nine circumferences of the moon, a distance already traveled by experienced sailors. What's more, he figured, it would take an express train only 300 days to travel to the moon. But Verne didn't stop with this simple reasoning. He went on to express his belief that one day soon people would travel to the moon, and that there was probably life on distant planets.

Verne and other dreamers spurred on scientists of the day and may have been partially responsible for early insights into space technology. Early speculations are credited to a Russian scientist, Konstantin Tsiolkowski, sometimes called the father of space travel. Tsiolkowski, writing in the early 1900s, was the first person to understand that the propulsion for space travel had to come from rockets. He grasped the basic and important concept that gas escaping into space would cause the rocket's thrust, and that a rocket could function in a vacuum, essential for a vehicle leaving the protection of earth's atmosphere.

Meanwhile, in the United States, another young scientist, Robert H. God-

Do You Remember?

Most of us recall some key event in the U.S. space program: days when youngsters were yanked out of class to watch fly-bys approaching a distant planet, or people gathered around TVs to see Neil Armstrong's footprints on the moon's surface. Those were the days when it was not unusual to talk about manned missions to Mars or space stations equipped with homes and spacemobiles.

Today we've taken the space program pretty much for granted, although events can command national intrigue from time to time. Still, it's not like the good old days. To keep those heady days in mind, here is a warp-speed time line of some of the highlights, inspiring us to keep reaching for the stars.

1958: *Explorer 1*—first scientific discovery in space, the Van Allen radiation belts.
1959: *Explorer 6*—first television images of earth from space.
1961: Alan Shepard—first American in space, flying 116.5 miles up in a 15-minute trip.
1962: John Glenn rides the Mercury capsule *Friendship 7*, circling the globe three times in just under five hours.
1962: *Mariner 2*—first scientific discovery in interplanetary space: the direct observation of solar wind. *Mariner 2* also goes to Venus.
1965: *Gemini 3*—first flight in which scientists learned to switch orbits.
1965: *Gemini 4*—first U.S. walk in space.
1968: *Apollo 8*—the first manned mission to the moon.

1961—Ham, a 37-pound chimpanzee, survives the first American experimental space shot.

1969: *Apollo 11*—the first time humans land on another celestial body—in this case, the moon.
1971: *Apollo 15*—first manned roving vehicle to the moon.
1974: *Mariner 10*—first spacecraft to visit two planets: Venus and Mercury.
1976: *Viking 1*—first successful landing on Mars and the first spacecraft to search for life on another planet.
1979: *Voyager 1* reveals Jupiter's ring and the volcanoes of its moon Io.
1980-1981: *Voyagers 1* and *2*—first close-up study of Saturn, its rings, and moons.
1980-1984: *Solar Maximum Mission*—first satellite to be retrieved, repaired, and redeployed in space.
1981: The space shuttle—first manned reusable spacecraft, debuts.
1986: *Voyager 2*—first close-up look at Uranus.
1988: The flight of the shuttle *Discovery* brings the U.S. back into the space race.

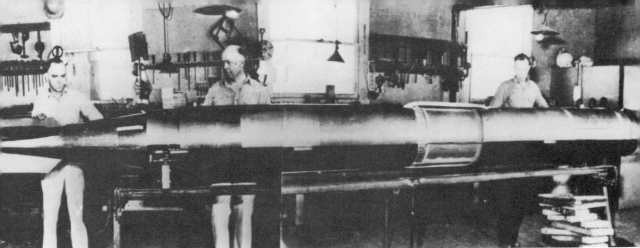

Robert Goddard and crew work on early rocket, circa 1941. Courtesy National Aeronautics and Space Administration.

dard, was developing very similar concepts. According to popular lore, at age 17, Goddard climbed a cherry tree to prune its branches and looked down at the countryside. He was so moved by this vision that he vowed to create a device that could travel to the planets, enabling others to watch the earth recede as they went. The event played such a powerful role in Goddard's life that he celebrated its anniversary each year.

Whatever the real reason, Goddard worked his whole life on rocket designs, launching the world's first liquid-fueled rocket in 1926. He continued to perfect liquid-fueled rockets until his death in 1945. Unfortunately, his work didn't capture the public's imagination—or the government's financial support—and by the time of his death, he had all but vanished from the public eye. The Soviets, meanwhile, combined drive, technical skill, and government backing to push ahead with their space efforts.

Soviet scientist Sergei Korolyev was the inspiration behind Russian rocketry. Working with the Group for the Study of Jet Propulsion, also known as GIRD, he perfected both rocket propulsion and space travel. As a result, the Soviets launched the first *Sputnik* satellite in 1957.

This historic event took the United States by surprise. Although there were a few research programs in place by the late 1950s, Americans hadn't yet managed to put an artificial satellite into orbit. Much work needed to be done. And there was public clamor to compete with the Soviet Union, whose nuclear capabilities had made it the United States' global rival for political supremacy. Should the Soviets maintain and enhance their technological superiority in space, it was reasoned, they could be well positioned to gain worldwide dominance.

Moreover, it soon became evident that the Soviets' lead in space research pointed up an even bigger problem for Americans: a lack of technical expertise, particularly among children. For example, everything from telephone communications to intercontinental ballistic missiles required complex calculations; so too did the new computing machines, capable of calculating *pi* to more than 3,000 decimal places in just minutes. One result was "the New Math," an attempt to inspire mathematical prowess in American schoolchildren, in hopes that they might be better prepared to meet the technological challenges of foreigners—Soviet or otherwise—head-on. It's a challenge Americans are still trying to meet.

As for the United States' space efforts, one problem was that there was no effective government agency in place to

John Glenn, the first American to orbit the earth, rides in a celebratory 1962 parade through Washington, D.C., accompanied by his wife, children, and Vice President Lyndon Johnson.

oversee the massive operation needed to catch up with—and surpass—the Russians. The military was involved in some research, but popular opinion held that space travel should be under the control of civilians. It turned out that a small office existed; called the National Advisory Committee for Aeronautics, it had been set up in 1915 for aeronautical research. Given new life by the spirit of international competition, this small agency was to become the National Aeronautics and Space Agency—later the National Aeronautics and Space Administration—better known as NASA.

The rest, as they say, is history.

THE STATE OF THE SPACE PROGRAM
by Keay Davidson

Just two decades ago the United States dominated the heavens and the earth. It was the world's richest and most advanced nation, and proved it by planting the Stars and Stripes on the moon in July 1969. Nothing, it seemed, was impossible. If Americans could go to the moon then surely they could conquer poverty, cancer, racism, crime—even the common cold. Back then top NASA officials expected that by the 1970s and 1980s Americans would have established a permanent manned space station, built a manned lunar base, and landed humans on Mars. None of these has come true.

Since the 1960s the world has changed dramatically: The Vietnam War, the oil shortage, the Iran crisis, the skyrocketing deficit, and the invasion of Japanese cars, VCRs, and semiconductors have all eroded Americans' faith in the future. Not all is gloom, but as the nation's economic and technological strengths have waned, so has its space program.

❏ Going to the moon is no longer possible—the fleet of Saturn 5 rockets which first flew Neil Armstrong, Buzz Aldrin, and Michael Collins to the moon has been scrapped; some blueprints for the rockets reportedly have been lost.

❏ NASA's brightest dreams—a space station, a lunar base, a manned flight to Mars—are starving from lack of political support. Congress is still debating how much to fund the proposed station; experts agree its cost will be double the original estimate—$8 billion—and perhaps top $30 billion.

❏ The solar system is littered with a quarter century's worth of American high-tech debris—the ruins of space spectaculars gone sour. The U.S. moon program was cut off early; *Skylab*, America's first stab at a space station (which was bigger than the Soviets' *Mir* space station), plummeted back to earth because the shuttle was not built in time to boost it into a higher orbit.

❏ The ashes of the space shuttle *Challenger* are buried in silos at Kennedy Space Center in Florida—the ultimate discredit, critics say, to the ill-run program that made promises it couldn't keep. The disaster virtually halted the U.S. space program for two and a half years.

❏ The sky is full of Soviets. Cosmonauts are conducting experiments aboard their *Mir* space station. In 1988 the Soviets launched an unmanned spaceship on a historic trip to Phobos, a tiny moon of Mars. They also have begun providing launch space aboard their rockets to satellite customers, including Americans.

❏ And spaceships from Japan, China, and a consortium of European nations may also clutter the heavens in coming years, stealing satellite-launching business from the United States.

Yet hope springs eternal at NASA. In interviews with NASA personnel across the nation, most—but not all—expressed confidence the agency would weather its current woes as it weathered past crises—the launch pad fire that killed three astronauts in 1967, the *Apollo 13* explosion that could have stranded Americans in lunar orbit, and the long and embarrassing delays in the development of the

How to Become an Astronaut

The childhood dream of becoming an astronaut and heading for the stars may not be as outlandish, or as impossible, as it once seemed, although it's no piece of cake. Today NASA accepts applications on a continuous basis for what it calls *pilot astronaut candidates* and *mission specialist astronaut candidates*. The process goes something like this:

By filling out several simple forms, applicants start the process rolling. Mission specialist astronauts may be military or civilian. They must have a bachelor's degree in engineering, biological science, physical science, or mathematics and three years of related professional experience, or a doctoral degree. They must pass a NASA space physical, which is similar to a military or civilian flight physical. Requirements include visual acuity of 20/100 or better, blood pressure of 140/90, and a height of between 5 feet and 5 feet, 4 inches. Candidates who make it to a final screening undergo additional tests to evaluate cardiovascular health, exercise capacity, pulmonary function, and tolerance to acceleration forces.

Those qualifications are checked during a six-month period, beginning with NASA's selection cycles. Accepted candidates are hired temporarily and asked to report to the Johnson Space Center, Texas, to spend a year contributing to ongoing NASA programs and participating in the astronaut training program. Final selection does not come until after completion of the training program and successful medical evaluation. At that time applicants become permanent NASA employees; they are expected to stay for at least five years.

During that time they may receive a space assignment.

On space shuttle flights mission specialist astronauts take responsibility for projects such as crew activity planning and experiments conducted in space. Astronauts who pass more stringent physical tests and who enter the space program with at least 1,000 hours commanding jet aircraft may become pilot astronauts. Aboard a spaceflight, they take responsibility for the vehicle, the crew, and the safety

and success of the mission.

Only a few lucky candidates become part of a space shuttle crew. A typical shuttle crew consists of a commander and pilot—both pilot astronauts—and three mission specialists.

For more information, write NASA, Johnson Space Center, Astronaut Selection Office, Attn.: AHX, Houston, TX 77058.

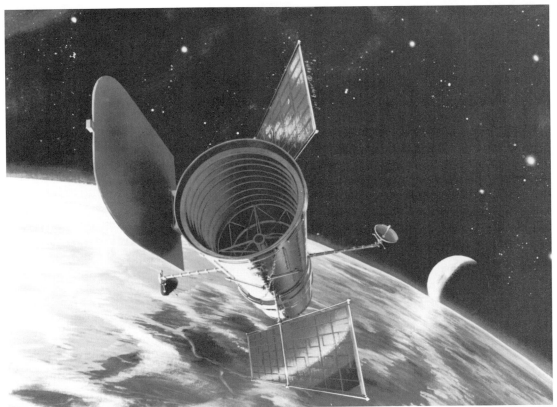

An artist's view of the Hubble Space Telescope, as it might appear in earth orbit at an altitude of over 300 miles. Courtesy National Aeronautics and Space Administration.

shuttle orbiter. They have refused to stop dreaming, and some envision the eventual settling of the solar system: mining operations on the moon and asteroids, scientists turning Mars from a red desert into a green world, and thousands of humans living like suburbanites within huge orbital cities with clouds, hills, and rivers.

But space enthusiasts disagree vehemently about what the United States should do next. Some support the manned space station; others denounce it as a waste of money and say the nation should instead join the Soviets in a joint manned mission to Mars. Still others want to go to the moon and build a colony; and some say there is no need for astronauts at all, rather robots should explore space.

Now in its middle age, "NASA needs to sort out its priorities," says Daniel S. Greenberg, who edits the respected Washington, D.C.-based publication *Science and Government Report.* "There's no need for a manned space station and the talk about a Mars mission is absolutely nutty."

NASA is undergoing "the transition from what I call the romantic era of spaceflight into the realistic era of spaceflight," says former NASA historian Alex Roland. He compares it with the early days of aviation, which began with utopian forecasts of "an airplane in every garage."

"We've been to the moon," says Roland. "We have made heroes of the Lindberghs of our age. But we're reaching the limits of that. Now the most exciting thing we can think of is to put astronauts in [a space station] and watch them float around. But there's not much for them to do up there."

The Soviets disagree. In 1988 three cosmonauts, one of them Bulgarian, returned from a week-long trip to the Soviet manned space station *Mir*, where they had studied stars, manufactured metal alloys, purified the drug interferon, and studied pollution in Bulgarian waters. The Soviets' new heavy-lift launch vehicle, the *Energia*, allegedly can lift 100 tons at a time—three to four times as much as the shuttle. They may use the *Energia* to launch either a much bigger space station than *Mir* or a manned mission to Mars.

Meanwhile, the French are luring the commercial satellite-launching business away from the United States; a consortium of European nations plans to develop its own space station; and the Japanese are training astronauts and have invented the world's most advanced communications satellites. Even China, Brazil, and India are getting into the rocket business. But, critics say, Americans shouldn't become hysterical as the hammer and sickle, rising sun, and fleur-de-lis ascend to the stars.

For now, "no single country is 'ahead' of all the others in space," said a report issued in 1988 by the Congressional Research Service. Although the Soviets have much more in-flight experience than the Americans, they "are only now beginning to have a space station with the technical capability of the 1972 U.S. Skylab."

"We've got to get over the idea that we're in a decline if we don't lead in space," historian Roland says. "Unless there's a military advantage or a commercial advantage, countries just can't afford to pour that much money into these romantic escapades."

And a great deal of money it has been. NASA has about 23,000 employees, almost 40 percent fewer than during the Apollo era. And its annual budget—$9 billion—is less than 1 percent of the federal budget, compared with 4 percent during the moon program.

In the 1980s NASA's fortunes have mirrored those of the nation as a whole— an age of tightened budgets and lowered expectations. Delayed by the shuttle's "stand down" (the experts' euphemism), more than 50 satellites—including the long-awaited Hubble Space Telescope and *Galileo* probe to Jupiter—are awaiting launch, and some won't get into space before the mid-1990s.

Only a few years ago, space buffs envisioned turning the shuttle into a cruise ship that could carry several dozen passengers to a space station in orbit, á la the resort space station in the film *2001: A Space Odyssey*.

But when Christa McAuliffe died in the *Challenger* explosion, all talk ended of passenger shuttles into space. Not even Walter Cronkite could wangle a ride aboard this bird, which reminded Americans what they had forgotten: that space is a dangerous new realm.

How NASA Works

At its birth in 1958, the National Aeronautics and Space Administration was mandated to manage all nonmilitary research, exploration, and conquest of space. This awesome burden demanded that the fledgling agency delegate responsibilities to appropriate research facilities.

So NASA quickly took control of a network of existing government facilities—Langley in Virginia, Ames in California, and Lewis in Ohio. These would be at the forefront in research and planetary satellite technology. Contract work with California's Jet Propulsion Laboratory expanded. NASA acquired a site in Maryland—soon named the Goddard Space Flight Center—for communications and data processing, tracking, and satellite development. A large portion of the Army's Redstone Arsenal in Alabama became the Marshall Space Flight Center, which developed an expertise in rocketry. At Cape Canaveral, Florida, NASA used air force rocket facilities until it completed the Kennedy Space Center. And it built a new Manned Spacecraft Center—now the Johnson Space Center—near Houston, Texas.

All these facilities and more make up the complicated agency that goes by the name of NASA. Over the years the roles of each part have become more firmly defined. Today six program offices at national headquarters in Washington, D.C., are responsible for monitoring different aspects of NASA's operations. Here are descriptions of each of these offices, as well as of NASA's major field installations.

Office of Aeronautics and Space Technology (400 Independence Ave. SW, Washington, DC 20546; 202-453-2643) monitors programs designed to develop advanced technology in aeronautics and space. This office also coordinates NASA facilities with the U.S. aerospace industry.

Office of Exploration (700 D St. SW, Washington, DC 20546; 202-453-8928) was established in 1987 to assess what the next step should be after completion of the manned space station. Currently this office is studying the possibility of sending manned missions to Mars and to the moon.

Office of Space Flight (400 Independence Ave. SW, Washington, DC 20546; 202-453-1132) manages the space shuttle program and other advances in space transportation. It also monitors the work of the Johnson Space Center, Kennedy Space Center, Marshall Flight Center, and John C. Stennis Space Center.

Office of Space Science and Applications (400 Independence Ave. SW, Washington, DC 20546; 202-453-1409) coordinates NASA's efforts to understand the origin, evolution, and structure of the universe; the origin and evolution of the solar system; and the functioning of our own planet. Research efforts include programs to explore surviving in space and evaluating space communications.

Office of Space Station (400 Independence Ave. SW, Washington, DC 20546; 202-453-2405) manages all aspects of the space station program. Goals of the program include development of a permanently manned space station by the late 1990s, involvement of other countries in the program, and the promotion of private-sector investment in space. This office oversees the work of the Johnson Space Center, the field station responsible

If you were wondering what to do with your favorite young scientist this summer, you might want to consider sending him or her to space camp. For an eventful five days, your child can don a flight suit and experience the thrills of weightlessness and the culinary delights of freeze-dried foods. (It might even lead to a newfound appreciation for home cooking!) Here are some highlights of the programs:

Kansas Cosmosphere and Space Center (1100 N. Plum, Hutchinson, KS 67501; 316-662-2305) offers a program for children in 7th through 9th grades. The program offers courses in space survival that includes handling life-support equipment in space suits, studying spacecraft design, and learning about the unique qualities of space food. Students also study the principles of rocket propulsion and spaceflight and learn about NASA's space shuttle program. The highlight of the five-day event is carrying out a simulation of a space shuttle flight. The program costs $415 for Level I (basic course), $495 for Level II (advanced). Students also have access to the center's sophisticated planetarium and Hall of Space, which includes more than $100 million of space artifacts and a chronological history of the space program.

Space Center (P.O. Box 533, Alamogordo, NM 88311; 505-437-2840) has eight sessions of camp, each lasting a week, for children in grades 3 through 9. Younger children go for half a day and do hands-on science activities, culminating in building a rocket that each child gets to launch. Older kids do increasingly complex projects. Tuition for the day program is $150; for overnight camp, $250.

Happy campers in U.S. Space Camp's space shuttle mockup in Huntsville, Alabama.

U.S. Space Camp (One Tranquility Base, Huntsville, AL 35807; 205-837-3400) has a three-day and a five-day program for the same age group. Highlights of the three-day program include experiencing a microgravity trainer that simulates the experience of walking on the moon, eating freeze-dried food, and simulating a space shuttle flight. Tuition is $275, including room and board. The five-day program is similar, with more benefits, such as attending shows at the center's planetarium and touring the nearby Kennedy Space Center. The space shuttle simulation is the climax of this program as well. Tuition is $550, everything included.

Youngstar Star Academy (2400 Bel Pre Rd., Silver Spring, MD 20906; 301-460-7822) offers trips to the Goddard Space Flight Center, classes in aerodynamics, and tips to remember if you want to be an astronaut. Two sessions are offered: a half-day, two-week program for children in grades K through 3 ($250) and a full-day program for older children, also for two weeks ($750).

for coordinating the space station, as well as the work of the Marshall Space Flight Center, Goddard Space Flight Center, and Lewis Research Center, all of which have roles in developing the space station.

Office of Space Tracking and Data Systems (400 Independence Ave. SW, Washington, DC 20546; 202-453-2030) coordinates the complex communications systems that enable contact with space. The global communications network links tracking sites, control centers, and data-processing facilities that provide real-time computations and calculations for mission control and routine processing of data for space missions. Links in the communications chain include the Deep Space Network (DSN), the Space Flight Tracking and Data Network (STDN), the first of the Tracking and Data Relay Satellite Systems (TDRSS) spacecraft, and support facilities.

Field Installations
NASA also has several key locations outside Washington, D.C., where the real work is done, from research and development to assembling and launching the space shuttle. Most are open to the public for tours; in some cases the library facilities are open as well.

Ames Research Center (Moffett Field, CA 94035; 415-694-6370) conducts research on fundamental aerodynamics, aeronautics and flight dynamics, and flight simulation. Activities oriented to the space program include planetary and deep-space probe development, space-human factors and life support, space biological and biomedical research, and technology for extended human stays in space. Ames's visitors' center is open 8:30 a.m. to 4 p.m. daily except Christmas. Tours are also offered.

Goddard Space Flight Center (Greenbelt, MD 20771; 301-286-8981) operates six scientific laboratories that specialize in the design of flight instruments and conduct basic research on astronomy, the earth, and the space environment. One of its most prominent current projects is managing the development of the scientific instruments and ground operation system of the Hubble Space Telescope (HST). When placed into its 320-mile-high orbit by the space shuttle, the HST observatory will allow astronomers to view extremely faint objects with more clarity than previously seen by earth-based telescopes. The HST is designed to last at least 15 years, during which Goddard will manage its operation.

Other major projects at Goddard include the Cosmic Background Explorer satellite, designed to gather evidence about the validity of the "Big Bang" theory; the Gamma Ray Observatory, another pioneering astronomical telescope in orbit; the Upper Atmosphere Research Satellite, designed to study chemical changes in the earth's upper atmosphere; and the space station *Freedom*, designed as a permanent facility to support people in space. Goddard also operates the Wallops Flight Facility, located on the eastern shore of Virginia near Chincoteague. This facility conducts experiments using rockets, balloons, and aircraft to gain a better understanding of earth's upper atmosphere.

Goddard's visitor center offers exhibits about the history of the space program and information about the space shuttle program. The center is open to the public Wednesday through Sunday, 10 a.m. to 4 p.m., except federal holidays. Special events such as model rocket launches are held on the first and third Sundays of each month. The Teacher Resource Laboratory has printed materials and videotapes for classroom use.

Jet Propulsion Laboratory (JPL, Califor-

A fully equipped Saturn V launch vehicle and Apollo payload, at the Johnson Space Flight Center's Spaceland Park in Houston, Texas.

nia Institute of Technology, NASA, Pasadena, CA 91109; 818-354-5011) was transferred from the U.S. Army to NASA in 1958 and is operated for NASA by the California Institute of Technology. The JPL has overseen unmanned missions to the moon and the planets. Among its accomplishments are the Ranger and Surveyor lunar projects, the Mariner missions to Mars, a survey of the sky at infrared wavelengths by the *Infrared Astronomical Satellite*, and exploration of Jupiter and Saturn by *Voyagers 1* and 2 and of Uranus by *Voyager 2*.

Planetary flights currently in development include *Galileo*, which will orbit Jupiter and probe the planet's cloud-covered atmosphere; *Ulysses*, a spacecraft built by the European Space Agency to fly past Jupiter and over the poles of the sun, which will look at regions of the sun never explored before; *Magellan*, which will orbit Venus and map its surface with imaging radar; *Mars Observer*, the first of a new class of spacecraft, the Planetary Observer, which will study the climate and geology of Mars; and *Mariner Mark II*, one of another new spacecraft class, earmarked to rendezvous with comets and asteroids, investigate the Saturn system from orbit, and study the atmosphere of Titan, Saturn's principal satellite.

The JPL also manages the Deep Space Network, which includes communications facilities in California, Spain, and Australia. Each of these complexes includes antennas up to 210 feet wide. These centers facilitate communication with spacecraft in almost any region of the sky.

The JPL has no formal visitors' center or exhibits for the general public. It does, however, hold two visitors' days each month, announced about a month in advance. Groups of about 50 are shown a film on space and a scale model of the *Voyager* and other spacecraft. Schools may make reservations for groups of at least 10, in the eighth grade or higher. The JPL begins accepting reservations in August for the upcoming school year.

Lyndon B. Johnson Space Center (Houston, TX 77058; 713-483-4321) focuses on the manned space flight program. The center's responsibilities include the design, development, and testing of manned spacecraft; selection and training of astronauts; and operation of manned space flights. An additional mandate includes developing medical, scientific, and engineering experiments. The visitors' center offers exhibits of moon rocks and other space program paraphernalia; viewings of the mission control briefings; and a chance to walk through the Skylab trainers used by astronauts to practice complex tasks in preparation for scientific missions. Hours are 9 a.m. to 4 p.m., everyday except Christmas Day. There is no admission charge.

John F. Kennedy Space Center (Cape Canaveral, FL 32899; 407-867-7110) also known as Cape Canaveral, has been NASA's primary launch facility since 1962. Obsolete launch pads from the Mercury and Apollo programs of the 1960s, among others, are on display, as are exhibits about the Mercury, Gemini, and Apollo programs. The visitors' center, which houses these shows, is open 9 a.m. to 6 p.m., daily except Christmas. Bus tours of the space center and Cape Canaveral are available; fees are $4 for adults

and $1.75 for children. Tours are offered every day except Christmas. If you can plan your trip several weeks in advance, you may be able to get one of the limited number of special passes available from members of the U.S. House and Senate. These congressional tours are a bit longer than the regular tours, although seats are limited. Contact your member of Congress for details.

Langley Research Center (Hampton, VA 23665; 804-864-1000), founded in 1917, focuses on aeronautics research, spaceflight, and aircraft structures. Programs now under way include developing technology for an advanced aerospace

A display of space hardware at the Kennedy Space Center, Cape Canaveral, Florida.

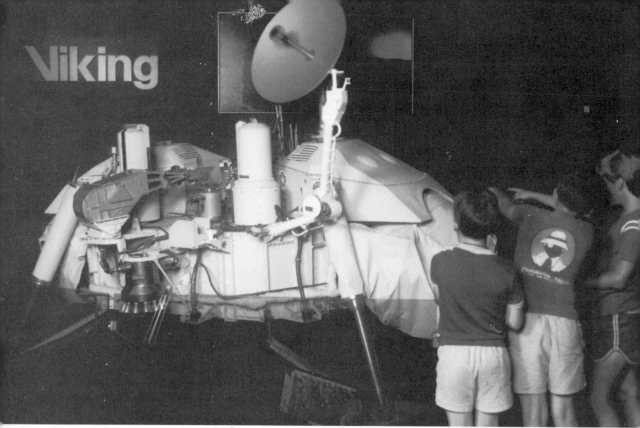

Viking

The Viking Mars Lander, one of two spacecraft that explored the "red" planet, on display at the Langley Research Center, Hampton, Virginia.

plane and materials and methods for building large structures in space. Langley scientists are also developing technology for environmental monitoring of earth's resources. The first U.S. manned space program, Project Mercury, was operated out of this center. In addition, researchers here developed space probes to map the moon's surface in preparation for manned landings and to travel to Mars to photograph and analyze its surface. Langley's visitors' center has an aeronautics gallery that traces the evolution of flight from the Wright brothers to future plans for the National Aero-Space Plane. The center also has a space gallery that displays memorabilia from space missions. Hours are Monday through Saturday, 8:30 a.m. to 4:30 p.m.; Sunday, noon to 4:30 p.m. Admission is free.

Lewis Research Center (Cleveland, OH 44135; 216-433-2001) is NASA's lead center for research and technology development in aircraft propulsion, space propulsion, space power, and satellite communications. It also manages the Atlas-Centaur launch vehicle and the Centaur upper stage for use with the shuttle space transportation system. For the Department of Energy, Lewis manages selected terrestrial energy programs. Its visitors' center includes exhibits on earth-orbiting satellites, flight in the atmosphere, space exploration, space spin-offs, and Lewis's role in the development of the space shuttle. Hours are Monday through Friday, 9 a.m. to 4 p.m.; Saturday, 10 a.m. to 3 p.m.; and Sunday, 1 to 5 p.m. The center is closed on New Year's, Easter, Thanksgiving, and December 24, 25, and 31. There is no admission charge.

Marshall Space Flight Center (One Tranquility Base, Huntsville, AL 35807; 205-837-3400) was transferred from the

U.S. Army to NASA in 1960. This facility develops large launch vehicles used in the manned space program. Its accomplishments include the solid rocket booster and major portions of the space shuttle. Visitors are invited to tour the facility to see scientists at work. The tour lasts an hour and 45 minutes, including the bus trip. Also available on-site is the Space and Rocket Center, which offers hands-on exhibits such as firing a model rocket engine, taking the controls of a moon lander, and stacking cubes with a robotic arm. Other displays: Neil Armstrong's "quarantine van," monkeynauts trained for shuttle flight, and history-making spacecraft such as the Apollo moon ship and a Mercury spacecraft. The museum is open 9 a.m. to 5 p.m. in the fall, winter, and spring; 8 a.m. to 6 p.m. June through August. Call for information about group and family admission rates.

John C. Stennis Space Center (Stennis Space Center, MS 39529; 601-688-3341) is responsible for managing research and development activities in space and terrestrial applications; space flight; and oceanography, meteorology, and environmental sciences. The laboratory coordinates research between NASA and other government agencies. Stennis also is involved in testing the space shuttle. The visitors' center is open 9 a.m. to 5 p.m. daily except Christmas. Tours to the testing site are offered several times a day.

SPACE SOCIETIES

Not everyone can be an astronaut, but space societies provide an opportunity for both amateurs and experts to play a role in our pioneering efforts in space. Most clubs offer members a wide range of publications and activities that suit the interests of both hobbyists and professionals in the field, although the membership of one organization is made up entirely of astronauts and cosmonauts.

All of these organizations maintain that continued exploration of outer space is a natural and vital step to the further development of humankind. Members of the **Association of Space Explorers** speak in rather metaphysical terms of the results of their ventures, emphasizing new perspectives on the vastness of space, the finite nature of earth, and the achievements and limits of humans. By contrast, the **National Space Society** interprets the benefits of space technology in very practical terms, citing diverse applications of manmade satellites such as wildlife and natural resource management, as well as long-term weather predictions that can give relief organizations sufficient time to prepare for potentially disastrous droughts.

Because the costs of space exploration are extremely high—particularly in an era of budget consciousness—space societies often have political agendas as well, advocating that the federal government allocate more funds for the research and development necessary for a state-of-the-art, competitive space program. Although most of these groups promote international cooperation in space, they also note that the United States must make a

Right: Astronaut John Glenn, in his historic 1962 flight, raises his face plate to eat from a collapsible tube filled with apple sauce.

greater effort to keep up with the Soviet Union if America is to retain its leverage in world politics. After all, the mind-boggling prospects for colonization of space become increasingly attractive to countries seeking new territory as the earth's natural resources and territories dwindle.

Despite their pursuit of these serious goals, space societies are also fun. Some, such as the National Space Society, offer space buffs a chance to experience vicariously astronauts' adventures in space, maintaining hotlines that carry live communications between ground control and orbiting spacecraft. Because famous personalities such as Carl Sagan and Sally Ride belong to these organizations, members can feel a kinship with their space heroes. Local meetings and national conferences sponsored by space groups allow all enthusiasts opportunities to share information and ideas. Operating under the premise that a better-informed public is more likely to support further space exploration, the organizations also publish a wide variety of periodicals and books, describing for all levels of readers the exciting research and discoveries that have resulted from space technology. Publications such as the **Planetary Society's** *Planetary Report* stimulate the imagination with features on the search for extraterrestrial life and the feasibility of a manned mission to Mars.

As space societies continue to generate enthusiasm and funds toward an understanding of the vast unexplored territory surrounding earth, perhaps some members will see the day when excursions to the moon, or even Mars, are as common as trips to Europe.

Here are some of the national membership space societies:

American Astronautical Society (AAS, 6212-B Old Keene Mill Ct., Springfield, VA 22152; 703-866-0020). An organiza-

tion geared toward professionals and hobbyists alike, AAS seeks to promote the American space program, encourage international cooperation in space exploration, and urge young people to pursue interests in astronautics. Founded in 1954, AAS conducts conferences and meetings locally, nationally, and internationally, including the AAS annual meeting, an annual AAS classified military space symposium, and the Goddard annual symposium. Among the society's publications are the *Journal of Astronautical Sciences*, a quarterly geared to scientists and mathematicians, featuring articles such as "Approximate Description of Attitude Motions of a Torque-Free Nearly Axisymmetric Rigid Body"; *Space Times*, a less intimidating bimonthly for lay readers with articles such as "What the Well-Dressed Astronaut Will Wear"; the *AAS Directory*, published approximately every two years; and a wide spectrum of books.

AAS members receive free subscriptions to the *Journal of Astronautical Sciences* and *Space Times*, as well as discounts on AAS proceedings, technical publications, and registration fees at AAS-sponsored meetings. The society encourages members to establish local chapters. Currently, there are three local regional chapters: Southwest region, Rocky Mountain region, and Washington, D.C., region. Annual membership fees vary from $20 to $75, according to membership type. Corporate memberships are available for $200 to $1,000; memberships for colleges and universities cost $100.

Association of Space Explorers (ASE, 3263 Sacramento St., San Francisco, CA 94115; 415-931-0585). The fifty-odd members of the Association of Space Explorers hail from over a dozen countries and are all astronauts or cosmonauts with trips into outer space under their belts. Since its inception in 1985 the association

A spacesuit exhibit at the Johnson Space Center, Houston, Texas.

has promoted international cooperation in space, urged that our understanding and exploration of space be used to benefit all humankind, and worked to bring public awareness to the achievements and significance of space programs and to the "transformative experiences" of those who have ventured into space. The association holds an annual planetary congress and issues a report on its proceedings and recommendations. The 1987 congress recommended international cooperation to bring about a manned mission to Mars. During ASE-sponsored lectures, members seek to dispel the common misconception that space exploration is a frivolous undertaking, emphasizing that its long-term benefits enrich the lives of all.

Aviation/Space Writers Association (17 S. High St., Ste. 1200, Columbus, OH

43215; 614-221-1900). An organization of reporters, editors, and public relations professionals covering aviation and aerospace, the Aviation/Space Writers Association provides information about upcoming space events through individual contacts, seminars, booklets, and newsletters. Dues are $75 a year for active members, $25 for retired members and military, and $10 for students. There is also a $20 initiation fee for all but student members. Membership includes the monthly newsletter.

National Space Society (NSS, 922 Pennsylvania Ave. SE, Washington, DC 20003; 202-543-1900). The result of a merger of the National Space Institute and the L-5 Society, the National Space Society hopes to create "a space-faring civilization which will establish communities beyond earth." Boasting close to 100 local chapters in the United States and abroad, the organization strives to increase U.S. commitment to pioneering in space, using the Soviet space program to point out deficiencies in ours, and to educate the public about the benefits of space technology. The NSS furthers its political agenda through an affiliated lobbying organization, Spacecause, and a political action committee, Spacepac.

Particularly accessible to amateur space buffs, NSS's programs for members include discounts on its Space Shop merchandise (see "Space Stuff") and on registration fees at NSS international space development conferences; the opportunity to participate in one- to three-day national and regional meetings; a subscription to *Ad Astra*, a monthly magazine that addresses political aspects of space exploration; access to the NSS Space Hotline, providing the "latest Washington, D.C., space news rumor and gossip"; free annotated bibliographies on a wide variety of space topics; and a visitors' guide to "space-oriented sites in the nation's capital". The society also conducts seminars and conferences to commemorate and celebrate special space-related events, such as the space shuttle launching of NASA's Hubble Space Telescope. The society offers guided tours of NASA facilities, including the opportunity to watch lift-off from a prime vantage point near the Kennedy Space Center, and a "900" Dial-a-Shuttle telephone number (900-909-6272) that allows callers to hear live communications between ground control and the shuttle. Annual fees for a basic NSS membership range from $18 to $30. Higher levels of membership cost $50 to $100.

Planetary Society (65 N. Catalina Ave., Pasadena, CA 91106; 818-793-5100). The society, by far the largest space-related group, is presided over by Carl Sagan. It advocates international mobilization for a manned mission to Mars and promotion and funding the search for extraterrestrial life. It sponsors the Mars Institute and a funds a National Merit Scholarship as well as New Millennium scholarships for students pursuing space science. In 1987 the society hosted Spacebridge, a satellite-linked meeting between 48 Soviet and American scientists and engineers, who discussed prospects for the exploration of Mars.

Members of the Planetary Society receive a free subscription to the *Planetary Report*, a colorfully illustrated bimonthly, and discounts on merchandise. The society also publishes *Mars Underground News*—the title refers to the theory that conditions under the surface of the red planet may be amenable to life—a quarterly newsletter chronicling advances in Martian research that is available for $10 per year to members and Mars researchers. The society's annual membership fee is $20.

Space Studies Institute (P.O. Box 82, Princeton, NJ 08542; 609-921-0377). This institute is devoted to using extraterrestrial materials to build space equipment. Its first research project was to design and build a "mass-driver," which can accelerate payloads to escape the moon's gravitational pull. Other accomplishments: research into the most feasible way to build a solar-powered satellite using materials from the moon and the development of mining techniques in a lunar-simulated environment. Membership is $25 a year ($15 for students and senior citizens), which includes a bimonthly newsletter detailing key events. The institute sponsors a biennial space manufacturing conference.

U.S. Space Education Association (USSEA, International Headquarters, 746 Turnpike Rd., Elizabethtown, PA 17022; 717-367-3265). Describing itself as the

A spectacular view of comet Bennett photographed with an F/2 Schmidt telescope camera at the NASA/Goddard Space Flight Center in Greenbelt, Maryland.

"world's first citizen support space organization," USSEA was founded in 1973 to educate the general public about the significance of advancements in space technology in the hope of "securing a solid technological foundation for a future full of optimism." The organization pursues this goal through displays in shopping malls, schools, and libraries; a small museum exhibiting "a collection of space material covering the entire space field"; and the bimonthly *Space Age Times*, a periodical carrying news stories on space exploration and features covering topics ranging from supernovas to the television series "Star Trek: The Next Generation." Annual membership dues are $20. Members receive a membership card, a membership certificate, an international membership handbook describing USSEA services and programs, a subscription to *Space Age Times*, a monthly news bulletin, free samples of USSEA photographs distributed on an "irregular basis," access to free publications, and a discount on advertising in *Space Age Times*.

World Space Foundation (P.O. Box Y, Southern Pasadena, CA 91030; 818-357-2878). Founded in 1979, the foundation provides a medium through which "all persons interested in space exploration may participate in the development of the final frontier." The foundation researches and builds spacecraft, raises funds for space research, and provides information on space topics through publication of three quarterlies: *Foundation Astronautics Notebook*, devoted to topics of interest to professionals in the space field; *Foundation News*, covering projects sponsored by the organization; and *Under the Stars*, which provides information for beginning astronomers by tracking positions of the moon, planets, stars, comets, and other heavenly bodies. Two major activities sponsored by the World Space Foundation are the Solar Sail Project and the Asteroid Project. Participants in the Solar Sail Project are constructing a solar-powered spacecraft that will be able to operate in the vacuum of space without conventional fuel. The Asteroid Project

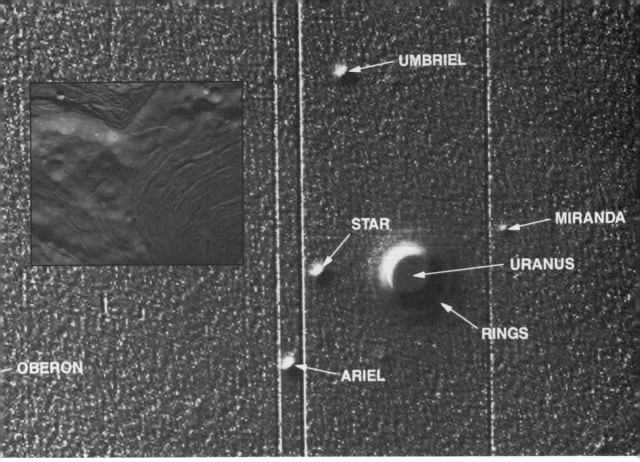

UMBRIEL

STAR

MIRANDA

URANUS

RINGS

OBERON

ARIEL

The first definitive photograph of the rings of the planet Uranus, as recorded by the Voyager 2 *spacecraft. Inset: Close-up of Miranda, one of the Uranian moons.*

funds the study of asteroids, particularly those near earth.

The foundation also funds seven space business roundtables, located in southern California, Houston, New York, Washington, D.C., Central Florida, Dallas, and Seattle. These roundtables provide business contacts and support for those involved in the commercial aspects of the space industry. The World Space Foundation's contributing associates receive subscriptions to *Foundation News* and *Foundation Astronautics Notebook*, and discounts on the foundation's merchandise; foundation associates receive a subscription to *Under the Stars*. Membership is $15 a year for contributing associates and $8 a year for foundation associates. Project associates contribute $25 to $100 a year to the Solar Sail or Asteroid project and are automatically registered as contributing associates.

Young Astronaut Council (1015 15th St. NW, Washington, DC 20005; 202-682-1984) provides curriculum materials related to space for both school and home use. The series Adventure includes activities for children in grades 1 through 9 and for children ages 3 and 4. The council has 25,000 chapters, reaching 500,000 children. Membership is $40 and includes mailings of curriculum materials every three months except in the summer. The materials for very young children are mailed only once a year.

SPACE SPIN-OFFS

What is the value of the space program? Once you get to the moon or to Mars, for example, you can't move around freely or set up space colonies easily. And what good is the information we gain going to do us anyway? Who cares if we know what moon rocks are made of, or that Mercury has no atmosphere? What's the point?

One point is that through space technology have come many products—more than 30,000, in fact—that we use daily, which few people realize have their origins in the space program. These products, often referred to as space spin-offs, may be reason enough to probe the boundaries of the last great frontier.

The link between space program technology and private industry is NASA's Technology Utilization Program. It uses several methods to inform the private sector about space technology, beginning with *Tech Briefs*—a catalog of new products, processes, and advances originating at NASA. Once a company finds what it is looking for in *Tech Briefs*, it can request a technical support package for more detailed information. More than 100,000 packages are requested every year. Most are free and can be obtained by simply filling out a card. For information about the Technology Utilization Program, contact Technology Utilization Division, NASA Scientific and Technical Information Facility, P.O. Box 8757, Baltimore, MD 21240; 301-859-5300 ext. 2410. Each of the field installations also has a technology utilization officer; see "How NASA Works" for addresses and phone numbers.

Computer software developed by NASA, the Department of Defense, and other government agencies is also listed in *Tech Briefs* and available to industry. COSMIC, the Computer Software Man-agement and Information Center, provides additional information at 382 E. Broad St., Athens, GA 30602; 404-542-3265.

Here is a sampling of some favorite space spin-offs. If this list whets your appetite, and you want to know what the other 29-some-odd thousand are, contact the Centralized Technical Services Group, NASA Scientific and Technical Information Facility, P.O. Box 8757, Baltimore/ Washington International Airport, Baltimore, MD 21240. There is also an annual publication, *Spinoff* (S/N 033-000-00989-5, $6.50), published by the Government Printing Office. Write: Superintendent of Documents, U.S. Government Printing Office, Washington, DC 20402.

Medical Advances: The material of the Jarvik-7 artificial heart, the concept of a pump to deliver insulin to diabetics, and a highly abrasive-resistant coating used on plastic contact lenses all are here because of space-related activities. Magnetic resonance imaging (MRI) uses the computerized image enhancement technology developed to interpret satellite imagery to "see" into the bones and provide thematic "maps" of the human body. False color can be added to each type of tissue, making tumors or blood clots stand out. In the future: new techniques, once used to examine the mirror surface of the space telescope, will be applied to surgery of the cornea. Scientists think that these developments will lead to improved eye surgery, eye transplants, and contact lenses.

Advanced Wheelchair: Developed by NASA's Langley Research Center in conjunction with the University of Virginia's Rehabilitation Engineering Center, the new wheelchair was designed

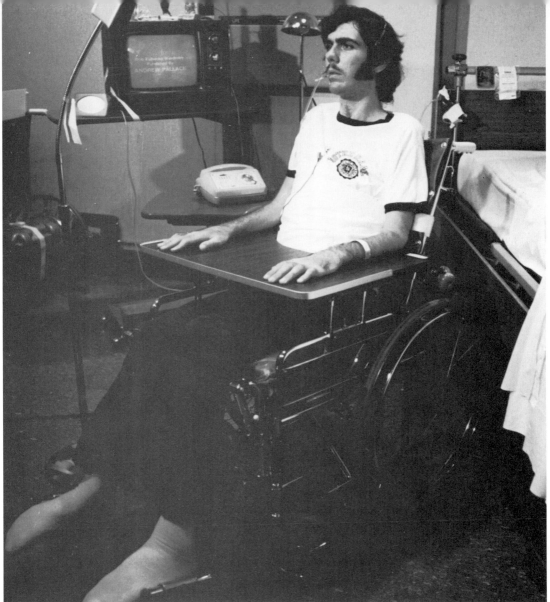

An electronic device designed to activate controls in a spacecraft in case the astronauts lost use of their limbs is now used to aid handicapped individuals.

using aerospace computerized structural analysis techniques and composite materials, which are generally lighter and stronger than metals. The result is that the new 25-pound chair offers the strength and weight-bearing capability of a 50-pound stainless-steel wheelchair but can be collapsed for storage and transport.

Handicapped Vehicle Controller: Using technology developed by NASA for the Lunar Rover vehicle, scientists have created a system that offers severely handicapped people a chance to drive automobiles. The vehicle's control system combines the functions of a steering wheel, brake petal, and throttle pedal, permitting people with no lower-limb control and only limited use of their arms to drive. The driver simply moves the joystick forward to accelerate, backward to brake, and from side to side for steering. The system can be adapted to any automobile.

Weather Forecasting: The widespread use of meteorological satellites to forecast the weather comes from aerospace technology. These satellites not only make it possible to understand our environment better but also protect us from its dangers. Weather satellite forecasts enable us to warn people of impending danger from hurricanes, tornadoes, or other violent storms.

Voice-Controlled Wheelchair and Manipulator: Based in part on robot technology developed for the space program, a voice-controlled wheelchair and its manipulator have been tested as a future aid for paralyzed and severely handicapped persons. The core of the system is a voice-command analyzer, which uses a microcomputer. A person repeats commands several times into the microphone connected to the computer. The analyzer can recognize these commands and translate them into electrical impulses, which activate appropriate motors and cause the desired motion of the chair or manipulator. The manipulator can pick up objects, open doors, turn knobs, and perform other functions.

Water Recycling: The water-recycling industry has started to use aquatic plants in the treatment and recycling of wastewater. The application of these plants comes from years of research by the Space Technology Laboratories, and they operate at a much lower cost than previous methods of sewage treatment. The glossy green water hyacinths, as they are called, absorb and digest nutrients and minerals.

Reading Machine for the Blind: A spin-off of optical and electronic technology, the device called OPTACON—for *OP*tical-to-*TA*ctile *CON*verter—converts regular print to a readable, vibrating form that responds to the sense of touch. This enables blind people to read anything in print, not just Braille transcriptions. As a blind reader moves a miniature camera across a line of print with one hand, he or she senses, with the fingers of the other hand, a vibrating image of the letters the camera is viewing on a special screen. For school use OPTACON makes the instructional materials of the sighted available to the blind.

Breathing System for Fire Fighters: The current breathing system used by fire fighters weighs only slightly more than 20 pounds and includes a face mask, frame and harness, warning device, and air bottle. This replaces a system that was so uncomfortable to wear that many fire fighters risked smoke inhalation rather than be burdened with the device.

Left: Volunteers from the Houston Fire Department demonstrate the firefighting garments made from fire-resistant fabrics developed for use in manned spacecraft.

ALL ABOUT UFOs

You say you don't believe in unidentified flying objects? Well, come on. How do you think the elusive Bigfoot manages to visit the Bermuda Triangle and the Loch Ness Monster each year on his vacation?

Seriously, the debate about the existence of UFOs has raged for years, and it's sure to continue for many more. Skeptics claim that not one scrap of undeniable evidence from a UFO sighting has ever been identified. Believers think they have history on their side. Reports have turned up over the centuries describing lights and strange noises emanating from the sky. Some believers say that UFOs have been visiting this planet for thousands of years.

The modern rash of UFO sightings can probably trace its origins to June 24, 1947. Veteran pilot Kenneth Arnold spotted nine disks that seemed to be flying in formation over the state of Washington. He stated that the disks looked "like a saucer would if you skipped it across the water." His description stuck. The term *flying saucer* became part of the American vernacular.

At first the U.S. Air Force was quite interested in the phenomenon. It was concerned that the nation's security might be at stake. Some officials even suspected that the Soviet Union had invented a new type of flying craft. But after a number of serious efforts to catalog and explain the various sightings (including Project Sign, Project Grudge, and the extensive Project Bluebook), the air force could offer no evidence either to prove or to disprove the existence of UFOs. It investigated literally thousands of reports and found that most sightings could be explained by weather balloons, strange cloud formations, or aircraft. But many sightings were destined to carry the

designation *unidentified* forever. There just wasn't enough information to explain them.

Some believers have accused the air force of covering up important facts in its investigations. Claims by people who said they had not only seen a UFO but had been picked up and examined by aliens, increased over the years. Finally, in the late 1960s the University of Colorado was given a $500,000 government contract to sift through UFO data and prepare a scientific report. The final report concluded that "the study of UFOs is not likely to advance science."

On December 17, 1969, the air force closed the UFO investigation division, and it has not officially pursued UFO research since. Some researchers considered the move an intelligent choice as a way to trim costs by eliminating a pointless government office. But others continue to insist that the air force is hiding something. They point to a supposed crash of a UFO in New Mexico and claim that there are unreleased government papers detailing this accident.

Recent books, such as *Communion* by Whitley Strieber (1987), have brought UFO abductions back into the spotlight. Several New Age personalities who promote things such as reincarnation and the healing properties of crystals have once again made UFOs a popular topic at conferences throughout the country. Skeptics have pointed out that many of the stories now being discussed by this new wave were actually exposed and explained years ago. No matter who you believe, it is obvious that the UFO question will rage on—whether flying saucers are a reality or not.

Here are several clubs and publications that deal with UFOs. Most clubs are

GGS FROM SPACE ARE ABOUT TO HATCH!

Scientists await 'the greatest event of the century!'

Space alien eggs that were found floating in the Atlantic near Antarctica in 1967 are definitely going to hatch, possibly by the end of spring!

That's the word from Soviet geneticist Alexei Okulov, who has monitored the condition and development of the watermelon-sized eggs for the past 22 years and now says their gestation is almost over.

The hatching of these eggs — and there are 22 of them — will be the greatest event of the century," Dr Okulov told reporters in Moscow. "The gestation period has been unusually long but I'm convinced they will hatch by May or June.

"At that time we'll have the opportunity to observe an extraterrestrial species develop from infancy to adulthood. There is no limit to what we can learn from these creatures that come of these eggs."

Dr Okulov refused to say where the green, leathery eggs are being kept or why the Soviets waited so long to tell the world about Project Starchild, their incredible effort to hatch the eggs from the starship...

Web-footed alien embryos have wings like birds, say docs

...

Top UFO expert's shocking claim: space aliens use flying spheres of light to spy on us

LIBERACE SIGHTED IN A YELLOW UFO!

Liberace isn't dead — he was kidnapped by aliens from another ... returned for a visit in a yellow UFO.

... of several eyewitnesses who swear that they saw the UFO appear like a flash out of the nighttime sky and hover over a farm pasture

Then a door in its side opened and ...came Liberace in a glittering silver suit — literally walking on air. He sat on an invisible seat and played on an invisible piano

"It was the most beautiful music I ever heard," said Miguel Ortiz Diago, farmer near Collie, Mexico.

...and it glowed with a ye... wanted to run when the th... but Maria held me

"When Liberace came u... rub my eyes I recognized h... evision. It was him.

And when he played th... piano and that music came ... where I knew it was him. Maria and Liberace were ... his teeth sparkled as if they ... of diamonds

After about 15 minutes ... went back inside the craft

Wacko refuses to wear clothes to court, say cops

A man was arrested for his ...ing a mass during church ... police, but wasn't aware ... for his complaint a bawling ... because they refused to we... clothes. Authorities wa... reinstated Larry Tubbs because ...'unruly' and disruptive be... ing church services at the be... and Christmas ('butch in Las ... rence, Kansas Tubbs was b... r... led for biting a woman se...

...ved beautiful... an invisible ... witness...

'The thing tried to kill me — so I shot...'

ANGRY TRUCKER FIR 5 BULLETS INTO UFO

Crippled starship glowed green and wobbled away, say 50 wit...

Some Have Called It The Greate Mystery Of The Space Age — Oth The Biggest Hoax.

UFOS, THE SHAVER MYSTERY & THE INNER EARTH

By Gene Steinberg

IS THE CIA INVOLVED IN A SI CONFUSE THE PUBLIC IN RE THOUSANDS OF UFO REPORTS VALLEY?

...HE MYSTE...

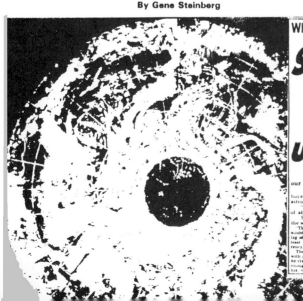

Whopping real estate deal will rock the universe!

Space aliens put Earth up for sale!

$3 trillion

...and the new buyers just might send us packing, warns scientist

A leading scientist says space aliens have staked a claim on our planet — and put it up for sale!

"Our world is going to the highest bidder and we can only hope that the buyers are friendly," Dr Tom Meerbach, the Dutch astronomer, told reporters in Amsterdam.

"The wrong kind of civilization might strip Earth of all its resources.

Such a civilization might not care anything about the welfare of men — they might even send us packing.

The mineral deposits alone would give our planet a price tag of $3,000,000,000,000 — at least — in intergalactic currency," said Dr Meerbach.

The expert's report met with plenty of skepticism but he claimed to have more than enough evidence to support his view. "The simple fact that space aliens and UFOs visit Earth proves that we've got something they want," said Dr Meerbach.

I also think we can assume that these extraterrestrials come here from more than one planet — and that the first visitors staked a claim

That claim would entitle them to use or dispose of Earth as they wish.

"I truly believe that every UFO we see is carrying a potential buyer.

"Our planet is for sale." Richard Kiern, the West German UFO expert, couldn't

agree with the Dutch expert more.

In his 1977 pamphlet Our Role In Space, he argued that Earth is a strategic point in the universe — and would fig ure prominently in any alien civilization's plan to conquer space. "If our planet is im

portant then why do so ma extraterrestrials come here he asked newsmen.

I don't want to ra.. undue alarm but we've got face facts.

Earth is definitely a pri.. piece of real estate.
— IRWIN FISH

staffed by true believers, a few by total skeptics. A few try to take a middle ground, approaching the question with an open mind.

Astronomical Society of Harrisburg (329 S. Front St., Harrisburg, PA 17104; 717-938-6041). This organization provides an excellent bibliography of suggested readings on UFOs. A note of caution to true believers: Several of the books on this list examine evidence scientifically and critically, and in many cases claim to solve famous UFO cases. This list also mentions a few regular publications dealing with UFOs, including journals such as *The Skeptical Inquirer*, which is devoted to debunking pseudoscientific claims (available from the Committee for the Scientific Investigation of Claims of the Paranormal, Box 229, Kensington Station, Buffalo, NY 14215; $15 per year).

Fair-Witness Project (4219 W. Olive St., Burbank, CA 91505; 818-506-8365) This project specializes in UFOs as well as New Age metaphysical and occult research. The organization offers dozens of UFO-related publications, many written by William L. Moore, whose publishing company happens to be located at the same address. Publications for sale include *Remote Viewing Studies* by Harold E. Puthoff (a 40-page reprint with illustrations from a 1983 symposium about using mental process to uncover information blocked from ordinary perception, $7) and a dissertation titled *Nazi Flying Saucers: Project V-7* by Moore ($10). The organization has spent a great deal of energy discussing the supposed cover-up of a saucer crash near Roswell, New Mexico, in 1947. Several publications deal with that topic.

Fund for UFO Research (P.O. Box 277, Mt. Rainier, MD 20712). FUFOR offers many government documents released through Freedom of Information Act requests and lawsuits. Copies can be obtained for suggested donations. You may inspect items such as *1986 Brazilian Air Force Sightings* ($5), *UFO Landings near Kirkland AFB* ($10), a report on pre-1945 sightings ($15), and the *Final Report on the Psychological Testing of UFO Abductees* ($30).

J. Allen Hynek Center for UFO Studies (CUFOS, 2457 W. Peterson Ave., Chicago, IL 60659; 312-271-3611). Hynek, who was involved as a consultant to the air force from 1948 to 1968, testified before the House Committee on Science and Astronautics and coined the phrase *close encounters of the third kind*. The center's bimonthly newsletter, *International UFO Reporter*, covers current sightings and related news. CUFOS also publishes the *Journal of UFO Studies*, which prints scholarly papers on UFO topics. If you sight a UFO you may call the center at any hour, and CUFOS will have one of its investigators contact you as soon as possible. Dues range from $25 per year (which includes a subscription to *International UFO Reporter*) to $1,000 per year (which includes a lifetime subscription and a choice of several items from the CUFOS library).

Mutual UFO Network (MUFON, 103 Oldtowne Rd., Seguin, TX 78155; 512-379-9216). MUFON calls itself a grass roots organization with leadership and motivation at the local level. This non-profit group assigns a state or other regional director to investigate UFO efforts in each region. The network has a board of consultants with experts in engineering, science, astronomy, psychiatry, and more. Prospective members can submit a membership application and dues. If judged "qualified," based on education and experience, they may serve as a consultant, state or provincial director, field investigator, research specialist, translator, UFO news clipping service, contributing subscriber, under-age-18 associate member, or in one of several other positions. A subscription to a 20-page monthly magazine, *MUFON UFO Journal*, is included with the $25 annual membership fee ($30 for foreign countries). A sample copy of the journal is $2.50.

National Investigations Committee on UFOs (14617 Victory Blvd., Ste. 4, Van Nuys, CA 91411; 818-989-5942). The committee's aim is research and education on UFOs, space, and science phenomena. Founder Frank E. Stranges says he began his research 40 years ago, when a roommate who was a former World War I squadron commander told him about three UFOs buzzing his formation. Membership is $20 per year ($25 foreign).

Society for Scientific Exploration (c/o Laurence W. Frederick, secretary, Department of Astronomy, University of Virginia, Box 3818, Charlottesville, VA 22903; 804-924-0311). The society seeks to provide a forum for responsible discussion of "anomalous" phenomena, or that which appears to contradict existing scientific knowledge. Its 100 founding members were drawn mostly from university faculties. Membership is open to people judged by a society council as being likely to contribute actively to furthering the society's aims. There are no official qualifications, but most elected members have doctoral degrees, an appointment to a university, or a record of publication in scholarly journals. Society publications include *The Explorer* newsletter and the scholarly *Journal of Scientific Exploration*.

UFO Newsclipping Service (Rte. 1, Box 220, Plumberville, AK 72127). Because articles about UFOs appear in newspapers around the world, there's no way that even the most well read UFO buff can catch all the writing. That's where this publication comes in handy. The editors scan English-language newspapers for UFO-related articles. They even have some articles translated into English. These stories are then reprinted, with photos, on legal-sized pages. A recent issue had articles from as far away as London and Australia. Subscriptions for the 20-page monthly UFO report are $5 a month, or $55 a year, including a special section on strange creatures and events, from Bigfoot to cattle mutilation.

Vehicle Internal Systems Investigative Team (VISIT, P.O. Box 890327, Houston, TX 77289). VISIT is dedicated to the study of vehicle systems as they are documented in UFO reports. The group is especially interested in physical evidence from UFO cases and similarities in several reports, with particular attention to the internal systems and the physiology of beings involved. Past reports of sightings have been analyzed by members and reformatted into VISIT data bases. The founders say that formatting the information this way allows them to find patterns among the thousands of UFO reports available.

UFO PUBLICATIONS
Flying Saucer Review (FSR Publications, Ltd., c/o The Editor, Snodland, Kent, ME6 5HJ, England). Rated by many as the best professional UFO journal in the world. Published for 33 years. $25 for an annual subscription; $5 for a single copy. For airmail to the Western Hemisphere, including the United States, add $10.

Just Cause Bulletin (Lawrence Fawcett and Barry Greenwood, P.O. Box 218, Coventry, CT 06238). $10 in the United States, $15 elsewhere.

Search magazine (Palmer Publications,

Inc., Amherst, WI 54406). $10 for one year, $16 for two years in the United States; add $2 elsewhere.

UFO: A Forum for Theories and Phenomena, published by California UFO: Vickie Cooper and Sherie Stark (1800 Robertson Blvd., Box 355, Los Angeles, CA 90035; 213-273-9409). Covers a wide variety of UFO topics, from frauds to abductions. One issue exposed the fact that at least one supermarket tabloid editor does not double-check so-called eyewitness accounts of space invaders before printing their stories. This same issue of *UFO* also contained an article scolding the media in general for not taking reports seriously enough. Annual subscription of the bimonthly is $18.

The above publications are primarily for UFO believers. Among books taking an opposing view are:

❏ *UFO Abductions: A Dangerous Game*, by P. Klass (1988, Prometheus Books)
❏ *UFOs: The Public Deceived*, by P. Klass (1983, Prometheus Books)
❏ *UFOs Explained*, by P. Klass (1974, Vintage Books)
❏ *The UFO Verdict*, by R. Sheaffer (1981, Prometheus Books)

The View from Up:
Aerial and Space Imagery

Learning to fly has given us a wonderful opportunity to photograph the earth from above. These images not only provide a way to chart development patterns below but also are the starting points for most kinds of land maps. Cartographers often use stereoscopic aerial photos—two aerial photos of the same site taken from different camera positions—to create the three-dimensional effect needed for certain kinds of maps. But people in many other professions also rely on aerial photographs. Farmers use the images to see how the distribution of cropland has changed over the years. City planners study aerial photographs to measure growth in an area. Preservationists evaluate aerial photographs of wildlife refuges and forests.

Aerial photos are taken by cameras in airplanes, which usually photograph the land section by section. The photos must then be corrected to eliminate distortion, camera tilt, and optical effects created by the land itself. Some aerial photographs being collected through coordinated federal programs are also infrared images. The National Aerial Photography Program is taking such images of the 48 coterminous states, as well as some in both color and black and white.

The Earth Science Information Center (ESIC), part of the U.S. Geological Survey National Mapping Program, maintains records of U.S. aerial photographs gleaned from reports from federal and state agencies. Records go back as far as the late 1930s. Standard photographic products vary in price, depending on the size and color of the print. A 9-inch black-and-white photo printed on paper costs $6; film positive and film negative images are $8. A much larger image, 9-by-18 inches, costs $12 on paper, $16 for film positive or negative. Color images are considerably more expensive. A 9-inch image costs $16; a 9-by-18-inch print is $50. Prices for intermediate sizes range from $24 to $45. A 36-inch print costs $65, the highest price on ESIC's list.

ESIC also has created an Aerial Photography Summary Record System on microfiche that displays descriptions of aerial photography projects in the United States. The lists are organized by state and can be purchased for $2 per state.

To order materials from ESIC, write to one of the following offices:

National Headquarters
Earth Science Information Center
U.S. Geological Survey
507 National Ctr.
Reston, VA 22092
703-860-6045

Mid-Continent Mapping Center
Earth Science Information Center
U.S. Geological Survey
1400 Independence Rd.
Rolla, MO 65401
314-341-0851

Stennis Space Center
Earth Science Information Center
U.S. Geological Survey
Bldg. 3101
Stennis Space Center, MS 39529
601-688-3544

Rocky Mountain Mapping Center
Earth Science Information Center
U.S. Geological Survey
Mail Stop 504
Denver, CO 80225
303-236-5829

Western Mapping Center
Earth Science Information Center
U.S. Geological Survey
345 Middlefield Rd.
Menlo Park, CA 94025
415-329-4309

Alaska Office
Earth Science Information Center
U.S. Geological Survey
4230 University Dr.
Anchorage, AK 99508
907-271-4159

Another major source of aerial photography is Earth Resources Observation Systems, or EROS (U.S. Geological Survey, Sioux Falls, SD 57198; 800-344-9993; 605-594-6151), the federal government's clearinghouse for aerial photographs as well as satellite and space imagery created by the federal government. NASA aircraft imagery can be ordered directly from EROS for between $8 and $50.

Aerial maps and photographs also are available from the following commercial sources:

Aerial Surveys
107 Church St. NW
Marietta, GA 30060
404-434-2516

Air Photographics Inc.
11510 Georgia Ave, Ste. 130
Wheaton, MD 20902
301-933-5282

Atlantic Aerial Surveys Inc.
803 Franklin St.
Huntsville, AL 35804
205-722-0555

International Aerial Mapping Company
8927 International Dr.
San Antonio, TX 78205
512-826-8681

Space Imagery

The famous picture of earth as seen from space has become a familiar icon of our planet, used in magazines, books, newspapers, advertisements, and on TV. The revolutionary tool that made that ubiquitous image and many others like it possible is called *remote sensing*, the process of detecting and monitoring chemical or physical properties of an area by measuring its reflected and emitted radiation.

Remote sensing is a direct by-product of the space program. The first experiments using this technique took place aboard the first manned earth-orbiting missions—Mercury, Gemini, and Apollo. Astronauts used hand-held cameras to produce historic pictures that were examined by scientists worldwide.

In 1969 the first scientific space photographic experiment was performed on *Apollo 9*. Four 70-millimeter cameras were mounted on a metal frame that fit the spacecraft's command module hatch window. A variety of pictures were taken of the Phoenix, Arizona, region, scientists later connected them and printed them as a single image. This process, called *mosaicking*, paved the way for highly sophisticated photo-mapping techniques using images produced from both manned and unmanned spacecraft.

Landsat I (originally called the Earth Resources Technology Satellite, or ERTS) was the first American spacecraft designed specifically to record images of the earth. Launched in 1972, it has been joined by four other Landsat satellites that have recorded hundreds of images of our planet. *Landsats 1, 2,* and *3* orbit at an altitude of 570 miles, while *Landsats 4* and *5* orbit at 438 miles. At one time all five circled the globe 14 times a day, scanning a particular area every 18 days, or about 20 times a year. Each image has the capacity to cover an area of about 115 square miles. The satellites can detect objects as small as 100 square feet.

To take these extraordinary pictures, the more advanced Landsats use two digital sensor systems called *multispectral scanner systems*. Digital cameras have several advantages over traditional cameras: they are lighter, easier to operate, and more reliable. What's more, digital information can be manipulated in a computer, allowing enhancement or suppression of images. For these reasons digital cameras have been used on almost all planetary space probes.

Multispectral scanning systems record information in two visible (red and green) wavelengths and two infrared wavelengths, not visible to the human eye. The procedure results in four separate black-and-white images, combined into a "false-color" portrait, in which healthy vegetation appears in shades of red; unhealthy vegetation in blue-green; water in dark blue or black; and most buildings and streets in shades of blue-gray.

In 1985, ownership of Landsat was transferred by the federal government to the Earth Observation Satellite Company (EOSAT), a partnership of Hughes Aircraft Co. and RCA Corporation. You may order products directly through this company. Available are black-and-white photographs in film negative, film positive, or paper in varying sizes and scales. They sell for between $160 and $250 per image. Color photographs are considerably more expensive; prices range from $360 (for film positive) to $500 (for large images on paper). Computer tapes containing digital data also are available. They range in price from $660 for a single set to $1,320 for a set of four. EOSAT also has aerial photographs in its files. To order either Landsat or aerial images, contact EOSAT, EROS Data Center, U.S. Geological Survey, Sioux Falls, SD 57198; 800-344-9933; 605-594-6151.

One marvelous set of space images was compiled by **Addison-Wesley Publishing Company** (Jacob Way, Reading, MA 01867; 617-944-3700) in the book *The Home Planet* ($38.95). The 150 photographs of earth were taken by 204 men and women from 18 countries who have flown in space, including many American astronauts and Soviet cosmonauts. These images reveal the beauty and fragility of the only planet in our solar system that can support life. The text comes from interviews, conversations with Mission Control, and other writings, and it shows the spirit and determination of those who have traveled to space. The book is available in bookstores.

SPOT IMAGES

In 1986 a French-owned satellite launched Spot, the first commercially owned satellite sensing system. *Spot's* sensing abilities enable it to record images of areas as small as 33 feet (about 10 meters) square—about half the size of a tennis court—and at a higher resolution than Landsat (whose resolution is about 100 feet, or 30 meters). The reason *Spot* can "see" so clearly is that it uses a system of mirrors that can "look" to the side as well as straight down. This unique feature allows the satellite to view an object from two or more directions. Among other things this means that stereoscopic images, which create a three-dimensional perspective, can be produced. In spite of these advantages, however, Landsat can produce bigger pictures than *Spot* can, and it can operate in more wavelengths.

To order *Spot* images, contact **Spot Image Corporation** (1897 Preston White Dr., Reston, VA 22091; 703-620-2200), the wholly-owned subsidiary of the French company created to market *Spot's* services. *Spot* data are available as black-and-white or color prints and transparencies and as digital information in computer-compatible tapes. Prices aren't low and depend on several factors, including which of the three types of radiation that *Spot* records (two bands of visible light and one of near-infrared radiation) is desired, resolution quality (either 20-meter or the sharper 10-meter), and the size of the print or transparency. Prices for transparencies range from about $700 to almost $2,000. Prints go for between $400 and $800.

SPACE FROM SPACE

In 1969 several amazing things happened in space. First and foremost was that *Apollo 11* reached the moon, and astronaut Neil Armstrong emerged from the space module and pronounced his prophetic words: "One small step for a man, one giant leap for mankind." Perhaps equally amazing is that we were able to watch the show in our homes, on our own television sets.

Such technological wizardry began even before the Apollo missions, however, and it now extends to unmanned spaceflights. Over the years NASA and other facilities have amassed extensive stockpiles of photos from dozens of missions ranging from the Ranger series to the Voyager space probes, which have explored the outermost planets.

Clearly astronauts on manned spaceflights take the images that are then viewed back on earth. But how can unmanned probes photograph the objects they were sent to study? The secret is to launch the probe perfectly from earth and to harness the gravitational pull of the sun and the planets themselves to guarantee that the probe moves in the right direction. So, for example, a Mariner mission to Mercury was launched toward Venus so Venus's gravitational pull would change its course, enabling it eventually to fly past Mercury. The result was remarkable pictures taken by TV cameras of a planet very difficult to see from earth.

A later Pioneer mission accomplished a very different task. It orbited Venus and used radar to penetrate the dense blanket of clouds that surround the planet. And whereas *Mariner 9* took vivid pictures of Mars, discovering what appeared to be dried-up riverbeds, the Viking probes were designed to look for signs of life on that planet. They came equipped with arms that could scoop up samples of Martian soil for chemical and biological testing. These experiments, along with the many pictures of the planet, have enabled us to map the Martian surface quite accurately.

ORDERING SPACE PHOTOS

You can purchase space photos through **Bara Photographic Inc** (P.O. Box 486, Bladensburg, MD 20710; 301-332-7900) at relatively high prices: $4 for an 8-by-10-inch black-and-white image and $8 for a color photograph the same size. Keep in mind that many organizations reproduce these images in the form of slide sets, postcards, and posters at lower prices. (See "Astronomy Stuff" and "Space Stuff" for additional information.)

The media can obtain free photographs from the **NASA Audiovisual Department** (Rm. 6035, 400 Maryland Ave. SW, Washington, DC 20546; 202-453-1000).

Members of the scientific community have access to the images from the space probes through **Planetary Image Facilities** located throughout the country. The Smithsonian Institution, in cooperation with NASA, has these archival sources available at the **Center for Earth and Planetary Studies of the National Air and Space Museum**. These images are available for use at the facility only, but if necessary it is possible to order them. They are kept at the **National Space Science Data Center**, Goddard Space Flight Center, Greenbelt, MD 20771; 301-286-8981.

The following institutions also house Planetary Image Facilities:

Right: Landsat image showing portions of western Bolivia, southern Peru, and northern Chile.

University of Arizona
Dept. of Astronomy
Tucson, AZ 85721
602-621-2288

Cornell University
Dept. of Astronomy
Ithaca, NY 14853
607-255-4935

University of Hawaii
2680 Woodlawn Dr.
Honolulu, HI 96822
808-948-7087

Jet Propulsion Laboratory
California Institute of Technology
4800 Oak Grove Dr.
Pasadena, CA 91109
213-354-2887

Lunar and Planetary Institute
Houston, TX 77058
713-486-2139

Washington University
St. Louis, MO 63130
314-889-6257

SPACE STUFF

Even us ordinary earthbound folks, who will never get much higher off the ground than you can go in a 747, can get closer to the magic of space by collecting some of the vast amount of "space stuff" out there in the wild blue open market. From embroidered patches to authentic pieces of *Skylab* preserved in lucite, space souvenirs abound.

The possibilities are sky-high: Members of space clubs meet wearing T-shirts boasting a club insignia. Children combine learning and fun while assembling rocket models, some of which actually fly. Those who dream of colonizing space amuse themselves for now by pasting huge murals of outer-space scenes on their walls. Culinary adventurers (and campers) snack on freeze-dried astronaut ice cream, peaches, strawberries, chicken, and beef, to name a few things on the menu. And, of course, there is a plethora of books, videocassettes, slide series, flight suits modeled after those worn by astronauts, and commemorative medallions and pins.

Much of this merchandise is available in toy stores, aviation and space museum gift shops, and bookstores, although the easiest way to get a look at the latest crop of collectibles is by browsing the several mail-order catalogs specializing in space products. Also, in addition to their many other services, some space clubs advertise merchandise—with discounts available to members—in journals, occasional flyers, or catalogs. Of these groups the National Space Society offers the largest and most intriguing variety (see its listing under "Mail-Order Houses"). And Uncle Sam gets in on the action too: NASA and the Government Printing Office both sell space memorabilia.

Here's a representative list of sources that offer something for every kind of space buff, and at a wide variety of prices:

MAIL-ORDER HOUSES

A-B Emblem (P.O. Box 82695, Weaverville, NC 28787; 800-438-4285), manufacturer of the original NASA patch, sells *the* authentic space patches. It offers Mercury, Gemini, Apollo, and Skylab patches, as well as those for recent space shuttles. Prices range from $16.95 for six patches from the Mercury program to $108.65 for 27 shuttle patches. Add $2 shipping.

Astronomical Society of the Pacific (390 Ashton Ave., San Francisco, CA 94112; 415-337-1100) offers posters, slides, and videos from space exploration, as well as spaceflight simulation software. For an illustrated catalog, send two first-class stamps.

Blackbird (P.O. Box 8607, Dept. FF 288, Scottsdale, AZ 85252; 800-272-7171; 602-966-7613) sells sweatshirts, T-shirts for adults and kids, and wall hangings from NASA's own collection. Prices range from $10 for kids' T-shirts to $35 for wall hangings.

Dover Publications (31 E. 2nd St., Mineola, NY 11501; 516-294-7000) offers 24 photo postcards from the archives of NASA. The postcards ($3.50) are representative of NASA's efforts in space since 1982.

The Easton Press (47 Richards Ave., Norwalk, CT 06857; 203-866-0101) sells a series called *America's Achievements in Space*, ten 90-minute videocassettes chronicling the history of the space program. Tapes are available by subscription only at $21.95 each.

Final Frontier Books (2400 Foshay Tower, Minneapolis, MN 55402; 612-332-3001) offers several books on the space program. Sample titles include *Race to Mars, The Astronauts: The First 25 Years of Manned Space Flight, History of NASA: America's Voyage to the Stars,* and *To the Edge of the Universe: The Exploration of Outer Space with NASA.* Most prices are under $20.

Final Frontier Magazine (P.O. Box 20089, Minneapolis, MN 55420; 612-884-6420), published bimonthly, is the only popular magazine exclusively on space exploration. This slick periodical covers topics such as international space travel, the latest in space technology, and adventurers of the new age of space exploration. Subscriptions are $14.95 in the United States, $19.95 in Canada, and $23.95 elsewhere.

National Space Society (NSS, 922 Pennsylvania Ave. SE, Washington, DC 20003; 202-543-1900) produces catalogs offering a huge selection of merchandise. The videocassette, poster, slide, and book selections, which include Government Printing Office publications, are mostly accounts and depictions of U.S. space missions. Among the more unusual products: a series of 9-foot-by-14-foot wall murals—"Columbia in Flight," "Clouds," "Earthrise" (as seen from the moon), and "Saturn and Moons"—which are sold with hanging paste; fragments of *Skylab* debris suspended in a lucite pyramid or in a hand-blown glass paperweight; and laminated full-color Landsat photos of various cities, including New York, Paris, San Francisco, and Washington, D.C., at resolutions high enough to indentify specific blocks—and even buildings—in these cities. Prices range from $10 to $20.

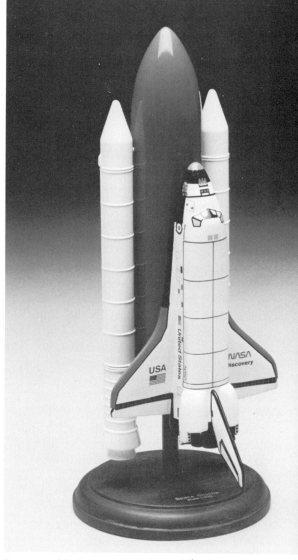

Preassembled space shuttle model, from the National Space Society.

The NSS also sells preassembled space shuttle, orbiter, astronaut, and space operations center models; NASA sport jackets, astronaut caps, patches, and flight suit reproductions; and games and toys. Prices range from $10 to $50 for slide series, $25 to $250 for artifacts and memorabilia, $2 to $35 for books, $40 for videos, $13 to $200 for models, $3.50 to

BEAM ME UP, SCOTTIE

For some people, "Star Trek" is a television show that ran some 79 episodes over three years beginning in 1966, in which Captain James T. Kirk, Mr. Spock, Dr. McCoy, Mr. Scott, and the rest of the crew did battle with Klingons, Romulans, and other alien forces. But to many, many other people, "Star Trek" is more than a TV show—it is a phenomenon that lives on and on. More than two decades after the show first aired, there are over 300 "Star Trek" clubs, more than 75 books, and a number of local and national—and international—conventions that celebrate the show. The original 79 episodes have aired more than 50 times each in almost every American city. More than 50 "Star Trek" books have been published since 1979. And in 1987, a Dallas financial services company issued a "Star Trek" Visa card, featuring a colorful picture of the Starship *Enterprise* embedded in plastic. (As one pundit put it, they don't call it the *Enterprise* for nothing.)

What's going on here? What is the attraction to this show? "Many people see `Star Trek' as a vision of a kinder world, where positive values are acted out during each episode," explains Barbara Walker of the Leonard Nimoy Fan Club. (Nimoy portrayed the character Mr. Spock in the series.) For others, it is the relationship between Kirk and Spock that has kept them tuned in these many years. Whatever the reason, there is no doubt that "Star Trek" has become a cult classic.

If you are interested in becoming part of this mania, there are several places to turn. The first is Star Trek: The Official Fan Club (P.O. Box 111000, Aurora, CO 80011; 303-341-1813), which is actually a business licensed by Paramount Pictures Corp., the studio that created "Star Trek." The club issues a bimonthly magazine, aptly called *Star Trek*, which features

Mr. Spock and Captain Kirk. Courtesy Broadcasting *magazine.*

interviews with stars, information about special effects, and other items of interest to the diehard fan. The club also offers products such as mugs, T-shirts, and models of important "Star Trek" figures. Membership ($9.95) includes the magazine.

Another key group, Star Trek Welcommittee, offers a wealth of services for Trekkies. Each year it publishes a directory that includes "Star Trek" clubs in the United States and abroad, actor fan clubs, people who sell "Star Trek" paraphernalia, and a listing of selected books available about the infamous show. The Welcommittee is not a club, however; there are no membership dues. To receive a copy of the directory, send a self-addressed envelope and $2 to Shirley S. Maiewski, Star Trek Welcommittee, 481 Main St., Hatfield, MA 01038.

Of the many books on "Star Trek," there are a couple you might want to check out: *The Star Trek Compendium* and *The Star Trek Interview Book*, both written by Alan Asherman, who is the closest you can get to being a "Star Trek" scholar. Both books have numerous anecdotes and interviews about "Star Trek," the show and the phenomenon.

$110 for NASA clothing and patches, and $5 to $60 for games and toys.

Neptune Pacific Company (953 E. Colorado Blvd., Ste. 201, Pasadena, CA 91106; 818-794-0177) markets the Voyager spacecraft paper model. Intended for ages 10 and up, the 15¹/₂-inch model comes in 24 laser-cut pieces. Accompanying illustrated literature details the purposes and the achievements of Voyager missions. The model sells for $14; a display stand is $25. Discounts are available for bulk orders.

Planetary Society (65 N. Catalina Ave. Pasadena, CA 91106; 818-793-5100) in the September-October issue of its bi-monthly publication, *Planetary Report*, offers an annual Holiday Gift Guide. Merchandise includes books for children and adults, posters, slides, videocassettes, and Planetary Society T-shirts. The books focus on space exploration, the possibilities of living in space, and the planets, particularly Mars; posters feature photographs from various space missions, as well as paintings; slide series, accompanied by fact sheets or audiocassette narration, reproduce photographs from the Viking and Voyager missions; and videocassettes offer footage of various planets and other heavenly bodies, including Halley's comet. Prices range from $7 to $28 for books, $5 to $9 for posters, $8 to $17 for slide series, $17 to $33 for videocassettes, $9 to $10 for T-shirts, and up to $70 for other products. Members of the Planetary Society receive discounts.

Shuttle Products International (1812 Park Ave., P.O. Box 5100, Titusville, FL 32783; 800-852-6272) publishes an annual catalog of mail order products. Its line of merchandise includes silk-screened T-shirts and sweatshirts, available in adult and children's sizes; official NASA caps

Paper Voyager *model, from the Neptune Pacific Company and the Planetary Society.*

and patches; a reproduction of the official NASA flight suit for children, and official shuttle medallions, including one for the *Challenger* with the dubious inscription "First in Flight Tragedy." Prices range from $10 to $38 for clothing, $3 to $5 for patches, and $5 to $35 for medallions.

Space and Rocket Center Catalog Sales (One Tranquility Base, Huntsville, AL 35807; 800-633-7280) publishes *Space Gear*, a catalog of mail-order merchandise. *Space Gear* offers a wide variety of books, clothing, astronaut food, videocassettes, and souvenir items bearing the Space Camp logo. Among the books are astronaut William R. Pogue's *How Do You Go to the Bathroom in Space?*, providing information on topics not usually addressed in mass-media coverage of space missions, and *The Space Shuttle Operator's Manual*, detailing the pilot procedures for lift-off and ascent. For those who dare to "eat like an astronaut," freeze-dried chicken or beef space dinners, fruit, and ice cream are waiting to melt in your mouth. *Space*

NASA flight suit for kids, from Shuttle Products International.

Gear's space and aviator clothing line features flight jackets, flight suits, and Ray Ban sunglasses. Videocassettes include *U.S. Space Camp*, filmed at the Space and Rocket Center; a space adventure film, *Space Camp*; and the immensely popular *Top Gun*. Items displaying the Space Camp logo range from cuff links to duffel bags. Prices range from $5 to $25 for books, $2 to $8 for astronaut delicacies, $55 to $290 for space and aviation wear, $30 to $50 for videos, and $5 to $30 for Space Camp memorabilia.

U.S. Space Education Association (Mail Order Sales, 746 Turnpike Rd., Elizabethtown, PA 17022; 717-367-3265) distributes to members catalog sheets for an eclectic array of space stuff. Merchandise includes a 2 1/2-inch-square piece of thermal blanket from Gemini test spacecraft, mounted on a certificate of authenticity ($10); the Wholearth Ball, an inflatable model of earth as it appears from space ($8); NASA space shuttle mission patches, displaying the exact multicolored embroidered design worn by astronauts on their flight suits ($4.25); and the "*Challenger* Accident Video," which features rare footage of the tragedy, a "frank, technical explanation of the events surrounding the accident," and a "brief analysis of the recovered debris" ($19.95).

World Space Foundation (P.O. Box Y, Southern Pasadena, CA 91030; 818-357-2878) sells a limited selection of merchandise. Recent offerings include T-shirts, sweatshirts, stoneware mugs, and silver or gold lapel pins, all with graphics and inscriptions related to the space shuttle program—such as "I Want to Go" or "Keep the Dream Alive"—or to projects sponsored by the foundation. Clothing prices range from $10 to $20; other products run from $5 to $150. Discounts are available on multiple orders.

GOVERNMENT SOURCES

Government Printing Office (Washington, DC 20402; 202-783-3238) publishes NASA books on just about every aspect of the space program. The GPO also publishes the *NASA Aerospace Bibliography*, which lists all of these publications. Here are a few choice items from the list:

❏ *Apollo* (S/N 033-000-00553-9; $4.75) uses black-and-white photos to trace the history of the Apollo program in the 1960s.

❏ *Pioneer* (S/N 033-000-00805-8; $14.50) explores the missions to Jupiter and then the journey farther on to Saturn. Contains color photographs and an analysis of the data from that journey.

Paperweight containing fragment of Skylab *debris, from the National Space Society.*

❏ *Voyage to Jupiter* (S/N 033-000-00797-3; $9) chronicles the Voyager mission to Jupiter, 1972-1979, especially the fly-bys in 1979. Includes color photographs of Jupiter and its moons.

❏ *Space Shuttle: NASA's Answer to Operations in Near-Earth Orbit* (S/N 033-000-00968-2; $1) describes the technological development and use of the space shuttle.

NASA Facilities. The visitors' centers at NASA headquarters in Washington, D.C., and NASA field installations (see addresses under "How NASA Works, page 287") sell a variety of space stuff: photographs, T-shirts, commemorative medals, emblems, flight patches, and other space-related memorabilia.

NASA Teacher Resource Centers. To ensure future generations' interest in the space program, NASA has developed teacher resource centers across the United States. The centers provide educational materials appropriate for kindergarten through 12th-grade students. Available educational tools include videocassettes, filmstrips, 35-millimeter slides, audiocassette-slide programs, lesson plans and classroom activities, NASA publications, software, and "telelecture" programs. The materials cover topics such as aeronautics, life science, earth science, physics, chemistry, astronomy, environmental issues, mathematics, and computer science. Duplicating equipment at the teacher resource centers allows educators to copy audio and videocassettes, filmstrips, slides, and publications. Teachers are asked to make an appointment and to bring their own blank audio or videocassettes. Those unable to visit may call or write for services at the appropriate teacher resource center. Many materials are free; some require a nominal fee. (A list of NASA Teacher Resource Centers can be found under "Uncle Sam the Weatherman," page 136.)

Index

Marv Golden Discount Store, 261
Maryland Science Center, 40
Mason & Sullivan/Classics in the Making, 165
Mattatuck Astronomical Society, 91
Maui Astronomy Club, 92
Mauna Kea Astronomical Society, 92
Mauna Kea Observatory, 22
Maximum Wind and Weather Instruments, 165
McAuliffe, Christa, 286
J. M. McDonald Planetarium, 41
McDonald Planetarium, 43
McDonnel Star Theater, 32
McGraw Hill Observatory, 21
McKim Observatory, 23
McLaughlin Planetarium of the Royal Ontario
    Museum, 32
McMath Planetarium, 40
McVehil-Monnett Associates, Inc., 152
Meade Instrument Corp., 59-60
MECC, 75
Melton Memorial Observatory, 26
memorabilia, aviation, 273-276
Memphis Astronomical Society, 102
Mercury (magazine), 74, 80, 114
meteorites, 112
Meteorological Applications, 152
Meteorological Evaluation Services, Co., 152
Meteorological Standards Institute, 152
meteorologists, 149-153
Metro Monitoring Services, 152
Miami Valley Astronomical Society, 100
Michiana Astronomical Society, 94
Michigan Spacelog, 96
Microillusions, 75, 79
Micro Prose, 263, 265
Mid-South Astronomical Research Society, 88
Middle Georgia Astronomical Society, 92
Middle Tennessee Astronomical Society, 102
Middletown Planetarium, 44
Midlands Astronomy Club, 102
Midwestern Astronomers, 94
military aviation, 216
military insignia collectors, 251
military uniform collectors, 251
Daniel B. Millikan Planetarium, 36
Milwaukee Astronomical Society, 104
Mindscape, Inc., 75, 76, 264, 265
Minneapolis Planetarium, 40
Minner Press, 202
Minnesota Astronomical Society, 97
Minnesota Valley Amateur Astronomers, 97
Minolta Planetarium, 36
Mission Soaring Center, 209
Maria Mitchell Observatory, 23
MMI Corporation, 110, 179
Mobile Astronomical Society, 87
mobiles, astronomical, 112
Model Airplane, 217
model airplanes and rockets, 210-214
Modern Talking Picture Service, 179
Modesto Society of Astronomical Observing, 89
Mohawk Valley Astronomical Society, 99
Montclair Telescope Club, 98
Montgomery College Planetarium, 40
moon, phases of, 119
Moorhead-Fargo Astronomical Club, 97
Moorhead State University Planetarium, 40
Morehead Planetarium, 35
Morgan Jones Planetarium, 45
Morrison Planetarium, 35
Mother Lode Astronomical Society, 89

Mt. Cuba Astronomical Observatory, 22
Mt. Cuba Planetarium and Astronomical Observa-
    tory, 37
Mt. Diablo Astronomical Society, 89
Mt. Hood Community College Planetarium, 43
Mt. Olive Astronomical Society, 93
Mt. San Antonio College Planetarium, 36
Mt. Washington Observatory, 160
Mt. Wilson Observatory, 21
MSU Observatory, 25
MTA-Sticks, 202
Ralph Mueller Planetarium, 41
Muller Planetarium, 43
The Multiple Mirror Telescope, 17
Murray and Trettel, Inc., 152
Muscle Shoals Astronomical Society, 87
Museum of Arts and Sciences Planetarium, 38
Museum of Flight, 232
Museum of the Rockies, 41
museums, aviation, 222-228, 237-243
Muskegon Astronomical Society, 96
Mutual UFO Network, 306

Naperville Astronomical Association, 93
NASA, *see* National Aeronautic and Space Admini-
    stration
National Aerial Photography Program, 309
National Aero-Space Plane, 292
National Aeronautic and Space Administration, 11,
    13, 282, 284, 285-286, 287-293, 312
    Ames Research Center, 289
    Astronaut Selection Office, 284
    Audiovisual Department, 312
    Cosmic Background Explorer, 289
    Deep Space Network, 289, 291
    field installations, 289-293
    Gamma Ray Observatory, 289
    Goddard Space Flight Center, 289
    Jet Propulsion Laboratory, 289, 314
    John C. Stennis Space Center, 293
    John F. Kennedy Space Center, 291
    Langley Research Center, 291, 300
    Lewis Research Center, 292
    Lyndon B. Johnson Space Center, 291
    Marshall Space Flight Center, 292
    Office of Aeronautics and Space Technology,
        287
    Office of Exploration, 287
    Office of Space Flight, 287
    Office of Space Science and Applications, 287
    Office of Space Station, 287
    Office of Space Tracking and Data Systems, 289
    Planetary Image Facilities, 312-314
    Scientific and Technical Information Facility,
        300
    Space Flight Tracking and Data Network, 289
    Teacher Resource Centers, 145-147, 320
    Technology Utilization Program, 300
    Tracking and Data Relay Satellite System, 289
    Wallops Flight Facility, 289
National Aeronautic Association, 246, 255
National Aeronautics Association, 214
National Air and Space Museum, 196, 222, 225-226
    Branch Library, 219
National Archives and Records Administration, 220
National Association of Flight Instructors, 255
National Astronomy and Ionosphere Center (NAIC),
    15-16
National Audiovisual Center, 179
National Aviation Museum of Canada, 243
National Balloon Museum, 240, 242

National Center for Atmospheric Research, 143
National Climate Program Office, 148
National Climatic Data Center, 138-139, 148
National Council for Industrial Meteorologists, 154
National Deep Sky Observer's Society, 107
National Environmental Satellite, Data, and
    Information Service, 139-141
National Geographic Society, 68, 71, 110, 170, 179
National Geophysical Data Center, 139
National Hurricane Center, 142-143, 155
National Investigations Committee on UFOs, 307
National Mapping Program, 309
National Marine Fisheries Service, 139
National Meteorological Center, 138
National Model Airplane Championship, 214
National Oceanic and Atmospheric Administration,
    137-142
    Atlantic Oceanographic and Meteorological
      Laboratories, 141
    Environmental Research Laboratories, 141-142
    Geophysical Fluid Dynamics Laboratory, 142
    Great Lakes Environment Research Laboratory,
      142
    National Climatic Data Center, 138-129
    National Environmental Satellite, Data, and
      Information Service, 139-141
    National Geophysical Data Center, 139
    National Hurricane Center, 142-143
    National Marine Fisheries Service, 139
    National Meteorological Center, 138
    National Oceanographic Data Center, 139
    National Ocean Service, 138
    National Severe Storms Laboratory, 139
    National Weather Service, 138
    Office of Oceanic and Atmospheric Research,
      141-142, 141-142
    Pacific Marine Environmental Research
      Laboratory, 142
    Satellite Data Services Division, 139-141
    Space Environment Lab, 142
National Oceanographic Data Center, 139
National Ocean Service, 255-258, 260
National Optical Astronomy Observatories (NOAO),
    11
National Parachute Industries, 207
National Radio Astronomy Observatory (NRAO), 14-
    16, 306
National Science Foundation, 10, 11, 15, 143
National Science Teachers Association, 199
National Scientific Balloon Facility, 143
National Severe Storms Laboratory, 139, 180
National Soaring Museum, 242
National Solar Observatory, 11, 13
National Space Science Data Center, 312
National Space Society, 294, 295, 296, 316
National Technical Information Service, 144
National Weather Association, 154, 160
National Weather Service, 137, 138
Nature Center and Planetarium, 38
The Nature Company, 112
Naval Aviation History Office, 220
navigation charts, *see* aeronautical charts
Neptune Pacific Company, 318
Neville Museum Astronomical Society, 104
New England Air Museum, 222, 242
New England Science Center, 40
New Hampshire Astronomical Society, 98
New Jersey Astronomical Association, 98
New York Public Library, Science and Technology
    Research Center, 220
Niagara Frontier L5 Society, 99

The NightStar Company, 71-72
The Ninety-Nines, 248
NOAA, *see* National Oceanic and Atmospheric
    Administration
Norfolk State University Planetarium, 46
North American Weather Consultants, 152
Northeast Bronx Planetarium, 42
Northeast Florida Astronomical Society, 91
Northeast Kansas Amateur Astronomers League, 94
Northeast OH AMS Chapter, 100
Northeast Wisconsin Stargazers, 105
Northern Illinois University Observatory, 22
Northern Indiana Astronomical Group, 94
Northern Sky Telescopes, 61
Northern Virginia Astronomy Club, 104
North Jersey Astronomical Group, 98
North Jersey Weather Observers, 160
North Museum, 43
NorthStar Imports Company, 72-73
Northwest Astronomy Group, 101
Northwest Oklahoma Astronomy Club, 101
Northwest Suburban Astronomers, 93
Novagraphics, 108
Robert J. Novins Planetarium, 42
Nowcasting, 152
NUS Corporation, 152

M. J. O'Brien Inc., 202
observatories, 10-28
    private, 17-28
OceanRoutes, Inc., 149, 152, 170
Odyssey, 80
Office of Oceanic and Atmospheric Research, 141-
    142, 141-142
Ogden Astronomical Society, 103
Oglethorpe Astronomical Association, 92
Ohio's Center of Science and Industry, 43
Ohio State University Planetarium, 43
Ohio Turnpike Astronomers Association, 100
Oklahoma City Astronomy Club, 101
The Old Farmer's Almanac, 151
Old Rhinebeck Aerodrome, 222, 242
Olympic Astronomical Society, 104
Omaha Astronomical Society, 98
OMNI, 77
Omni, 81
OMSI Astronomers, 101
on-line services, weather, 169-171
optical astronomy, 10-13
optical telescopes, 10-13
Orange Coast College Planetarium, 36
Orbic Systems, 112
Order of Daedalians, 248
organizations, astronomy, 85-107
organizations, aviation, 244-245
organizations, space, 294-299
organizations, weather, 154
Orion, 102
Orion Telescope Center, 61
Outback Boomerangs, 201, 202
Owl Boomerangs, 202
Owls Head Transportation Museum, 242

Pacific Marine Environmental Research Laboratory,
    142
Pacific Science Center, 46
Palomar College Planetarium, 36
Palomar Mountain Observatory, 18
paper airplanes, 212
Paper Airplanes International, 212
Para-Gear Equipment Co., 207

Vehicle Internal Systems Investigative Team, 307
Ventura County Astronomical Society, 90
Vermont Astronomical Society, 103
Very Large Array (VLA) telescope, 15
VFR charts, *see* aeronautical charts
videos, aviation, 276
Villanova University Observatory, 26
Virginia Weather Observation Network, 160
VIZ Manufacturing Co., 168
Von Braun Astronomical Society, 87
Vor-Tec Sports, 202

Wabash Valley Astronomical Society, 94
Wagner College Astronomy Club, 99
Wallace Astrophysical Observatory, 23
Ward's Natural Science Establishment, Inc., 179
Warner & Swasey Observatory, 25
Warren Astronomical Society, 97
Warren Blake Old Science Books, 114
Washburn Observatory, 28
Washburn University Planetarium, 39
Washington County Planetarium, 40
Washington State University Planetarium, 46
Watkins Aviation, 271, 272, 273
Watson-King Planetarium, 40
WDBJ Weatherwatchers, 160
WDIV-TV4 Weatherwatchers, 160
weather, 135-188
    agencies, state, 148
    clubs, 159-160
    federal government agencies, 136-147
    maps, 177
    state government agencies, 148
Weather Applications, 153
WeatherBank, Inc., 171
The Weather Channel, 160
Weather Consultants Incorporated, 153
Weather Corporation of America, 153
WeatherData, Inc., 153
weather forecast telephone hotlines, 140
WeatherMeasure Weathertronics/Qualimetrics, Inc., 167
Weather Research Center, 153
The Weather School, 173
Weather Services Corporation, 153
Weathervane Software, 171
Weatherwise, 153
Wehr Astronomical Society, 105
Weitkamp Observatory, 26
John C. Wells Planetarium, 46

Westchester Astronomy Club, 99
West Chester University Planetarium, 44
Western Amateur Astronomers, 53, 86
Western Connecticut State University Observatory, 22
Western Montana News Weather Watchers, 160
Western Observatorium, 90
Westminster Astronomical Society, 96
West Valley College Planetarium, 37
Wetherbee Planetarium, 38
Fred L. Whipple Observatory, 17
Whirlwind Designs, 113, 175
Whitworth Ferguson Planetarium, 42
Wichita Omnisphere and Science Center, 39
J. Calder Wicker Planetarium, 46
Wickware Planetarium, 37
Wilderness Center Astronomy Club, 100
Wilkens Weather Technologies Div., 153
Willingboro Astronomical Society, 98
Willmann-Bell, Inc., 68, 70, 76, 78
Wind & Weather Catalogue, 167
wind-chill factor, 169
wind speeds, 157
Wings Inc., 261
Wings (aviation stuff), 270, 271, 272, 273-274, 275
women in aviation, 219
Margaret C. Woodson Planetarium, 43
World Meteorological Organization, 137
World Paper Airplane Contest, 212
World Space Foundation, 298-299, 319
World War I Aeroplanes, 250
Wright, Orville, *see* Wright brothers
Wright, Wilbur, *see* Wright brothers
Wright brothers, 194-195, 197, 203, 220, 222, 243
Wright Brothers National Memorial, 243
writers, aviation and space, 253
WTJM Weather Center Observers, 160
Wyoming Infrared Observatory, 28

Yeager, Chuck, 196
Yeager, Jeana, 196
Yerkes Observatory, 28
Young Astronaut Council, 299
John Young Planetarium, 38
Youngstar Star Academy, 288
youth camps, space, 288

Z2 Computer Solutions, 78
Harry Zacheis Planetarium, 37